More Praise for *On the Trail of Genghis Khan*

"Vivid, insightful, thoughtful, with great narrative drive. A modern classic."
—John Man, author of *Genghis Khan: Life, Death and Resurrection*

"Tim Cope is a beautiful explorer—by which I mean that he explores beautiful places, but also that he does it beautifully. This is a young man possessed of extraordinary courage, but also great sensitivity and respect. His writing, like his journeys, speaks to a heightened soul, operating at its highest potential. He is an inspiration to me and I believe he will be an inspiration for many. To anyone who believes that there are no worlds left to be discovered, I offer up the evidence of this magnificent tale."
—Elizabeth Gilbert, author of *Eat Pray Love*

"Tim Cope's exploration across the continents on horseback grew into a quest through history and then an odyssey deep into the human heart. In exploring some of the most remote places on earth, he brings us back to ourselves and to a better understanding of our place in the world today."
—Jack Weatherford, author of *Genghis Khan and the Making of the Modern World*

"I suspect that here we have a classic, likely to inspire generations yet unborn."
—Dervla Murphy, author of *Full Tilt*

"Tim Cope has woven sensitive observation with scholarship to create a unique sharing of his experience. The result is one of the most meaningful, rewarding accounts of an odyssey I have yet read."
—Thomas Hornbein, author of *Everest: The West Ridge*

"I can honestly say that I've never read anything quite like it before, with its interweaving of heart-on-the-sleeve personal narrative, shrewd modern observation, and historical background."
—Tim Severin, author of *The Brendan Voyage*

"In some ways the most reassuring thing about On the Trail of Genghis Khan is that, in a world too full of people and connections and easy means of gratification, someone with enough courage and curiosity can still find a place to get lost. And, in doing so, can still come to understand life on totally foreign terms. That Cope also writes beautifully about the experience makes this book one to treasure and remember."

—Nick Reding, author of The Last Cowboys at the End of the World and Methland

"An epic tale of an epic journey, told with beauty and sensitivity. For anyone who loves adventure and travelling off the beaten track, this is a must read."

—Tim Macartney-Snape, first Australian to summit Everest

ON THE TRAIL *of*
GENGHIS KHAN

TIM COPE

ON THE TRAIL *of* GENGHIS KHAN

AN EPIC JOURNEY THROUGH THE LAND OF THE NOMADS

BLOOMSBURY

NEW YORK · LONDON · OXFORD · NEW DELHI · SYDNEY

Bloomsbury USA
An imprint of Bloomsbury Publishing Plc

1385 Broadway   50 Bedford Square
New York   London
NY 10018   WC1B 3DP
USA   UK

www.bloomsbury.com

First published 2013
This paperback edition published 2015

© Tim Cope, 2013
Cartography by Will Pringle

ISBN: HB: 978-1-60819-072-0
       PB: 978-1-60819-446-9
       ePub: 978-1-60819-447-6

LIBRARY OF CONGRESS CATALOGING-IN-PUBLICATION DATA

Cope, Tim, 1978–
On the trail of Genghis Khan : an epic journey through the land of
the nomads / Tim Cope.
pages cm
ISBN: 978-1-60819-072-0 (alk. paper)
1. Voyages and travels—Eurasia. 2. Horsemanship—Eurasia.
3. Eurasia—Description and travel. 4. Cope, Tim, 1978—Travel—
Eurasia. I. Title.
G490.C57 2013
950'.21—dc23
2013017599

2 4 6 8 10 9 7 5 3 1

Typeset by Westchester Book Group
Printed and bound in the U.S.A. by Thomson-Shore Inc., Dexter, Michigan

To find out more about our authors and books visit www.bloomsbury.
com. Here you will find extracts, author interviews, details of forthcoming
events, and the option to sign up for our newsletters.

Bloomsbury books may be purchased for business or promotional use. For
information on bulk purchases please contact Macmillan Corporate and
Premium Sales Department at specialmarkets@macmillan.com.

DEDICATION

IN JUNE 2004, at the age of twenty-five, I set out to ride on horseback from Mongolia to Hungary, approximately 10,000 km, across the Eurasian steppe. I called it the "Trail of Genghis Khan," referring to the inspiration I found in the nomadic Mongols, who under Genghis Khan set out to build the largest land empire in history. The aim of my journey was to honor and understand those who have lived on the steppes with their horses for thousands of years, carrying on a nomadic way of life.

When I reached the Danube more than three years later, in autumn 2007, one of the common questions people asked me was, "How did you cope for so long alone?" The truth is that I never thought of myself as being entirely alone. With me were my family of horses, two of whom, Taskonir and Ogonyok, carried me most of the way. Then there was Tigon, my Kazakh dog, who accompanied me on his own four feet. My animals were on the front line of this journey, bearing the brunt of the extremes of cold and heat, traversing deserts and mountains, and being subjected to the consequences of bungled bureaucracy and even horse thievery. It was through them I came to experience the tapestry of the Eurasian steppe, and in retrospect, I can think of no better explanation for my journey than the reward of riding with my steeds, Tigon running by their hooves, as we sailed over open steppe, where nothing—not thoughts, feelings, time, the earth, or animals—was fenced in.

It is also true that the journey would have been meaningless without the many individuals and families I met, several of whom joined me for parts of the way, and more than one hundred of whom took me and my animals in. Some of my hosts were desperately poor, others were rich, and many were afflicted by alcoholism or even involved in corruption and crime, but most cared for me like I was a friend and shared their food, fodder, and shelter generously—sometimes, as it turned out, for weeks and months. To be welcomed with a smile by a stranger after many days of hard riding, even though I was usually in a state of disrepair, provided a sense of camaraderie and closeness that not only enriched my life but in some cases saved me and the lives of my animals.

All of my hosts also shared the story of the circumstances of their lives, their culture, and their history with great honesty and openness. I realized later on that in some of them I had met the modern guardians of the steppe—those special people who are driving the culture into the future, fueling the pride of the nomad, saving the traditions, and keeping the memory of their ancestors alive.

This book is dedicated to all of these people I met on the Eurasian steppe, and to my animals.

CONTENTS

UKRAINE

HUNGARY

LIST OF MAPS

Before us now stretched Mongolia with deserts trembling in the mirages, with endless steppes covered with emerald-green grass and multitudes of wild flowers, with nameless snow peaks, limitless forests, thundering rivers and swift mountain streams. The way that we had traveled with such toil had disappeared behind us among gorges and ravines. We could not have dreamed of a more captivating entrance to a new country, and when the sun sank upon that day, we felt as though born into a new life—a life which had the strength of the hills, the depth of the heavens and the beauty of the sunrise.

—Henning Haslund
Mongolian Adventure: 1920s Danger and Escape
Among the Mounted Nomads of Central Asia

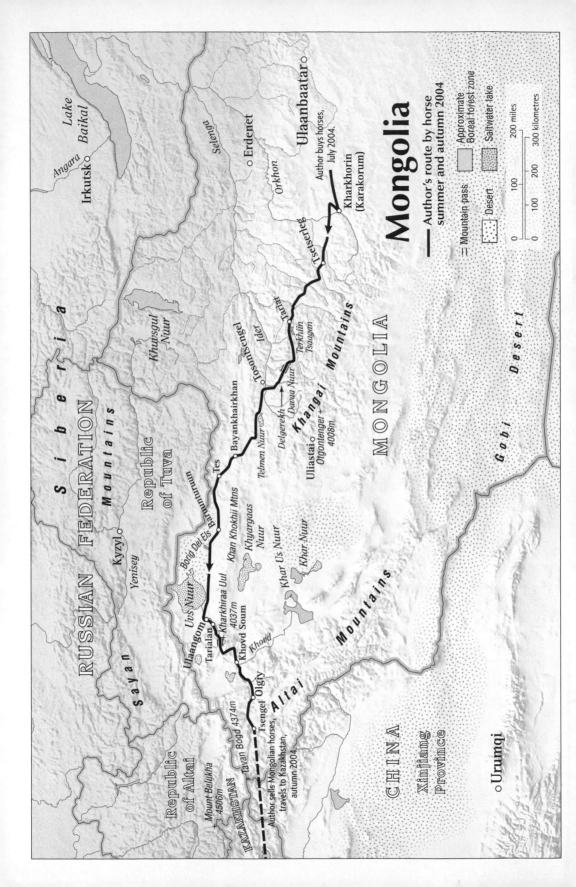

Mongolia

Author's route by horse
summer and autumn 2004

Mountain pass:

Approximate
Boreal-forest zone

Desert

Saltwater lake.

0   100   200 miles
0   100   200   300 kilometres

Lake
Baikal

Angara

Irkutsk○

S i b e r i a

RUSSIAN FEDERATION

S a y a n   M o u n t a i n s

Republic
of Altai

Mount Belukha
4506m

Kyzyl○

Yenisey

Republic
of Tuva

Khuvsgul
Nuur

Selenga

Erdenet○

Orkhon

Ulaanbaatar○

Author buys horses,
July 2004.

Kharkhorin
(Karakorum)

Tsetserleg

Ider

Tosontsengel○

Tariat○

Terkhiin
Tsaagam

Davaa Nuur

Delgerekh

K h a n g a i   M o u n t a i n s

Uliastai○   Otgontenger+
4008m

Bayankhairkhan

Telmen Nuur

Tes

Borig Del Els

Baruunturuun

Khan Khokhii Mtns

Khyargaas
Nuur

Khar Us Nuur

Khar Nuur

MONGOLIA

G o b i   D e s e r t

Uvs Nuur

Ulaangom

Tarialan

Kharkhiraa Uul
4037m

Khovd Soum

Khovd

A l t a i   M o u n t a i n s

Tsengel Olgiy

Tavan Bogd 4374m

Author sells Mongolian horses,
travels to Kazakhstan,
autumn 2004.

KAZAKHSTAN

CHINA

Xinjiang
Province

Urumqi○

1

MONGOLIAN DREAMING

ONLY TEN MINUTES earlier we had been bent forward over our saddles, braced against the nearly horizontal rain and hail, but now the afternoon sun had returned and the wind had gone. As I peeled back the hood of my jacket, details that had been swept away by the storm began to filter back. Nearby there was the rattle of a bridle as my horse shook away a fly; around us, sharp songs floating through the cleansed air from unseen birds. The wet leather chaps around my sore legs began to warm up, and the taste of dried curd, known as *aaruul*, turned bitter in my mouth. Ahead, my girl-friend, Kathrin, sat remarkably calm on her wiry little chestnut gelding. Below, the rocking of my saddle as my horse's hooves pressed into soft ground was steady as a heartbeat.

In a land as open and wide as Mongolia I was already becoming aware that it took just the slightest adjustment to switch my attention from the near to the far. With a twist in the saddle my gaze shifted to the curved column of rain that had been drenching us minutes before, but which now sailed over the land to our left. Pushed out by the wind in an arc like a giant spinnaker, it crossed the valley plain we were skirting and continued to distant uplands, fleetingly staining the earth and blotting out nomad encampments in its path.

During childhood, I had often watched clouds such as this, feeling envious of the freedom they had to roam unchecked. Here, though, the same boundless space of the sky was mirrored on the land. Scattered amid the faultless green carpet of early summer grasses, countless herds of horses, flocks of sheep and goats, shifted about like cloud shadows. For the nomads who tended to them, nowhere, it seemed, was off-limits. Their white felt tents, known as gers, were perched atop knolls, by the quiet slither of a stream, and in the clefts of distant slopes. Riders could be seen driving herds forward, crossing open spaces, and milling by camps. Not a tree—or shrub, for that matter—fence, or road was in sight, and the highest peaks in the distance were all worn down and rounded, adding to the feeling of a world without boundaries.

Clutching the reins and refocusing my sights on the freshly cut mane of my riding horse, Bor, I wavered between this simple, uncluttered reality and the trials of a more complex world that were slipping behind.

For the past twelve months I had been preparing for this journey in a third-floor apartment with a static view over the suburbs of inner-city Melbourne, Australia. In theory, the idea of riding horses 10,000 km across the Eurasian steppe from Mongolia to Hungary was simple—independent of the mechanized world, and without a need for roads, I would be free to wander, needing only grass and water to fuel my way forward.[1] One friend had even told me: "Get on your horse, point it to the west, and when people start speaking French, it means you have gone too far."

In reality, there were complexities I needed to plan for. I knew, for example, that bureaucracy—getting visas and crossing borders with animals—would likely be a major obstacle, and taking the right equipment could mean the difference between lasting two hundred days on the road or just two. Perhaps more significant were the challenges ahead that remained unknown, and of a type unfamiliar to me. At that point, early in my planning, not only was the scale of the journey beyond my comprehension, but the sum total of my experience as a horseman amounted to ten minutes on a horse almost two decades earlier, when I was seven years old. On that occasion I had been bucked clear and shipped to the hospital with a broken arm. I was still deeply scared of these powerful creatures, and couldn't quite picture myself as a horseman—a feeling shared by my mother, Anne, who was a little bewildered when I first mentioned the idea.

Notwithstanding the uncertainties, I had pressed ahead with plans, and by the spring of 2004 I felt reasonably well prepared. With valuable direction from the founder of the Long Riders Guild, CuChullaine O'Reilly, I had studied the realities of traveling with horses and gathered together a trove of carefully selected equipment. I had also managed to make contact with people in embassies, visa agencies, and those who had promised to help me on the ground.

Not all preparations had proven fruitful. I hadn't managed to raise enough money to reach my target budget of $10 a day (for a journey I expected to take eighteen months), and assurances I would receive long-stay visas were vague at best. Since planning had begun, it was also true that I had not accumulated as much experience on horseback as I had hoped. In addition to that disastrous long-ago ride, I had managed to join a five-day packhorse trip through the Victorian Alps in southeastern Australia— courtesy of the Baird family, who were kind enough to take on the white-knuckled novice that I was—and a three-day crash course with horse trainers and an equine vet in Western Australia. Nevertheless, I was buoyed by the firm belief that because the difficulties of the journey ahead would prove to be of a scope beyond my imagination, not even another forty years of planning would have been enough. And besides, who could possibly be better teachers than the nomads of the steppe who I would soon be among?

From the time I booked my air tickets and canceled the lease on my apartment, there had been no turning back. Life as I knew it was disassembled, and I went through the process of farewells with my family. After saying goodbye to one of my brothers, Jon, I slumped up against the wall in my emptied apartment in tears. Setting off on such a long journey as the eldest of four close-knit children, I felt as if I was severing ties, and it frightened me to think how much we might grow apart. Finally, at Melbourne airport my existence was stripped down to an embrace with my mother. The longer I lingered in her arms, the more strongly I felt that, as a son, I was doing something that bordered on irresponsible.

After making my way to Beijing, and from there by train to Mongolia's capital, Ulaanbaatar, I had spent a few weeks persuading Mongolia's Foreign Ministry to grant me a visa extension (and very nearly failing), gathering together additional equipment, and, finally, searching for the horses that would be my transport, load carriers, and traveling companions.

A young English-speaking Mongolian man named Gansukh Baatarsuren had taken me to the home of a nomad family 300 km southwest of the city, where he promised to find me "hero's horses." The process had proven tricky. There was a general belief among nomads—in my case warranted—that "white men could not ride," and upon discovering the buyer was a foreigner, several previous offers to sell had been rescinded. No one wanted to be responsible for exposing a foreigner like me to danger, let alone risk maltreatment of their prized horses.

In the end I had been helped in my quest by a stroke of luck—there had been a general election, and voting was an opportunity for nomads to ride in from all corners of the steppe to socialize. Gansukh had gone to a polling place and put word out that he was looking for three good mounts. The following day, while I hid in a ger, he covertly negotiated with sellers on my behalf. In this way I had managed to buy two geldings and had purchased a third from the nomad family with whom we were staying.

Just six days ago I had assembled my little caravan and taken the first fragile steps, albeit most of them on foot, leading my little crew. Since then I had rendezvoused with Kathrin, who planned to ride with me for the first two months of the journey.

Lifting my eyes again to the steppe between my horse's ears, I felt the stiffness in my joints ebb away. Perhaps it was just the effect of *airag* seeping in—alcoholic fermented mare's milk that Kathrin and I had been served by the bowlful during lunch with nomads—but for the first time since I'd climbed into the saddle, a sense of ease washed over me. With reins in hand, compass set, and backpack hugging me from behind, all I could think was that ahead lay 10,000 km of this open land to the Danube, and across all of these empty horizons, not a soul knew I was coming.

WHEN THE SUN began to edge toward the skyline and the heat wilted, I watered the horses, then chose a campsite halfway up a hillside that over-looked the country we had ridden through. As would become my regular evening routine, I set about hobbling the horses and tethering them around the tent using 20 m lines and steel stakes. The camping stove was fired up, dinner was boiled, and Kathrin and I rested up against the pack boxes to watch herds of sheep and goats pouring over troughs and crests on their way back to camps scattered below. The sweet smell of burning dung and calls of distant horsemen carried through to us on the breeze, and when our dinner pots had been scraped clean, we lay down on mat-tresses of horse blankets listening to the crunch of horses chewing through grass. Thereafter the prospect of unbroken weeks and months of travel held me lingering in a dreamy state of semiconsciousness.

I must have eventually fallen into a deep sleep, for when I opened my eyes again, the bucolic scenes of evening had vanished. In their place the tent clapped and bucked in a roaring wind. Something had woken me, and although I wasn't sure just what, I crawled out of my sleeping bag and clutched blindly for my flashlight. When I failed to find it I lay still, held my breath and strained to listen for my horses.

Minutes passed. There were no telltale jingles of the horse bell that had been tied around the packhorse's neck, or indeed any other sound indi-cating the horses were grazing. I tried to convince myself I was experi-encing a moment of paranoia and that the horses were sleeping, but then from somewhere beyond camp I heard muffled voices and the thunder of hooves. I forced my way out and ran barefoot to where I had tethered the animals, only to find my white riding mount, Bor, alone, pulling at his tether line and madly neighing into the black of night. Somewhere be-yond the perimeter of camp the sound of galloping was fading fast.

Holding Bor's tether tight, I stumbled my way farther until I felt the other two tether lines between my toes. When I reached the end of one I fell to my knees clutching the only remaining evidence of the other two horses: the bell and a pair of hobbles.

Even as Kathrin woke and came running from the tent with a flashlight, warnings I'd brushed aside from seasoned nomads in recent days came flooding back: *What are you going to do when the wolves attack? When the thieves steal your horses? Are you carrying a gun?* In response I had naively pointed out my axe and horse bell. Sheila Greenwell, the equine vet in Australia who had so kindly helped me prepare, had suggested that if I put the bell on my horses at night I would wake up if thieves did approach, because the horses would become nervous and sound the bell. In reality, the sound of the bell as the horses grazed in the dark had led the thieves straight to my camp. They had quietly slipped off the bell, untied the horses, and made their escape.

As futile as it might have been, Kathrin and I continued to trawl the steppe in the hope we might have missed something. But by the time we returned to the tent, frozen, there was no denying that on just the sixth day of my journey some of my plans needed revision. In fact, I thought, perhaps the whole journey needed a rethink.

卐

THE VISION OF riding a horse on the trail of nomads from Mongolia to Hungary had been incubating since I was nineteen. At the time I'd abandoned law school in Australia to study wilderness guiding in Finland. There I'd learned about the travels of Carl Gustaf Emil Mannerheim—the legendary Finnish general and explorer who began his career in the Russian Imperial Army and went on to lead Finland's move to independence, eventually becoming Finland's president during the final stages of World War II.

At the age of thirty-nine, in 1906, he set off on a two-year ethnographic expedition from St. Petersburg through Central Asia to Beijing, the last part largely on horseback. In truth, Mannerheim was not the ethnographer he was dressed up as, but a covert spy for the Russian tsar.

Nonetheless, he impressed me as someone interested in the continuity between the ethnic groups of Central Asia and the origins of the Finnish people. The Finns are part of the Finno-Ugric group of peoples, and are related to many different indigenous peoples that stretch right across the belt of forest and tundra regions of Russia and Siberia, as far as the Pacific. The story of Mannerheim's journey inspired in me the idea that connections between cultures, based on a common environment and way of life, transcend modern state boundaries.

After completing the wilderness course in 1999 I canceled my return ticket to Australia and set off with my friend Chris Hatherly to ride recumbent bicycles from Karelia, in European Russia, to Beijing. It was to be a fourteen-month journey during which we lived on a budget of $2 a day, surviving by camping in the forest, drinking from roadside ditches and being rescued by kind villagers who took pity on us. The world expanded with every new challenge, from frostbitten toes to the dark clouds of mosquitoes that came with summer in Siberia. But most of all it was the people who left an impression on me. In the throes of the traumatic times of post-Soviet Russia and the more recent 1998 economic collapse, the people were resurgent with pride in their many varied origins, whether they were Buddhist Buryatians or the lesser-known Udmurtians of the pre-Urals. Above all, I found it astonishing that in the midst of an adventure I experienced more comradeship and connection with many of these people than with those where I had grown up in Australia.

It was more by necessity than by desire—it was the most logical and shortest route from Siberia to Beijing—that Chris and I found ourselves in Mongolia in the autumn of 2000.

While pushing our bikes through the sands of Mongolia's Gobi Desert we would pause, exhausted, and watch as horsemen materialized from the horizon at a gallop, their long cloaks flying, eyes trained forward, and sitting so composed it was as if they were not moving at all. After stopping to take a look at the two young Australians, bogged in the sand of the only track in sight, they would remount and gallop off in whatever direction they pleased.

I was struck by their world: unscarred by roads, towns, and cities, it was a place where even homes left impermanent marks on the land. Free of fences and private land ownership, the natural lay of the earth was unhindered, defined only by mountains, rivers, deserts, and the natural ebb and flow of the seasons. What's more, with little more than a thin piece of felt to protect them against annual variations in temperatures that spanned more than 82°C, the nomadic people had a connection to the land I had never dreamed existed in modern times.

Until that point of our travels, bicycles had been freedom machines for Chris and me, allowing us to break away from the pull of a conventional path in life. But it began to dawn on me that because we were confined to roads and wheel tracks, the realm of nomads was off-limits to us. I was merely a tourist passing through.

⊞

OUR JOURNEY TO Beijing was over rather quickly after reaching the Chinese border, and within a month of dropping down from the Gobi Desert to China's bustling megalopolis, my bike was gathering dust in my parents' garage. The memories of Mongolia still burned bright, though, and from that point on I not only craved to return to Mongolia but grew enchanted by the history of the Mongolians' ancestors, who had once ruled supreme under the leadership of Genghis Khan.

Drawing on the same hardy qualities that enable the nomads and their steppe horses to survive in the harsh environment of Mongolia today, horsemen of the thirteenth century had trotted out of the vast Mongolian steppe and thundered into Poland and Hungary, crushing some of Europe's most prestigious armies. I was captivated by stories of these warriors who were renowned for mounting up in the dead of winter, smearing fat on their faces against frostbite, and drinking blood from the necks of their horses when food supplies were low. The Mongolian armies were able to travel a remarkable 80 km a day, and among many military accomplishments they defeated Russia in winter—something neither Napoleon or Hitler could achieve. Later, when they conquered Baghdad in 1258, they also managed in one attempt what the Crusaders had been trying to do for more than a century, and which wouldn't be repeated until the 2003 American invasion.

Just as impressive as the military prowess of the Mongols was the ability of Genghis Khan and his successors to make the transition from conquering and pillaging to governing and administration. They established an empire that remained more or less intact for a century, and which left a sophisticated model of government and military that long outlived the Genghisid dynasty. Many contemporary historians point out how taxes levied by the Mongols during their reign were by and large used to serve the diverse people they ruled. They implemented legal codes, funded public works projects, patronized the arts and religion, and promoted international trade and commerce. Under their stewardship, trade routes and communication lines across Eurasia were perhaps safer and more efficient than they had ever been, enabling the first direct relations between China and Europe.

It is remarkable to think that at the zenith of Mongol power nomad herders of the little-known steppes of East Asia ruled an empire that included some of the most populous cities on earth and stretched from Korea in the east to Hungary in the west, the tropics of South East Asia in the south—the Mongols even campaigned in Java, Indonesia—and the sub-Arctic in the north. Western Europe could have become yet another corner of their lands if it weren't for a stroke of fate. In 1242 when Mongolian scouts reached Vienna, the great khan in Mongolia died—at that time it was Genghis Khan's son and heir, Ogodei—and the army packed up and went home to elect a new leader. Ambitions to rule western Europe were never revisited.

As I learned about the scale and significance of the Mongol Empire, I began to think the only thing more astonishing than the achievements of the Mongols was how little I'd known about them, not to mention my ignorance of the broader history of mounted nomads on the steppe.

When Chris and I were en route by bicycle to Mongolia, many ethnic Russians we met had hardly been enlightening. We'd been warned time and time again that Mongolia was an impoverished and backward country where the "primitive" and "uncivilized" people who still relied on horses would surely bring an end to our journey. There was a permeating sense of disbelief that these people who "didn't even know how to build a house" could ever have ruled Russia, let alone many of the great civilizations of China, Europe, Central Asia, and the Middle East. And yet at a time in history when most medieval Europeans were still limited to the distance they could walk in a day—the original meaning of the word *journey* in English—these Mongolian horsemen had been galloping across the globe, expanding their knowledge as rapidly as their empire assimilated the religions, technologies, and cultures of those they conquered.

Significantly, the Mongols were not some kind of isolated nomad phenomenon. To the contrary, they reflected a historic trend of nomadic empires that had begun thousands of years earlier with one of human history's most significant yet unheralded turning points: the domestication of the wild horse.

Recent discoveries suggest that this revolution began around 3500 BCE in what is now the northern steppe of Kazakhstan. There on the primeval plain where the steppe mingles with the southern edge of Siberian forests, hunter-gatherers first began to tame, breed, milk, and ride this four-legged creature with which they had shared the land since time immemorial.

On the sweeping, largely waterless tracts of land on the Eurasian steppe the marriage of human intelligence and equine speed enabled flat-footed hunter-gatherers to gallop beyond the known horizon and prosper in ways previously unimagined. Free to search out better pasture, water, and game, they rapidly expanded their concept of the world and revolutionized the way they communicated, farmed, traded, and waged warfare. As Bjarke Rink puts it in his book *The Centaur Legacy*, the union between man and horse represented "a qualitative leap in human psychology and physiology that permitted man to act beyond his biological means." In other words, the horse liberated humankind from its own physical limitations.

Over time the domesticated horse gave rise to nomadic societies from Mongolia to the Danube River in modern Hungary. The Greek historian Herodotus dedicated his "fourth book" to one of the first such known horseback people, the Scythians, who rose to prominence in the eighth century BCE and ruled the steppe from the Danube to the Altai Mountains.

The realm of the Scythians was at the very heart of what would become the platform for the countless nomadic empires that followed them—the ocean-like plain in the heart of Eurasia, where the horse had evolved over millions of years. On the northern shores of this land lay the boreal forests and tundra of Russia and Siberia, while to the south it was rimmed by the baking deserts of Central Asia and Persia, the great walls of the Tien Shan and Pamir ranges, and, farther to the west, the Caucasus and the shores of the Black Sea. Some areas of the steppe were rich grasslands and others semi-arid zones, deserts, high plateaus, and even forests, but far away from the moderating effect of any ocean, it was all characterized by a harsh continental climate.

For settled people who lived beyond the boundaries of this realm—clinging to the safety and protection of more-fertile soils, river systems, and plentiful forests—the steppe was a mysterious, inhospitable, and almost impenetrable world. For nomads such as the Scythians, however, who relied on grazing their herds of sheep, goats, cattle, camels, and horses, the steppe formed a corridor of pasturelands that linked Asia with Europe, and Russia and Siberia with Asia Minor and the Middle East. Apart from the Altai Mountains in the east and the Carpathians in the west, it was largely free of natural obstructions, and the east-west axis meant that despite vast distances the conditions varied comparatively little. Nomads could therefore apply very similar principles of pastoral farming in Mongolia as they could in Hungary.

It was inevitable that, once domesticated, the horse would carry nomads beyond the shores of the steppe and into conflict with sedentary society. Nomads, after all, could not survive exclusively on the milk, meat, and skins of their animals, but to a degree were dependent on trade with, and plunder of, the earth-tilling societies in the lands that bordered theirs. The horse gave the nomads a crucial military advantage, and a pattern of conflict began that would endure as late as the seventeenth century: nomads would make raids on settled lands and retreat to the steppe with their spoils.[2]

Among the many nomad powers to follow in the wake of the Scythians were the Sarmatians, Huns (who under Attila rocked the foundations of the Roman Empire), Bulgars, Avars, and eventually the Magyars, who founded the modern nation of Hungary in 896. Two hundred and fifty years later the greatest nomad force of all time, the Mongols (also known in the west as Tatars), were at the height of their powers.

Even after the breakup of the Mongol Empire in the fourteenth century, Turkic-Mongol peoples with nomad heritage took over much of the fallen Genghisid dynasty. The much-renowned Tamerlane modeled himself on the Mongols and went on to carve out his own empire of historical renown.

It wasn't until the advent of the musket in the seventeenth century that nomads began to go into permanent decline. The last great migration of nomads across the steppe took place in 1771, when the ethnically Mongolian Kalmyks migrated from the Caspian region in Russia to China and Mongolia. The final descendant of Genghis Khan to hold power was Alim Khan, emir of Bukhara, who was deposed in 1920.

OVER THE MONTHS and years following my bicycle journey I continued to read about the Mongols, and nomads more generally, and became struck by two disparate and rather extreme images of the steppe people.

On one hand, there was the entrenched stereotype of Mongols as primitive barbarians who, in their time of power, had senselessly pillaged, raped, and murdered before returning on their horses to the east. It is a reputation that, it should be acknowledged, is not without some justification. The Mongol tactic of conquest was brutal, designed both to decrease the population to prevent rebellion and to instill fear so that future enemies would surrender without a fight. There are, consequently, cities across Central Asia, Persia, the Middle East, Russia, and China that suffered irreparable devastation. When the city of Merv surrendered, historical sources suggest, nearly the entire population was put to death. Urgench was famously submerged by the waters of the Amu Darya after the Mongols broke dam walls. In Iran, the Mongols are still bemoaned for the destruction they wreaked on life-sustaining irrigation networks that took centuries to re-build; the famines caused by the devastation probably caused more people to die than did the initial conquest. There is even evidence to suggest that the early destruction by the Mongols under Genghis Khan left a problematic legacy for his successors. In China, Khubilai Khan—Genghis's grandson, who went on to become both grand khan and emperor of China—spent decades struggling to reconstruct towns, cities, and agricultural lands that had borne the brunt of the initial Mongol invasion.

Passing moral judgment on the Mongols based on their violent con-quests is nevertheless not a fair way of interpreting the nature of the Mon-gol Empire or the Mongols as a nomadic people and culture. As historian Charles J. Halperin writes, "Empire building is an invariably destructive process, unwelcome to the conquered," and in this regard the Mongols were "no more cruel, and no less," than empire builders before or after them. It is important to consider that the history of the Mongol Empire was predominantly recorded by the vanquished, and filtered by religious ideol-ogy. Nomads were often judged on the premise of being pagan infidels and presented as harboring some kind of innate depravity. In 1240, the year before the Mongols crossed the Carpathians into Hungary, the renowned English monk of St. Albans, Matthew Paris, described the Mongols as "the detestable people of Satan" who were "inhuman and Beastly, rather Mon-sters than men, thirsting for and drinking blood, tearing and devouring the flesh of Dogges and Men."[3]

Such typecasting was not limited to the Mongols. The Roman soldier Ammianus Marcellinus described the Mongols' predecessors, the Huns, as "so prodigiously ugly and bent that they might be two legged animals, or the figures crudely carved from stumps which are seen on the parapets of bridges." Of the nomadic way of life, he wrote: "They have no home or law, or settled manner of life, but wander like refugees in the wagons in which they live. In these their wives weave their filthy clothing, mate with their husbands, give birth to their children and rear them to the age of puberty."[4] As late as the seventeenth century some Europeans still believed the myth—as recounted by the French traveler Beauplan—that Tatar ba-bies were born with their eyes closed, like dogs.

On the other hand, the achievements of the Mongols, military and otherwise, have been widely lauded as evidence of a highly sophisticated and worldly people. The Mongols created not only the largest contiguous land empire in history but an empire that, despite the terror it raised, initiated broad social programs, showed remarkable religious and cultural tolerance, and ushered in a relatively stable era of economic prosperity. During Khubilai's reign over China he attempted to introduce public schooling, encouraged the widespread use of paper money (which was later used as a model by his Mongol counterparts in the Ilkhanate of Persia and the Golden Horde in Russia), provided grain to widows and orphans, and instigated the development of granaries across the country to ensure against famine and natural disasters. He set up governmental institutions to protect and promote the interests of traders, artisans, farmers, and religious faiths, and he used some of the tributes collected from conquered lands for state projects, such as the extension of the Grand Canal—a venture that never fully succeeded but employed an estimated three million laborers.

Mongols also administered urban centers of culture and commerce that are inconsistent with assumptions that Mongols—as uncultured "barbarian" nomads—conquered and ruled exclusively from the saddle. The purpose-built capital of the Golden Horde, Sarai, which lay on the Volga River, was a flourishing city exhibiting paved streets, mosques, palaces, caravansaries, and running water supplied by aqueducts. Khubilai's capital in China, Khanbalikh (also known as Ta-tu or Dadu), was symbolic of the way Mongol rulers amalgamated the diverse cultures, beliefs, and skills of their domains. In it were built a shrine for Confucians, an altar with Mongolian soil and grass from the steppes, and buildings of significant Chinese architectural influence. As historian Morris Rossabi points out, Khubilai "sought the assistance of Persian astronomers and physicians, Tibetan Buddhist monks" and "Central Asian [Muslim] soldiers." One can only imagine it must have been a city of grand cosmopolitan dimensions.

To me, these two somewhat conflicting portraits—the cruel barbarians bent on wanton destruction versus the empire builders with governing and administrative genius—were surely two sides of the same coin. But time and again I reflected that neither image bore relation to the hospitable herdsmen and herdswomen I had met in the Gobi.

Whenever a map of the world was in front of me, I couldn't help but be beguiled by the vast swath of fenceless land at the heart of Eurasia that stretched from Mongolia to the Danube River in the heart of eastern Europe. The history of empires aside, who were the people who had once roamed across this land? What must their lives have been like? What would it have been like for a young Mongol man to climb into the saddle and ride halfway across the world into Europe?

It was in 2001, about six months after arriving back home from my cycling expedition, that it first occurred to me to ride a horse across the steppe. Over time, the idea took shape and form, and I was excited by what appeared to be a very simple concept: using packhorses to carry my equipment, and camels where necessary, I would start from the former capital of the Mongol Empire, Kharkhorin (also called Karakorum), and make my way west through the heart of the Eurasian steppe until I reached the Danube. While this was a similar route to that taken a thousand years earlier by the Mongols under Genghis Khan and his successors, it wasn't my intention to follow any one trail, and I was not interested in visiting old battlegrounds, following a warpath, or even venturing to cities in the sedentary nations that once had been vassals of the Mongols. By climbing into the saddle, I wanted to discover the human face of the nomadic cultures, which seemed to have been lost in so many of the superlative-filled histories. The end goal of my journey, the Danube, represented the western boundary of the Mongol Empire, but more important, it was the very western fringe of the steppe, and therefore the end of the traditional nomad world.

From the beginning of my planning I was very conscious that I wasn't the first traveler to attempt a ride by horse across the Eurasian steppe. Apart from the untold thousands or perhaps millions of nomads who had crisscrossed the steppe through time, there were several standout examples

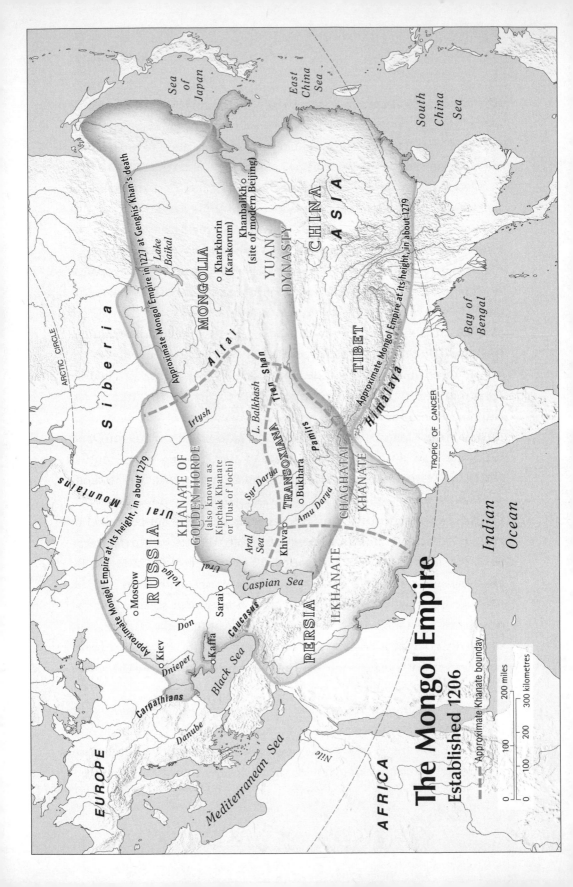

The Mongol Empire
Established 1206

Approximate Khanate bounday

EUROPE

AFRICA

ASIA

CHINA

Siberia

Ural Mountains

MONGOLIA

YUAN DYNASTY

TIBET

RUSSIA

PERSIA

ILKHANATE

KHANATE OF GOLDEN HORDE
(also known as Kipchak Khanate or Ulus of Jochi)

TRANSOXIANA

CHAGHATAI KHANATE

ARCTIC CIRCLE

TROPIC OF CANCER

Sea of Japan

East China Sea

South China Sea

Bay of Bengal

Indian Ocean

Mediterranean Sea

Black Sea

Caspian Sea

Aral Sea

L. Balkhash

Lake Baikal

Caucasus

Carpathians

Himalaya

Altai

Tien shan

Pamirs

o Moscow
o Kiev
• Kaffa
o Sarai
o Kharkhorin (Karakorum)
Khanbalikh o (site of modern Beijing)
o Bukhara
Khiva o

Danube
Dnieper
Don
Volga
Ural
Irtysh
Syr Darya
Amu Darya
Nile

Approximate Mongol Empire in 1227 at Genghis Khan's death

Approximate Mongol Empire at its height, in about 1279

Approximate Mongol Empire at its height, in about 1279

200 miles

300 kilometres

100   200

0

0   100   200

of intrepid Europeans who had made the journey at the peak of Mongol power.[5]

Among the more intriguing of these was a mysterious Englishman employed by the Mongols as a chief diplomat and intelligence adviser. A renowned linguist, he had accompanied the Mongol army during the conquest of Hungary in 1241 and was eventually caught by the Austrians during the Mongolian siege of Wiener Neustadt—where, remarkably, he was recognized by Austrian royals from the arena of the Holy Crusades more than twenty years earlier.[6] Had the Englishman been given an opportunity to write about his experiences, he would have been uniquely qualified to present history from the point of view of a nomadic regime at the height of its power. Unfortunately, he was hanged in Vienna, and the only glimpse we have of his life is from the writings of a heretic French priest who survived the siege of Wiener Neustadt.

Shortly after the death of the Englishman came the first two European travelers to make it to Mongolia and back to Europe and write accounts of their experiences—Italian friar Giovanni di Plano Carpini and, later, Franciscan friar William of Rubruck.

Carpini, who set out in 1245 from France with the Pope's blessing, traveled first to Kiev, where he was told to leave his European-bred horses because "Tartars have neither straw nor hay nor fodder, and they would all die." With various Mongolian entourages he carried on east through the steppes of what is Russia and Ukraine today, then onward to Mongolia through the Kazakh steppes, traveling an astonishing 3,000 km in just 106 days. No doubt still wrapped in the bandages that had apparently helped keep his body intact for such an exhausting ride, he arrived in the "Golden Tent" of the Khan in July 1246 and wrote:

> So great was the size of the tent which was made of white fabric
> that we reckon it could hold more than 2,000 men . . . they called
> us inside and give us ale because we did not like mares milk in the
> least: and so did us a great honor. But still they compelled us to
> drink so much that we could not stay at all sober, so we com-
> plained that this bothered us, but still they continued to force us.

Only five years after Carpini's miraculous return to Europe, William of Rubruck—on a mission to convert the Mongols to Christianity—set out on a route similar to Carpini's and became the first European to reach the capital of the Mongol Empire, Kharkhorin. His description of an animated debate that he participated in between representatives of the Buddhist, Muslim, and Christian faiths—and which was hosted by the khan—has gone down in legend.

Upon returning to Europe, both William and Carpini brought a wealth of information about the mysterious Mongolians, and their accounts are still a valuable resource offering historians and anthropologists a firsthand look at the inner workings of Mongolian society of the thirteenth century. It is also true, however, that as Dominican friars traveling from west to east, they inevitably interpreted the nomads and their way of life through the prism of their Catholic faith and their upbringing in sedentary Europe.

What I wanted to do on my journey was, in effect, the reverse. Leaving my Western baggage behind as much as possible, I wanted to start in Mongolia as an impressionable novice horseman, immerse myself in the lands and ways of the nomadic people, and travel steadily west to arrive at the far end of the steppe in Hungary, where I would try to view Europe firmly through a nomad's eyes.

In the twenty-first century a westward trajectory was all the more important for another crucial reason: the Eurasian steppe, and the western half in particular, was no longer the realm of nomads it once had been. In recent centuries the Russian Empire had reversed the trend of their subjugation to nomads and had come to dominate the vast bulk of steppe societies. The land between Kharkhorin and the Danube, albeit fenceless and much of it wild and remote, was now carved into modern states. In the west they included Hungary, Ukraine, and southern Russia, and in the east Kazakhstan, Mongolia, and those regions less relevant for my journey, western China and the Central Asian nations of Kyrgyzstan, Uzbekistan, and Turkmenistan. With the exception of China these were countries emerging from the shadows of Soviet rule, during which the people had been largely uprooted from their traditional way of life.[7] Only Mongolia, as a satellite Communist state, had been spared the full brutal effects of Stalin's collectivization policy. Partly by virtue of this, and the inherently isolated nature of Mongolian geography, the Mongols had managed to retain a vibrant nomadic culture, whereas their cousins in countries to the West had lost theirs.

Given this reality, the purpose of my journey wasn't just to understand how nomad life had once been on the steppe. I wanted to know whether there were still living, breathing connections between the nomadic and formerly nomadic peoples now scattered across Eurasia. Were Hungarians, for example, conscious of their nomad roots at all?

Even more important, what had happened to the nomadic societies during the violent upheaval of Stalin's industrialization campaign, and what did the future hold for them in the wake of the collapse of the Soviet Union? In the long run, would the nomadic way of life survive?

To have any hope of recognizing living traces of nomad heritage, I first had to come to understand it. And in reality, that was what had led me to Mongolia in the first place.

IT WAS HARD to know how many hours had passed since the horses had been stolen, but eventually my faith in the journey, like the dullest of predawn light, began creeping back into the world. Still, I needed to do something. So I did what any modern adventurer might when in a bad situation: I picked up the satellite phone. The person I called for advice was my longtime friend Tseren in Ulaanbaatar.

"Well, Tim," she told me, "here in Mongolia we say that if you don't solve your problems before sunrise, then you will never solve them. You better get on that last remaining horse of yours and start looking!"

At 5:30 A.M. I pointed Bor into the pale hues of the eastern sky. Smoke had begun curling its way out from the outline of the nearest ger, and people were already emerging to milk the goats. Sitting high and straight in the saddle, I put on the most intimidating look I could muster and willed the horse into what I imagined was a gallop but was probably no more than a trot. As we approached the first ger, a large dog shot out, Bor reared, and I struggled to hold on as we followed it back the way it had come. Visits to other camps proved more elegant, but all brought little more than shrugs.

Then, around 8 km from camp, a woman waving from her ger caught my attention.

"Hello!" she called in English.

No sooner had I dismounted there came a herd of horses thundering over a rise, throwing clouds of dust into the path of the sun. Squinting hard, I could just make out the shape of two horses trailing behind, and beyond them a horseman. As he maneuvered the herd down toward us, I looked closer. My horses!

The herder, who was in fact the husband of this woman, approached, and I explained that two of those horses were mine.

"I know," he said. "They came to me themselves this morning. You must have tied them *really* badly."

In my poor Mongolian I asked him to explain how it was that my horses no longer had any halters or lead ropes. He shrugged. It was irrelevant now.

I was invited in to share a drink of fermented mare's milk while new halters were made from rawhide. The herder sat on the dirt floor looking me over, then said something in Mongolian: "Tanilgui hun algiin chinee. Taniltai hun taliin chinee."

With the help of a pocket dictionary I was able to translate: *A man without friends is as small as a palm. A man with friends is as big as the steppe.*

It was an old Mongolian adage, and in hindsight I would be left to wonder whether indeed the whole drama had been an intentional lesson. Gansukh even suggested that it could have been the original owners of my horses who had tracked me down and stolen them just to prove the truth of their warnings. Whatever the case, it didn't really matter now.

With the horseman from the family riding by my side, I cut a trail through the lingering dew of morning in high spirits. Somewhere during the search for my horses I had left my worries of the past twelve months behind. What mattered now was that my family was intact—I had been given a second chance—and I was returning to Kathrin and camp with two bits of newfound wisdom: if I camped alone I was fair game, and if I was to have any hope of making it another 100 km, let alone 10,000 km, my horses were not to be taken for granted.

2

THE LAST NOMAD NATION

"To the mounted nomads who rode and resided along the Equestrian Equator [Eurasian steppe], possessions were for using, not hoarding. Life to them was a bridge; one should cross over it, not build a house on it."

—CuChullaine O'Reilly, F.R.G.S.,
    Founder of the Long Riders' Guild

AS I CAME riding back into camp with the reclaimed mounts, Kathrin emerged from the tent, her blond hair all wispy and her blue eyes aglow in the morning light. It was those eyes that had caught me off guard some nine months earlier. Two years older than I, she was a schoolteacher from Germany who had been living in Australia for a year to work and travel. We shared a passion for travel, and I'd been drawn at once to her down-to-earth humor and warmth. Our relationship got off to a quick start after she responded to an advertisement to rent one of the two bedrooms in the Melbourne apartment where I was living. For me, then twenty-four, it was the beginning of the most serious and important relationship of my life until that point, and in the time since we had met she had become the person who knew me better than anyone else probably ever had.

At the same time, it remained the case that our paths had crossed after I had set my sights on riding from Mongolia to Hungary. I had also long dreamed of traveling alone. Solo, I reasoned, I would be able to render myself more vulnerable, and therefore pledge a much greater trust in the humanity of strangers. With no familiar companion or culture to lean on, I would be forced to appeal to the better side of human beings no matter who they were. Doing so would offer me the kind of immersion—in the landscape and in the lives of people—that I craved.

Kathrin was aware of my plan and initially did not intend to join me, but she probably didn't expect the degree of my preoccupation in the intense six months of planning leading to departure. Kathrin felt neglected, and questioned at times what she was doing living with me, commenting that she might have been better off traveling around Australia, as had been her original plan.

Eventually we had decided to travel together for the first two months, until the end of August, when she was due to return to Germany to start a teaching job. It would be an opportunity to share this first part of the adventure and spend some precious time together after my prolonged "absence" at home.

Beyond these first two months together lay what I expected to be another sixteen months to Hungary, during which time we had rough plans for her to join me during her summer holidays. In the end, that's not what prevailed. The following summer Kathrin would be diagnosed with a life-threatening illness, Cushing's syndrome, triggered by a brain tumor that required surgery, and it would take me three and a half years to reach the Danube. By the time I was riding the last kilometres in the saddle, she would already be married. For the time being, though, that was all in the future.

Five days prior to the horse theft, Kathrin had emerged from a dusty van and dropped her bags onto the dirt in the town of Kharkhorin—the once proud capital of the Mongol Empire that lies in the upper Orkhon River of Central Mongolia. The following morning her humor helped me through a rather shaky start when my horse, Bor, went into a spin as I tried to mount. In front of a crowd assembled to send us off, I fell forward with my butt up and my face planted in Bor's mane. When the horse calmed down I leaped to terra firma and followed Kathrin's lead in towing my horse on foot out of town. Since then I had come to appreciate her presence and optimism, which made the trip's initial problems somewhat easier to bear.

⚞⚟

THE MISADVENTURES OF our beginnings were hardly becoming of a journey in the spirit of the great horse people of the steppe. We could take heart, however, that we were setting out from a region of esteemed nomad heritage.

Even before the time of Genghis Khan, the upper Orkhon River valley—in which Kharkhorin was built—had been the fabled seat of imperial power for successive steppe empires. Such was the veneration felt for the Orkhon that the Turkic Gokturks, who reigned over much of Mongolia and Central Asia between the sixth and eighth centuries, believed that he who controlled the Orkhon region had a divine right to be grand leader of the Turkic tribes. Later the Uighurs—who at one stage claimed to rule from the Caspian Sea to Manchuria—usurped the Gokturks and built their own capital, Khar-Balgas, on the same site, the remains of which still lie just 30 km from Kharkhorin.

Part of the significance of the Orkhon lay in a belief that a special power resided in the sacred mountains through which the Orkhon meandered. A glimpse of a map provides a more obvious strategic importance. Draining the gentle foothills of the Khangai Mountains, the upper reaches of the Orkhon lie near the geographic heart of Mongolia, where the main east-west and north-south routes pass and the three dominant land types of the Eurasian steppe very nearly intermingle—the deserts of the south, the forests of the north, and the grasslands of the center. With a plentiful supply of water and its own relatively mild microclimate, the Orkhon River valley transforms in late spring and early summer into a carpet of olive-green grasslands where all five of the prized types of steppe livestock—horses, bovines (yak, cattle), sheep, goats, and camels, the five known collectively in Mongolian as *tavan tolgoi mal*—are grazed in abundance. In particular, the horse has always thrived here, roaming in the kind of free-running herds that one might imagine existed before its domestication. As such, the Orkhon has always been a cradle of the quintessential no-madic, pastoralist way of life once aspired to by peoples across the steppe.

Befitting a man who would create an empire that overshadowed all others on the steppe before it, Genghis not only designated the upper Orkhon the administrative capital but fought here one of the most impor-tant battles of his long path to consolidating power.[1]

In 1204, as the ruler of the tribes in the eastern half of Mongolia, Gen-ghis had become aware of a plot against him by enemies in the west—the powerful Naiman tribe, which had formed an allegiance with, among others, his childhood friend turned archenemy, Jamukha. In anticipation of attack, Genghis rallied an army in the spring and set out west in a dar-ing preemptive campaign. To reach the vicinity of modern-day Kharkho-rin, they had ridden across vast distances, risking their horses becoming fatigued at a time of year when pasture was scarce and all livestock were at their weakest. His men were also greatly outnumbered by the enemy, who were under command of the leader of the Naimans, Tayang Khan.

Using tactics that would become associated with the Mongol Empire for centuries to come, Genghis ordered that every man light several camp-fires at night, therefore fooling the enemy as to the true size of his army. In the future, the Mongol army would also go to the additional effort of plac-ing human-like dummies on reserve horses, thereby appearing to be at least two or three times their real number.

When scouts brought word of Genghis's advance to Tayang Khan, the Naiman leader considered retreating to the more familiar territory of the Altai Mountains in the west. Had the Naimans followed through, Genghis and his men would have had to pursue them for about 1,000 km, which could have proven disastrous given the weakened condition of their horses. However, Tayang Khan's son, Kuchlug, dismissed the idea as cowardly and convinced his father to commit to battle.

It was a fatal decision. The Naimans were cut down in vast numbers, Tayang Khan was mortally wounded, and Kuchlug, together with Jamukha, fled west into what is modern-day eastern Kazakhstan, where they were eventually hunted down.

Following defeat of the Naimans and the subsequent folding of the western tribes, Genghis Khan, now forty-three years old, was both reaching the end of a lifetime of struggle to unify the tribes of the Mongolian plateau and on the cusp of founding the Mongol Empire.[2] To come this far Genghis had overcome almost unthinkable odds. Twelfth-century Mongolia, into which he had been born, was a land engulfed in perpetual conflict as nomad tribes of mixed Mongol and Turkic origin engaged in an age-old series of tit-for-tat raids, as well as broader power struggles that were defined by ever-shifting alliances and an endless narrative of revenge and betrayal.

Genghis, originally known as Temujin, was a member of the Borjigin clan, which practiced a mix of hunting and pastoralism in the northern reaches of Mongolia where the southern rim of the vast Siberian taiga, the coniferous belt of subarctic forest, greets the open steppe.[3] Around the time of Genghis's birth, his father, Yesugei, was known to have killed a chief from an enemy tribe, the Tatars—in fact, it is believed Yesugei named his newborn Temujin after the slain Tatar.[4]

It was a killing that would have consequences.

When Temujin was but nine, Yesugei was poisoned by Tatars and died. Temujin's widowed mother, Hoelun, was abandoned by the other Borjigin families, beginning a tenuous existence in which Temujin fought with his elder kin to become head of the family, narrowly escaped violent raids, and experienced multiple spells in captivity.

Genghis Khan—whose new self-chosen title approximately translates to "grand leader of all"—had dealt with many enemies since that time. It was emblematic of how far he had come that just three years prior to the defeat of the Naimans, in 1201, he had exacted revenge on the Tatars, wiping them out as a future threat. According to various sources, male Tatars were put to the slaughter and the survivors distributed among other various tribes. And although the term *Tatar* has endured to the present as a general term for nomad people of the Eurasian steppe, European visitors to the Mongol Empire in the thirteenth century were told that the Tatars had once been a people, but that the Mongols had conquered them.

On a personal level for Genghis, the Upper Orkhon valley must have been a gratifying vantage point from which to survey this remarkable path to ascendancy. To the north and east among the mixed forest, mountains, and steppe lay his spiritual home, where he had spent his formative years and proven his ability as a charismatic leader. Southward from the upper Orkhon stretched the Gobi Desert, which spoke more of future aspirations. It was home to various nomadic and semi-nomadic peoples, including the Uighurs, from whom Genghis would eventually borrow a script for his previously illiterate tribe. Beyond all that sand and arid steppe also lay China—a land of immeasurable riches that would be the first in his sights once Mongolia had been consolidated. Genghis would eventually die in 1227, after falling from a horse during one of many campaigns to conquer his southerly neighbor.

For a shrewd leader such as Genghis Khan, though, who frequently implied that his rule was mandated by Tengri, the great god of the sky, it was the symbolic importance of conquering the upper Orkhon that would have been at the front of his mind. As long as he held sway over the Orkhon, he would have both an omnipresence among nomads that would help to keep the Mongolian tribes in unity and a strategic gateway to the corners of his growing empire.

Such was the significance of the conquest of the Naimans in the Orkhon River valley, in fact, that just two years later, in 1206, he had the confidence to declare himself the leader of the Mongols, or, more specifically, "The leader of all those who dwell in felt tents." Steppe history is complex, but of everything I'd read, it was this line about felt tents that gave my journey its primary sense of direction and purpose. Understood in the context of the modern day, this reference would only include Mongolians and a few scattered nomads in China, Russia, Kazakhstan, and other former states of Soviet Central Asia. In the thirteenth century, however, it would have applied to the plethora of nomadic tribes that inhabited the Eurasian steppe. While the vast majority of these nomads would never

have heard of Genghis Khan or the Mongol tribes at that time, the unifica-
tion of the Mongols was to lay the foundation for an empire that would
eventually encompass the steppe as far as the Danube and fulfill Genghis's
audacious claim to sovereignty.

Therein lay my journey: I wanted to ride from the symbolic cradle of
Mongolian nomadism, where Kharkhorin still stands, through countries
and cultures that shared a landmass and a common way of life. The end
goal of my journey, the Danube, not only represented one of the approximate boundaries of the Mongol Empire but, more important, the very edge
of the steppe, and therefore the farthest people who ever lived in felt tents.

IN 1204 GENGHIS KHAN might have been able to unite the warring
tribes of Mongolia, but eight centuries later on the same land, Kathrin and
I were content to successfully navigate our way out of the horse-theft valley intact. We spent the night camped hidden between the folds of some
hills, waking regularly to check on our trio. At dawn the shadows, like
our fears of thieves, began to retreat, but the sunrise only seemed to illuminate the scale of the task at hand.

In this first leg of the journey there lay approximately 1,400 km of
steppe, desert, and mountains to the Altai Mountains in the far west of
the country, and horse rustling was just one element of the greater challenge. To see out a single day safely we needed to learn to see other, less
obvious threats, such as an ill-fitting saddle that could fast injure a horse.
Without supplementary feed such as grain and hay, we knew one of our
main tasks would be learning to recognize and search out grasses that
were nutritious for the horses, not to mention learning steppe etiquette
and mastering riding. Viewed in this light, the coming three months of
summer were a narrow window to earn my nomad credentials. Beyond
Mongolia, if I made it, I would face the less forgiving conditions of winter
and the prospect of countries where nomadic life and wisdom had long
been in decline.

At the heart of the steep learning curve was coming to terms with the nature of the horse. Although all Mongolian breeds are stocky animals that survive the winters by digging through the snow to find feed, they apparently fell into two broad categories. The first included horses with a calm temperament; these were known as nomkhon. The second comprised wild, untamed horses that can nevertheless tolerate humans. Two of our horses—my old white gelding, Bor, and the chestnut gelding, Sartai Zeerd (the name meant "moon crescent chestnut"), were definitely of the latter variety. Just the touch of a brush or a blanket could send them into a wild display of bucking and rearing, and pig rooting—an Australian expression that describes the behavior of a horse when it kicks out with the hind legs while keeping the head down and forelegs planted. Grooming, blanketing, and saddling each morning were therefore nerve-racking procedures. Packing the gear was another art unto itself. Even a small difference in weight between the pack boxes could risk saddle sores and injuries. The boxes subsequently had to be meticulously weighed using hand scales before being hoisted up onto our little bay gelding, Kheer, who by virtue of his calmer nature had become our designated packhorse.

A year would pass before I had learned enough to begin taking the rigors of riding and horse care in stride, and in these first few days it required all our energy and focus just to cope with getting from one camp to the next. The situation wasn't helped by a regime of night watch shifts that Kathrin and I had decided on. Nonetheless, the predatory feeling to the land did seem to fade with each passing day, and as the horses tired, they became slightly more agreeable.

After a week of straight riding, I found myself reawakening to the romance of the land and settling into a rhythm that was intimately involved with the moods of summer. Casting off from camp down onto a wide treeless plain on what was our twelfth day out from Kharkhorin, I felt the sun's early rays gently warming us from behind, while the pink hues of the western sky gradually flooded with incandescent blue. Ahead and around us the steppe spread out in vast sheets of luminescent green, appearing utterly empty until the sun revealed the white flecks of gers nestled at the base of tall mountains on the plain's perimeter. The agent for the changing of the guard from morning to midday was a breeze that came whispering over the young, supple summer grass, bringing a sortie of clouds, the shadows of which bent and twisted gracefully over the curvature of the earth. Also drifting across this sea-like grandeur were nomad riders sitting high in the saddle, their horses' legs a blur.

In a pattern that would become familiar, the climbing heat of midmorning coincided with a rising symphony of cicadas and the melting of the horizon into a haze. Herds of cattle, yaks, sheep, and goats disappeared in search of shade and water, and at the sun's zenith, when the temperature exceeded 30°C, the few horses we passed stood nodding their heads and swishing their tails. Nomad camps, meanwhile, appeared abandoned and lonely. Swept up in pungent clouds of dust and fine particles of dried animal dung, the only sign of movement came from foals lying flat, tied to tether lines, and big wooly guard dogs that lay low in whatever sliver of shadow they could find.

Come late afternoon, the sun had burned a path from our backs over our left shoulders and now dangled from the western sky before our eyes. Like the incoming tide, herds converged and piles of smoldering dung were placed around camps, keeping the swarms of mosquitoes at bay. Looking for a place to spend the night, we fixed our course on two nearly imperceptible gers that lay below a rounded peak in the distance.

By the time we reached the gers, the land was basking in golden evening light and the family in camp had been watching us through a spyglass for a couple of hours. Even before we could dismount, children came running with fresh bowls of yogurt, directing us to a place where we could set up our tent. While the horses were taken to a spring-fed trough, a team of young and old descended to help us unpack.

Ever since the horse-thieving incident we had been somewhat wary when it came to getting to know the people, but imbued with the magic of the day's ride, we happily surrendered. Our ensuing stay became typical of much of our time among nomads in the coming months, but particularly characteristic of central Mongolia, with its abundance of animals and summer dairy production.

With about eight pairs of helping hands, our tent was soon set up and the family piled in. An elderly man wearing a silky green *deel*—the universal long cloak of the nomads, fastened at the waist with a tightly bound sash—inspected the zips, fabric, and poles, then lay down on its floor as if he were a prospective buyer. Next he inventoried our horse tack and was particularly fascinated by my saddles and rope halters. Much to his disbelief, we had come riding in without a bit in the horses' mouths, instead using a rein tied to the rope halter. This was a technique the Watson family—who had given both of us our crash course in horsemanship—had encouraged us to do because it allowed the horses to eat and drink freely. The old man shook his head and waved his finger at this bitless riding technique, and was equally unhappy about the packsaddle with its heavy boxes. Horses were considered the aristocrats of the steppe, and by loading mine with deadweight, treating it as a beast of burden, I was breaking an ancient taboo. Today, just as in the time of Genghis Khan, horses were used only for riding, the task of haulage strictly delegated to camels, cattle, and yaks.

My riding saddle was an entirely different matter. The man fetched some spectacles held together with grotty old Band-Aids and ran his hands over the saddle's every feature, from the deep leather seat to the soft panels underneath. It was an Australian stock saddle with an adjustable gullet—a feature that enabled me to change the width of the front of the saddle according to the size of my horse's withers. Although I was still somewhat flummoxed by horse tack in general, the old man most definitely wasn't. He planted my saddle on his own horse and took turns trying it out with several of his sons. By the end of the session he came to me with what would be the first of hundreds of offers for my saddle right across the steppe. In some cases hanging on to it proved more difficult than keeping tabs on my horses, and often I was forced to sleep with the saddle inside the tent.

As the sun began to sink behind the mountains, the matriarch of this family group came out firing off orders, and within seconds everyone had scattered from our tent and returned to their duties. We now turned to the activities of the family with the same sense of fascination with which we had been inspected.

In this camp, which was nestled on a slight rise overlooking the plain, there were three gers that housed three generations. An elderly couple lived in one at the far end of camp together with their youngest, unmarried son, while the other two were home to two of their other sons and their wives and children. We found that keeping track of whose child was whose was especially difficult, since the number of children at any nomad camp swelled in the summertime, with relatives from the provincial centers and Ulaanbaatar sending their children to the countryside for the long school break. At the same time, babies seemed to be frequently handed from one mother to another depending on who was busy and who was not.

There was a distinct structure to nomadic family life, however, that had remained the unwritten law since the earliest records on the steppe. For one, daughters were required to move away to live with their husband's family, while males generally stayed closer to their parents. The youngest son was shouldered with the responsibility of looking after the parents in their elderly years, but was also given the title of otchigin— guardian of the family's home and livestock.

Although Genghis Khan broke with many nomad traditions, he stuck ardently to the tradition of otchigin when dividing up the Mongol Empire between his sons. His eldest son, Jochi, was given the lands farthest from the center of Mongolia, "to as far west as our hooves have trodden," which at the time of Genghis's death included the area from the Irtysh River to the Ural River, in modern Kazakhstan. As the Mongol Empire expanded, Jochi's sons became the founders and leaders of what became known as the Golden Horde, which included modern-day Russia, Ukraine, and much of Kazakhstan.[5] Genghis's youngest son, Tolui, was entrusted with the heartland, Mongolia, and inherited the responsibilities of chief administrator after Genghis's death until one of the other sons, Ogodei, was elected grand khan.

Prior to our arrival, the boys of the family had driven immense communal herds of sheep, goats, and yaks back to camp, where the women were ready and waiting with their milking buckets and stools. The goats were the first in line to be milked, and as we watched, every member of the family took part in what was a nightly production line being repeated by tens of thousands of other nomad families across the country.

There were scenes of hysterics as the little children were tasked with rounding up the most mischievous goats. They sprinted after the animals, diving to catch whatever body part they could lay a hand on, whether it be the leg, ears, or even tail, but often ended up facedown in the dust. When one particularly large and courageous goat made a break for the open steppe beyond camp, one of the boys, probably no older than ten, swung up onto a horse bareback and, with his chest pushed out like a little man's, went galloping off with a shriek.

One by one the goats were tethered head to head with ropes made from yak- and horsehair. Young girls under the watch of their mothers moved from animal to animal, milking away until the pail was full, at which point it would be taken to a ready pot for boiling.

While nomads of the steppe rely largely on meat for survival, in the summer, dairy is a staple. From the boiled milk of goats, yaks, and cows—and, in desert areas, camels—they are able to make a diverse array of products, including creams, butters, cheeses, and yogurts. This is not to mention the renowned fermented mare's milk, *airag*—better known by the Turkic term *kumys*—that Marco Polo remarked was like "a white wine." It is known from archaeological digs in northern Kazakhstan, where the earliest horse culture has been discovered to date, that this drink, or unfermented mare's milk at the very least, has been an important part of the diet on the steppe since the earliest of times.

Perhaps the most universal food for horsemen of the steppe, however, was aaruul, which was what the grandmother of the family was preparing this evening. The fresh milk carted into her ger was boiled over a dung-fired stove, left to curdle, and then strained. The resulting curds were then compressed between pieces of wood weighted down by large rocks. These large pressed cakes would be made into various shapes and then put on the roof of the ger in trays to dry. Aaruul could be soft when fresh, but in the dry climate of the steppe it was often hard as rock, to the point where it was have to be sucked rather than chewed, and would last for a very long time. By carrying a bag of this bitter snack, it is said, warriors in Genghis's day were able to survive ten days without any other food. Kathrin and I had already been loaded up with aaruul by other nomad families,

and although I found it overwhelmingly bitter, I eventually came to appreciate the way it staved off hunger during long hours in the saddle.

Midway into the milking process, Kathrin and I were beckoned into a
ger and ushered to the grass at the rear, behind the hearth. One of the
mothers, a bandy-legged woman with an angelic, youthful face but the
creased, worn hands of someone in middle age, passed us cups of tea even
before we were seated.

As I took a sip of the salty milk tea, the lingering sound of the wind in
my ears died out. In this felt tent, just steps from the doorway, it seemed
as though the vast land and sweeping sky that had so dominated our lives
had vanished.

I looked across to Kathrin and said nothing. She sat with her cup cradled in her hands, her eyes wandering about the ger.

Feeling the teacup warm my fingers, I gazed up at the woman who
stood next the stove. She was illuminated by a shaft of dying light that passed
through the circular opening in the ceiling. She lifted a ladle of milk into
the air and let the milk pour back down, then fluidly repeated the process.
Steam wafted up, condensing fleetingly on her cheeks, which were as broad
and splayed as wings, darkened by the sun but still soft. Her eyes were
gracefully elongated, feather-like in shape, emanating femininity, yet her
shoulders were wide, big-boned, and brimming with strength.

When the woman retired to an old steel spring bed to cradle her baby,
my eyes shifted to the details of the ger. The frame was constructed with
six collapsible lattice wall sections that could be swiftly dismantled and
tied to the back of a camel or, as was the tradition in this region, strapped
to a yak-drawn cart. From the top of the walls more than seventy intri-
cately painted wooden roof poles—much like spokes—angled up to the
circular opening at the apex of the ceiling.

Wrapped around the wooden frame like flesh on bone, thick sheets of
felt were nearly impervious to sunlight, insulating against the cold and the
heat. The felt so effectively damped the sounds from the world outside that
one could easily converse in whispers while sitting at opposite sides of
the structure, even in the midst of a storm—a quality I could only com-
pare to what I had experienced in a snow cave.

When the milking was finished, everyone crowded into one ger for a dinner of meat and homemade noodles—known as *gurultai shul*—after which we passed around my photo album from Australia. The elder of the family, who had been so interested in my saddle, tried to ask a series of questions, but our poor Mongolian left us hanging. I was fluent in Russian, but like communism itself, it was a language that had never really held currency among a people who had remained more or less self-reliant through the centuries.

It was dark outside before we knew it. An oil lamp was lit, throwing a glow across to the woman who had been cooking earlier; now she sat with her husband, their little one fast asleep between them. Outside there came the almost inaudible sound of bleating and farting as the sheep, goats, and yaks settled in around the gers, adding to the sensation we were sitting in the nucleus of an extended family.

Although I didn't quite grasp it yet, much of my journey across the steppe to Hungary would be spent trying to imagine how life might have once been before the Russian Empire and the era of industrialization in Soviet times brought about an effective end to the nomadic way of life. It was also true that even now in Mongolia, the urban population, particularly in Ulaanbaatar, was growing exponentially, and there were whispers of multinational mining giants negotiating agreements to exploit Mongolia's untold deposits of gold, coal, copper, and uranium.

For most Mongolians in 2004, though, the looming mining boom and its potential impacts still seemed far off and unfathomable, and here, cradled by the ger, there was no thinking backward or forward, only a feeling of completeness, for this was nomadic life intact, virtually unchanged from the days of Genghis Khan eight hundred years before.

3

WOLF TOTEM

FROM THE NOMAD camp we continued northwest through the Khangai Mountains—a sprawling range that dominates central Mongolia and separates the dry deserts of the south from the Siberian forests. We were cutting through a narrow finger of the Khangai range to reach the gentler plains and river valleys on its northwestern perimeter. As we rode, I found myself absorbed by the unfolding terrain that grew in scale and wildness.

Meandering rivers led us among peaks as bony as the backs of malnourished old horses and past lakes where we watched the mist roll across the glassy water at dawn. The higher peaks were generally sleek, round-edged and emerald green, with dense clusters of forest concealing much of the upper slopes.

Perhaps it had something to do with a confidence newly found during our stay with the nomad family, but a feeling of cadence and routine emerged. Flecks of white on the horizon grew into gers as we rode, filling our day with characters, sound, and color, then melted over our shoulders just as the taste of fermented milk and dried curd faded from our palates. In a world without fences, where communities lifted and moved as unpredictably as the weather, our usual ways of keeping track of time and place were beginning to change. The only reference point for one particularly empty valley was a vulture pecking away at the flesh of a yak carcass under an oppressive sun. An entire day was defined by an incident when herders who borrowed Kathrin's horse to catch their own runaway mounts left us for hours wondering if, in fact, they had stolen it. A whole afternoon was marked out by one of many storms that came roaring through, breaking the heat and slamming us with a barrage of hail. For an hour we stood, like the horses, tail to the wind, shivering cold, yet within another half hour the black wall had given way to blue, and under the baking sun I was searching the sky for shade-giving clouds.

Ten days after our stay with the nomad family we made a decision to deviate from the main valleys and travel over a wild mountain pass known as Davaa Nuur (Mountain Pass Lake). Although we had begun to camp regularly with nomad families for the protection they offered, the grass around these camps was usually eaten down to dry stubble, and our horses were growing hungry and thin. Just as important, crossing Davaa Nuur would take us up away from the heat and provide a shortcut through the northern fringes of the Khangai Mountains to where the land promised to settle into broader slopes and plains.

Upon hearing about our plan, the family with whom we had camped at the base of the river valley loaded us up with dried curd and yak cheese. As we were on the point of departure, our host, a gruff toothless herder in a torn, threadbare deel that reeked of tobacco and mutton, emerged from the ger shaking his head and repeating, "It's dangerous up there!" The bowlegged elderly matriarch of the family waddled out carrying a bucket of milk. As we turned and rode away she flicked three ladles to the sky. "Ayan zamdaa sain yavaarai!" she called, wishing us good luck on our journey, as the milk rained down on our backs and the rumps of the horses. In a land where every journey away from home presented the risk of misfortune and even death, this was a ritual that had been preserved from ancient times long before the era of Genghis Khan. White represented luck and purity, and painting the road with this sacrifice of milk asked the gods to favor us with safe travels.

Several hours later, the family ger had contracted to an anonymous speck below, and what had been a wide river valley was a boxed-in ravine at the feet of giant mountain ridges that leaned toward one another. We had long lost any hint of a trail and followed a stream that cascaded down a trench through swamp and loose rock.

It was just coming on to evening as the tall seeding grasses gave way to dense, short alpine varieties cradling delicate colonies of dew and rain-drops. Not far above, 3,000 m peaks swam in frothing mist and cloud, revealing a different character each time I lifted my eyes. For one short period the sun bore through to the silvery scree slopes, highlighting orange and yellow lichens. Soon, however, the whole mountain was stained with dark cloud shadow, betraying no pigment at all. Then the clouds boiled over, and again all was lost in a soup of rain and mist. The sheer fragility of calm in this mountain environment brought a welcome clarity absent in hotter climes.

When we crested a final pinch of rock and grass, the source of the stream opened up. Davaa Nuur was a tawny lake nestled between the rocky peaks we had been aiming for all day. By now muscular black storm clouds had cut the sunlight short and banished any sense of romance.

In the morning we woke to waves of rain and hail that drove into the tent with such intense gusts that the tent threatened to tear apart. When it was particularly strong we sat hard up against the fabric feeling the blows from rain and hail pepper our spines. At last the wind abated somewhat and we lay cuddling in the sleeping bag. It was no secret that Kathrin had been looking forward to the sense of privacy to be found out here in the relative wilderness. It had become the norm to wake at the break of dawn greeted by children and adults sitting at the entrance of the tent watching our every move. When we packed up to leave, they would often inno-cently pull everything out of our boxes and sprawl things about. Men would also gallop in begging to see our saddles. Coping with this atten-tion, as well as managing the horses and everything else, left no room for romance. Our relationship had become a businesslike, working one, not helped by the fact that I could barely manage a weary "good night" before falling asleep each evening.

At around lunchtime, however, it seemed that even here in the wilderness time to ourselves was limited. Just as one of many thunderclouds surged over and the light went dim, two bedraggled men crawled in unannounced. It was a small, two-person tent—cozy at the best of times—but this didn't seem to concern the men, who unraveled tobacco bundled in old silk sashes, and began smoking.

"Where are you traveling?" they eventually asked.

I explained we were traveling to the Danube, but their eyes glazed over. "Tosontsengel," I then said, referring to a town on the far side of the pass. In turn, they explained they were searching for 150 missing yaks.

I offered them tea and aaruul. For the next hour or so they sat quietly smoking, flicking through our photos, and talking among themselves.

The rain eased, and the herders left the tent. I seized the opportunity to hike to the peak directly above camp. Perched on a rock that nearly breached the ceiling of cloud, I took in the land we had been riding through. First I cast my eyes over the lake. For a brief time the water was still, but then, brushed by the wind, it all went opaque and gray and an isolated rainstorm drifted across its breadth before smacking into rocky slopes on the far shore. To the north beyond the lake, where we planned to cross the pass tomorrow, mountains and clouds choked off the view, but to the south the horizon was indefinitely far. In places light spilled through patches of blue to the earth far below where flocks of sheep could be seen like fine grains of salt and pepper in a slow avalanche down the valley sides. Across on the opposing mountains patches of forest nestled into sheltered indentations, watched over by pyramids of green. I imagined the many hidden crevices and unhampered woods crawling with wild animals, which warily monitored the life of the humans below, just as I was doing.

The longer I concentrated, the more I became aware of the multitude of gers and the presence of horsemen, particularly on the bottom of the valley slopes. Together with their animals, nomads were carrying out a cycle of symbiotic life as old as the domestication of the sheep and the horse—the animals turned the grass into meat, milk, and dung, providing food, shelter, and heat. In return, the nomads offered their flocks protection from wolves and storms.

Some horsemen, however, like those who had been in our tent, could be seen picking their way up through the wild mountains to summits far from their homes and flocks. At the same time kites were diving down to clean away the tossed-aside remains of carcasses near gers and pick off rodents such as ground squirrels and mice from the grazing areas. Unlike where I had grown up in Australia, where the land was demarcated into national parks, logging zones, farmland, and residential areas, here there was an overwhelming sense that animals and humans coexisted on the margins of survival, each knowing its unique role.

By the time I made my way back down to camp, hail was beating down once more and the view had closed in. I was more than happy to return to a slumber in the tent, where the world was small and snug. The sun faded early behind the dense clouds, and we slept longer than we had since beginning our journey.

Two days later we were still confined to the tent by the weather and I was craving the long horizons of the steppe. With dwindling food supplies and only a sprinkling of diesel left for the stove, there was, in any case, no choice but to give the pass a try or retreat back down the way we had come.

We woke at 5:00 A.M. and by seven o'clock were skirting around the edge of the lake. A hint of sunlight that promised to break through the moody clouds stirred hopes of better weather, but there was no denying we had left summer behind in the valley. My toes turned to ice, and from the bare, wind-lashed slopes the only trees that dared grow were dwarf birch and willow, rising up all disfigured and little higher than ground creepers.

No sooner had I contemplated dismounting to warm up my toes than Bor fell knee deep through a frozen crust into a bog and I was very nearly thrown from the saddle. We dismounted and continued on foot, but time and time again were forced to backtrack from bogs with panicked horses, or became blockaded by fields of jagged rocks reminiscent of an old moraine. When Kathrin's horse suddenly flew at me with his back legs, hooves clearing my head by a hairsbreadth, we lay back in the bog to take stock. My hands trembled with adrenaline, and my vision blurred from hunger. Kathrin looked defeated. We had only just reached the northern end of the lake, and judging from my map, the pass was another 8 km away, the majority of which remained smothered by mist. Getting up there was beginning to feel beyond us.

As we sipped tea from the thermos, however, we noticed something that rekindled hope. Delicately marked out between two rocks was the unmistakable shape of a hoofprint. Sensing the significance, we leaped to our feet, and only a little farther on found a similar indentation. Then we laid eyes on something that told us all we needed to know: the butt of a cigarette.

Over the next three or four hours there were times when we lost all sign of the horse tracks, but just when we were convinced we had gone astray, they would materialize again. Meanwhile, a picture of this phantom rider grew. He was a gentle man, I decided, probably in his middle years, riding with a gun slung over his shoulder and a cigarette lolling in his mouth. At times he sang, but as he neared the pass he grew quiet and sober. In truth, though, nothing fazed him. While we pushed and fell and fought against every obstacle, he passed by with lightness and subtlety along a path that was clear as day to him and his horse. This grand adventure of ours was possibly an ordinary day's ride for a nomad returning home after a visit to friends.

Over the course of the journey, the companionship I felt from the sight of these hoofprints was something I would come to experience time and time again. In remote areas, the tracks of wild animals, horses, or humans provided solace, comfort, and clues to the puzzling lay of the land. It helped me ignore my fears, engaging me in a guessing game as to where the tracks might be headed and why. When finally we would depart from one set of tracks, it was like saying farewell to an old friend.

After six hours of heavy trudging, we were heartened when the mist dissipated slightly and the triangular silhouette of a cairn, known as an *ovoo*, came into view. It was a humble pile of rocks scattered with fragments of dried curd and a tattered blue silk scarf known as a *khadag*. A few craggy tree branches were planted in the middle of the pile. Ovoos like this had been a familiar sight on mountaintops and passes across Mongolia for centuries, if not thousands of years, possibly originating as marker cairns for navigation but also, and more important, functioning as sites of worship where travelers paused to venerate the mountains and offer acknowledgment and prayer to *tengri*, the eternal blue sky. The triangular structure, sometimes created with timber rather than stone, was, according to some, meant to symbolize the shape of the rising sun and pay tribute to its life-giving rays. This reflected the ancient animistic beliefs of Mongolians who, since time immemorial, considered the sky their father and the earth their mother. Ovoos were usually only found in the highest places, since it was there that sky, sun, and earth all married.

Following tradition, we walked around the ovoo in a clockwise direction three times, offering a new rock to the pile with each circle. In another context we might have felt like foreigners going through the motions of performing another culture's ritual, but here it provided a sense of comfort to know that something had borne witness to our presence there.

Just below the ovoo we dropped down a crumbly slope of clay and rock and emerged from a curtain of mist into daylight.

Boggy permafrost gave way to sturdy ground, and the sun's rays gently filtered down, bathing us with warmth that had been unimaginable in recent days. The only sign of storms here were wispy trickles of mist that boiled over the lip of the east-west-running ridge we had crossed, evaporating in the face of the sun. While the southern side had been treeless and windswept, the slopes here were thickly carpeted with larch forests that extended as far north as we could see. Following the tracks of the horseman, we descended at a good pace until the wind came to a standstill and we began to hear the bubbling of a stream, the cackle of birds, and the whine of cicadas. The cold and storms had become a memory, packed away like the rainproof coats and warm layers of clothing we had been living in for days.

We remounted the horses, and for the next few hours followed the twists and turns of the stream as it led us ever deeper into a forested valley. The horses pushed through the same waist-high grass where the phantom rider clearly had been, and I fell into rhythm with my horse, imagining that the mountain pass had delivered us into another time.

It was precisely this kind of high, forested backcountry that had so shaped the outlook and beliefs of Genghis Khan. Unlike nomads of the open steppe grasslands, he had grown up on the southern fringes of the Siberian forests, where reliance on grazing sheep and cattle wasn't possible. Hunting was a mainstay of his small tribe's survival, and whenever there was trouble in his life, he learned to retreat to the forest, where nature afforded him sustenance and protection. In one legendary episode, at the age of sixteen he managed to narrowly escape a deadly raid on his family by fleeing to the forested Khentii Mountains, not far from the place of his birth in present-day northeast Mongolia. There, surviving on marmots, rats, and whatever else he could find, he managed to evade capture. According to The Secret History of the Mongols, the future leader later voiced his gratitude to the highest mountain in the Khentii range, Burkhan Khaldun, by removing his belt and throwing it over his shoulder, then dropping to the ground nine times toward the south. "The mountain has saved my life. I shall not forget it," he said.[1]

Right up until the end of his days, Genghis would return to Burkhan Khaldun Mountain to worship and pray before going off to war or making any important decisions. Victory was always a sign that he had been given divine power and permission from Tengri, the eternal blue sky.

Just as the yellow disc of the sun began to touch the jagged skyline of the forest, our mood swung. We had lost the horseman's tracks, and the slopes of the valley side had become so steep we were forced to lead the horses along narrow ledges and crisscross from one riverbank to the other. The forest had been gutted by a wildfire, and where trees might have once bloomed with color and crawled with birds and squirrels, bare, sooty trunks fingered their way toward the sky. A sea of willow-herb had been the first to seed on the ground below us, and its millions of bobbing purple flower heads were the only living thing to catch the lingering light. No nomads had been here for a long time, and perhaps they had never grazed their animals in the upper reaches of this valley.

By the time dusk came on we were feeling marginally more positive. After negotiating the steepest section of the valley, we had reached a broad, open meadow on the riverbank, and set about making camp. Just as we were tying down the guy ropes, there came a howl from down the valley.

"There must a be a nomad family down there after all!" I said to Kathrin, fixing my eyes downstream, expecting to locate a nomad encampment. As I strained to focus in the fading light, the only white tinge to the landscape came from a ghostly rock that glowed from a slope of blackened, dead trees.

The howl came again, long and hound-like. From up the valley a similar cry echoed, then another from high in the forest on the far bank. Kathrin tripped over our canvas duffle bag, then sat where she had fallen with her panicked eyes skirting the forest. Nothing moved, and again things fell silent.

"You—you secure the horses! I'm going for firewood!" I stammered.

Nomads had long cautioned me about wolves and thought us mad to be traveling without a gun, but I had always dismissed their warnings as scaremongering. During my studies in Finland, I had learned that despite all the rumors and fear about wolves, there had only been a handful of recorded stories in history about attacks on humans, and even then the victims had been babies or young children.

It was only now that the real threat dawned on me. The wolves were interested not in us but in our horses. If the horses were frightened enough to break free of their tethers and escape, what would we do?

Night flooded in fast as I chopped away at standing trees, the axe first smashing its way through charcoal before hitting a core of dead dry wood that was hard as steel. After an hour's work I barely had enough wood to fill my outstretched arms, but nevertheless hurried back to camp.

Without a gun, there were only two courses of action available. I urinated near each of the three horses—a trick long suggested to me by veterinarian Sheila Greenwell. Second, I lit a fire and rationed out the meager wood supplies that would need to see us out until dawn. According to Mongolians, a fire would keep the wolves at bay.

Once the fire was going we relaxed somewhat and sat gazing into the flames, eating a mash of rice and rehydrated meat. As my tummy filled, I watched a deep blackness spill into the eastern sky and stars flicker on.

After an hour or two had passed with no sign of wolves, I collapsed in the tent while Kathrin took the first shift by the fire.

I woke after what felt like just minutes. Kathrin was shaking me.

"Relax, Tim! Apart from the fact that I'm freezing, everything is okay. No wolves so far. It's one in the morning, so it's your turn, you lazy Australian!" she said, her German accent, as always, more pronounced when she was tired.

I swapped my sleeping bag for the down jacket she had been wearing, and I settled in beside the gentle crackle and spitting of the fire. The flames licked the night air and cast a circle of flickering light that just reached the horses. All three of them had eaten themselves silly in the afternoon and now stood like statues, their heads hanging. The sky was giant above, yet as we nestled in this tall grass in the bosom of the hills, there was an intimacy that cradled us. I couldn't help wonder what it would be like after Kathrin went home and 9,000 km to Hungary yawned. The longest journey in the wilderness I'd ever done alone until now was a mere ten days.

By three o'clock an invisible heaviness tugged at my arms and legs. I rested my head on a rolled-up coat and drifted off.

When I felt the thudding of hooves vibrate through the soil beneath me, I thought sleepily that I was in the tent. I assumed Bor was attempting to move in the hobbles that bound his two front legs to his back left leg. While the others had mastered the art of walking at a reasonable speed with the hobbles on, Bor stumbled awkwardly.

Then, however, I heard furious pounding coming in toward me from all directions.

No sooner had I pried open my eyes than a howl shot through the darkness. This time it was from somewhere right behind us, perhaps no more than 100 m away, on the edge of the forest. I lay low, not daring to breathe. It was black all around—I had let the fire burn down to a few glowing coals.

When the fire was again ablaze I picked up the axe and checked on the ropes and tethering stakes. The horses' necks and withers were tense and their heads were raised high, ears twitching this way and that. Over thousands of years they had evolved as a supreme animal of flight, able to reach top speed within seconds and escape at the first hint of predators. By hobbling them, however, I had turned them into easy prey.

For the next few hours I sat, axe at hand, convinced our lives hung in the balance. When the fire sputtered and it seemed my pile of wood wasn't going to make it to dawn, I was sure I could make out the furry outline of wolves prowling the perimeter of camp. I even began to think there might be hundreds of them, half crazed by starvation in the cremated remains of the forest. Feeding my remaining branches into the fire piece by piece, I prayed for dawn and rued my formerly dismissive attitude. No matter what I might have previously thought about wolves, there was something deeply petrifying about these howls in the dark. Perhaps through thousands of years of coexisting and competing with the wolf, humans, like horses, had evolved an innate reaction to them—one that was surely not without reason.

I recalled what my friend Gansukh had once told me: "It's not for nothing you call a dog in your country 'man's best friend'—we Mongolians know they were the first animal to be domesticated! We believe the wolf is the wisest and most spiritual of animals. Look how cunning they are, how they survive in such tough conditions. To see a wolf, in our belief, is a good omen. It means you will inherit some of its wisdom. To kill a wolf is to be wiser than a wolf. We eat wolf meat for strength and use it for medicinal purposes."

The significance of the wolf for Mongolians went beyond Gansukh's words. There was a legend that the ancient Mongolian people had been born from a union between the blue-gray wolf and a deer. Wolves carried the spirit of the Mongolian ancestors, the link proven by what was called a "Mongolian spot"—a bluish patch found on the lower back of most Mongolians in their infancy. It was also understood that when a wolf howled, it was praying to the sky, making it the only other living being that paid homage to sacred tengri.

Perhaps most important for nomads was the belief in the symbiosis that existed between wolf and humans on the steppe. Wolves were an integral part of keeping the balance of nature, ensuring that plagues of rabbits and rodents didn't break out, which in turn protected the all-important pasture for the nomads' herds.

Although they caused havoc when they attacked sheep, when it came to horses wolves were known to mostly attack the injured and the weak, therefore aiding natural selection and ensuring that only the strongest horses lived on to breed. Reflective of the deep sense of gratitude and respect Mongolians reserved for wolves, there was a belief that only through wolves could the spirit of a deceased human be set free to go to heaven. When a person passed away, his or her body would be taken to a mountain and left for the wolves to eat. A good person would be eaten by wolves quickly, while a bad person would be left to rot for days. According to legend, wolves would fly up to the sky with the ingested human flesh and release the person's spirit.

As Kathrin and I would later discover, this "sky burial" was a practice still carried out among modern nomads. In Uvs province, only a day's ride from Ulaangom, we came across the skeleton of a young man on the steppe with only a few remaining pieces of sun-dried flesh and a torn khadag lying nearby.

In the safety and comfort of a nomad ger this philosophy might have made for engaging storytelling. But as the fire wavered it was difficult to feel gratitude toward the wolf. How could I reconcile the benevolent creature that Mongolians so worshipped with the ruthless animals that were surely about to attack my horses, and perhaps even Kathrin and me? And how was it that Gansukh could speak about worshipping the wolf and then in the same breath about killing and eating it?

I didn't know it yet, but these were questions that would linger for me well beyond the end of my journey. Over time I would come to believe that to dismiss the wolf as a bloodthirsty enemy would be akin to labeling nomads in the same ignorant way that Europeans had done for centuries.

The reality was that survival on the steppe was a fine balance, and wolves, like the humans, were no more cruel than was required to survive. Perhaps the relationship between wolves and nomads was best described in the fictional tale "Wolf Totem." In it an old Mongolian herder recounts to a Chinese student that the "wolf is a spiritual totem but a physical enemy." Of course, this understanding was still light-years from my mind where I sat now, barely a stone's throw from the beginning of my journey on the way to the distant Danube.

In the end, the test between night and my fire went down to the wire, and there were times when I was sure the fire would not hold out. When finally the night began to wilt away, however, there had been no howls for hours. I placed the last morsel of wood on the flames and lay until the sun's glow had eclipsed that of the coals. Soon the fire I had so clung to was nothing more than a gray bed of ashes.

By the time we were ready to go, the sun had painted out the shadows, and, just as the mountains around us appeared to shrink in the daylight, the threat of the wolves began to seem exaggerated. I started to think that had I been a more experienced horseman, I might have taken the night's experience in my stride. As if to leave us with a reminder of the danger, however, only a stone's throw from camp we passed the fresh tracks of a wolf on the muddy banks of the river.

In the future, particularly on the open steppe of western Mongolia and Kazakhstan, I would not have the advantage of firewood, nor the company of Kathrin. While carrying a gun seemed out of the question, it was clear I might have to come up with some kind of plan. For the time being, though, I was just grateful to be riding away.

4

A FINE LINE TO THE WEST

WHEN WE EMERGED from the forest into the grazed slopes of the lower valley, thoughts of the dangers posed by wolves faded and I was comforted by thoughts of a bigger picture of the journey. The mountain river we followed from the pass, known as the Delgerekh, was part of a greater watercourse I had crossed paths with during previous travels. Not more than three days' ride downstream it entered the Ider River, which in turn flowed east and north, joining the Selenga, and emptying into Lake Baikal in Siberia.

Four years earlier during the cycling journey across Russia, Chris Hatherly and I had crossed Baikal's pristine waters by ship and ridden our bikes along the Selenga. The following year I had returned to the shores of Baikal to join three others rowing a wooden boat more than 4,000 km northward through Siberia to the Arctic Ocean. Following first the Angara and then the Yenisey River and rowing twenty-four hours a day, we spent four and a half months meandering through steppe, then dense taiga, and finally frozen tundra. Having reached the Arctic coast at the river's mouth on the Kara Sea, we abandoned the boat with a reindeer-herding community and made our way home.

Now, three years later, riding alongside the humble waters of the Delgerekh that would someday make the same journey to the Arctic, I was on a very different trajectory. Heading west into the center of Eurasia, I could never hope for the abundance of firewood, water, and fish that had come to characterize those earlier experiences. For nomads, pasture held currency above all else, and so I was destined to remain on the steppe, picking a line between the boreal forests of the north and the deserts and mountains found at more southerly latitudes. Although the river tempted me with the possibility of greater plenty, I was looking forward to breaking away from its predetermined course and returning to open horizons. Just a few days' ride from here lay the prospect of exiting the Khangai Mountains, from where our route promised to take us into the broader and drier terrain of western Mongolia.

Before we could leave the valley and recover some rhythm, however, the Delgerekh had some important lessons in store for us.

We had only just made camp near one of the first gers we had seen in days when the distant rumble of a Russian four-wheel-drive from down the valley rapidly grew into a roar. I was attending a pot of boiling water when the headlights found us. As Kathrin ran to pull the horses in close to the tent, the car motored in over the tethering lines and jerked to a halt half a metre shy of my stove. The engine cut out and there was momentary silence, but then a door opened and from beyond the blinding glare of headlights the silhouette of a man stumbled into view, a waft of vodka preceding him.

"Do you have whiskey? Vodka? Airag?" he screamed in Russian, digging his index finger into my chest. Infuriated by my blank look, he lunged for the knife on my belt. When I resisted, keeping it out of his reach, he clenched his fist and drew it back, ready to punch.

"I take two of your horses now! They are mine!"

What had begun as a calm evening in what we assumed was the safety of peopled, wolf-free lands was about to become an all-night ordeal during which we managed to narrowly save the horses but had our crucial navigation maps stolen. When the attacker drove away, we took refuge with a nomad family, only to find ourselves in the throes of more drunken antics. Arguments, the odd prod and jab at Kathrin and me, and the coming and going of horsemen lasted until dawn, when, upon checking the horses, it was clear we were still not out of the woods. We found Bor sitting on his haunches trying to lick a swelling that had appeared on his spine. It was on an area of his back well behind my saddle, in a spot where I had earlier noticed multiple scars—signs, according to vet Sheila Greenwell, of a possible warble fly infestation. The larvae of this fly were known to burrow into the flesh, causing painful swellings and then sores when the mature flies resurfaced.

Staying to rest the horses was not an option, and so I loaded my backpack and set off on foot with Bor and the packhorse, Kheer, in tow. It was a relief when two young men rode up to us with the stolen maps, although they promptly threatened to tear them up unless we paid for their services. After negotiating a fee of $10, we carried on aware that while we had escaped serious misfortune this time, there was no guarantee we would always be so lucky.

Even before we threw ourselves on the mercy of a friendly nomad family that night, it was obvious that one of the main challenges of this journey would be treading the fine line between the dangers of the wilds and those of a human sort. More important, the coming days and weeks of travel would confirm that navigating between these perils was a defining reality of life and survival for the nomads themselves.

⌗

AFTER TWO DAYS' rest we parted ways with the Delgerekh, crossed the Ider, and headed northwest. As expected, the bottleneck of the Khangai Mountains gave way to open, barren plains and sleepy hills where the land faded from an early summer green to a brittle golden yellow. The temperamental weather of the mountains mellowed, and nomad camps, like our troubles, grew sparse and thin.

On the shores of a brackish lake known as Telmen Nuur, we were able to buy a new horse from a nomad family and thereby allow Bor to travel load-free. The new addition was a calm eighteen-year-old gelding, bigger than most Mongol horses, with a sharp odor and unusual coloring. His torso was white, speckled with rusty flecks of chestnut, while his hindquarters were splashed with large chestnut spots. Rusty, as we named him, led from the front with a fast pace, which, coupled with the wide-open land, enabled us to stride out and cover around 40 km a day—far more distance than we had previously.

It was just over a week after leaving behind the Khangai Mountains that our respite from trouble ended and the rigors of the land began to test us once more. The northwest of Mongolia, which we were entering, is part of a semi-arid basin known as the Great Lakes Depression. Dominated by desert, shallow saline lakes, and salt flats, it is a dry and sparsely populated corner of the country where the distance between watering points for the horses would turn out to be farther than we could cover in a single day.

The challenge began in earnest with a precarious route between a rocky range known as the Khan Khokhii and the southern fringe of the Borig Del Els, a desert renowned as the most northern in the world, which spreads out in a series of sand dunes beyond Mongolia's border into the republic of Tuva, in Siberia. According to nomads we had spoken to, there was no border fence, and, owing to the remoteness of the Borig Del Els and lack of patrols, the dunes were a favored route for horse thieves who specialized in smuggling into Russia.

Our departure from the river Tes coincided with a heat wave, and by 9:00 A.M. the temperature had already reached 30°C. Although our horses were hardy, while working in the heat they required a minimum of 20 litres of drinking water a day—more than we could ever hope to carry. For the next two days we saw no one and were only able to water the horses courtesy of a chance thunderstorm that left rainwater collected in a handful of puddles along the wheel tracks we followed.

Three days farther on, the heat was taking its toll. Kathrin's face was sunburned to nearly burgundy, her lips were swollen, and her hands were a mess of splits and cracks.[1] I had long lost my sunglasses and, after days staring into the raging sun, my pupils felt seared. We were both weary and dehydrated, and so were our horses.

Hungering for water and a day or two of rest, we stumbled into an isolated camp of two gers beyond the dusty village of Baruunturuun. A mother and her children took us to a well in a riverbed, then invited us to join in picking apart the boiled head, organs, and trotters of a freshly slaughtered goat. We were ravenous, and so the rubbery boiled scalp, lips, ears, and intestines—which only weeks ago I had found nauseating—slid down with ease.

For all the refuge this family offered us, they were in a particularly difficult predicament themselves. In the summer months they ordinarily retreated to the cool of the Khan Khokhii Mountains, but their remote pastures had been overrun with wolves, and so they had recently migrated to the slightly more populated corridor between the mountains and the Borig Del Els. As we would come to learn during our stay, however, life on these baking hot plains that lay wedged between the wolves and the dunes was by no means a perfect solution.

Early in the morning after our arrival I woke with my eyes glued shut by gunk and dust and a terrible throbbing at the back of my retinas. Trying to ignore the pain, I lay listening to what sounded like the soft patter of rain, but which I knew to be a thousand goats and sheep being herded out. The long grueling summer days were what nomads dreaded most—it was crucial to take the sheep and goats as far as possible to graze between dawn and dusk so that they would grow enough muscle and fat to see them through the winter. In some respects winter was an easier life—long dark nights meant lots of sleeping, and during blizzards the animals would not leave the pens.

After the sound of the sheep tailed off I put my head down for a bit more rest. When I woke again, I was struck by suffocating heat and the sound of an approaching motorbike. Kathrin came to as well, and together we ripped open the door to emerge dazed into the searing white light of midmorning.

As the motorbike hurtled closer, there was no mistaking the familiar sound of drunken singing. We fast retreated into the tent, from where we watched events unfold through a gap in the entrance zipper.

A short distance from camp, the driver expertly cut the engine and used the remaining momentum to steer his craft to the doorway of a ger. As it rolled to a halt, two men clinging on behind dismounted and staggered off—one lumbering away for a pee, the other falling unbalanced to the ground.

When all three had gathered themselves and dusted off their tattered deels, they charged inside, demanding vodka and food from the mother of five who had served us so generously the night before. Not having gotten what they wanted, two of the men went to the second ger, where her in-laws lived. There were several comings and goings before the young brother-in-law of our host ushered the driver out. An argument ensued, and after the driver carelessly knocked over the family's own motorbike, the gloves were off. A crack cut through the air as the young man's fist slammed into flesh and bone. The driver stumbled backward, clutching at his face, and fell, butt first, to the ground. Some uneasy moments passed while he recovered, but then he steamed forward, picked up his opponent, and drove him into the ground. No one emerged from the ger. The dogs lay low, unbothered.

Eventually the brother-in-law and the driver gave in to exhaustion, helped each other up, and then drove off together on the family's motorbike, leaving the other one there. All fell still and quiet. The white-hot sun crawled across the empty sky, and the dunes of the Borig Del Els wobbled on the horizon. Perhaps drunkenness and the trouble it brought, I speculated, was a welcome distraction in a land that was so desperately lacking in movement.

When the heat became unbearable we emerged from the tent and stumbled nervously into the mother's ger, where we found the two drunks fast asleep and the family drinking tea. One of the men was a special guest arrived from Ulaanbaatar, and the other two were family friends. The fight was never mentioned.

With time I learned that the drunken episode was not only an ordinary feature of steppe life but synonymous with summer. Coinciding with the peak production of milk, summer on the steppe is the nomad's age-old opportunity to partake in socializing—and drinking. The drunken men had been imbibing *nermel arkhi*, also known as "Mongolian vodka"—a clear, wine-strength drink distilled from fermented cow and yak milk. When Carpini arrived in Kharkhorin after his long journey from Europe, it is most likely this drink that he witnessed wreaking havoc. "Drunkenness is honorable among the Tartars, and when someone drinks a great deal he is sick right on the spot, and this does not prevent him from drinking more," he wrote. "In short, their evil habits are so numerous that they can hardly be set down."

Years earlier, Genghis Khan also had bemoaned the culture of drinking: "If there is no means to prevent drunkenness, a man may become drunk thrice a month; if he oversteps this limit he makes himself punishable of this offence . . . What could be better than that he should not drink at all? But where shall we find a man who never drinks? If however such a man is found, he deserves every respect." Despite Genghis's apparent will to curb alcohol consumption, his son and successor, Ogodei, was known as a lifetime drinker whose death in 1241—rumored to have occurred during a drinking bout—forced Mongolians to return to the homeland to elect a new leader, and in doing so abandon plans to invade Western Europe.

On the second morning of our stay I woke feeling overcome by nausea. The semi-broken-down trotters, lips, ears, and boiled intestines from the arrival feast seemed to be inching their way through my bowels like some slowly dying creature. Soon enough the sun surfaced with a vengeance. Stripped down to my underwear in the tent, I couldn't help but look on in horror at my bloated stomach. As my belly grew taut and round, it seemed to accentuate just how bony my arms and legs had become. After a mere seven weeks on the road, the muscle and fat appeared to have shriveled away, leaving my knees and elbows—knobby at the best of times—more skeletal than I had ever seen them.

By midmorning the temperature was 40°C. I staggered into the shade of the main ger and joined the family, who were lying on the dirt floor. To keep the ger as cool as possible, the felt was hitched up about 30 cm from the ground, allowing some limited airflow. Just beyond the collapsible wall in the sliver of shade cast by the ger, the mother of the family lay in dry dust and animal dung on her side, her young infant cradled in her arms.

For the remainder of the day I lay where I had fallen, taking in the world from ground level—every detail of which suggested that even in the paralyzing heat, surviving winter remained at the forefront of their minds. Directly above hung a curtain of meat strips being dried to produce what is known as *borts*. When dry, the strips would be cut into pieces, then ground into a fibrous powder, ensuring that the meat would be light, easy to carry, and would keep for months. Gansukh had told me that using borts in the old days Mongolian warriors could keep a "sheep in their pocket." Indeed I had discovered that a kilo of this—a portion of which each night we would add to rice—would last a couple of weeks between Kathrin and me. Next to me in the ger, under a bed, lay a cow stomach freshly filled with the cream known as *urum*, and beyond the door outside a pile of dried manure—the only fuel for cooking and heating in a land where the temperature could drop as low as −50°C.

There was no escaping the slim separation from the elements, and as compromised as this family might have been on the plains, where the pastures were thin, the heat was oppressive, and they were vulnerable to the intrusion of summer drunks, I was beginning to understand that there the herds weren't as threatened as they had been in the mountains. To lose animals, whether it be to wolves, frost, or drought, would be the undoing of any nomad family.

When finally I emerged feeling better in the cool of evening, both the remaining drunken guests had gone. The herds had arrived from another day of grazing, and children were busily tying up the goats for milking.

By dawn the next morning we were up and moving.

ALTHOUGH NOMADS DO not own land, there are some who are more fortunate with the land they inhabit than others—historically the cause of territorial conflict between tribes. One long day's ride west, we reached a nomad camp nestled into a relative oasis formed by a delicate brook flanked by slender shoulders of silky green grass. Where dust had reigned supreme the previous day, children splashed about in the water, and the women lay out their washing on a carpet of grass. Welcomed by five adult brothers and their extended families, who lived in five or six gers strung out along the stream, we felt a sense of life and prosperity sorely lacking in recent days—and, as would become clear, none of the drunken aggression we had come to expect. Such a camp was all the more welcome given that we were now just a day's ride from the driest and most challenging leg of the journey to the west.

By the time we had set up our tent and watched the family's herd of eighteen fat camels thunder down the steep, dusty banks for a drink, we knew it was a watershed moment for our little troupe. Although Bor, who had been running free without a saddle for two weeks, had improved, we were reluctant to put him back to work. More significantly, Kheer—our loyal packhorse and the mainstay of our caravan—was beginning to show fatigue and early signs of friction sores on his withers. It was nothing a few days of rest and a slight adjustment in the pack saddle wouldn't cure, but such was our affection for Kheer that we couldn't bear the thought of pushing him on longer than we needed to. Although it was true he was the kind of horse I would have liked to ride on with to the Danube, quarantine laws forbade the export of Mongolian horses on the basis that they are a "national treasure," meaning I would have to sell them before leaving the country.

The idea of trading Bor and Kheer for a new, fresh horse had only occurred to us in the past couple of days, but presented with such an idyllic setting, we were convinced we had found their new home.

There was great excitement among the families when they realized we were offering two horses in exchange for one, and by dusk children came galloping bareback into camp on an array of mounts. The first horse we checked was tame but had a fresh injury on its back hoof, and the second tore away and bolted to his herd before I had even looked him over. The third horse stole our hearts. A small bay gelding with a long matted mane and dark eyes, he was younger than Kheer at around six years, but equally calm. To prove he was a nomkhon—quiet-natured and tame—six children climbed onto his back, while another clambered underneath and gripped his penis. Through all of this the poor horse stood resigned to his fate, the only sign of any impatience the trembling of his rubbery lower lip.

The following day we stayed put and celebrated the exchange. Continuing a long-standing tradition, the herder took his horse out onto the steppe with his children, where they plucked hairs from its tail and mane. We too took our horses aside, pulling out a few strands, while stroking them, and whispering heartfelt thanks.

Mongolians believe the spirit of a horse can live on in its hair, even long after death, and in the past, nomad warriors collected the hair from their best stallions to weave into a *sulde* or "spirit banner," which served to bring good luck and as a way of harnessing the spirit of nature. Genghis Khan had famously used a white spirit banner in times of peace and a black banner for guidance during war, and it was thought that after death the soul of the warrior was preserved in these tufts of stallion hair.[2]

On this occasion, the herder selling us his horse simply strung up the hair in the ger so that a part of the horse's spirit would forever be with the family.

"You should keep the hair from your horses close to you as well, especially when in danger, for it will protect you from bad people. Also, do not give away your halters, or anything else together with a horse that you are selling, because it means you haven't entirely let go," he explained through the translated words of Gansukh via satellite phone. I pledged to keep hair from all the horses I used until the Danube.

After the horse exchange ceremony, we retired to the ger of the elderly parents, where we feasted on a meal of noodles and mutton, and sat watching a Korean soap opera on their shoe-box-size black-and-white TV. Like most well-to do Mongolian nomads, they had a satellite dish parked outside and a solar panel on the roof trickle-charging a 12-volt car battery, which in turn powered the TV. This cobbling together of the nomadic way of life with elements of the modern settled world had appeared a little incongruous to me at first, yet gradually I was coming to accept it as part and parcel of the evolving story of nomad life.

While the constant need to pick up and move had always ruled out any possession or technology that couldn't be carried on camels or yaks during migration, whenever something came along that was suitable and could improve their lives, it had historically been embraced with unique nomad ingenuity. In the twentieth century, for example, access to tight-weave cotton led to white canvas ger covers becoming the norm, whereas for thousands of years before, there had been no available material to protect the felt walls and ceilings from rain and wind. During the Soviet period, metal stoves and flues had also come to replace open hearths in gers, dramatically decreasing the prevalence of lung disease and lifting the average life expectancy of nomads. Although TV was perhaps more intrusive than these other innovations, the nomadic way of life out here was master and remained fundamentally unchanged.

Even if the advent of solar power, batteries, and TVs was an invasion of sorts, it certainly proved invaluable for me. By using a 12-volt adapter, I was able to recharge my video camera, satellite phone, and laptop computer. The system had its downside, though. As had happened on previous occasions, the family sighed and moaned when the TV went dead. My charging had flattened their battery.

With the TV out of action, dinner was washed down by nermel arkhi and the family's attention deftly switched from this modern, borrowed form of entertainment to one that was as ancient as nomadic life.

It was the matriarch of the family, a woman in her seventies, thin and creased as an old bedsheet, who pulled out a stringed instrument known as the morin khuur, or horsehead fiddle. Boasting a trapezoid-shaped box, carved horsehead at the top of a long stem, and two long, parallel strings—one made from 135 tail hairs of a stallion, the other from 105 of a mare's—it had been handcrafted in a tradition probably unbroken for at least a millennium. The morin khuur's predecessor, the chuurqin, was believed to date back to the sixth century, supporting a widely believed theory that bowed string instruments originated on the steppes somewhere in Central Asia. Once established by horseback nomads, the tradition is thought to have spread first through Persia and the rest of the Islamic world, reaching western Europe in the eleventh and twelfth centuries.

As this old woman moved the bow back and forth, the shaky, bony fingers of her left hand pressed on its two strings at the top of the stem, just below the green-colored carved horsehead. The sound coming from the wooden box between her legs was like a scratchy, drawn-out cry, but nevertheless her husband, a bandy-legged old man ignited by vodka and the special occasion, began swaying back and forth rhythmically, his hands and arms twisting this way and that. The music and vodka settled together in my own system and I found my eyes wandering from the fiddle to various points around the ger: the horsehair ropes that tied together the ger, the airag in the corner, and a piece of horse dung dangling from the ceiling for good luck. According to one Mongolian legend, the morin khuur had originated from a boy whose slain horse came to him in a dream to instruct him to make the fiddle using its body so that they would forever be together. In the present day, it was clear the morin khuur was a celebration of this crucial union between horse and man—a relationship that not only made life possible on the steppe but which, like string instruments, had been adopted in Europe and become a part of the making of history across the globe.

WHEN WE WERE saddled the next morning, the man from whom we had bought the horse came to our tent with his ten-year-old son. If the grief we felt in leaving our horses behind was difficult, then it was hard to imagine how it was for them. The horse we had bought, named Bokus, was the boy's favorite and had been raised from birth by the family. Over the years the boy had no doubt learned to experience and interpret the world around him from the back of Bokus. Now Bokus was abruptly about to leave for good, and as his father lifted the boy onto the horse for the last time he sat looking pale and bewildered.

Just before riding out, the boy's father pressed a gift into my hand—a wolf's ankle bone tied onto a necklace. "Keep it with you for luck," he whispered.

The boy cried at first, but by the time we had crossed the brook, I turned to see that everything was returning to normal. The camels had been released for a day of herding, and the boy was moving them out on a different horse. A woman was wandering down to collect water, and a sheep was being slaughtered in the morning cool. Bor and Kheer were mingling with the family's herd and didn't raise their heads from the grass as we moved away.

⊞

A DAY'S RIDE west from the family's oasis-like camp, the corridor between the Borig Del Els and the Khan Khokhii mountains widened to a thirsty plain extending west to where sand dunes in the north gave way to the shallows of the giant saline lake Uvs Nuur, and the Khan Khokhii in the south became the foothills of the greater Altai range. Not far from the southwest corner of the lake lay the provincial capital, Ulaangom.

Even before I'd left Australia, a quick scan of maps suggested that the greatest obstacle in traversing Mongolia would be crossing these wide, dry deserts and plains, which separate central Mongolia from the western provinces. I had trusted that a way through the driest zone would come to light en route, but nomads we had met of late had been adamant there were no gers or fresh water for at least 100 km. The only solution we could think of was to start in the evening, ride through the cool of night, and keep going for as long as necessary.

In theory, this first attempt at night riding—a routine that would become the norm a year later in Kazakhstan—was a prospect that excited me. In practice, it became a farce.

We started late in the dark and not far from camp became disoriented and rode into a swamp. Rusty sank up to his chest in mud, and it was a good half hour before he extricated himself. For a couple of hours thereafter we made swift progress, but then the absence of the moon and a suffocating cover of clouds conspired to render the world a soup of blacks and grays, inducing a feeling of motion sickness. The flashlight batteries went dead, and we spent a frustrating hour searching for my compass after I accidentally dropped it. Most unfair was the cold—expecting a sultry night in prelude to a searing hot day, we instead found ourselves hunched over in a damp breeze. The only way to stay warm, awake, and nausea-free was to walk.

When the world resurfaced, it came in a series of fragments between long periods when my eyes struggled to break open. At first an endless black, empty plain materialized, preyed upon by swirling gray clouds. A couple of hours later, the silhouette of mountains grew from the south, tapering off into the western horizon. To the north a slim flicker of silvery gray indicated the waters of Uvs Nuur, the hills beyond which lay in Russia. We had come far closer to the southern mountains than we intended but were still half a day's ride from their base. The lake was even farther.

Come midmorning, the sun suddenly seemed to be upon us, but with the air still cool, what might have otherwise been terrifying appeared exquisite. The mist lifted, revealing a band of fresh snow on the mountaintops, and a slither of blue in the direction of Uvs Nuur. The breeze died, and the pale, naked land we trod on turned mute, amplifying the sense that we were far from any shore. It was only after midday, when the crippling heat began to beat down and the horses slowed to a crawl, that our spirits withered.

In search of water, my eyes scanned the mountains to the south, where a web of cracks and crevices on the slopes promised to collect at the base in some kind of stream or river but was thwarted by what appeared to be the buildup of millions of years of rockfalls and landslides. Through these mounds a few rivulets thus reached the plains with barely enough momentum to limp out of the shadows into the baking sun.

By keeping my head down and focusing on the end goal of each day, I was ordinarily able to keep the bigger picture of traveling to Hungary at bay, but not today. The great plain that rolled out into a horizon of heat haze was inescapable. It was too big to fathom, yet amounted to nothing in the scheme of the overall scale of the steppe. It would have been easier to drift off into the anesthesia of half-sleep and let the horses carry me, but thoughts about the great distances the Mongols once traveled in their many traverses of Eurasia kept me bolt upright.

For a Mongol cavalry just to *reach* the enemy typically involved a journey of weeks, if not months. During these campaigns their armies were known to routinely travel 50 to 80 km a day. At the zenith of the Mongol Empire, horseback messengers could even gallop from Kharkhorin to Hungary in

a matter of weeks, a legend seemingly confirmed by the great Venetian traveler Marco Polo, who wrote that Mongol couriers could cover 400 or even
500 km in a single day.

Reading historical tales about such exploits, one could be forgiven for
imagining the steppe as a single flat grassland through which horsemen
moved with a sense of freedom and ease. Here on horseback, though, it
was clear the cavalry were negotiating deserts, mountains, rivers, swamps,
heat, and frosts, and somehow keeping their horses fed and healthy, even
before leaving Mongolia.

There were, of course, secrets to the Mongol ability to travel over such
immense distances, which seemed all the more ingenious to me now. The
much feted courier system, *yam*, which remains a great symbol of the efficiency and discipline with which the Mongol Empire was ruled, relied on
staging posts known as *ortoo* every 30 to 50 km, where fresh mounts,
food, and water were permanently stationed. As the rider approached, a
special bell would warn the ortoo master of the impending arrival, and
for urgent deliveries the rider would leap from one horse to the next and
continue at a gallop. Unlike the Pony Express of the mid-nineteenth century in the United States, which was based on riders changing every 160 km
or so, the Mongol messenger entrusted with the communiqué from the
beginning was bound to deliver it to the very end. To protect his body
from the rigors of such sustained rides and keep him upright, even when
sleeping, he was bound in special strips of material and wore a thick
leather belt around the waist. Today, the silk sash most Mongols wear per-
forms a similar purpose, holding their lower abdomen tightly in place.
The yam system reportedly remained in existence in Mongolia well into
the twentieth century, until the Soviets began introducing roads and a
mechanized postal service.

In terms of the great roaming campaigns of the Mongols, the sheer
number of horses available to them was no doubt a key to their success.
Historical accounts suggest that every Mongol soldier traveled with at least
one spare horse, and up to three or four. This way, they could constantly
rotate the horses and ride fresh mounts. Carpini even commented that "the

Tartar does not mount for three or four days afterward the horse he has ridden for one day; so they do not ride tired horses because of the great number that they have."

Carpini may have been describing the Mongol transport system rather than the mounted soldier, but in any case, by way of contrast with European armies at the time, the majority of European soldiers fought on foot, and their cavalry units used heavy warhorses reliant on hay and grain supplements. It is also true that the geography of Europe, with its forests, mountains, and fertile cultivated land, could not cope with the kind of large free-grazing herds that had always been an indigenous feature of the steppes. Not only was it the case that Europeans could never have hoped to achieve supremacy over the Mongols in the open terrain of the steppe, but they were also at a disadvantage when the Mongols attacked them on their own home ground.

We plodded on until late evening, at which point we had been moving without a break for more than thirty hours but covered little more than 50 km as the crow flies. Without the energy to carry on, we made camp and collapsed.

COME MORNING I was woken by a rather zealous Kathrin, who prodded and laughed until I peeled my eyes open. She had been up early to check on the horses and had scanned the distant lakeshore with our binoculars.

"Tim! I think I can see gers!"

I stumbled out of the tent, wiped away the dried toothpaste crusted around my lips, and brought the glasses to my eyes. Sure enough, there appeared to be nomad families on the shoreline.

Several hours later we stumbled into a camp and were led to a well. At first it was a relief to see the horses empty out several troughs of water, which were filled by hauling up buckets from a shallow well. As we rode on along the shore through more camps, however, we began to wonder why just 65 km earlier nomads had sworn there were no people or drinking water to be found on the shores of Uvs. We had been directed to follow the main way—a series of wheel tracks—to the capital of Uvs Aimag, Ulaangom, which cut through a largely waterless desert halfway between the mountains and the lake. Had the nomads intentionally misinformed us, or did they simply not possess enough knowledge of the region?

The experience remained a mystery until later on in the journey, when I realized that when modern nomads travel more than about 25 km from camp, they typically use mechanized transport.[3] This led me to consider the vastly different experience of riding a horse versus traveling via machine, and the effect this had on traditional knowledge of the land. On a horse, one was constantly monitoring the pasture and the general lay of the terrain, keeping an eye peeled for natural paths that might preserve the horse's energy. The slowness of the travel enabled the rider to absorb the details of each unfolding chapter of the landscape. It was inevitable, therefore, that nomads of the past would have possessed far more intimate knowledge of far greater tracts of land.

One might argue, of course, that the convenience of a motorbike or car outweighs the importance of traditional knowledge garnered from horseback. For those nomads remaining out here, where the elements have never really changed, I couldn't help feeling that the loss of knowledge was not to be taken lightly. In a drought or severe winter, nomads are routinely required to move beyond their usual pasturelands, and details such as being able to identify plants and their uses, or knowing where to take the animals to cover in the midst of a blizzard, can mean the difference between a herd being wiped out or clinging on.

HAVING EMERGED FROM the desert plain earlier than expected, we had reached the last chapter of this leg of the journey, which would take us along Uvs Nuur, then on to Ulaangom.

Uvs Nuur and the vast but dry basin it drains is one of Central Asia's most northerly depressions and thought to have once been the bottom of an ancient inland sea. While nowadays a relative puddle, the 70 km stretch of water is still the largest lake in Mongolia by area, and it transformed our perspective of the landscape. Panning out to the north, its flawless surface mirrored the pale blue above, creating the giddy feeling that if I stumbled, I might fall from the saddle into the depths of the sky. It was an illusion shattered only by herds of horses that forged into the shallows from time to time, and flocks of gulls that bobbed idly about. To the south, meanwhile, the plain that had so dominated our thirsty ride was reduced to a thin yellow line, overshadowed by the range beyond, which was still dusted with snow.

At the southwest corner of the lake we left the shore and reached the edge of a sprawling delta of salt marshes and dry, seasonal riverbeds. During an overnight stay with a prosperous nomad family, we discovered a drunken horseman attempting to steal our horses, providing another night of sleepless drama but also the consolation of affirming we had left the dry belt of land in our wake and returned to problems of a human-made kind.

Tired, but quietly proud that we had more or less taken the horse-stealing attempt in our stride, we rode on through lowlands of luscious tall grass that grew upon the salt marshes. There were Soviet-era bores where the horses were able to drink, and pastoral scenes of nomads grazing the prestigious *tavan tolgoi mal* (herds of five species). After the uncertainty of the desert, and with just 90 km to Ulaangom, we hoped to keep a low profile and settle in for a few excitement-free days. One encounter in particular, however, would prove to have far-reaching significance, although the importance wouldn't become clear to me until more than a year and 4,000 km later.

From a distance, there seemed to be nothing unusual when a horseman came galloping our way, his deel and whip flying, but up close I was intrigued by his unusual features. His eyes had the typical Mongol shape, long and slender, but they were a clear, translucent blue instead of brown. Assessing us, he sat groping a long gray goatee, baring some rather twisted, yellow Russian-like teeth. He wasn't the first Mongolian I'd seen with distinctly Turkic and Caucasian features, but combined with his obvious dialect, there was something so exotic I couldn't tear my eyes away. It wasn't long before we were sitting in the man's ger, where, over tea, he explained his origins.

"We are Oirats, and our ancestors traveled to the Caspian Sea and back here. Our brothers, the ones who didn't come back, still live there, so please bring greetings from us when you get there."

While *Mongol* is essentially an umbrella term that describes the many different tribes of the Mongolian plateau that were united under Genghis Khan, the history and identity of the Oirats, like the geography of western Mongolia, has always been somewhat distinct. A confederation of the Choros, Durvud (or Dorbet), Torghut, and Khoshut tribes, believed to have originated from the forests of southern Siberia, the Oirats fought fiercely against Genghis until the crushing of their allies the Naimans in 1204.

Over the course of the thirteenth century, the Oirats proved to be a loyal force for the Mongols, known for their role in the battle of Homs and as Genghis's personal bodyguards, but despite their loyalty they were never fully accepted within the circles of Mongol society.[4] The Oirats were certainly not considered to be of Genghis's lineage, and according to the unwritten laws of the empire, no Oirat could take the reins of power as khan.[5]

In the wake of the collapse of the Mongol Empire, the Oirats nevertheless rose to ascendancy on the steppe, establishing a vast empire known as Zhungaria. While the story of their empire is a history unto itself, it is really after the beginning of the demise of this empire in the seventeenth century that a fascinating tale of triumph and tragedy—and an important chapter in the history of the steppe—unfolds. I will recount the details later, but here suffice it to say that the Oirats eventually fled west to the steppes north of the Caspian Sea, where they formed a new khanate known as Kalmykia. Less than two centuries later, under repression from the Russian tsar in 1771, they embarked on a mass exodus back to their roots in Asia, during which more than half perished on the steppes of Kazakhstan. Those who survived the journey regrouped as the four Oirat tribes in western Mongolia and what is today Xinjiang province in China. Those who stayed behind in Russia remained known as Kalmyks.

The man who was now sitting before me was a Durvud, of the Oirat tribe that nowadays forms the majority in Uvs province, and whose name derives from the verb meaning "to escape." While it is true that it is nearly impossible to distinguish Durvud Mongolians from other ethnicities by physical characteristics alone, and the features of our host might well have been due to Russian heritage from the Soviet era, I liked to think those blue eyes might have been a remnant this man had carried from his ancestors in the distant Caspian steppe.

Taking his words seriously, I imagined for a moment relaying his greetings to his fellow countrymen on the steppes of Russia. It was, after all, a journey I was far more likely to make than this man or any of his family in their lifetimes.

Filing away his image for another time, we climbed back onto our horses, waved goodbye, and turned again to Ulaangom.

5

KHARKHIRAA: THE ROARING RIVER MOUNTAIN

A DAY'S RIDE from the camp of the Durvud man—whose name I never knew—we crested a rise at sunset to lay eyes on a glittering ensemble of mud huts, fence-enclosed gers, and a handful of Soviet-era apartment blocks. It was the end of August, and having traveled more than 1,000 km from Kharkhorin, we had reached the remote capital of Uvs province, Ulaangom.

For three days we stayed with a family on the outskirts, relishing the chance to sleep in and taking turns traveling to the town center. Symbolic of Ulaangom's isolation from Mongolia's more populated central regions—and a measure of how far we had come—it was a town that relied exclusively on electricity from the power grid in the republic of Altai, in Russia, which was closer. Due to unpaid state debts to Russia there had been a summer-long blackout, and owing to this the streets were particularly quiet. There were, nevertheless, some private generators in operation, and we were able to delight in such luxuries as ice cream, sweet biscuits, and carbonated water.

Our celebratory mood was tempered only by the fact that within a week Kathrin was scheduled to begin work as a schoolteacher in Germany. The dirt runway in Ulaangom was her ticket home, and so this far-flung town had come to represent not only a milestone on my journey to Hungary but the end of our trip together.

As we approached this crossroads, a feeling of unease had been growing in me, and I reflected with a sense of regret that in the last two months we had been so tested and stretched simply by coping with day-to-day events that we had spent precious little time concentrating on each other. More to the point, we had barely discussed the uncertainty looming over us as a couple: Kathrin was about to disappear to the other side of the world, while I would carry on for at least another sixteen months, and that was only if everything went according to plan.

"So what should we do?" Kathrin uttered nervously after darkness and silence had fallen on Ulaangom one night.

Although we had been together for almost a year, Kathrin well knew I was committed to my dream of riding across the steppes, and that the dream had only grown stronger along the way. There was no turning back, and so the only way to spend time together would be if Kathrin came to join me during her vacations. At the same time, while Kathrin was ready for a more serious stage in our relationship, to me the concept of real love involved a commitment I knew I wasn't ready for or capable of at this stage.

Perhaps I was wrong, but I had a feeling that Kathrin, like me, sensed that breaking up was the most realistic way forward. Yet I couldn't fathom casting off alone on this without Kathrin's support. From Kathrin's point of view, she was about to plunge into a new job and life in Germany, and the uncertainty she felt must have been far more immediate.

After buying a plane ticket for her to Ulaanbaatar, we spent our last day riding south across a vast plain that angled toward the base of a dark wall of mountains known as the Kharkhiraa-Turgen massif. We had been watching these mountains grow for over a week, the 4,000 m apexes of the glacier-encrusted peaks at times coming into view and inviting thoughts of alpine pastures and river valleys. The name *Kharkhiraa* itself was a word that describes the roar of a river's rapids.

As we had come to expect in the openness of western Mongolia, what appeared to be a short ride became eight hours. We spoke little but managed to articulate a desire to remain in a relationship and see how things worked out when I arrived in Hungary, or whenever she could join me again.

The following morning we hurried on horseback into the village of Tarialan, where we had arranged a lift back to the Ulaangom airport. Then it was all over in a heartbeat. The driver cranked the engine into life, Kathrin leaped in, and I waved goodbye. Within minutes the only visible sign that Kathrin had ever been with me was the sweat marks from her saddle on the back of her beloved Saartai Zeerd, who by now was the only remaining horse that had been with me from the beginning.

Even as the dust trail of the car carrying her began to fade, I turned my thoughts to immediate plans. Digesting the significance of what had just happened would have to wait for another time.

LIKE MY OWN state of mind, the village of Tarialan was a place on the edge of two very different worlds. Built on the banks of the glacier-fed Kharkhiraa River at the point where its waters spew from a gorge into the sun-baked plains, it was both the end of the road for motorized vehicles and the gates to the mountains.

From here I hoped to begin the first chapter of my journey without Kathrin by traveling west over the Kharkhiraa-Turgen range to the sandy basin on the far side. On one hand, crossing the mountains was a practical decision—the alternative was to make a lengthy detour around the massif to the north—but there was something more important that had led me to Tarialan. This humble little village was the central, and only, settlement of a minority known as the Khotons, who still live a traditional nomad life among the inaccessible slopes and valleys of Kharkhiraa-Turgen. Numbering no more than two or three thousand, the Khotons are thought to be descendants of a Turkic tribe that originated in Central Asia. Over time they had adopted the Oirat Mongolian tongue but remained distinct from other Mongolian groups, practicing customs and beliefs that are a mesh of Islam, Buddhism, and the shamanic faith of Tengrism.

Tseren Enebish, my longtime friend in Ulaanbaatar, had told me about the Khotons and suggested I find a local friend of hers named Dashnyam. I was hoping he might guide me through the high passes that would be impossible for me to tackle alone.

After being pointed in multiple directions, I found Dashnyam's ger near the mouth of the gorge. As soon as I dismounted, his children ushered me inside to the ger's back wall and slid a bowl of dried curd and stale pieces of deep-fried dough (known as *boortsog*) under my nose. While children from neighboring gers massed about the entrance, Dashnyam's wife ladled boiling tea into a cup, then, with her left hand supporting her right elbow, passed it to me in traditional fashion.

Dashnyam knelt, cradling a chipped teacup with an open palm, balancing his elbow on his raised knee, and brought his face down to drink.

"Drink tea, eat boortsog," he said gently.

Even at a glance, Dashnyam was different from other Mongolians. In the absence of the pronounced cheekbones that keep the skin stretched taut into old age for most Mongolians, his cheeks fell away in a series of saggy folds and wrinkles. His eyes were wide and almond-shaped, sunken deep in their sockets, framed by bushy eyebrows. The most prominent telltale of his Turkic origins, though, was the craggy, hooked nose that reached out from his otherwise rather hollow face.

Quite apart from Dashnyam's Khoton ethnicity was his gentle, kind character. Even as he looked me over, his eyes were thoughtful, betraying a sense of curiosity without hint of opportunism.

When the tea had begun to revive me I pulled out the map and asked whether he would guide me. At first he scanned the map with narrowed eyes and a pained look of bewilderment, but when I made myself clearer, he cast it aside.

"When do you want to leave? Today? Tomorrow? I need to fetch a camel!"

He agreed to travel with me for eight days—time enough to make it over the highest passes. A camel, he explained, was essential, since my horses were tired and unshod, and the way ahead was rocky. It was imperative we leave at the first opportunity, since the passes could soon be blanketed with snow.

Dashnyam, who was in his late forties but had the stiff, stringy body of someone ten years older, launched himself into action and rode with me into the village. After shopping for supplies, he sent me home. "Take the bag of flour back to my wife and tell her to make boortsog. I am going to find a camel."

I SPENT THE day preparing in camp and getting to know Dashnyam's family, who, it became clear, were sorely destitute.

The father of five children all under the age of fourteen, Dashnyam owned one old horse and seventeen goats. In the evening, when other families herded sheep and goats by the hundreds, Dashnyam's eldest son, Tsagana, walked up a slope not far from camp and shooed his flock home. Milking was over within twenty minutes, and the little pail it filled held barely enough for a day's worth of milky tea. There were no strips of drying meat (borts) hanging in the ger nor pouches of yogurt being stirred, or even the ubiquitous trays of curd drying on the roof. With so few animals, Dashnyam neither had the means or reason to migrate with his family from pasture to pasture, and so shifted no more than about 3–4 km between winter and summer camps. As such, he was caught between sedentary and nomadic lives, without the security of a "five-animal" herd or the safety net of town.

Come dusk, when Dashnyam returned with a small female camel, I had decided I wanted to give him a horse. With Kathrin gone, I didn't need a third animal, and Saartai Zeerd, who wasn't happy on rocks at the best of times, was not suited to the mountains.

When I first placed the horse's lead rope in his hands, both Dashnyam and Saartai Zeerd looked at me blankly. But as my offer registered, a nervous smile spread across Dashnyam's face, revealing a not quite full set of yellow, crooked teeth. Rather than make him a gift outright, I proposed trading the horse for two days of guiding, which Dashnyam said would normally cost $27 (I would pay for the other days in cash). There was a degree of dignity about such a deal that made us both happy.

AT DAWN DASHNYAM entrusted Saartai Zeerd to his son and told him to take the animal away to pasture. Then we packed the camel, Dashnyam's wife threw a single spoonful of milk in the air, and we were off.

Not far upstream we entered the head of the Kharkhiraa River canyon. Mountains drew like curtains over the sky, and the steppe shrank to a puddle behind. The river, which lower down had been nothing more than an unremarkable braid of channels leaching into the thirsty steppe, tumbled through with the momentum of a thousand ice-melt tributaries, carving out a gap through an otherwise impassable wall of rock.

In the initial stages of the canyon we avoided the river, riding along the bank beneath the shade of tall, elegant poplars still fragrant with the life of summer. After the monotony of the treeless steppe I was struck by the poplars' leaves, still supple, but turning bright yellow. Cast against the deep blue of the river, the pale sun-bleached river stones, and the red rock of the cliffs, they were an addition to a world full of contrast.

Where the trees ended, the canyon's walls drew in tight. Dashnyam forged paths from one riverbank to the other sitting casually with camel in tow, gently tapping the rump of his horse with a whip. I lifted my stirrups to avoid the rapids, gripped Rusty's mane with one hand, and tugged at Bokus with the other.

Eventually the river became so deep and concentrated we were forced to ride along a precarious ledge. I was beginning to lose confidence in

Rusty, whose hooves slipped about on the loose rock, but then, as abruptly as the canyon had begun, the cliffs parted.

The plains had now completely slipped from view behind, and before us lay a glacier-carved valley where the river was dwarfed by a wide, rocky flood plain. Within another few minutes, the canyon had become an imperceptible shadow between the overlap of ridges, and ahead grew a sight confirming we had been squeezed through a portal into a different world.

Weaving through a maze of river boulders came a camel train. From a distance these elegant animals seemed to move in slow motion, their long curved necks extending and retracting with each gait cycle, and their baggage-laden humps bobbing to and fro. The rapid rate at which they grew in size, however, suggested they were moving with remarkable speed. By the time my eyes had focused on the three or four men and women who led the caravan, they had drifted right before us.

"Good journey!" cried Dashnyam, overcome with such a smile that his pointy chin reached out to greet them.

"Good journey to you!" they replied, dismounting to join Dashnyam cross-legged on the earth.

I was too excited to dismount, and rode to the woman who controlled the lead camel. For nomads migration is a special occasion when the wealth and pride of a family is paraded, and this woman embodied the tradition. Sitting in a silver-coin-encrusted saddle embellished with yak horn and decorated with red velvet, she wore a silky golden and green deel with matching earrings and a fluorescent green sash pulled tight in around her thin waist. Traditionally, sashes and belts were important symbols of status and wealth. Men wore them low around the waist, while women wore them high. An unmarried Mongolian would not wear one at all.

I reached out to shake the woman's hand, and she obliged me in this unusual gesture with a giggle. Her hands were strong, wrinkled, and worn, yet the twinkle in her eye and the full set of blinding white teeth spoke of a woman younger than me, in her early twenties. When she smiled her eyes and mouth spread as wide as her broad fleshy cheeks, radiating a naivety and wisdom that in my experience are common among young nomad mothers who juggle giant responsibility with the gaiety of youth.

But the overwhelming emotion that flowed from this woman now was her pride. She motioned to the five camels behind, where, apart from the family's herd, which had been driven down a day earlier, her entire earthly belongings were on display. Each camel—carrying as much as 300 kg—was packed with segments of two family gers. Lattice wall pieces, cupboards, and milking buckets and cans were all packed on the sides of the camels, while the wheel-like ceiling structures were cast over the humps. On the heels of the last camel came a huge guard dog of the bankhar breed—the large Mongolian mastiff that is a quintessential of nomad herders—with the beginnings of a new winter coat, and last year's still hanging off in dung-encrusted dreadlocks.

The woman pointed to the camel immediately behind her, where the kind of wooden baskets used to collect dung were brimming with odds and ends. Only when she dismounted and pulled the camel to its knees did I realize these baskets contained more than possessions. From the far basket, a young girl, perhaps three years old, raised her head shyly above the humps. Her hair was long and untamed, her cheeks rendered a deep red through exposure.

The woman lifted a sheet covering the basket immediately in front of me, and there, wrapped in a cocoon of sheepskin, was a newborn. Lying as placidly as the camel, the baby gazed up to a world framed by the wooly outline of the skin.

I was humbled by the thought that for much of the morning I had feared my horse might make a misstep on one of the narrow ledges or be knocked over by the river's current. This woman trusted her animals with the precious lives of her most fragile loved ones—showing more trust in those camels than many people in my own society would bestow on another human being. For these people, animals were part of the broader family, and, as such, they carried great responsibilities.

After bidding farewell to the family, we carried on buoyantly. Dashnyam seemed immensely pleased I had witnessed the camel train.

"Up there in the mountain they live in the summer camp." He pointed to the high mountains. "Very, very good grass!" He shook his head passionately, then leaned down from the saddle, picked some grass, and brought it to his mouth.

Down on the lower steppes where I had traveled with Kathrin, the driving force behind migratory patterns was cryptic, but here it was relatively clear. Nomads spent summer in the high mountains, where the pasture was rich and they could avoid the heat and insects of lower down. The family we had met was moving to the plains for autumn, where dew promised to reinvigorate the grass. Some families would remain on the lowlands for winter, but many would return to camps here in the mountains, where it was marginally warmer. Where nomads moved to depended entirely on the needs of their animals.

It was, of course, this drive to search out greater pasture that had seen nomads and their animals spread out across the breadth of the steppe all those thousands of years before. And while families in this region might only have been migrating a relatively small distance a year, I was reminded that my journey was not only on the trail of nomads who might have ridden the steppe in the space of a lifetime but, perhaps more important, in the spirit of the people who had shifted across Eurasia on their horses through the space of millennia.

In the evening as the sun began to fall more steeply, the tips of the ice-encrusted peaks of Kharkhiraa and Turgen breached the horizon. We rode far above the river on a grassy shelf, marveling at cliffs on the far side smattered with splotches of white—signs of ancient kite and eagle nests. On this evening, though, it was signs of continuous *human* habitation that would leave the deepest impression.

On a particularly straight stretch, the shifting columns of light illuminated a series of embedded stones in a variety of shapes and patterns— signs of nomad grave markers. Dashnyam led me up the slope to a spot from which we had a bird's-eye view. The pattern below was a perfect circle, perhaps as much as 50 m in diameter. At the core lay a circular pile of stones from which four straight lines of stones spread out to the perimeter like the spokes of a wheel. As a whole, it resembled a giant sundial, or perhaps the circular wooden ceiling of a ger.

This was most likely a grave type known broadly as khirigsuur, dating back around 2,700 years to the Bronze Age. Some archaeologists theorize that the nomadic culture of the period was influenced by the Scythian tradition of burying horses and tack together with the deceased. I had read that during excavations of some burial grounds up to forty-five horses had been discovered in a single grave—a sign of the nomad's enduring belief that the horse carried them into life, through life, and beyond into the afterlife.

Beyond this grave marker lay many more, of tens if not hundreds of different types. Of the circular kind alone there were numerous intriguing variations. Some were surrounded by a square perimeter, while others were squares surrounded by circles. Many were circles filled out with a cobblestone effect, and still others were circles containing no central pile of stones or spokes.

While it was impossible for me to judge, some of these were probably those of the Xiongnu, a nomadic people who ruled an empire in greater Mongolia during the Iron Age from the third to the first century BCE. It was their constant attacks on China, including a war with the Han dynasty, that is thought to have triggered the building of the Great Wall of China. Although the origin of the Xiongnu is subject to ongoing controversy and debate, many historians believe they were the original Hunnic people, whose descendants charged into Europe centuries later under the helm of Attila.[1]

In a kind of collective cemetery that evidently spanned thousands of years, we rode through silently and slowly, taking in monuments from untold eras and peoples. Among them were long columns of around fifty small vertically standing stones. At the northern end of each column, facing the east, were the figures of men carved from granite. Each man held a cup in one hand and the dagger on his belt with the other. Flowing mustaches hinted at the Turkic origins of the makers, as did sculpted noses more resembling Dashnyam's features than the average Mongolian's. These were balbal stones—a kind of engraved headstone found across Central Asia and thought to be memorials to individuals of the diverse Turkic peoples of the steppe.

Just as remarkable were the large red standing megaliths, known broadly as deer stones, that stood solitary on the periphery of the cemeteries, thousands of years since their makers had placed them there. Although the particular stones we saw had no sign of engraving, other similar standing stones in Mongolia are renowned for extravagant depictions of deer and for some of Mongolia's—and Central Asia's—earliest known images of human beings.

At the far end of the cemetery, we stopped to examine some deer stones. When Dashnyam climbed back onto his horse, I watched him closely. Observing a custom universal among horsemen the world over, he carefully approached his black gelding from the left-hand side and eased into the saddle. Horsemen in the Western world believe this tradition originates from a time when cavalrymen carried swords on their right leg. On the steppe, however, among the descendants of those who introduced horses and cavalry warfare to the West, there is a belief about this custom that is probably older than both the Iron Age and Bronze Age. In a culture where the sun has always been worshipped and gers still strictly face south toward the life-giving orb, the word for "left" in Mongolian, baruun, is the same as the term for "east." To approach a ger from the east or mount a horse from the left is to approach in the same direction as the sun passes through the sky. To approach from the right and therefore the west is the sign of an enemy and can only invite trouble.

When the cemetery was behind us, I asked Dashnyam what he thought about the graves. With a distant look in his eyes, all he could tell me was they were in memory of his ancestors, and that those who lay here had been heroes.

⊞

IN THE MORNING we reached the confluence of the Turgen and Kharkhiraa rivers, then continued up the main Kharkhiraa River valley as it turned sharply south. The mountains grew taller and the valley sank so deep and narrow that we waited for what seemed an eternity for the shadows of night to peel away down the far western valley side, then up to where we rode high above the rapids on the eastern side. When finally the sun reached us, the frost burned away and my tense, cold muscles eased. Rather than ride alongside Dashnyam, I fell in behind the camel, too tired to speak.

After leaving the grave markers the previous day we had spent a sleepless night camped with a herding family. From the moment we put our heads down to rest, the mountains had come to life with howling wolves and the crack and echo of gunshots. Men had been coming and going to check on their animals, and every time I seemed to be falling asleep the ger door would creak open and bang close again.

Now, with the sun melting any remaining resistance to sleep, I leaned back in the saddle, let the horse guide me forward, and surrendered. Where the stars had been, kites and eagles circled against an incandescent sky painted with streaks of cloud. Where wolves had prowled, the herders from the family we stayed with pushed their flocks high to the lesser-eaten pastures. As my hands loosely gripped the reins, eyelids heavy with gravity, it all passed by in lucid fragments.

Several hours on, hunger pulled me from my slumber. The river had mellowed to a knee-deep meander, and we descended to ride along the water's edge through spongy alpine grasses. For the rest of the day the only person we saw was an old man out watching his yaks. He dismounted ahead of us and sat waiting with his sleeves hanging past his hands. I joined him and Dashnyam on the grass and watched as the man's horse leaned in with its bottom lip quivering and pushed its nose over its master's forehead. The horse groaned and lifted its head, and turds dropped to the earth in a series of muffled thuds. A waft of fresh dung mixed with the sweet aroma of horse sweat drifted between us. Just as the man appeared oblivious to the cold wind, he didn't acknowledge the horse, the smell, or the trail of saliva on his scalp.

Come midafternoon the snow-dusted shoulder of Kharkhiraa peak was emerging at the far end of the valley. I was eager to make progress and disappointed when Dashnyam pulled up at a lonely ger, insisting at first we were stopping for a cup of tea, but later suggesting it was too late to carry on. But my feelings of frustration didn't prevail long.

The dim interior of the ger hummed with a dung-fired stove, and a cauldron of salty tea breathed moisture into the air. The walls and ceiling were hung with antique rifles, a fresh wolf skin, rows of drying goat meat, and ornate horse tack. Dashnyam pulled out his stone snuff bottle and offered it with both hands to the elderly man of the family, Davaa. In return, Davaa, who had a long, narrow sun-blackened face and a white goatee, produced his. The two men sniffed each other's in a sign of respect, then sat back to drink tea and smoke from long pipes. Back down on the plains beyond the gorge, Dashnyam was a poor man, but here he could partake as an equal in the broader traditions of nomad life. It moved me to see how he was treated with a sense of high dignity.

Dinner was freshly boiled goat head and a cup of bouillon to wash it down. When our bellies were taut as drums, a silver bowl of nermel arkhi was passed around. Then we lay down our bedding—me my sleeping bag, Dashnyam an old winter deel—and passed out to the muffled sounds of settling sheep, goats, and yaks.

I slept heavily, and in the morning rode away feeling as sharp and crisp as the frozen needles of alpine grass that crunched under my horse's hooves. The sky was clear and the horses, alert from a good night of grazing, twitched this way and that, drawing attention to marmots and foxes that darted away from our path, and a kite that dove to earth in pursuit of a ground squirrel. Unlike on other journeys, when my own body had been on the front line, on this trip it was the horses that were in that position, and it was through their needs, senses, and toils I experienced the land-scape. They had become my conduit with the land, and perhaps it was more accurate to suggest I was riding to Hungary learning to view the world through their eyes rather than those of a nomad.

Within an hour we reached a great sweeping corner of the valley where the river swung around in a right-angle turn to the northwest and split in two. The drama of 4,037 m Kharkhiraa slid into view. Gentle spurs climbed skyward to a craggy, indomitable peak entombed in a sar-cophagus of glaciers. From the summit a cloud of wind-driven snow plumed into the sky, and, as I watched, it cascaded down the northern face past giant chunks of glacial ice that clung to the cliff midway down. Where the plume settled at the bottom, the main glacier slalomed through black rocky spurs, disappearing into the bowels of the mountain, then reappearing as a slender, cascading stream forming the headwaters of the Kharkhiraa River.

A little farther on Turgen emerged. Capped with a helmet of ice, its sheer northern face of dark rock looked more like the cross section of a mountain.

After pausing for lunch, we began climbing high above the respective valleys to the 3,000 m pass between the twin peaks. I leaned forward, gripping Rusty's mane, following Dashnyam along a zigzag of narrow ledges. The camel cried every time its soft, wide feet became wedged between rocks. Only the pain from the nose peg Dashnyam pulled was enough to egg her on.

The climb eased off abruptly when we reached an ovoo and rode out onto the broad grassy pass. Directly ahead, a series of hazy blue mountains aglitter with ice rose from the horizon. They were peaks of the Sayan range, on the distant border with the republics of Altai and Tuva in Russian Siberia.

We had made good time, so when we crested the highest point, we resolved to spend the next day and night camped just below the pass. The clear, stable weather provided an opportunity to explore the higher mountains on foot. Leaving Dashnyam with the animals, I trekked to a razorback ridgeline at around 3,700 m, where I spent a couple of glorious hours gazing down upon snaking glaciers, and a series of turquoise lakes at their tail ends. Up so high, it was as if life in the thinner air had been distilled. The sweat and difficulties of the last few months fell away.

On the second morning in the pass we woke to cluttered skies. Clouds like floating battleships had gathered, and wind tugged and pulled at our tents. Curved columns of snow raked across the slopes. We rode through scattered snow showers, passing hills pockmarked with hundreds of lakes, and in the evening maneuvered down a gully to arrive in camp ravenous and cold. As would become a ritual for me as far as Hungary, we sat with our eyes glued on the stove, waiting impatiently for the water to boil.

In the morning snow came thick and hard. Dashnyam was worried.

"The camel's pads will slip on this snow, and we will have a very bad accident if we continue. Better wait till tomorrow, when the snow might have melted," he explained.

I was more than happy to spend the day in the tent, using the undisturbed time to catch up on my diary entries, although it soon became clear we were not as alone as we thought.

After breakfast there came the standard Mongolian door knock—the clearing of the throat and a loud spit—before three men carrying rifles and bearing frozen, chapped cheeks clambered into Dashnyam's tent.

"How is your journey going? Good?" they asked.

"How is yours?" asked Dashnyam, offering them tea.

I sat squeezed up against the tent wall watching the tea breathe life back into the men. Like the snowflakes in their hair and eyelashes, which soon liquefied, sending rivulets of water running down their faces, their rigid expressions melted and the tent became abuzz with chatter.

The men—one in middle age, the others in their twenties—were marmot hunters who had been living for a week in a rock shelter not far from our camp. Their aim was to collect as many marmot pelts as possible, which they would sell to traders on the plains. All was going well, so they planned to stay another week.

In the late afternoon when the weather cleared we joined the hunters as they checked their marmot traps. With little emotion they hauled out their victims and methodically snapped their necks. When this was done we returned to the cave, where the limp carcasses were skinned and tossed into a pot of boiling water, and vodka was passed around. Before drinking, each man flicked a drop to the sky and one to the earth, then rubbed a little on his forehead. Dashnyam shared his snuff bottle and tobacco, talking with the men in the measured cadence I had become used to.

As the vodka set in I leaned up against the rock wall and studied my hosts. Their deels were shredded and impregnated with oil, dung, and soil. They had nothing to sleep on, and no food bar the marmots they caught and a few morsels of stale boortsog. The older man's face was a landscape to behold. His nose rose in a broad plateau from the steppe of his cheeks, below which a mustache as frayed as his deel grew unchecked. His life had clearly been hard, yet there was no hint of complaint. When he laughed, the features of his face parted elastically, giving vent to a happy soul.

When the meat was done, a single knife was produced, and fatty chunks carved out and brought to mouth. The older hunter chewed ungraciously on a jawbone. He then picked pieces up and slurped on them before licking his fingers and hands clean of the rich marmot oil. It was a scene that had played out through the ages. The same oil had once widely been used by warriors who would rub it over their skin to prevent frostbite during marches in the winter. Today the oil is still valued as a treatment for burns, wounds, and rheumatism, although eating marmots, as these men were doing, is frowned upon. A ground rodent, the marmot had been one of the first known carriers of the Black Death, which went on to contribute to the fall of the Mongol Empire and threaten entire civilizations from China to Africa. Marmots are still carriers of the disease, outbreaks of which occur annually in Mongolia.

"What about the Black Death? Are you scared?" I asked them through Dashnyam.

Their laughter said it all. Ignoring the taboo about eating marmot meat, I bent forward and accepted a piece of the fatty meat. As it slipped down my throat, I had no doubt these were the hardest men I had ever met—not in the aggressive, macho sense, but in their gracious acceptance of the difficulties and privations of their lives. On the steppe when the grass was rich and thick, herds flourished, and the people rejoiced and gave thanks to tengri. When the land was in drought, or stung by a bitter winter, their herds shrunk and the people accepted it. Life and death were at the whim of the earth and the sky, and there was nothing inherently wrong with that.

Their world fostered an uncomplaining attitude I would have liked to think I could adopt and carry forth to Hungary—but which I knew was probably beyond me.

TWO DAYS FROM the hunters' cave, we paused by an ovoo from which the mountains dropped away to a vast crater-shaped valley. Through the middle of this, a single wrinkle of a stream flowed its way to the west, funneled out by the mountains onto a distant desert-like plain where it spilled into a wide shallow lake. We were about to drop down to a rugged landscape of sand and rock where alpine grasses gave way to little more than hardy desert bushes.

On the horizon, beyond this immediate landscape there were too many layers of mountains to count, each riddled with thousands of shadowy crevices, gullies, and peaks that would absorb a lifetime of exploring. For now, though, my mind was sated by the journey that had just passed.

I rode behind Dashnyam, admiring the way he held the camel's lead rope with one hand and smoked with the other, still managing to tap gently at his horse's rear when necessary. "Aha aha," he called every time the camel threatened to slow or panic. I didn't have the heart to tell him that for days he had been wearing my backpack upside down.

In the evening we reached the abandoned summer community of Khovd Brigad, where a few old shoes and round circles of yellow grass indicated that the community had recently packed up and gone. We were still a good day's ride from where I could expect to find people again, but it was here that our journey together would come to an end. Dashnyam needed to return before the winter snows blocked the pass, and with only one serving of porridge, a handful of pasta, and some dried strips of meat remaining of our food stocks, one more day together meant that we would run out completely.

In light of our humble prospects for dinner, my heart sank when two men on motorbikes came to us at dusk. They were hunters, had been riding all day, and had no food or shelter. Dashnyam offered them half our meal, and we went to bed ravenous. The hunters lay down on the earth and pulled their deels over their heads. In the morning they stood up, dusted off the frost, and climbed back on their bikes.

Over breakfast, I took the time to appreciate the idiosyncrasies of Dashnyam's character one last time. As always, he ate his share of semolina by dunking his head into the buckled old pot and licking until it was shiny clean, his hooked Khoton nose needing a wipe afterward. I still couldn't work out whether he had forgotten to bring a spoon and was too proud to borrow mine or simply thought it unnecessary. Afterward he rolled a cigarette along the edge of his worn soldier's boots, and then, while he smoked it, took supreme care to fold up his tattered but treasured tent. When he was ready to pack, he ambled bowlegged to his camel and brought her over to his gear, tugging gently on the lead rope to make her sit.

Without my cumbersome equipment, the packing that had taken us over an hour required but ten minutes. I looked on with envy as he swung his tent, pot, brick tea, and tobacco up between the camel's humps. The distance that had taken seven days for us to cover together, he said, he could manage on the return in two and a half—and judging by his light load, I could partly understand how. In the end, I was a westerner and would never master the art of traveling light the way he did.

When he was ready to go, I gave him a packet of Russian cigarettes and paid him for an extra couple of days. He presented me with a packet of matches, which I accepted with two hands and brought to my forehead, according to custom. The packet hit the headlamp that was still strapped on my head, and went tumbling to the ground, to my embarrassment, since in Mongolian culture dropping a gift was a grave sign of disrespect.

Lastly, I split our meager rations—a few pieces of curd and some old sand-encrusted jellybeans from the bottom of the boxes. He lifted the collar of his deel over his head so he could tightly wind the sash around his waist. Then he mounted up and swung his arm in an arc to the northwest, indicating the way I was to travel.

I watched him shrink into the distance until he disappeared beyond a ridge. The melancholy cry of his camel lingered for a few moments, but then I was alone.

FROM THE KHARKHIRAA-TURGEN range, there remained about 250 km until the point where the borders of Mongolia, China, Kazakhstan, and Russia converge in the heart of the Altai Mountains—a two-week journey. Just two days after saying goodbye to Dashnyam, however, I crossed the Khovd River, and it was there that my Mongolian journey effectively came to an end. I had reached Bayan-Olgiy Aimag, at Mongolia's western-most extent, where Kazakh nomads have been in the vast majority since migrating to the region in the mid-nineteenth century. Nominal Muslims who speak a Turkic tongue, many I met gravitated culturally more toward my next destination, Kazakhstan, than to Ulaanbaatar, and certainly they were geographically closer to the former.

With hindsight, I would come to understand that because the Kazakhs from Bayan-Olgiy had been isolated during the period of Soviet revolution and Stalin's ensuing rule, these people had retained a more traditional and authentic culture than their brothers and sisters in Kazakhstan itself. At the time, however, I felt that Bayan-Olgiy simply represented the end of my Mongolian experience, and a prelude to a land that would dominate the next twelve months of my life.

Short of the border itself, I decided to finish up my journey beyond the village of Tsengel. There I managed to sell my horses to a Tuvan school-teacher who promised to use Rusty and Bokus as work animals and not slaughter them for winter meat. Since neither the border with Russia nor China in Mongolia's West was open to foreigners, getting to Kazakhstan by horse through either country was impossible. I had therefore decided to fly over the mountains into Kazakhstan and buy horses as close as I could to Kazakhstan's eastern border.[2] It would prove to be the only stretch of terrain—about 250 km as the crow flies—that I would not be able to travel by horse to the Danube.

6

STALIN'S SHAMBALA

IN MONGOLIA I had ridden for more than seventy days and 1,400 km from east of the old empire capital, Kharkhorin, to the far western province of Bayan-Olgiy. It had been a time crowded with challenges—among them learning to ride, familiarizing myself with nomad ways, and getting through the daily test of finding water and grass. And yet in the scheme of my journey to the Danube, it had been little more than a prelude to the challenges that lay ahead. I had, after all, been riding through the forgiving conditions of summer in a land where nomads were often nearby to lend a hand.

It was with feelings of trepidation and excitement that I looked ahead to the next broad chapter of my journey: Kazakhstan. The trepidation was because I knew Kazakhstan would be the make-or-break leg of the journey—not simply because of the sheer distance involved, the topography I could expect, and the fact that winter would be on my heels, but because of the social legacy of the Russian Empire and the Soviet Union, which I would confront in its many forms.

And yet I would also be heading into the heart of my journey—the remote center of Eurasia, which had been pivotal in the history of steppe nomads. Somewhere out there in the immense and sparsely populated deserts, steppe, and mountains—during a crossing that promised to be more than twice as far as that of Mongolia—there beckoned the kind of freedom of travel and cultural immersion I had dreamed of.

One of the first times I had heard anything about Kazakhstan had been in 2000 during the bicycle journey. Chris and I had stayed for some days with an ethnic German family in Siberia who had recently moved from the Kazakh steppes, where they had lived in exile since Stalin deported the Volga Germans during World War II. They had told of a land so hot in summer that Kazakh nomads wore heavy sheepskin coats and hats to insulate from the sun. In winter, the wind and the cold were more severe than in Siberia—compounded by the absence of the shelter and firewood found there in the dense taiga forest. Since that time, I had been fixated on maps of Kazakhstan, and my fascination with the country had steadily grown.

Almost equal in size to Western Europe, and the largest of the former Soviet nations behind Russia, Kazakhstan occupied what for many in the Western world is a geographical blind spot, stretching from the north Caspian Sea in the west (that technically lies in Europe) to China and the Altai in the east. In the south its borders pass through the legendary Central Asian deserts of the Kyzylkum and Karakum, and the ridgelines of the Tien Shan, China's "Celestial Mountains." To the north, sweeping grasslands merge with the beginnings of the Siberian taiga.

Significantly for me, Kazakhstan lay at the geographical heart of the Eurasian steppe, encompassing the most extreme terrain and climate of the nomads, and it was home to the world's oldest continuous horseback culture. Historians believe it was in the country's north, where present-day Akmola province lies, that an ancient people known as the Botai (c. 3700–3100 BCE) became the first humans to domesticate the equine.

Since that early period of nomad history, the Kazakh lands had played a central role in the rise and fall of steppe empires, including that of the Mongols. While the grasslands, desert, and mountains stretching from

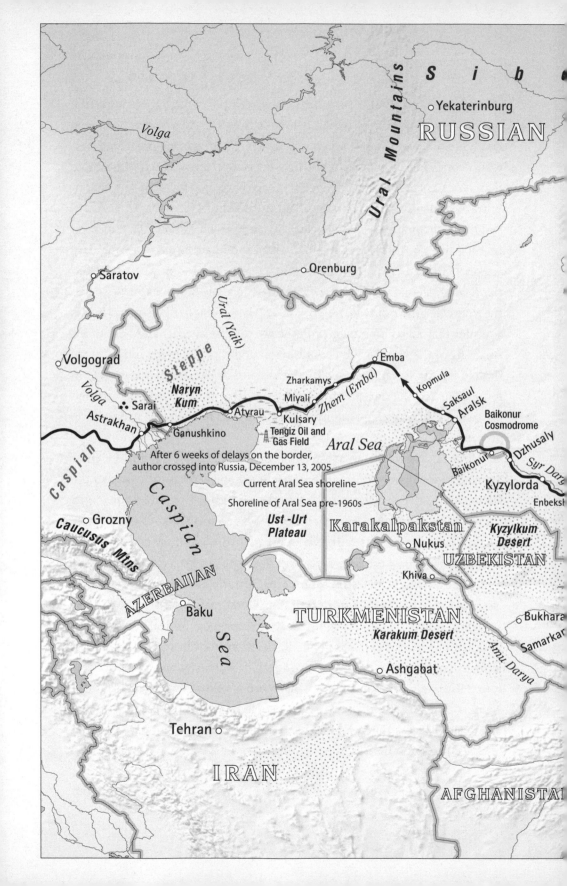

Yekaterinburg

Sib

RUSSIAN

Ural Mountains

Volga

Orenburg

Saratov

Ural (Yaik)

Volgograd

Steppe

Emba

Zhem (Emba)

Zharkamys

Kopmula

Volga

Naryn Kum

Miyali

Saksaul

Aralsk

Astrakhan

Sarai

Atyrau

Kulsary

Baikonur Cosmodrome

Ganushkino

Tengiz Oil and Gas Field

Aral Sea

Baikonur

Dzhusaly

After 6 weeks of delays on the border, author crossed into Russia, December 13, 2005.

Syr Dary

Caspian

Current Aral Sea shoreline

Kyzylorda

Shoreline of Aral Sea pre-1960s

Enbeksh

Grozny

Caspian

Ust -Urt Plateau

Karakalpakstan

Kyzylkum Desert

Caucusus Mtns

Nukus

UZBEKISTAN

Sea

Khiva

Bukhara

AZERBAIJAN

Baku

TURKMENISTAN

Samarkar

Karakum Desert

Amu Darya

Ashgabat

Tehran

IRAN

AFGHANISTAI

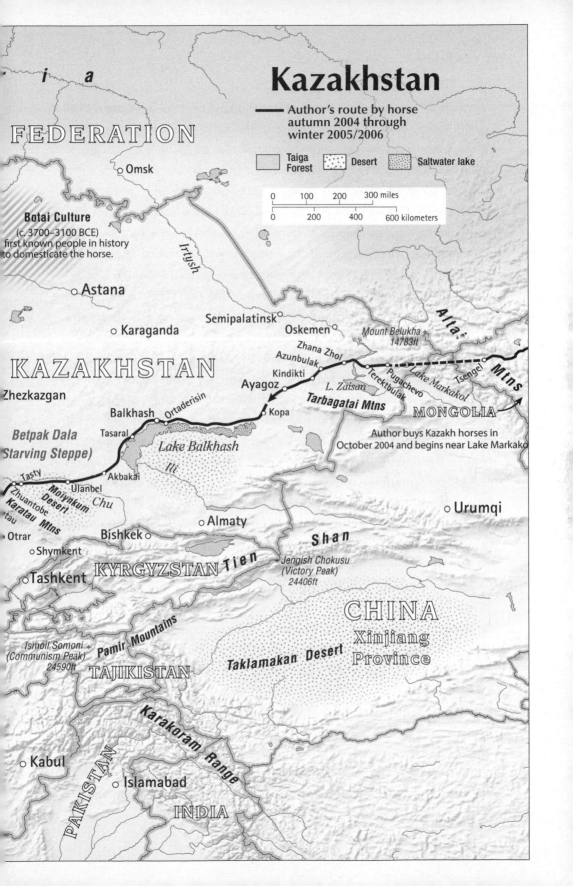

Kazakhstan

━━ Author's route by horse autumn 2004 through winter 2005/2006

☐ Taiga Forest ⬚ Desert ▨ Saltwater lake

0　100　200　300 miles
0　200　400　600 kilometers

FEDERATION

○ Omsk

Botai Culture
(c. 3700–3100 BCE)
first known people in history
to domesticate the horse.

Irtysh

○ Astana

○ Karaganda
　　　　　Semipalatinsk ○ 　Oskemen ○ 　*Mount Belukha +*
　　　　　　　　　　　　　　　　　　　　14783ft
　　　　　　　　　Zhana Zhol
KAZAKHSTAN　Azunbulak
　　　　　　　　Kindikti　　　　　　Terektbulak　Pugachevo　　*Altai*
Zhezkazgan　　　Ayagoz ○　　L. Zaisan　　　　　　Lake Markakol　Tsengel　　**Mtns**
　　　　　Ortaderisin　　　　　**Tarbagatai Mtns**
Balkhash ○　　　　　Kopa ○　　　　　　　　　　**MONGOLIA**
Tasaral　　　　　　　L. Zaisan
Betpak Dala　*Lake Balkhash*　　　　　Author buys Kazakh horses in
(Starving Steppe)　　　　　　　　　October 2004 and begins near Lake Markakol
　Tasty　Akbakai　*Ili*
Zhuantobe　Ulanbel
Karatau *Moiynkum*
Mtns *Desert* Chu　　　　　　　　　　○ Urumqi
tau
○ Otrar　　○ Almaty
○ Shymkent　　　　　　　　*Shan*
　　Bishkek ○
○ Tashkent　**KYRGYZSTAN**　*Tien*　→*Jengish Chokusu*
　　　　　　　　　　　　　　　　(Victory Peak)
　　　　　　　　　　　　　　　　24406ft　　**CHINA**
　　　　　　　　　　　　　　　　　　　　Xinjiang
Ismoil Somoni +　*Pamir Mountains*　　　**Province**
(Communism Peak)
24590ft　　　　　　*Taklamakan Desert*
TAJIKISTAN

Karakoram Range

○ Kabul
PAKISTAN
　○ Islamabad
　　INDIA

the Caspian Sea to the Altai did not have the kind of treasures sought during the conquests of China, Europe, and the more fertile regions of Central Asia, it was a strategic steppe heartland that could be used as a horse highway bridging Asia with Europe, and a vast sanctuary where millions of horses could be grazed. In Genghis Khan's own lifetime, some of his most important conquests were launched from here, including the crushing of the Khwarezm Empire in Central Asia. These were also the lands that Genghis's oldest son, Jochi, had been given control of after his father's death, and which became entrenched as part of the Golden Horde.[1]

Just as important as the strategic nature of the Kazakh territory for the Mongols were the people who inhabited it. Tribes of mixed Turkic descent, they shared a common nomadic way of life with the Mongols, in some regions moving as much as 1,000 km a year in pursuit of pasture. The inherent rigors of this life made them formidable soldiers, and although the Mongols initially faced fierce resistance during their probing campaigns—most notably from the Kipchaks—historians estimate that the Mongolian army that invaded Europe consisted of only around 10 percent Mongolian soldiers; the bulk of the remainder were of Turkic extraction. In fact, as the Mongol Empire fractured into autonomous khanates in the late thirteenth and early fourteenth centuries, Turkic came to replace Mongolian as the language of the ruling class in much of the southern, central, and western regions, including the Golden Horde.

It is unclear when the identity "Kazakh"—a term that means "free rider"—emerged, but in the eighteenth century, three Turkic hordes, known as the Ula Juz (Elder Horde), Orta Juz (Middle Horde), and Kishi Juz (Junior Horde), united to form what would become the modern nation of Kazakhstan. Riding through their country would be to ride through the nucleus of the nomad's world—the original steppe melting pot.

IN A FORESHADOWING of the complex bureaucracy I would have to deal with as I traveled west, just getting to Kazakhstan proved difficult. As previously noted, the borders of China and Russia were closed to foreigners in western Mongolia. I'd tried nonetheless to wangle some way to transit the small stretch of Russia that lay between Mongolia and Kazakhstan by horse, presenting my visa invitation to an official at the Russian embassy in Ulaanbaatar. But he held up my invitation in anger and growled, "You understand Russian? The border is closed! And you know what? This invitation is toilet paper. That is what it is!"

With little choice, I bought a ticket on a charter for the short flight from Olgiy to the city of Oskemen (also known by the Russian name Ust-Kamenogorsk) in eastern Kazakhstan. My plan from there was to drive east, deep into the Altai—home of the mythical *shambala*, a paradise on earth that, according to Buddhist beliefs, will reveal itself upon the destruction of humanity—and as close as possible to the Mongolian border, to look for tough mountain breeds. From there, I hoped to quickly descend from the mountains before the winter hit and begin the long ride west toward the Caspian Sea. The complete crossing of Kazakhstan from east to west amounted to more than 3,000 km in a straight line—much more by horseback—and I estimated it could take anywhere between six months and a year.

I landed in Oskemen, a small industrial city that had once been a Russian fort town, during the first week of October, when the mountains were dusted in fresh snow. A couple of weeks later, a taxi driver known as Meirim was awash with excitement as we loaded his car in front of a central Oskemen hotel. With the trunk full and the backseat loaded to the ceiling, I handed over half of the agreed-upon sum of money—about $100—for him to drive me out of the city and begin searching for horses.

Meirim's eyes were alight like those of a young boy plotting an adventure. "I have told my wife that I will be away for just two days," he said. "When we are out there, I will call and explain we have been delayed."

It was not without reservations that I had agreed to hire Meirim. I had come to know the middle-aged father of two after accepting a ride in his taxi from the Oskemen airport. On the way into the city a speeding car had run down a pedestrian right before our eyes, and instead of stopping to help, Meirim had mouthed off at the traffic holdup, tooted his horn in fury, and then driven up over the curb and around the scene. There was a tough survival instinct just behind his disarming friendliness, and I wasn't sure I could trust him.

On the other hand, I had learned that Meirim was a Kazakh from Bayan-Olgiy province in western Mongolia. During Soviet times he had served as a tank operator in the Gobi Desert and gone on to become a professional translator for the Soviet army, specializing in Mongolian, Russian, and Kazakh. With the fall of the Soviet Union, he had spent several years trading marmot furs between Siberia and Mongolia before taking the opportunity to emigrate from Mongolia to the "motherland" in search of a better life.

Because I spoke Russian I could communicate freely with Meirim, and I was hoping his knowledge could help me reestablish a sense of continuity between Mongolia and Kazakhstan that had been broken not just by my plane flight and modern political boundaries but also by more than two centuries of dramatic social and political change. Although Mongolia and Kazakhstan might once have resembled each other as pastoral, nomadic societies, the Russian Empire had been encroaching on the Kazakh steppe as early as the latter half of the eighteenth century. By the 1880s most Kazakh lands were firmly under Russian control, and Russia's designs were such that the Russian commander in chief of the Kazakh headquarters in Almaty had the audacity to declare: "There is a requirement to admit with sincerity that our business here is a Russian one, first and foremost, and that land populated by Kazakhs is not their own, but belongs to the state. The Russian elements must force them off the land or lead them into oblivion."[2]

In the twentieth century Stalin initiated an intense industrialization of Kazakhstan that included the forced settling of nomads in collectives, the plowing up of steppe for grain production, and a process of cultural russification. Kazakhstan's remoteness also made it his favorite dumping ground for enemies. Some of the better-known prisoners of Kazakhstan's many gulags included Trotsky and Alexander Solzhenitsyn.[3] By 1989, the Kazakhs had long become an ethnic minority in their own lands, eclipsed by Russians, and it was estimated that 40 percent—mostly those living in urban areas—had lost proficiency in their native tongue.

Since then, of course, the Soviet Union had unraveled, and I was entering a country going through incalculable upheaval as it made the difficult transition to both independence and a free market economy. In these times of change it seemed likely that Kazakhstan's emerging identity would have less to do with its renown as the birthplace of horsemanship than as a resource powerhouse. The discovery of massive oil reserves on the Caspian Sea had attracted billions of dollars of foreign investment since the breakup of the Soviet Union, and some analysts were predicting that Kazakhstan would be among the world's top five oil producers by 2015.

If there was any chance of getting beneath the multiple layers of change that had coursed through Kazakhstan and reconnecting with the spirit of the horseback nomad, then Meirim, I reasoned, was surely a good start.

On the edge of the city a dacha village gave way to the open steppe—an undulating sea of pebbly earth sprinkled with hardy tufts of sun-bleached grass. The sky was gray and stagnant, casting dreary light onto the earth, which seemed to be resigned to the coming winter. I wound down the window, letting the cold air whisk away the mental cobwebs that had gathered around my senses in the city.

Meirim began to tell stories about the land around us. There was a mountain pass called Ayultai, which means "dangerous" in Mongolian. "When you ask the locals if they know what these names mean, they just say, 'Oh, there was a man called Ayultai.' They don't realize that so many of the places here have Mongolian names." As if to prove the point, we dropped into a valley thick with a pall of wood-fire smoke and came into a village hugging the bend of a shallow river. It was named Targyn— according to Meirim, a corruption of the Mongolian word *targan*, which means "fat" and is often used in describing horses.

"There are many Mongolian Kazakhs living here," said Meirim. "I lived here to start with for the first year as well, with relatives." He explained that many families occupied overcrowded homes while they searched for work and a new beginning.

The wooden homes were dark and gray, and the streets largely deserted. Among the locals, there were few if any Russians to be seen. Barely a soul acknowledged our car as we roared through.

The mass exodus of Kazakhs from Mongolia—and from other regions including China and Iran—to Kazakhstan began in the wake of the Soviet Union's collapse. In 1992, in a move to increase the native population, the president, Nursultan Nazarbayev, convened a kurultai, or council, and adopted a resolution appealing to all Kazakhs to unite under a single flag on the soil of Kazakhstan.[4] While sixty thousand Kazakhs had left Mongolia for Kazakhstan over the next few years, many had since returned to Mongolia, disenchanted. Many more likely wound up in impoverished villages such as Targyn.

AN ENGLISH LONG rider (equestrian traveler), Claire Burges Watson, who knew the area, had given me the name and address of a man who I hoped would be able to help me in Kazakhstan.[5] Ruslan was a herder and fisherman in his mid-twenties who at one time had traveled with her on horseback into Kyrgyzstan. Late in the evening, we arrived at his home in the village of Slavyanka.

Still smelling of fish, Ruslan and his brother met us with open arms. Ruslan was an athletic-looking man with coarse hands, thick eyebrows, and a strong jaw. Unlike Meirim, who had a classic, open face, Ruslan's was more chiseled, and he had a large, almost Russian nose. His charisma and strength must have made him popular among village girls, and when he spoke in his gentlemanly manner, I imagined he charmed the hearts of little old ladies. Meirim, by contrast, was a short, wiry little man with delicate hands who seemed to speak loud and gesticulate with his arms in order to enlarge his presence.

After a night in Ruslan's family home, we spent a day searching for horses in the nearby village of Terektbulak, to no avail. The horses we inspected were either old and scarred or untrained and dangerous. Without exception, they were also expensive, averaging $500.[6] Because I had been banking on a budget of $10 a day, the prices made my blood run cold. Ruslan did everything but soothe my concerns.

"Tim, if you want a really good horse, you will need $1,000. The price you are being offered is purely meat value." He explained how trucks from slaughterhouses in the city often came around to the villages. Whoever was in need of money sold their horses.

I wasn't ready to accept the high prices, so we set out early the next day east along the Kurchum River to a remote mountain valley near an alpine lake called Markakol. Meirim's spirits rose as we snaked through the rocky slopes. The territory had lain beyond the reach of Stalin's plans for Kazakhstan's north and looked more like the untamed environment of Mongolia. Ruslan, on the other hand, was becoming *more* anxious, perhaps because we had now gone well beyond his network of loyal friends and family.

The gentle slopes became sheer ridges that blocked out much of the low sunlight and the road gradually deteriorated. It was in the village of Maraldy that Meirim decided his city car could not go on. There we negotiated with a local who owned a Russian Niva with four-wheel drive to take us to Pugachevo—the end of the road and the last place in the valley where I might find horses.

The Niva lurched through puddles of snow and mud, often on the edge of a sheer drop down to the river. Eventually we pulled over a rise onto a wide, open stretch of the valley, revealing a vista of peaks rising seamlessly into brooding gray clouds. Pugachevo, a village of about 160 homes, lay nestled below, among the gentle slopes on the river's edge.

Our party was now four—me, Meirim, Ruslan, and our driver—and in Pugachevo, this became eight. The idea was to find someone who knew someone. We stopped at every second house, asked questions, then rolled on. Those who approached the car were obliged to shake each passenger's hand, which was becoming difficult, since we all had to lean through the driver's window. The standard greeting used by the nominally Muslim Kazakhs, "As-salam aleikum," was followed by the standard response, "Wa aleikum as-salam," and sometimes by "Zdrast-vuy-tye"—"hello" in Russian—when they realized there was a white man in the car.

Nurkhan, a short, robust man with a clean crew cut, wearing camouflage and Russian army boots, considered us his personal guests. He made sure word circulated that a horse buyer was in town. There was something tough yet fair about him. His long, slender Mongolian eyes set into a broad, open face conveyed the maturity of a patriarch. He bonded quickly with Ruslan, the two of them talking avidly in Kazakh; I could still understand much of their conversation, though, because they often swore fluently in Russian midsentence.

With Nurkhan yelling out demands to anyone who crossed our path, it wasn't long before the horses began to line up. There was an old nag, "the best in the village," that had a back sunken like an old couch. A mare that had open back wounds and a foal by its side was touted as "the perfect horse for the job." When I said that I couldn't possibly ride such an injured horse, they told me, "Tim, you can sell this horse for twice the price when you get down to the steppe and buy yourself another!"

Nurkhan promised better horses and after lunch took me to a man renowned for his workhorses, which regularly lugged 70 kg loads of fish from Lake Markakol for trading. The man seemed reluctant to sell, but Nurkhan and others urged him to consider. I was led to a white gelding in a yard, followed by half of the village men. The horse's withers and spine were thick with muscle, his legs tough and sinewy. Like Mongolian horses, he was a stocky, heavily built horse. With feigned confidence, I took a close look in his mouth—I had been given a crash course in reading horse teeth, but in reality had little experience—and took him for a ride. He seemed to have stiff legs. Perhaps the gelding was recovering from work, but more likely was very old. I was sure he was at least fifteen.

"He is ten," said the owner.

"But how could that be? I can see he is much older!" I replied.

A man from the crowd vouched for the owner.

"I remember when this horse was born. The horse is no more than ten."

I took another look at the teeth, then at Ruslan and Meirim. They were silent. After much mediation by Nurkhan and others, I accepted that I was probably mistaken and was offered a price of 65,000 tenge (about $550). But I wasn't buying yet.

As darkness fell, a man arrived on a young chestnut horse that he had brought down from a herd in the mountains. Named Ogonyok—which meant "small flame" in Russian, but was also the namesake of a local wildflower—it had short, stocky front legs and a powerful chest. Although the animal was flighty, I liked him, and the owner invited us home for dinner.

Messages were run to relatives near and far before they decided it was in fact for sale, and in the process vodka began to flow. It began as a three-shot toast, but whenever the bottle of vodka was near empty, another replaced it, and I lost count. Somewhere in the midst of broken flashes of detail, I agreed to buy the chestnut horse and return the following day with payment.

Before leaving Pugachevo, Nurkhan secretively ushered us into his home, where he pulled up a trap door under a rug and produced a glass bottle filled with a dark red liquid. "This, my friends, is a secret, worth a fortune. It is blood from deer antlers. You know, good for . . ." He panto-mimed that it was an aphrodisiac. The three of us raised a toast and swilled down a shot of the stuff, followed by more vodka, then bundled into the Niva. It wasn't until we were sitting in the car that I wondered what good an aphrodisiac might do at that particular moment.

The Niva bucked and swayed in the night, and my head began to swim. I couldn't work out whether it was motion sickness or vodka, but I was overcome with nausea by the time we reached Maraldy and stepped out of the car into the freezing air. Meirim slumped into position behind the wheel of his own car, and Ruslan spread out on the backseat and fell asleep.

After negotiating just two bends, during which we very nearly veered off the edge of the road, I took over the wheel and guided the car down the winding valley road into the foothills. Meirim passed out, his head on the dashboard, where it rattled and rolled.

I must have been driving for a couple of hours when the shuddering of the car in the gravel suddenly became so violent it woke Meirim from his stupor.

"Stop!" he yelled. We stumbled out.

"Fucking Australian! If you were riding a horse and it had a broken leg, would you notice? This wheel is square! Don't you know they are meant to be round?"

The front right wheel had but a few shreds of tire remaining.

"Yeah, well, you didn't notice either, did you?" I retorted. "Because you are so drunk you can hardly stand up!"

Meirim took the tire off, threw it off the roadside in a rage, and fitted the spare.

"I will never let you drive again!" he shouted, handing the keys to Ruslan.

IT WAS WELL after midnight by the time we neared Slavyanka, but the night for us was only beginning. Eleven kilometres short of home Ruslan veered away to a ferry crossing point on the Irtysh River, where his wife-to-be worked twenty-four-hour shifts at a café. Inside, Ruslan greeted the patrons—mostly sleep-deprived truck drivers and local drunks—with a handshake, then announced to Meirim and me that we were his guests. I told him angrily that we needed to get home and back to Pugachevo by midday, but this only strengthened his resolve. On our table landed a bottle of vodka, which he and Meirim quickly finished . . . then another.

When Meirim began casting a steely stare at an aggressive-looking drunk in a soldier's uniform, I knew things were hurtling out of control. The soldier came and sat next to me, his breath heavy with alcohol. Ruslan stalled the face-off with a fresh round of vodka. I dragged Meirim outside.

"You know, Tim, I feel like I am young again! Those fuckin' Russians, these Russian Kazakhs, they know nothing! I just want to fight! You know that feeling, when you just want to break someone's nose?" I could only hold him out there for so long before he went back inside. It was the first of many close shaves when Meirim decided to pick a fight. Ruslan, meanwhile, ended up arguing with his girlfriend, then stealing her away in Meirim's car.

It wasn't until eight o'clock in the morning that we were back on the road, and upon pulling in at Ruslan's home I was so tired I could barely stand. I went straight to sleep, and when I woke, both Meirim and Ruslan had left.

A day passed before Meirim sheepishly showed up. I'd promised the villagers that I would be back within a day with the money for the horse, so by now they had probably given up on me. I had been paying Meirim a generous daily allowance, plus covering the fuel and food bills, and, sensing that I was ready to heap him with abuse, Meirim refused to look me in the eye, all the while protesting that he saw the situation differently.

"My wife needs me. I can't just drop everything for you! I have two children. They need to be fed. You need to pay me for the broken wheel, then I am going home." I gave him $50, and he drove off.

Ruslan, in the meantime, was nowhere to be seen, and although his father and brother tried to convince me that he would turn up sooner or later, panic crept up on me despite my resolve. I retreated to a pit toilet in the village, where among piles of frozen shit and cigarette butts I squatted, struggling to hold myself together. The first flakes of winter were beginning to fall from heavy gray skies, and I listened to the sounds of a drunken argument drifting over from somewhere nearby. Perhaps I was just coming to terms with my decision to travel alone, but the past few days had not been the kind of experience I had envisioned on my journey. I was overwhelmed by an unshakable feeling that journeying across Kazakhstan would be one long trial.

IT WAS TWO days before Ruslan showed up, and when he did, I was not taking chances. I helped him into the back of a 1960s Moskvich—a small sedan of the Soviet era—where he collapsed into a deep hangover-induced sleep. The smell of beer and cigarettes rising off him was worse than the cold, and so we set off with the windows wide open, rising and dipping along the same road where my journey had earlier disintegrated. Ruslan slept until well after dark and woke remarkably sober as we crashed our way through the last icy potholes and puddles to Pugachevo.

The locals complained that I had kept them waiting, with their horses standing around eating valuable hay, but I made them laugh with stories of Ruslan's antics, and any sense of guilt vanished when an old man approached me and whispered to me that the white horse was in fact fifteen years old—he had apparently wanted to tell the truth at the time, but it was a tradition to keep to the script of a fellow villager.

Though I'd agreed to buy Ogonyok, the chestnut horse, I announced that I was not leaving until I found two decent horses that could take me to Hungary. The wheeling and dealing began again, and every time a horse was offered I was told I "would not find a better one."

Eventually an elderly man trotted in on the back of a large bay horse. Nurkhan, who had again taken me under his wing, looked surprised.

"Take a look if you please. If you want it, buy it now. If you don't, I will release it back to the herd," said the man gruffly.

The horse's name was Taskonir,[7] which roughly meant "brown stone." His back was straight and sloped away at the hindquarters, while his mane was coarse and untamed. In his dark eyes was a look of fire I recognized as that of a wild horse, independent and strong-willed. Yet he was also comfortable and calm in the presence of so many people, suggesting he was a veteran work animal. Like most of the horses in Pugachevo, he was a breed known as dzhabe. Renowned for endurance and ability to hold their weight— and subsequently the choice of preference for horsemeat—Kazakhs say that their nation "rode the back of a dzhabe."

I took Taskonir for a ride with no bridle or bit, just an old goatskin thrown over his back, then fitted my Australian stock saddle. He moved instinctively, with only the slightest of commands, making me appear more of a horseman than I really was. I asked the owner, whose name was Altai, the price.

"Seventy thousand tenge!" he replied, quoting me a figure roughly equivalent to $520, before adding, "But for that price I keep the horseshoes!"

"How about sixty-five thousand with the horseshoes?" I asked.

"Fuck you!" he shouted. "What kind of person are you? Take your fucking saddle off my horse." He threw my saddle into the mud and stormed off with the horse. The crowd that had gathered fell silent.

Nurkhan came to my aid.

"He is an old, honored man. Maybe that is why he will not bargain."

The crowd followed me to Altai's home. Altai refused to come out. His son emerged, and I sent him back to make an offer of seventy thousand tenge—but only if it included the horseshoes. It was some time before the son appeared and waved us in.

I joined Altai at a small wooden table. In the light that drifted through the old warped glass, he sat still, glistening eyes shifting back and forth from the window to the cup of tea in his weathered hands. He had removed his fur hat and coat to reveal a bald scalp and a wiry figure that was sinking with age. In the wake of his temper, sadness filled his pale brown eyes. Later I understood that he was selling his horse to pay for medical treatments and his daughter's education at college. He was probably torn between a love of his horse and the need to support his family, and I was the unwelcome catalyst for deciding his loyalties. It wasn't just sentimentality, though. Horses here were essential for survival and work, and Taskonir had been a reliable work animal.

I wondered what Altai was thinking. Having lived his life true to the Soviet mantra that labor brought reward, he was selling his pride to a young foreigner who had not an inkling of the hardship he had seen. Like so many of his generation, he had entered retirement just as the Soviet Union collapsed, and now he found himself with nothing to rely on but his own hands, which were already worked to the bone.

I counted the money out onto the table, where it was counted again by his wife, then by his son.

"This horse," he boasted, "will take you all the way to Hungary."

"Will it?" I asked. "I will not forget your word."

I shook his hands, raised a shot of vodka, and reminded Altai: "In my culture it is a sign of disrespect to throw someone's saddle in the mud." He apologized, and then with a grin admitted the horse was probably twelve years old, not ten, as he had maintained.

We took photos together with Taskonir, and I promised to send a photo from the Danube. I could see now that I was taking away a part of his soul, and I pledged to myself never to forget the privilege of having Taskonir and the many years of training and wisdom that Altai had invested in him.

Negotiations for my second horse, Ogonyok, were more straightforward, but in the light of day, this big chestnut horse was more fiery than

I remembered. His eyes were untrusting, and he jumped nervously when I reached out to stroke his back. He was clearly the kind of horse that would bolt at the sound of his own fart and minutes after handing over the money I was told a story that confirmed my fears. It had been several months since anyone had ridden Ogonyok and the owner had been willing to sell only because Ogonyok had fallen on him and crushed his leg the previous winter.

Given the risk Ogonyok posed, I heeded Nurkhan's advice to have him shod with special studded winter shoes for gripping on the winter ice and snow. What I didn't know was that he had never been shod before. Only moments after being secured in a special wooden stall built for farrier work, he exploded in a frenzy of kicking. Nurkhan and the other men leaped for cover, and by the time they lifted themselves out of the mud Ogonyok had ripped apart the wooden frame and stood shaking his head.

The second time round they tied Ogonyok's tail to the top of the stall, then winched it up so high that his back legs barely touched the ground. Extra girths were fitted to his belly and every time he dared move a man beat his side with a steel pipe. This was still not enough to subdue Ogonyok, who managed to bust away the girths kicking back and forth until he was hanging upturned by his tail. It was only on the third attempt that they managed to tie his leg to a post and forcibly bang the shoes on.

During the fiasco I stood holding Ogonyok's bridle and peering into his eyes, which were wide with terror. Although monstrously strong, he was oblivious to his power. He was an honest horse, with none of the cunning of older, more experienced steeds. Even so, overriding any sympathy at this point in time was my own fear—how would I cope with Ogonyok on my own in the wilds?

RUSLAN, NURKHAN, ANOTHER villager known as Orolkhan (and nicknamed "the Chechen"), and I decided to get away from the village and find a fresh starting point for my journey in the loftier reaches of the surrounding peaks. I hoped to use this trip to purify my own spirits with something other than vodka, as well as to find some redeeming traits in Ruslan. I had hardly been able to look him in the eye since his misadventures with Meirim and was frustrated by the reluctance he had shown in helping me bargain during the negotiations over the horses. In the summer months Nurkhan lived and worked at a cooperative deer farm at a remote mountain station. The excursion into the mountains would double as a chance for him to return to his hut and gather the animals and goods he'd left behind.

We set out, and the village of Pugachevo shrank below in a mash of autumn browns and grays. After a heavy sleep in Nurkham's hut that night, Ruslan and I picked one of the peaks and set off to climb as high as we could.

Air gushed into my lungs as Taskonir attacked the slope. I sat snugly in my saddle, daypack hugging my shoulders, my eyes drifting from the few wisps of cloud that caressed the open blue to the freshly powdered crests that curved skyward. On the far horizon, the custodial pyramid of Mount Belukha—the highest peak of the Altai at 4,506 m—stood head and shoulders above everything else.

It was a relief to be looking at the world from horseback again. With every step, the self-doubt and snafus that had plagued me in recent times receded like a single tree in the landscape below.

When the slope became too steep we tied the horses to trees and set off on foot up a rocky spur and into the descending front of winter. After a couple of hours of scrambling through knee-deep snow we emerged from the cover of Siberian larch and pine and finished our climb on a rocky crag. From there I gazed over the land through a multitude of filters. Before us lay invisible trails of the original hunter-gatherers, their descendants who had spread out over the steppe with their horses, Mongol armies that had surged past these natural ramparts in their thousands, explorers who had arrived on a quest to find lost worlds, and imperialist Russians and Chinese who had only recently drawn up artificial borders. I imagined the enchantment for explorers who might have traveled here, beyond the Himalayas and Tibet, in search of *shambala*.

Some believe this Buddhist concept of a celestial kingdom, accessible only to those on the most evolved spiritual path, is a place of the spirit alone. Others write of a physical hidden world in the Altai, in Tibet, in India, or somewhere in between, where all inhabitants are enlightened. Whether or not the legend is true and there is a mysterious world that has camouflaged itself from modern-day cartographers, the Altai, encompassing a mix of taiga, tundra, glaciated peaks, and desert, would surely accommodate such a dream.

Yet to me, it was the view to the west over the steppe that most captured my imagination. I ran my eyes down the spurs to where they merged seamlessly with a sea of brown. There were no forests out there, or sheltered valleys of thick grass. Even rivers turned north on the edge of this exposed abyss. How many people had stood here like me and wondered just how far this land stretched, and what lay beyond the horizon? From here the open land continued unabated to the Carpathian Mountains on the fringes of central Europe. And regardless of the modern, post-Soviet reality of Kazakhstan and countries farther afield, I felt confident that the horses that would carry me were an ancient link whose primary needs, grass and water, had never changed.

"C'mon, Tim, I'm getting cold, and we have no food or water. Let's go!" I shifted my stare. Ruslan had finished his cigarette and, having thrown the butt in the snow, was trudging back down.

WE ARRIVED AT the hut after dark and found Nurkhan and Orolkhan cooking up the heads of freshly shot wild boar.

"Two wild pigs were guests in our home today. They left their heads behind but they themselves ran away," said Orolkhan as he plunked the two boiled skulls on the table.

We laughed, cutting away flesh from the jaws, eyes, and ears. The three men with me didn't have any problem enjoying the meat, even though pork is typically forbidden to Muslims.

"Mr. Cope," Nurkhan reminded me, "keep this to yourself. We are Kazakhs, but we can eat these pigs because they are clean, they are from nature!"

Our descent back to the valley in the morning was a fitting send-off. Nurkhan gathered some geese and a cat into a couple of potato sacks and loaded them onto an old cart that he harnessed to his horse. One tire was blown, so the cart moved precariously down the steep, icy trail. The geese honked, the cat meowed, and Nurkhan swore violently at them to shut up. I sidled up with my horse and pulled my camera out.

"Don't you dare! With geese and a cart people will think I am a bloody Russian!" he said.

By afternoon Pugachevo was behind us. We rode on after dark until we found refuge back in Maraldy with a family whose eldest son had served in the army with Ruslan. In the morning word reached the patriarch of the family that his brother had just died. Later we saw him, his wife, and their children huddled on the back of a truck rattling down the valley to the funeral procession.

Farther along the Kurchum River where it deepened into a gorge Ruslan led the way up into a maze of bald peaks riddled with rocky gullies. We spent the night at a remote herding station, where we were stirred awake in the early hours by an old man who strode outside and began howling. He had been wakened by a wolf, and this was how he scared them away. Before leaving the man offered us a gun for the remainder of Ruslan's time with me, but Ruslan refused the offer on the grounds that he didn't have a license. The man's question to us would be repeated many more times during the journey: "Why don't you carry a gun? What will you do about the wolves? Thieves?"

A long day of around 50 km brought us to the village of Terektbulak, where I bought my third horse, Zhamba. He was one of the old scarred workhorses I had seen during our first day of horse searching. For the remainder of the journey I regretted this decision. I bought Zhamba because he was much cheaper and in the short term would cause less trouble. This, however, meant forgoing a flighty young black gelding on offer that might have been expensive and dangerous but in the long term would have had what it would take for this kind of journey.

From here on, Ruslan felt he was on home territory, and with around 70 km to cover we moved at a trot, weaving our way up and over bare wrinkled hills and through frozen reed-choked gullies. Every now and then we caught sight of wild goats and deer moving like flecks being picked up on the path of a whirlwind across the slopes.

Ruslan was impressed with Ogonyok, whom he had nicknamed "The Tank."

"This is a great horse. I like him—he reminds me of my own. He is wild, that is true—all ginger horses and redheaded people are like that— but he will settle down after a few days on the road. If you teach him to trot and not be lazy, you will be able to cover a lot of distance every day," he said.

Taskonir was proving himself agile and determined as well. To the as- tonishment of Ruslan and others, I had ridden him without a bridle or bit, able to control him with a rope halter and the lead tied as the reins. With winter looming, I had extra incentive to dump the use of a bit, given how uncomfortable the freezing metal would be in a horse's mouth.

By contrast with Taskonir and Ogonyok, the third horse, Zhamba, was already struggling although he was carrying no load. We renamed him Maral, which means "roe deer," since he looked more like a mix between a deer and a donkey than a horse when he moved.

There was little time to settle into a walk and we seldom spoke, but dur- ing a short rest break Ruslan seemed anxious to talk. He had never acknowl- edged the days of riotous drunkenness with Meirim, and I thought perhaps he wanted to clear the air. With a look of sincerity he took a long drag on his cigarette and began.

"Tim, how much do girls cost in Australia?"

I tried not to look surprised.

"What do you mean?"

"Well, for example, Russians here, I have tried plenty of them. When I lived with my uncle for a while in Astana, I just watched TV during the day and could pay about a thousand tenge an hour when I needed it. I was even able to try a Korean—they are the most expensive at around three thousand. And the Germans come at a high price too."

He said it so solemnly that I wasn't sure how I could answer without either offending him or leading to the impression that I was homosexual.

"Well, I don't know, to be honest."

"But how do you fuck girls, then?" he interrupted.

I thought a while.

"Well . . . I guess you could say it is free."

Ruslan's eyes lit up, and he gave me a grin that showed his gold teeth.

"I thought so! You know Kazakh girls—they never put out unless you are married to them."

I didn't believe him, but I did know that many people I had met in the former Soviet Union during my previous trip had had conflicting views about Western women and very rarely had the chance to ask for themselves. The word in rural areas in particular was that either they "wore pants like men" and were highly nonsexual because of the feminist move= ment or they were all willing to offer themselves at will like in American movies. This was one of hundreds of such frank conversations that I would have with men, often herders in the saddle, right across the steppes. One colorful man later told me that Shymkent was his favorite city because "watermelons are twenty-five kopeks and Uzbek women two hundred."

I tried to explain to Ruslan that things were a bit more complex than what he had concluded, but another, more pressing problem had surfaced; Ruslan had clean run out of cigarettes, and he needed to think about going home.

THE MOMENTUM AND camaraderie of my time with Ruslan waned quickly in Slavyanka. Ruslan had his mind on other things. He was planning to get married, but more important, the next couple of weeks would be his last chance to fish before the Irtysh River weir froze over for winter. While I could only offer him $15 a day, which was a stretch for me, he claimed to be able to earn almost $100 with a good day's catch. Like many others in his village, he was able to pay off the fishing inspector and send his fish by car to Oskemen for lucrative sales at the market. (Later I was told that because of this kind of poaching, the Irtysh was headed toward being fished out within a matter of years.)

In truth, though, Ruslan's news that he could guide me for just two more days was a mutually convenient way of parting with our rapport intact. I was already tired of trying to understand the world as it was filtered through his eyes, and I was looking forward to a new chapter.

The remaining time with Ruslan was just long enough for us to cross the Irtysh onto the open steppe farther west, where my hopes of finding someone to travel further with me rested on locating a stranger I had met briefly during a taxi ride in Oskemen, and whose address I had scribbled on the back of an old cigarette box. Aset, as he was known, lived in the small village of Zhana Zhol, which happened to fall along my route.

7

ZUD

"Those who suffered as we did wept bitterly for their losses and cursed those who had introduced such inhuman laws: for people whose lives revolved around their animals, it was worse than being invaded by Genghis Khan's hordes. Their suffering was shared by their relatives in the aul, and the tears continued for weeks in these communities."

—Mukhamet Shayakhmetov,
  The Silent Steppe: The Memoir of
  a Kazakh Nomad Under Stalin

ACROSS HIS KITCHEN table, without the pitchfork in hand and heavy coat he had been wearing outside, Aset resembled the soft-natured man I remembered from our brief meeting in Oskemen. His face was broad and full, framed by a crop of silver hair above and patchy bristles that skirted his chin below.

He spoke in a husky, gentle voice that seemed poised to break into laughter.

"Ah, Tim! Tim! Don't be shy—drink, eat! This is Kazakh potato. Best in the world!"

It wasn't until I had filled my belly that I broached the subject of finding a guide to ride with me for a couple of weeks. He was excited and proudly recounted working as a horse shepherd for a collective farm in his youth.

"I used to work twenty-four hours moving with the herd to keep wolves and thieves away. At night I slept in the open holding the tethering rope of the lead stallion."

He recalled his experience nostalgically and suggested that although he hadn't ridden much in recent years and now worked as a laborer on demolition sites in the city, he was more than qualified to ride with me.

What impressed me more than Aset's credentials as a horseman were his qualities as a father. Aset's only child, Guanz, was a ten-year-old boy afflicted with cerebral palsy. When Guanz hobbled into the kitchen, Aset lifted his atrophied, buckled-looking frame into the air in an almighty embrace. Guanz giggled, and Aset's almond eyes squeezed into slender crescents, mirroring Guanz's own expression of joy. Over dinner Guanz clung to Aset's arm, stealing glances at me whenever I wasn't looking and burying his face in Aset's shoulder when I smiled back. Later, as he became a little emboldened, he attracted my attention by picking up the family cat and rubbing it against his cheeks, closing his eyes and laughing. In the grim reality of post-Soviet Kazakhstan it was hard to imagine a bright future for the young boy, yet Aset's visible love and affection seemed to transcend all else.

The evening took on a festive atmosphere as Aset's home crowded with villagers, and I spent hours sharing my photo album from Australia and telling stories. When it became late we went outside to mingle on the street. Guanz and many other children giggled, and dogs from all over the village brushed past my legs in the dark. It was only after most visitors had left that I felt two warm paws on my chest. The moist breath of a dog reached my cheek, and for a protracted moment the animal was still. I glanced down in time to see two white paws vanish into the night.

"He likes you," murmured Aset.

When the children began to tire, we returned inside, and Aset, his wife, and I settled in around the kitchen table. A little earlier Aset had told me that I needed to ask permission from his wife to have him accompany me. Now, when I put the question to her, she put on a serious face and replied with conviction: "You can take him all the way to Hungary if you like!"

TWO DAYS IN Zhana Zhol were set aside for preparations but became filled with leisurely hours drinking tea with villagers and visits to speak to students at the local school. In the company of Aset, who was a teetotaler with none of the coarseness or immaturity of Ruslan, I used the opportunity to slow down and let my nerves recover from the edgy, alcohol-fueled chaos of the past few weeks. A couple of long sleeps were enough for me to wake with a more measured eye and view my surroundings less through the prism of my own challenges and more in light of the recent history through which Kazakh society had passed.

Zhana Zhol—the name means "new road"—was a huddle of fifty or so tired timber homes cast in a sea of dreary gray steppe. Its one muddy street was lined with poplar trees that stood like skeletons against the opaque, clouded-in skies. Autumn was turning, and while in Mongolia nomadic families were no doubt preparing to migrate to winter pastures, Kazakhs here were instead gathering coal, firewood, and hay to see out the long months of cold. Most families had a milking cow, chickens, and even a horse or two, but there were none that boasted the kind of herds I'd been accustomed to in Mongolia. It was a life that closely resembled that of hundreds of Russian villages I had seen on previous travels.

At the school we met with young, wide-eyed children who had never seen the inside of a yurt and had only ever known the tumult of life in post-Soviet Kazakhstan. There were, however, others in the village, including Aset's elderly mother-in-law, who were just old enough to recall a time when Kazakhs lived and breathed a horseback life, moving with the seasons. For her generation, the collapse of the Soviet Union was just one of the many cataclysmic events that had not just changed the course of their individual lives but shaped the future of the country.

By any standards, the twentieth century was one of immense upheaval and tragedy for Kazakhs. It began on the back of more than a century of Russian colonization. In 1916, 150,000 Kazakhs—mostly nomad herders—were killed during a widespread but doomed rebellion against their colonial rulers, triggered by tax hikes, expropriation of livestock, and an order for men between the ages of eighteen and forty-three to be conscripted into the imperial army.

Only a year later, the Bolshevik revolution—which led to the formation of the Soviet Union in 1922—fanned hope that communism might bring equality and independence, but successive Soviet leaders came to see the steppe as an uncivilized backwater to be exploited, and the nomads as itinerant wanderers.[1] The seventy years of Soviet rule would prove an assault on almost every aspect of nomadic culture, the landscape of the Kazakhs, and ultimately their way of life.

For many Kazakhs, nuclear tests carried out at the Semipalatinsk test site, some 400 km northwest of Zhana Zhol, were indicative of the open disregard with which Kazakhs were treated. In 1947 a piece of land chosen for testing by the Soviet Atomic Agency was officially deemed "empty" although the area was home to nomads. During the first detonation in 1949 local teachers were ordered to take children outside the schools to watch the explosions, so their bodies' reaction could be observed and studied. A total of 116 atmospheric explosions were conducted before ground tests were banned, and another 340 underground tests had been carried out by the time the site closed in 1991. The United Nations believes that between 1947 and 1989 one million people were exposed to radiation, leading to high suicide and cancer rates, infertility, and deformities. Aset had grown up in a village adjacent to the testing zone and had only recently moved to Zhana Zhol. He believed that his disabled son, Guanz, was just one of untold thousands of children in the towns and villages of the region still being born with genetic abnormalities.

There were many other tribulations wrought by politicians in faraway Moscow, such as the decision to dam and siphon off the main river arteries of Central Asia—the Syr Darya and the Amu Darya—for cotton production, which led to the calculated death of the Aral Sea. There was also the so-called Virgin Lands Scheme announced by Nikita Khrushchev in 1958, which involved plowing up the steppe of northern Kazakhstan for wheat fields in one of the Soviet Union's biggest agricultural experiments. The steppe is a fragile environment, and although many of the wheat fields were initially productive, many eventually became abandoned dust bowls.

All of these calamities led in one way or another to an erosion of the traditional way of life, but ultimately none was as far-reaching as the early policies of Stalin. Above all, it was the collectivization that took place between 1928 and 1931 that spelled an abrupt end to nomadic life, a national tragedy from which Kazakhs have still not recovered. Although I couldn't yet grasp the scope of the upheaval, over the many weeks and months ahead I would come to realize that without an understanding of events that transpired in those years, any insight into modern Kazakh society was hollow.

The era of collectivization, which affected societies across the Soviet Union, began with the expropriation of property from the wealthy in the mid-1920s and was driven by Joseph Stalin's push for industrialization. The Soviet Union needed grain, plus gold and other minerals in order to buy foreign machines and tools. In 1927, when the grain supply dropped, Stalin blamed the wealthy peasants, or *kulaks*, for hoarding, and ordered them to increase supply. There began a terrifying period when anyone found with the tiniest quantity of bread was sent to prison—a policy that led to an artificial famine in Ukraine in the early 1930s, known as the Holodomor, that claimed the lives of five million.

For Kazakhs confiscation of land and the imposition of grain quotas did not have the same initially productive result as it did in Russia and Ukraine, largely because nomads did not own land. To remedy this, Fillip Isaevich Goloshchekin, a Russian dentist turned politician, was named secretariat for the Kazakh republic. He attempted to solve the problem by declaring that livestock was the equivalent of land for nomads, and in 1928 ordered animals confiscated from the rich (known in Kazakh as *bai*). The truly wealthy nomads—the real bai—had been dispossessed or incarcerated several years earlier, prior to collectivization, and so instead the middling nomads, and even poor ones, were accused of hoarding and forced to hand over their animals.[2] Around this time local Kazakh Soviet authorities—mostly Kazakh political activists who had sided with the ideals of communism, and were known as *belsendi*—became notorious for their pillaging. They often took everything from families, right down to blankets, clothing, and cooking utensils. Nomad families were left with barely enough animals to warrant traditional migration in search of pasture. Officially, the confiscated goods and animals were to become the property of state-owned collectives, but the real intent was for Kazakhstan to supply meat to the cities of the Soviet Union. From every region a quota was demanded, in some cases right down to the last animal.[3]

The scenes of mayhem during these times are difficult to fathom. Train stations across Kazakhstan became mass holding and slaughter yards, where livestock was jammed into rail cars to be sent to Moscow, Leningrad, and other large centers. There was no veterinary control, and an epidemic of brucellosis and tuberculosis broke out. In some cases, the carcasses of animals slaughtered in winter were not transported until spring, by which time they had begun to rot. As an indicator of how poorly Goloshchekin and his government understood the conditions of the steppe, wool quotas were demanded on the eve of winter, which led to entire herds freezing to death. Many nomads destroyed their animals rather than turn them over to authorities, and even animals in collectives died en masse because of mismanagement.[4]

The result of Goloshchekin's policy meant that from 1928 to 1932, cattle and sheep numbers declined by around 90 percent.[5] People began to go hungry in 1930, and it is believed that by 1933 somewhere between 1.7 and 2.2 million nomads—around a third of the Kazakh population at the time—had starved to death and another estimated 653,000 had fled to China. Simultaneously, most nomads ceased their annual migrations, and by 1933, 95 percent of Kazakhs had settled in collective farms. The term *aul*, which once had referred to a community of nomads who moved together from pasture to pasture, now meant little more than a permanent Kazakh settlement.[6]

Zhana Zhol was one such aul—a community anchored permanently on the steppe where their forebears had once roamed. And yet, although the events of collectivization had created the underpinning realities of everyday life, it was an era largely unspoken of. For Aset's mother-in-law and others her age, memories of the famine and dispossession were too painful to be recounted. Aset and others of his generation also spoke little about the subject, perhaps partly out of respect for their elders, but also because the effects of the more recent Soviet collapse for them overshadowed the difficulties of the past.

The very nature of the famine nevertheless remained one of raw contention. Academics, ordinary citizens, and politicians across Kazakhstan and abroad continue to debate whether the famine was accidental, a consequence of Goloshchekin's gross ignorance, or an intentional genocide of the Kazakh people. One traditional school of thought among internationalists—those Kazakhs who supported Sovietization—is that the heavy loss of human life, culture, and language under Stalin, while regrettable, was an inevitable part of modernization. But I couldn't help thinking that for the people in Zhana Zhol, such gross human sacrifice must have been all the more abhorrent, given that it was for a system that would ultimately fail its own people within just a couple of generations.

THREE DAYS AFTER my arrival in Zhana Zhol, Aset and I led the horses out onto the muddy street for a public farewell. The plan was for Aset and me to ride 250 km southwest across rugged steppe and hills to the town of Ayagoz. From there I would go on alone.

Many of the villagers who had assembled considered the prospect of our ride a death sentence. "The frost! The cold! It will be here soon, and it will hit you! There will be snow up to your neck," said one man, running his hand across his throat.

"Yes, but the most dangerous of all are drunks," an old babushka wrapped up in a shawl cackled. "We have many of them—don't go near them!"

This was too much for Aset's wife, who broke down in tears. Despite her joke earlier about my taking him all the way to Hungary, she had been

fretting over Aset for the past two days, and today she had spent all morning helping to dress and equip him. To me it now appeared that the poor
man was more likely to die of constriction than cold. Up top he wore two
thick woolen sweaters, a neck warmer, and a denim jacket stretched so tight
it couldn't be buttoned. For emergencies his pockets had been stuffed with
sunflower seeds, pig fat, and garlic, and on the belt holding up his pair of
thick Russian winter overalls was a knife big enough to chop down a tree.
With only fractional movement possible at the knees and elbows, he waddled with great difficulty over to Ogonyok and heaved himself up.

When finally we turned to leave, the old babushkas and children alike
didn't know whether to laugh or cry, and so most did both. The last image
I caught before turning my attention beyond the village was of Guanz,
standing with one arm hanging in a fixed clench and laughing ecstatically.
He wasn't worried about the dangers out there in the wider world; he was
only filled with feelings of pride to see his father set off on such an exciting
adventure. When we pulled away from the crowd, he lifted his better arm
in an attempt to wave, and called out in stilted Russian: "Write to us!"

From Zhana Zhol we headed for the open steppe, and within half an
hour the drab timber homes had sunken into the creases of the land behind. The horses charged ahead, full of energy, and as the world around us
seemed to expand with its wide, empty horizons, my own world shrank to
the company of my animals and Aset. It was the kind of movement I had
been craving. Bristling with impatience, I moved into a fast trot uphill.

"We can go at a trot on the flat, but not up! The road is long. We need
to save the energy of the horses!" Aset called out.

"We also have to make the most of the good weather before winter
sets in!" I replied.

It was then I noticed the little black dog with white front paws like
socks running behind us. I recognized him as the dog from my first night
in Zhana Zhol and had since learned it was Guanz's puppy. All ribs on long
matchstick legs, he had a skinny trunk and snout followed by a frenetic
wagging tail. From the skeletal frame rose two large ears, rather like that
of a hare.

"Aset! What is this dog?" I demanded.

"Traveling on horse without a dog is incomplete," he replied.

"No! How will you take him home after we part?"

He said nothing, merely spitting out a few sunflower seed shells.

The way the dog peered up at me with those innocent, loving eyes was infuriating. I didn't know who was the more presumptuous, he or Aset.

That evening the sky cleared, and as the last light retreated, the breeze slowed to a halt and cold fell like a heavy blanket. I found my calm once more in the quiet of camp, and reveled in the feeling that there was little separating us from the stars. As the temperature dropped, Aset, on the other hand, grew nervous and withdrawn.

After dinner he looked worryingly into the food pot. "And for the dog?"

I reluctantly pulled out a can of meat. "If he is going to eat, he has to earn his keep. He must be a guard dog and stay outside."

My argument was nonsense. The poor dog, barely six months old, was a short-haired variety of sight hound, known as a *tazi*. He looked as if he might struggle to stay upright in a stiff breeze, let alone cope with sleeping in frosty weather. Later I pretended to be asleep when Aset pulled the poor shivering dog inside the tent to sleep at our feet.

In the morning, my hopes of making significant headway before winter were dashed. It was just the third of November, but when sunlight speared across the horizon it was hollow of warmth and splintered through a forest of hoarfrost on the entrance to the tent. A heavy panting from outside had woken me, and zipping open the door, I locked eyes with Aset, who was bundled up and jogging around the tent.

"It's freezing in there! It's much warmer out here!" he cried.

The temperature overnight had plummeted to around -15°C, and unfortunately we had just one sleeping bag and mat between us. Aset had shivered through the night under my horse blankets, and later he admitted it had been his first night in a tent.

When the sun rose higher there was some reprieve from the cold, and we rode out into a honey-yellow sea of wild grasses and heath. To the northwest a sliver of earth blanketed in snow rose across the horizon like a rogue wave. We met only one man during the day, a sheepherder who drifted across and away from us as if on the ocean currents.

It was the kind of autumn riding I had dreamed of, when the horses didn't overheat, there was plentiful pasture, and the air had such clarity it seemed that only the curvature of the earth prevented me from seeing what lay far ahead. As soon as the sun began to dip again, however, there was no more denying that winter was setting in. My leather boots froze solid and my feet became numb. I pulled out my knee-high Canadian-made winter boots and attached my wide Mongolian winter stirrups, which provided another layer of protection against the cold and wind.

At around four o'clock all concessions from the weather vanished. The grass howled with random, menacing strokes of wind, and the ambiguous sky of shifting clouds and scattered light was eclipsed by a dense, sweeping curtain of black and gray.

Terrified by the prospect of another night in the cold, Aset was determined to find somewhere indoors to regroup. Reluctantly I folded up the map and we moved into a fast trot toward the nearest aul.

IN THE LAST dying minutes of dusk we slowed the horses to a walk on the edge of Azunbulak. Aset wasn't familiar with this remote community and warned we might not find a place to stay. As we reached the sprawling carcass of Azunbulak's former collective farm, however, a young man came out on foot and greeted us with particular charm.

"What the dick? Yes, we have dick weather here, but true, we also have grass up to the dick!" he exclaimed. We could only take this as a warm welcome.

Even before we were led into the animal yards of the old collective farm I felt like I knew our host-to-be, Baltabek, who was steely and short, with a gold-toothed grin that belied his age, which was only twenty-one. It didn't come as a surprise to learn he had only recently been released from prison.

"Silly me! Young and stupid! I stole a few horses from the village! But I learned a lot in jail. In fact, that is where I learned Russian language. Before that I could speak only Kazakh!" he told us.

With the benefit of experience, I came to think that Baltabek's real crime had probably been not so much the stealing of horses as being young and, more important, getting caught. He was passionate about horses, and if he was to be believed, he had stolen them not to sell but because he didn't have enough money to buy the good ones he loved. That somehow seemed fair in a land where, until nomads were dispossessed of their animals during Stalin's era, Kazakhs had viewed their world almost exclusively from the saddle.

Nowadays Baltabek was getting on with his life. He worked for his father, who had established a small farm amid the wreckage of the defunct collective farm, and owned a black stallion that he couldn't wait to show us. Furthermore, his father empty bachelor pad—the former administration office of the collective farm—was about to be transformed into a family home.

"My wife has just given birth, and if only you wait two days, you could join the celebration when she and the baby return from hospital!" he said feverishly. According to him, my arrival was good luck, and it was "crazy" for me to continue through the winter. There was a better option: I could live and work on the farm with him and his family.

We stayed up talking with Baltabek late into the night, and come morning his proposition to stay for the winter no longer seemed far-fetched. About 20 cm of snow had fallen, transforming the landscape, and the storm showed no signs of abating. Snowflakes choked the sky, blowing in horizontally, caking everything in their path.

There was no choice but to stay put, and as the day wore on, my disappointment at being delayed turned to one of morbid fascination. While in Zhana Zhol I had reflected on the effects of collectivization, here in Azunbulak I was offered a glimpse of the tragic fallout following the collapse of the Soviet system.

The small farming operation run by Baltabek's father, which involved modest numbers of horses, sheep, and cattle, was dwarfed by the graveyard of the original collective. Gutted buildings stood falling in on themselves, and scattered all around were dismembered combines, tractors, and trucks, lying twisted and rusting. So violent and swift had been the death of the Soviet era, it seemed, that its remains had not been given the dignity of burial.

"Yes, fuck your mother!" Baltabek told us, surveying the farm. "It has all gone to fuck."

His father, an old man whose body was used to working uncomplainingly, was a little more enlightening. In its prime during the 1970s and 1980s, the collective had employed 250 people and supported three hundred families in Azunbulak. Now just thirty families were involved in the new cooperative, and the village had shrunk to seventy homes. Baltabek's father couldn't really explain where all the animals and machinery had gone, but he did recall a time in the 1990s when the only way to acquire 1 litre of diesel was to trade 10 kg of meat. It had been in this disastrous era that the collectives were transformed from state-owned enterprises into collective entities, and later into largely failed privately run cooperatives. To pay off debts, farmers had flooded the market with mutton, causing the price of meat to plummet. Between 1991 and 1998 grain production also fell by over 50 percent and the transport system ground to a halt, meaning there was no longer enough fodder getting to livestock in state farms. Many animals either were slaughtered or simply starved. To make matters worse, many collective directors, as in Azunbulak, had taken the opportunity to steal or sell most of the collective's assets and abandon the community.

By the end of the 1990s the majority of Kazakhs in collectives had been left to scavenge among the remains for anything they could sell or use as spare parts. People such as Baltabek's father had turned to subsistence farming, surviving on the meager food rations they could produce themselves with animals they privately owned.

"In my father's time," Baltabek's father told me bitterly, "the Soviets dispossessed us of our animals and way of life. It was a terrible time, but over the years we grew accustomed to state-run farms. Now though, we have been abandoned by the Soviets and left without any of the skills of our ancestors. We feel betrayed."

Whichever way one looks at it—whether from the point of view of city dwellers or that of country folk—the chaos of the 1990s, during which

Kazakhstan emerged as an independent nation, was a staggering time of hardship and lawlessness. To the masses, perestroika meant the severe shrinkage of industry, the breakup of agricultural collectives, the dissolution of social services including pensions, and the departure of educated experts, largely to Russia, Germany, and Korea. Power shortages were rife and not helped by a burgeoning trade in scrap metal as organized crime groups stripped and sold huge lengths of power lines. Between 1991 and 2000, the population of Kazakhstan dropped by almost two million.

It was no wonder that most Kazakhs, like Baltabek's family, rued Gorbachev and recalled Soviet times with nostalgia, even though they knew full well the horrors that the Soviet era had inflicted on their people. Then again, as Baltabek's father later told me, a quizzical expression on his face, "To be honest, life, as far as I can remember, has always been hard, no matter who had the reins, Moscow or Astana."

In the evening we rode into the aul of Azunbulak proper for an extravagant dinner with Baltabek's family, and the appalling reality around us vanished. We swapped photo albums, sifting through each other's lives, and celebrated long into the night. Baltabek's father saw my arrival as a great omen and wished me luck.

THE STORM HAD lulled by the time we rode out the next day. Stony clouds swooped over the steppe, blocking the sun that seemed to begin its downward trajectory before the day had begun. The poor dog, experiencing the first winter of his short life, was suffering from frozen paws. Whenever we stopped for a break he whined and peered up with a look of bewilderment. Once, in a desperate attempt to escape the cold, he leaped up onto my back with his front paws clinging to my shoulders. I had dismounted and was taking a pee at the time, and he caused me to lose aim.

For an unbroken few hours Aset rode in front of me, singing sorrowful-sounding songs in Kazakh and spluttering between verses: "Ah, Tim, when you have vodka, you have a voice. No vodka, no voice!" I wondered if the soft rocking motion of his horse, the trackless land before him, and the presence of a loyal dog by his side was bringing his nomad roots out of dormancy.

In the late afternoon we cut across a plain and climbed through a tangle of snow-laden spurs toward a plateau. My legs were beginning to ache and I could think only of retiring in camp with dinner on the boil. But just as we were nearing the top of a gully the light dimmed and there came a gust of wind carrying a sortie of airborne shards of ice and snow. Then the cloud was upon us, like an avalanche from somewhere above, wiping out all before it. Aset stopped singing in the middle of a verse, and within seconds the world had hemorrhaged away all shape and form. There was no sky or earth anymore, just a swirling, soupy sea of white. The sun was still up, casting weak, diffuse gray-blue light onto the snow, but illuminated little. Leaning forward and clinging onto Taskonir's mane I flicked my head back to see Aset's silhouette melting in and out of focus. When he caught up, Taskonir nudged forward, uneasily probing for solid earth. I urged him on, but for every step forward our circle of vision closed tighter.

For the next hour there was no telling where we were or when this rushing cloud might dissipate. Several times I lost Aset, only to scream out for him, and he would reappear. Every ten minutes I checked my GPS and compass bearing. The horses plodded on up slopes, down into gullies, and up again.

Eventually we crested yet another hill, the terrain surrendered to a plateau, and there came an acute change in the temperament of the air, as if the world were drawing a breath. I stopped, and as the wind eased and the mist about me scattered, I looked to the west. Dark, jagged clouds on the wings of the wind began to lift, and a purple-blue light flooded over the wavy troughs and crests of the frozen earth. It glowed ever brighter until a shaving of cobalt-blue sky blinked into focus. The tail end of the sun had just slithered over the horizon leaving a trail of fading watercolors— blue on the clouds, purple on the ground, a hint of orange here and there.

The truce was short-lived. Darkness fell, the wind recoiled, and cold took its grip.

"The closer to people the better!" Aset ranted. While the raw feeling of this place had evoked in me a sense of awe, Aset was beside himself with fear.

For the hundredth time I stopped and spread the map out over the reins from the saddle, studying it with the light from my headlamp. We were aiming for the aul of Kindikti, two days' ride to the southeast, and were somewhere in the stretch of deserted hilly steppe in between. Since the map had a scale of 1:1,000,000, I could only hazard a guess at where we were.

"We have food, we have a tent!" I told Aset. "We can stop now, make ourselves warm, cook dinner, sleep, and see how things are in the morning light,"

"To hell with your tent!" he replied. "What if a snowstorm really comes in? What about wolves? We have to get to a kstau!" he replied, using the nomad term for a herder's winter station. Finding one would be a long shot, even with the GPS I carried and the approximate directions Baltabek had given us, but Aset was willing to bet his life on it.

One of my rules of travel was to stop before dark and, more important, before the horses were too tired and cold. On previous journeys I had learned that I was never lost as long as I still had food, my wits, and shelter. But I gave in, and we trudged on.

My hands turned stone cold and stiff. The horses became so exhausted they were immune to the kick of my heels. The sky cleared, but the wind was so ferocious it brought a stinging swarm of ice particles that hit like glass shards.

At half past ten we arrived at the coordinates where we thought the kstau might be, but there was nothing. I had given up trying to figure out the landscape.

"It's got to be somewhere here! We have to make it," shouted Aset, his words garbled by his nearly frozen face. At that moment he struck me as mad. His hankering for civilization was such that any sign of human life, even a piece of old horse crap that we stumbled on, sufficed to calm him.

As a last resort, he ordered that we release the reins and let the horses guide us. This is a custom found across the steppe—when lost or in search of water, always let the horses guide you. To my surprise, the horses seemed to know where they were going, and half an hour later we stumbled into the dark shape of something man-made. There was no one to greet us, but this was good enough to console Aset, who dismounted achingly. Hypothermic, he crawled into the cocoon of my sleeping bag and passed out.

In the morning I woke with the residual hum of wind in my ears. Stillness ushered in the new day, and as shadows turned to real shapes and lines, it became clear we had camped in an abandoned concrete pumping shed littered with frozen manure and graffiti.

Outside, nothing had escaped the fury of the storm. The stands of heath looked like a bleached, exposed coral reef, the intricate form of each twig entombed in finger-thick ice. Every blade of grass was also encased, rising from the earth in a million stalagmites. The horses stood stiffly in half sleep. As Taskonir turned his head to me, ice cracked and fell away from his mane. Ogonyok woke, automatically lowered his head, and crunched through a carrot of ice with his teeth.

When Aset woke, slit-eyed and puffy, he was worried. The storm had passed for now, but this kind of weather apparently foreshadowed the beginning of a zhut—a harsh winter, more universally known by the Mongolian term zud, that sweeps through the steppe every few years, traditionally ensuring that only the hardiest animals, and humans, survive.

"At first the ice weighs down the grass, snapping it off. If this is followed by a warm period, the ice and snow will melt before freezing again to form a cap of ice. On top of this may come deep snow, which means even if the animals dig to the ground they will only find ice and won't be able to break through. If any horses survive, they will be naked by spring because as a last resort they eat each other's hair," he told me.[7]

There were different kinds of zuds—some caused by an impenetrable layer of ice, others by the sheer depth of the snow, and others still when there was no snow at all. Common to all of them was that if they were preceded or followed by drought in summer, it typically meant the nail in the coffin for large numbers of livestock. By way of example, the year that

I had ridden across Mongolia by bicycle, Mongolia had been in the midst of a series of three consecutive zuds and droughts. Come the end of the winter in 2002, 11 million animals had been wiped out. There was one Kazakh in western Mongolia I was told about who had just one of three hundred horses remaining by spring.[8] Kazakh herders would later describe to me how, when the grass was particularly lean, they kept their animals alive by feeding them a combination of horse dung mixed with sheep tail fat and a grain by-product that was like wheat bran.

Given the carnage that zuds could wreak, it wasn't difficult to understand why for thousands of years zuds had been the common enemy of nomads on the steppe. In the case of the Kazakhs, a new foe, the Soviet regime, joined the zuds as threats to the people's survival. This new enemy proved unbeatable, and the famine that resulted from forced collectivization and the destruction of aul life remains known among Kazakhs as the "Great Zhut."[9]

After feeding the horses the remaining bag of crushed corn that we had picked up in Azunbulak, we loaded up and wrenched ourselves away from the shelter. The horses moved hesitantly, like barefoot children on sharp gravel. Spikes of crystalline ice shattered, popping and exploding under their hooves. The poor dog remained curled up in the pump shelter until it dawned on him that we were not coming back. He came whimpering, tail between his legs and whiskers all frosted up.

An hour of riding took us over the sweeping face of a hill where another scabby piece of civilization broke the emptiness. This time smoke tendrils rose timidly from it, and a herd of flea-like sheep and goats inched across the otherwise inanimate landscape. It was the kstau we had been searching for, and as we drew closer, a herdsman on horseback pulled away from his animals and approached.

"As-salam aleikum," he said, extending his hand. The man had swollen, chapped cheeks and was struggling to control a violent shiver. He looked how I felt. The wind cut like razors, and no matter how I slouched into my jacket and pulled the hood tight over my face, it was inescapable.

I was happy for Aset to take over the introductions, and as we rode I learned that the herdsman was originally from western Mongolia. He and his wife had decided to carry on a semi-nomadic existence, traveling to higher pastures with a yurt in the summer months—a camp known in Kazakh as the *jailau*—and retreating to the kstau in winter.

When we reached the cattle shelter of the kstau, I watched as our host skillfully climbed onto the roof of the shelter despite the wind and with a fork peeled off hay for my hungry horses. This man embodied the *chaban*—the iconic herdsman of the Kazakh steppe, who was fast passing into legend in the modern era. Using knowledge inherited from untold generations of experience, he was unequivocally hunkering down to survive the winter, zud or not. As I sat there immobile in the saddle, my elbows frozen at right angles and my feet freezing in the stirrups, I experienced a crisis of confidence. I could barely consider myself a horseman, I didn't know how to look after horses in such conditions, and I doubted I could manage alone with three of them.

We stopped in briefly with the herder's family, enjoying fresh deep-fried dough—known in Kazakh as *baursak*—and hot milky tea. I secretly hoped we might turn in for the day, but all too soon we were back into the cold and riding under a sky that was wilting into dark gray. The storm was gathering again, and as the frozen earth meshed with the sky, we pushed the horses into a trot. This time I had no objections to Aset's urgency—we would ride for as long as it took to find shelter.

♯♯

THE LIGHT WAS fading fast and the snow was falling nearly horizontally when we came across the trail to Kindikti. First there came the muffled bellow of cattle and the cry of herders, then two figures materialized from the bleakness, hunched in their saddles, whips in hand, sweeping from one side to the other of a large herd of horses and cattle. Up close I could see they were wearing *valenki*, traditional Russian knee-high felt boots, and rode atop saddles with thick cushions—the kind that Aset had recently been encouraging me to get for my own saddle to prevent hemorrhoids.

From tightly drawn hoods, the men squinted against the snow and wind. Then, despite the conditions, they took off the mitts they wore and reached out to shake our hands. As luck would have it, we had caught the men herding the animals home to shelter for the night.

When the glow of homes emerged from the pall of snow, cattle peeled off to their respective owners and we followed a herder to a mud-brick house. Askhat, as he was called, dashed inside and came out with his father, a tall man named Bakhetbek. There were handshakes all around before we rushed to unload. Askhat was sent to the roof to gather hay, a young boy was given the job of preparing a barn, and Bakhetbek must have told his wife to prepare things in the house.

Accustomed to making sure the horses were cared for before I could think about relaxing, I was hesitant to go inside until everything was done. Ruslan had taught me that when we were finished riding for the day, it was unthinkable to remove the saddle and offer the horses water and feed until they had rested for two or three hours, or until their backs were warm and dry under the blankets. As I later understood, this was a kind of universal law on the steppe and possibly one that had been around since before the time of Genghis Khan.[10]

I began to explain to Bakhetbek how important this system was for my horses, but he interrupted me.

"Tim! Tim!" he said, almost angrily. "Don't even say it—it is offensive. Everything will be done, you don't have to worry about your horses. You are our guest!"

Aset pulled me aside. "Trust him and watch carefully—a sign of a Kazakh host who respects his guests is that he will feed the guest's dog before his own."

True to Aset's words, Bakhetbek fed our ribs-on-legs dog a pot of lamb innards and stale bread, sinking his boots into his own dogs when they tried to join in.

As tired as I was, somehow I got through dinner, and a few shots of vodka too, before tumbling into sleep. At some point in the night I woke in panic from a dream: we were on a creaking ship, but where was the exit? Then I remembered where we were and surrendered to sleep, confident that the horses, like us, were under the watch and care of the family.

⊞

By THE TIME I woke it was late. Where Aset had been lay a pile of blankets, and from the kitchen drifted the homelike sounds of shuffling feet, muffled conversation, and tinny clanging of pots. Peeling my eyes open, I sat upright slowly. What I had assumed to be bright sunshine through the small window of our room was the glare of a snowdrift creeping up the windowpane. Outside, the storm, muted by the house's thick walls, raged on. Heavy clouds of snowflakes were being tossed about in violent gusts, and I could just make out the outline of an animal shelter, its timber frame encrusted by wind-driven snow and ambushed on one side by a drift banking up to the roof. On the shelter's lee side, a herd of sheep stood huddled in a pen, their wooly coats under a gathering blanket of snow.

The blizzard had all the hallmarks of a *buran*, the fierce winter windstorms of the steppe, accompanied by a whiteout, that could last for days, and which, I had been told, could bury livestock and people alive if caught in the open. It was for this reason Aset considered it reckless to camp alone on the steppe.

I found Aset and Askhat sitting idly by the softly crackling coal stove, looking over my Australian saddle. When he noticed me Askhat motioned to the window and joked, "You think this is winter? You should see winter here! There is usually *two metres* of snow!"

The family and I settled down with tea from the pot that was perpetually on the boil. I sat leaning up against the white-washed walls that were hung with nothing more than a couple of rugs and a horse whip. In the afternoon the blizzard briefly abated, and movement out a window caught my eye—a young boy riding bareback with a hypothermic sheep slung across the neck of his horse.

Bakhetbek was a tall and stately man in his fifties with leathery dark skin, green eyes, and a strong jaw line. When he moved, he did so mea-

Nomad encampment Arkhangai Aimag in Central Mongolia.

Me and Ochirbat, the elder of the nomad family with whom I stayed while buying my first horses. Packhorse recruit Kheer also pictured.

Kathrin, my girlfriend, traveled the first two months with me through Mongolia.
KATHRIN BENDER-NIENHAUS

Kathrin heading off into the steppe, packhorse in tow.

Scenes at a family camp on the shores of Telmen Nuur lake, Zavkhan Aimag. The ger is being deconstructed for migration.

Ukher Tereg—Yak (or cattle) carts, traditionally used by nomads of Central Mongolia for haulage, particularly for migration.

A family helps me to set up camp not far from Uvs Nuur lake—the same night that a drunk attempted to steal my horses.

The Oirat man of the Durvud tribe who explained that his ancestors had traveled to the Caspian Sea, where they became known as Kalmyks, before returning to Asia in the eighteenth century.

Looking north to the Borig Del Els—a sandy desert sometimes described as the most northern desert in the world.

The horses grazing in camp on an idyllic Mongolian summer evening.

Churning fermented mare's milk, known as Mongolian as *airag* (or *kumys* in Kazakh).

Inside a family ger near the village of Tes. The meat cut into strips and hanging to dry is known as *borts*.

Dashnyam (center), a Khoton Mongol who guided me across the Kharkhiraa-Turgen Mountaints, sits with his wife, several of his children, and a friend (left).

Dashnyam's oldest daughter, carrying her sister.

Dashnyam astride his one and only horse.

Dashnyam leading our hired camel towards Kharkhiraa Uul.

Rusty and I survey Khokh Nuur (Blue Lake) near the 9,840-foot high pass between Kharkhiraa and Turgen Uul. (This photo—like many others—was taken on a tripod with a timer.)

A marmot hunter.

Dashnyam leading us toward the high pass, with Turgen Uul in background.

A proud Durvud Mongol woman leads her caravan down from the Kharkhiraa-Turgen massif to the plains for autumn camp.

Khoton family descending the Kharkhiraa River valley.

A Durvud Mongol man carrying his loved one in the saddle. Note the charcoal dust mark on the infant's face—a traditional marking for warding off bad spirits.

Kazakhs of Bayan Olgiy Aimag in Western Mongolia were isolated from the privations endured by their compatriots in neighboring Kazakhstan during Stalin's era. In Mongolia, they live a traditional nomadic life, reminiscent of what life might once have been like for Kazakh communities from the Altai Mountains to the Caspian Sea.

suredly, with grace and power. He was the father of four, and both he and his wife worked as schoolteachers. His passion was geography.

"Tim, if I am correct, you are not the first foreigner to travel here. An Englishman once came prospecting for gold and other minerals. That was about eighty years ago. I am fairly sure, though, that you are the first Australian," he said, eyes twinkling. His hands, broad and strong, shifted gently in their embrace around his cup of tea.

Bakhetbek's wife, wearing a scarf that accentuated her moon face, smiled. "Yes, that is true. But my Bakhetbek is a traveler, a foreigner even, of sorts, too."

Bakhetbek had been born near Urumqi in China's Xinjiang province, and fled to Kazakhstan after his brothers were murdered in the 1960s. Later his nephews, who remained behind, were also murdered. At his wife's gentle prod, Bakhetbek began telling his story himself, hesitantly, but was swiftly overcome with emotion.

"They killed us simply because we are Kazakhs," he said. "Back then, and even now, Chinese authorities don't protect Kazakhs. Actually, it was probably the police who did the murdering."

There was a bitter irony in Bakhetbek's return to Kazakhstan that he was well aware of. His own grandparents had originally fled to China among two hundred thousand others when the Russian imperial army violently quashed the 1916 Kazakh uprising. At the same time, though, Bakhetbek acknowledged that the tragedy of his family had been the experience of his ancestors through the ages—whenever the Kazakhs found themselves under oppression or attack, they would historically flee to Chinese Turkestan, Siberia, and other parts of Central Asia, only to find themselves under another oppressive regime.[11]

After telling his story, Bakhetbek looked spent, but there was a sparkle in his wife's eye. "Actually . . ." She looked over at her husband. "We still have one relative alive in China. She is Bakhetbek's niece, and she is studying in Urumqi. She wrote to us one year ago, but we have never met. She gave us a phone number, but we have never been able to call."

It was dark by the time everyone assembled outside in winter coats and fur hats. I pointed the satellite phone aerial to the sky and experimented with a few prefixes until the call went through. A woman answered. After a brief initial silence, all of Bakhetbek's family members took turns talking, struggling to hold back tears but smiling.

The occasion called for a feast, and after the phone calls it was all hands on deck. Bakhetbek's brother, who due to his balding head was nicknamed "the Kazakh Gorbachev," raced to get a sheep. In an outbuilding the men gathered with cupped hands to say a prayer before its throat was cut. Had I been of the Muslim faith, I would have been asked to bless the sheep, since traditionally guests were required to ask permission from the animal's spirit to partake of its flesh.

Late into the night we sat around gorging on meat and being plied with vodka. A dombra, the traditional two-stringed mandolin of the Kazakhs, was passed around.[12] When Bakhetbek played there was a fire in his eyes, and he sat with his back even straighter and prouder than usual. Strong fingers moved instinctively up and down the instrument's neck. In Kazakh they say a good player can make the dombra sing. I was sure I could hear the beating hooves of horses. It was as if a stoic, unfaltering rhythm prevailed through the harsh realities of life and the land. I looked across to Aset, who was welling up with pride. The last beat ended, and Bakhetbek looked at me. His eyes arched into crescents; from them tears spread into the many channels of his weathered face and disappeared.

Kazakhs believe that when a guest walks through the front door, luck flies in through the window. It is a good omen: the sheep will give birth to twin lambs in the spring. Looking back on this occasion, the magic of this belief was embodied by my meeting with Bakhetbek.

AS WE PREPARED to leave Kindikti, Aset was whistling and calling angrily, with an undercurrent of panic—the dog was nowhere to be seen. I felt guilty for rushing but still held resentment toward Aset for bringing the dog in the first place. We couldn't afford to wait any longer. If we

didn't get out of Kindikti today and start heading south, there was the risk
I would be stranded here until spring.

"If he doesn't come, let it be that his destiny is here," said Aset at last,
playing down his distress. Just then there came a whoosh as a stringy
heap of bones and elastic tendons leaped over the fence of a pen and came
screaming toward us, eyes wild in panic. I had learned that the dog had
been notorious in Zhana Zhol for stealing eggs from under chickens in
the early morning, before they could be collected. As we rode out of the
village, I thought with a shake of my head that if he kept this up in places
such as Kindikti, he didn't have much hope of a long life.

For the first few hours we followed the compass southwest through a
mire of deserted hills and gullies. Jagged rock fisted through unbounded
white like compound fractures. Peaks of around 1,500 m gnashed at the
horizon. To the south we could see the foothills of the Tarbagatai range,
which slope from east to west out of the Tien Shan.[13]

The sky had been blown clear of clouds, but despite the white glow of
the sun, cold tightened its grip. Even the slight breeze landed heavily,
forging ice crystals in my eyelashes and nose hairs. On the horses it gathered as ice beards around their nostrils and chin. The air was powder dry,
and beneath the horses the snow exploded in puffs, then fluttered back to
earth in glittering clouds. Bakhetbek's tune strummed in my head.

When the sunlight withered we were stranded in the open. The earth
froze to a standstill and the temperature dropped to around −20°C. Aset
and the dog hung around my camping stove looking unconvinced we
would survive the night.

"In these conditions you should not only consider leaving the saddles
on the horses for three hours after you finish, but leave the saddle blankets on all night. We Kazakhs would even leave the saddle on for the
whole night in this situation . . . And of course without vodka you won't
survive. When your hands get cold, rub the vodka into your skin and drink
it before you go to bed," Aset said. After dinner I unfolded my cotton blankets so that they covered the horses from withers to rump, and tied them
on with spare belts and ropes.

Food and hot tea in our bellies, we climbed into the tent. Poor Aset bundled himself up in my down jacket under the remaining horse blankets and put on the insulated liners of my boots. The dog curled up at his feet.

In the morning it seemed that Aset had conquered his fear of camping in the open, or at least he could joke about it now. "Aaaaaawwww! Tashkent! Tashkent down there!" he said, shivering and pointing to his feet, where the dog was still fast asleep. "But up here it is bloody Yakutsk!"

The inside of the tent was covered in hoarfrost, and any slight move sent a shower of ice down on us. Outside, the wind had picked up again, and the sky was streaked with shreds of blood-red cloud. Overnight one end of my tent fly had suffered a rip nearly half a metre long, and the small transparent windows at the entrances had turned brittle and shattered. When Aset went for a piss he came back with more worrying news—not more than 50 m away there were fresh wolf tracks.

Saddling up proved harder than usual as I struggled to find dexterity in mitts, yet when I took them off, even briefly, my fingers went numb. It was always a gamble putting Ogonyok's crupper on, and this morning as I lifted his tail and slid the leather down onto the sensitive skin above his butt he shied away and threatened to kick.

Inspecting the horses' hooves, we realized that Taskonir had one loose shoe, and all the horses had snow balled up under their feet, so they could hardly walk. We improvised with an axe head to solve both problems, but it took more than three hours, all told, to pack up, eat, and load the animals. By the time we settled into the saddle my feet were numb. I didn't want to think about the state of Aset's feet, since he was wearing only my hiking shoes.

For once the GPS and map proved correct as we passed through the tiny aul of Chubartas, a collection of twenty ramshackle homes and barns inundated by snow. Dogs came running, snarls of teeth and fur, and I watched our little guy scuttle away under the legs of Zhamba, tail between his legs and his back arching up like a skinny feline's. Aset lashed out at the attacking dogs with his lead rope. Not a soul came out onto the street.

Clouds crowded in, the temperature rose enough so that the frost on our faces melted, and the wind blunted. Following telegraph lines and tracks, we no longer needed the compass. Two days' ride to the southwest from here lay Ayagoz, where I would part ways with Aset.

In the aul of Saariarka Aset promised we would be able to stay with a relative overnight. As the sun set we were greeted by a thin, pale woman who looked terrified at the sight of us. She talked briefly with Aset over a cup of tea, and soon after we left in the dark. His relative—the husband of this woman—had recently died, and it was inconceivable to stay in the house with a woman when there were no men at home. Traditionally a strict custom was adhered to by which a whip was always hung adjacent to the yurt or kstau entrance. I was told that a whip hanging downward meant a man was home. If it was pointing upward, he was away and one should not enter.

Aset insisted we camp by an old Kazakh grave not far from town. It was a tall mud-brick dome, worn away at the top, the overall shape reminiscent of a giant, upright, cracked eggshell. Perhaps as much as several hundred years earlier the deceased had been laid to rest inside; as the structure eroded, his or her spirit would be given passage to the sky. This particular type of grave, often found in clusters known as "silent auls," had emerged in the fifteenth century when wandering Sufi dervishes succeeded in persuading nomads in the Kazakh steppe to adopt Islam. But the tradition of holding ancestors in great reverence was a far more ancient one among nomads, part of the shamanic religion of Tengrism once shared with the Mongols. For millennia they had believed that spirits inhabited the sky and land and could provide favor or disfavor depending on a person's action.

The next morning Aset turned to me hesitantly.

"We had a visitor last night. The old man from the grave. Nothing out of the ordinary; he was just here to check on us, to see what we were doing." Then he added, "My recommendation to you is that if you are alone, always try to find these graves. The old men of the steppe will protect you. If possible, the best thing is to even sleep inside the graves." He also pointed out that, as prescribed by Muslim custom, he had washed himself in the snow before going to bed.

For the rest of the day Aset seemed quiet but content. His eyes scanned the landscape longingly. His whip hung limply from his right hand. Every now and then he raised it and gently slapped Zhamba's hindquarters. He spoke little except once, when he pointed to the horizon across a wide plain.

"Many hundreds, thousands of my men lie here. Here there were big battles." He said it with pride and emotion, as though these events had happened recently, but he was talking about the invasion by the Zhungars— Oirat Mongols who ruled an empire known as Zhungaria after the collapse of the Mongol Empire—in the eighteenth century.

It had been dawning on me gradually, but now I realized that Aset felt a sense of approval from his ancestors at his being out here. On a horse, on the steppe, under the sky, he was living, even if fleetingly, by customs that he inherently knew but which meant so little in settled village life. Like most Kazakhs I would meet over the coming months, he had pre-served a consciousness of Islam, but he clung even more closely to a belief in his nomadic heritage and the spirit of his ancestors—a blend that was symbolized in his behavior toward the grave we had camped by, and which defined the culture of the Kazakh nomad in recent centuries.

IN THE AUL of Karagash the specter of death followed us. We met a man called Kazibek who was out collecting firewood on his horse. He broke the news that Aset's relative in that aul, too, had just died. Kazibek, how-ever, was more than happy to have us for the night, and his wife was kind enough to sew up my ripped tent.

Just shy of Ayagoz, Aset called home to Zhana Zhol and received more bad news: another relative of his had been run down by a tram in Oske-men and killed. The funeral would be the next day.

The caretaker of a dacha village not far from Ayagoz took us in. Aset pulled out the city clothes he had been carrying all along and suddenly our adventure together was over. It was sad to see him without his winter breeches, knife-laden belt, and woolen sweaters, and sadder still to see him on foot, horseless. He looked like a man dispossessed. At the local market I bought him some Chinese carry bags, a new watch—he had lost his during our trip—and a bus ticket to Zhana Zhol.

I expected Aset to be upset about his cousin in Oskemen, but he seemed to be resigned to the news and more worried about parting ways with me. There was something he had been waiting to tell me.

"Tim, you need a friend on the long road, someone to keep you warm at night and protect you from wolves. His name is Tigon. Tigon means 'fast wind' or 'hawk.' He is a hunting dog. His father was a tazi, a breed of hound that is not afraid of wolves and can run quicker than the wind.

"And in our country dogs choose their owners. Tigon is yours."

I was not in the mood. Only half an hour earlier at the market he had told me I should buy a packet of condoms because one never knew what might be around the corner. His ancestors surely hadn't relayed that advice to him! He had also convinced me to buy firecrackers to ward off wolves. He seemed to know everything that was best for me in a way I occasionally found patronizing.

"But what will I do with him? What will happen to him when I get to the border? I won't be able to take him further. Can't you take him on the bus?" I was frightened of the commitment of having a dog, and anyway, I had long since decided that if I was going to get a dog, it would be one of the big wooly mastiff breeds used by nomads as guard dogs.

Aset glanced down sadly at his feet and shrugged. "I don't know. You can give him to someone if you like." Then he looked me straight in the eye. "But there is one thing. In Kazakh culture there are some things that you cannot receive as gifts, that you must buy or steal: dogs, knives, axes, and wives. This dog is not mine. It is Guanz's. You need to give me something for him; it doesn't have to be money."

I paid Aset $120 for accompanying me; gave him a toy koala, some photos from Australia, and $10 for Guanz; and promised to print and send all the photos we had taken together. I needed a second packsaddle, and so he offered to sell me his own saddle, the one he had been riding in. I bought that for $50.

We locked Tigon inside the caretaker's hut for the time being, and waved down a car on the road into town. Then Aset was gone.

Aset had traveled only eleven days with me, but he knew so much better than I the challenges that lay ahead. For that I am indebted.

8

TOKYM KAGU BASTAN

I BROKE OUT of the tent into a landscape that resembled the open, rolling tundra of the Arctic. The scant moisture in the air had snapped frozen overnight into floating particles of ice that twinkled like quartz. Delicate crystals, light as cobwebs, clung to fine tussocks of grass that skewered up into the light. Underfoot the snow squeaked, but when I had finished my morning pee and stood still, there was utter silence.

I felt as if on a precipice.

The previous day I had said goodbye to Aset and nervously maneuvered the three horses around the southern edge of Ayagoz. In doing so I crossed the tracks of the "Turk-Sib"—a railway completed in 1931 to connect the cotton industry of Uzbekistan (set to rapidly expand under Soviet rule) with Siberia and Moscow. To me, these lonely black lines dissecting the steppe from north to south were a kind of frontier, beyond which the rest of Kazakhstan yawned—still more than 2,500 km of steppe as far as the Caspian Sea. The absence of fences, borders, and even mountain ranges, seemed to suggest endless possibilities as if I could ride in whichever direction I

pleased. In truth I knew if I remained at this latitude, I would be ambushed by deep snow. Too far south, and I might find myself in a freezing
desert without snow—which would be the main source of water for both
myself and my animals during winter. Additionally, of the few rivers that
lay between here and the Caspian, most flowed on a north-south line, or
drained sluggishly into desert, or the Aral Sea, meaning that there would
be no consistent access to water as I rode west.

Late the previous afternoon, after Aset's departure, I had called home
to Australia on the satellite phone. I received bad news: our family dog of
sixteen years, a blue heeler we called Pepper, had died. After the sun disappeared I had lain awake in the sleeping bag recalling the doe-eyed, tail-
wagging presence that had filled our home throughout much of my
childhood. At the same time I was aware of the curled-up ball of fur and
bones pressing up against my thighs and snoring. It was hard to believe
that earlier that day I had nearly decided to leave him behind.

With Aset gone but Tigon yawning by my side, I now stood with the
morning sun on my back and gazed west. Yesterday I had dwelled on the
challenge of finding water, pasture, and shelter through all that emptiness. This morning the overwhelming feeling was that I would have to do
it alone.

᠅

IT HELPED ME somewhat to indulge in a fantasy, thinking of my journey
as that of a Kazakh boy born into the rigors of life on the steppe. Under
the guidance of parents and the circle of kinship, there were rituals that
guided nomads from birth, equipping them with the knowledge required
to rise to the challenges of their lives.

Central to the rite of passage for young boys was mastering how to ride
a horse, graze and protect sheep, and in earlier times how to make and
use a bow, hunt, and ultimately defend the family. One of the first important rituals was mounting ashami, when the boy was encouraged to emu-
late his father by taking a stick in place of a whip and riding out to see
how the animals were grazed. An ashami was a special children's saddle

without stirrups to which the boy's legs were bound so that he could not fall. Although this custom generally took place when the boy was seven years old, he would have been taught to ride much earlier; many children had their first experiences in the saddle before they could walk.[1]

By my reckoning, I had probably reached the metaphorical age of ten, and a custom known as *tokym kagu bastan*. At this age the boy was sent off alone on horse for his first long journey. The successful home return was anticipated with great fanfare—*tokym kagu* literally means "waiting for the boy to return"—and celebrated with a feast including the most sacred of drinks, *kumys*, fermented mare's milk. Aset had known that these first few days and weeks alone would be a great test, my own tokym kagu bastan.

In the absence of nomads to consult about my route, a hunting inspector in Ayagoz had offered valuable advice. On his suggestion, I had settled on the idea of traveling southwest toward the salty waters of eastern Lake Balkhash to beat the deep snow, before riding west along its northern shoreline into central Kazakhstan. There I would reach the Betpak Dala—a name that roughly translates to "starving steppe." My immediate goal was 150 km as the crow flies, to an aul called Kopa, where the hunting inspector had given me the details of a man known as Serik who might take me in.

After a pot of semolina, I set about the task of grooming, saddling, and packing, determined to overcome my nerves and set out in a positive frame of mind. Four hours later, however, I was still struggling to get the loads tied down on the two packhorses. Even when I finally got moving, the stiff leather of my seat had barely warmed before the load on Taskonir loosened and fell to one side. My original plan had been to use one packhorse and rotate load-carrying duties so that each day one horse was rested without a load. Recently, however, Ruslan and Aset had convinced me that it was better to spread the weight across two packhorses and carry 50 kg of grain whenever I could get it. Unfortunately, I had left in Mongolia the extra packsaddle that would have been ideal for this purpose. Aset's riding saddle, which I had bought to make do, was terribly ill-suited for carrying any load, let alone the wheat sacks I had rigged up as saddlebags. It was, according to my diary entry that night, "an absolute pig" of a saddle to pack.

It took another half hour to reload, but by then it was clear that the horses, tied for only the second time in a single caravan, had their own issues to iron out. I was riding Zhamba, with Ogonyok directly behind me and Taskonir bringing up the rear. But Taskonir, who had asserted his authority as the leader of my little herd, used every opportunity to take a bite of Ogonyok's butt. Ogonyok would suddenly bolt forward, the rattling green boxes brushing along Zhamba's flank and bashing into my right leg. Zhamba, who was the oldest but had retiringly taken middle ground in the hierarchy, was not pleased. His ears rested flat on his head while he bit and then kicked until Ogonyok was back in his place. I tried tying Ogonyok to Taskonir, making him last in our little caravan, but Taskonir continued the bullying by trying to kick Ogonyok in the head. Ogonyok pulled back until Taskonir came to a standstill and the lead rope was torn from my grasp.

Come darkness we had traveled only 12 km—and not particularly gracefully—but it was good enough that we had made it to camp intact. It wasn't until the horses had been staked out, hobbled, and fed, the stove turned off, and my stomach filled that everything felt remotely possible again. I sank back onto my big canvas duffle bag next to the tent and watched the crescent moon slope its way off the edge of the world.

For the next two days, any gathering momentum was interrupted by the same circus of hiccups, but even so I recognized the outlines of a routine that would become habitual in the coming weeks and months. In the morning Tigon bravely led the way. Then, when he tired, he followed behind like a tiny black shadow. As we rode through undulating hills, the cold white sun panned across our path and I took notice how in the morning the right side of the horses gathered a forest of sweat-frost, but by afternoon it was thicker on their left flanks. During the lunch break I knelt in the snow and watched the horses dig with their hooves and nibble on whatever they could find. Tigon sat in front of me, tail between his legs, bony spine in an arch, licking his chops and shifting his front paws. I tossed him rations of *kolbasa*, a Russian sausage, that disappeared in lightning snaps.

In the afternoon of the third day the air thawed and the snow grew thin and patchy—encouraging signs that I was making progress south and had begun to drop off the plateau toward the basin of Lake Balkhash. By dusk the vacuum of frozen silence had been filled with the sound of wind rustling through grass, and I trotted out along a rounded, dun-colored ridge.

Free of snow, the steppe turned black in the sinking light, and I made camp atop stony hills near the ruins of mud-brick graves. Only after setting up did it occur to me that without snow there was no water. It wasn't a prospect of great concern, though—I could make do with half a thermos of tea that night, and I was sure the horses wouldn't have to go thirsty for long. Winter was on our heels, and the scent of a storm brewing on the wind suggested that by morning it would have caught up.

That night I woke several times with sharp pains in my chest and the terrifying suspicion that the horses were gone. Each time it happened I unzipped the entrance and shot out, turning on my headlamp as I went. There was nothing unusual about this routine, which had characterized most nights since the horses were stolen in Mongolia. I had long since resolved to maintain a discipline of sleeping in my trousers with belt, knife, and headlamp fitted.

At some point after 3:00 A.M., however, the usual paranoia mingled with a powerful and lucid dream, the likes of which I had not previously experienced, but which would prove to recur almost nightly for the next six or seven months.

The dream began with me instinctually flicking my headlamp on and preparing to rip open the door. No sooner had I sat up, however, than Taskonir's head appeared in front of me. His eyes were as dark and shiny as maple syrup. There was a sheen to the long, dark winter hair around his face and under his chin. His floppy underlip quivered, and I had the urge to reach out and touch it. But then I realized Taskonir was looking not at me but over me, away into the night. In fact, now that I looked closer, all the horses were in front of me, their furry fetlocks at eye level, and I had all three of their lead ropes in my hands. They were pulling hard!

I held on for what felt an eternity, but just when I thought my arms and hands couldn't hold out any longer, I noticed the stranger. He stood in the darkness just around to my right—I could see him from the corner of my eye. He seemed old, I thought—balding, with gray hair and strong workman's hands. Unfazed, he walked toward me.

The rope began to slip from my grip, up and away. The heads of the horses lifted out of the beam from my headlamp and into the shadows. Before I could catch another glimpse of this man, my legs and arms gave way with heaviness. I closed my eyes and felt released into deep sleep. I had a strong conviction the horses were safe.

In the morning it was hard to get up. Outside, wind lashed the tent with thick wet snow. Inside, the dream hung around like a heavy fog. In time I would find the dream familiar and comforting—each time I would hold on to the ropes until an old man appeared and I would fall asleep. When I told Kazakhs about it, they were sure it was the spirits of the old men of the steppe, protecting me. This morning, though, the dream was still raw and frightening. I could still feel the tension in my arms.

In recent days, the steppe had spread out in a milky white and brown sea in which it was difficult to tell the difference between distant crags and clouds, the curves of both rolling sensuously out into emptiness. Now, as I moved on, the scale of the land contracted to depthless, throbbing squalls of snow. I caught only glimpses of the lay of the land—a warren of hills, a swamp, more hills, then a plain.

I had the feeling we had come in the wrong direction, but in the end my compass proved to be much better oriented than I, and at midday we stumbled on a track leading towards Tansyk—a village only 30 km from Kopa.

For the next two hours the tracks wound into fog and snow, and I shivered into a state of despondency. Stopping made me more aware of the wet sleet dribbling down my skin from neck to ankles, so I carried on without breaks.

I shouldn't have, but I caved in to tempting thoughts about spring and good times with Kathrin. Visions, smells, and distant feelings taunted— hot sand underfoot on the beach, the light-as-air sensation of shorts and T-shirt, Kathrin's soft, warm skin. They collided brutally with the reality around me. As I shifted my gaze to the snow in front, I thought I was dreaming. A snake was slithering feebly, incrementally, across our path. The odds against it seemed overwhelming.

Another hour of introspection passed, and when I lifted my head the tracks had turned to mud, it was raining, and there was no snow in sight. I paused to focus on a flock of sheep, tended to by a horseman—the first sign of life I had witnessed since leaving Ayagoz.

I could have taken hints from the herder and found someone to take me in, but this was my first stretch of the journey traveling fully alone in Kazakhstan, and I wanted to prove to myself that I could cope. That night I camped in sight of two large dome graves and shivered through till dawn in a wet sleeping bag. By morning the sky had cleared, and now, on my fifth straight day I took great satisfaction in pouring out the last of the bag of grain for the horses. The sun brought relief, and as steam poured off my thawing clothes I packed up for the first time in three weeks without mitts.

"Another half a day south to Kopa. It must be still summer down there!" I said to Tigon. The dog looked back at me, ears upright. He just wanted breakfast.

⊞

IN THE SAME way that Kopa would prove a fleeting but intense concentration of life and movement in the larger scheme of my winter journey, the aul of forty or so homes came into view as no more than an island dwarfed by a wild sea of brown and gray steppe.

Far out, a herd of sheep and goats was being driven home for the night, appearing from a distance like bobbing seagulls drifting in on the currents. I descended from the hills just as people emerged from their homes to welcome the animals and herders back. Had the animals grazed well today? No wolf sightings? Were all the animals accounted for? Then again things settled, the working horses in their corrals, the sheep in their pens.

I'd met two men on their way on foot to Kopa earlier in the day, and they led the way to a courtyard where others came out and helped unload the horses. There could be no mistaking my host, Serik, who motored into the aul and stepped out of a battered Soviet, crank-start jeep. He was a gentle but powerful man with a strong Russian nose, meaty hands that clutched on to me, and pale Kazakh eyes that looked at me intensely.

"Where have you been? We have been expecting you for two days!"

Serik was the *akim* of the aul and the local district, which meant he was at once an elected mayor and a man of recognized natural authority. It was a title reminiscent of leaders in nomad times, known as *biys*, who, along with *batyrs*—warriors—had been part of the old nomad aristocracy known as the "white bone" (*ak suyet*), which officially ruled outside the tribal system of nomads. In such vast territories, where loyalty always lay to circles of kin and not central administration, they were crucial for re-solving disputes, especially over rights to grazing land.

Although there were historical parallels to be drawn, Serik oversaw a very different aul than that presided over by biys. In Soviet times Kopa had been a dedicated haymaking collective—a type of farming created under Soviet rule that saw collectives developed into monoculture farm-ing productions and former nomads equipped with specialized skills such as haymaking, tractor driving, herding, and slaughtering. In post-Soviet times, this had left rural Kazakhs conditioned to be employees of the state but without the skills to practice the kind of wholesale farming intro-duced by the Soviets, yet also bereft of the knowledge that would allow them to contemplate a return to the nomadic pastoralism of their ances-tors. Many Kazakhs had subsequently departed to regional towns and cities to look for work. Kopa, a victim of this trend, was now a largely deserted village, where the dwindling population survived on subsistence farming and the barter and sale of the hay that was still produced.

Despite the somewhat depressing conditions, the tradition of hospital-ity remained firmly unbroken. Without hesitating, Serik ordered the aul's fodder vault to be opened, whereupon two of his workers hauled out giant bundles of hay and laid them at the feet of my horses. Tigon was promptly thrown some bones, and after I had been treated to a sauna-like *banya*, a dish of meat, and a couple of shots of vodka, Serik compelled me to stay for three days. This was a traditional period of time during which a

Kazakh host was required to ply the guest with hospitality and had no right to ask who the guest was or what his business might be. Perhaps more to the point, there was due to be a wedding in nearby Tansyk, the aul I had bypassed the day before on the way to Kopa, and it was essential—compulsory, in fact—that I be there.

Two nights later the old *dom kultura*—the Soviet-era "house of culture"—in Tansyk was pulsating with a crowd of several hundred. Against the backdrop of a Soviet-era mural and some hastily strung up lights that flashed robotically, men with drab but impeccable suits and women in camel-hair vests mingled with a throng of teenagers clad in skin-hugging jeans. In a rising fervor of anticipation, many danced, including elderly men whose faces pursed in concentration, as if they were trying to remember a long-forgotten style. It didn't matter if the music was Madonna or traditional Kazakh—their dance moves did not change.

To announce the beginning of the ceremony, a musician made a dramatic entrance in a flashy suit with a dombra cradled in his arms. He roamed about the hall demanding attention with his furious strumming, and as he began to sing, people left the floor. In the past a musician such as he might have been known as an *akyn*—a talented performer chosen to represent a certain kinship group or family. For centuries, in the absence of the written word, the continuity of nomadic life and a sense of national consciousness rested heavily on such artists.[2] In the twenty-first century the akyn evidently had to have a broader repertoire than his predecessor. A tangle of amplifiers, microphones, and speakers was part of the modern arsenal, and in addition to traditional music, many of the songs he performed were slow love melodies to clunky backing music from a synthesizer.

When finally the bride and groom walked in, the musician serenaded the bride as part of a custom known as *betashar*, "revealing the face" of the bride. The formalities that followed were as eclectic as the musician's gamut. A mullah stood alongside a bureaucrat from the registrar's office, and as the bride and groom, dressed in a generic gown and suit, respectively, signed some papers, the dombra went quiet and Mendelssohn's "Wedding March" blared from the speakers.

Throughout the ceremony, Serik and several old men chaperoned me, making sure I was propped right up close to the action. As a foreigner wearing dirty hiking boots and faded travel garb, I found the experience a little awkward at first. When the official matters were over, though, I was carried into the dining room by the heaving spirits of the crowd. There I paused momentarily in disbelief.

Three rows of long trestle tables were laden with dazzling platters of fresh fruit, horse sausage, dried curd, pastries, confectionery, salads, and nuts. By every third plate shiny bottles of vodka and sparkling water provided additional polish. I had long since become accustomed to preserved meat, rice, and semolina as the mainstays of my diet, not to mention the frugal existence of the people I had met, so I found this at once overwhelming and perplexing. Noticing my sense of awe, Serik explained that it was a small wedding—only three hundred guests. Kazakhs, I discovered, put their life savings into wedding ceremonies.

I fell into it all. As a hundred different toasts were raised to the newlyweds, I relished the kaleidoscope of faces that seemed to reflect all corners of the steppe. There were men with large ears, sunken cheeks, and blue eyes, and others with broad faces and olive skin stretched taut over formidable fist-like cheekbones. A woman two seats up from me had large dark eyebrows, a slight red tinge to her face, and a pointy nose. A woman opposite had glowing porcelain skin that blanketed the rounded contours of her wide, open face like snow. Her eyes were almond-shaped, so, depending on her expression, she could swing from an Eastern look to a Western one in an instant.

After Serik had proclaimed his toast and the akyn made everyone aware over the PA system of the special guest from Australia, we moved back to the other section of the hall. The floors and walls there vibrated with a throng of old and young dancing to contemporary Kazakh music. There were middle-aged women twirling in shrieks of laughter, and grooving old men whose shirts had popped out from their belts and shook like flags in the wind. Judging by the number of empty vodka bottles lying around, there were a lot more festivities to come. Sensing this, and wisely choosing to censor my experience, Serik signaled that it was time to go.

MUSIC FROM THE wedding echoed in my head as I saddled up and rode out from Kopa. The horses were similarly buoyant—they had gorged so much under Serik's watch that I was forced to lengthen their girth straps. They were wound up, and happy to move into a trot with the gentlest of commands, but just as inclined to use their excess energy to misbehave. Something a Kazakh herder later told me was partially true: "It is dangerous to rest a horse too long, or a man, for they will soon relax and become weak, lazy, and disobedient."

Only a short distance beyond Kopa, a sobering headwind stole away any residual warmth from my stay. The horses also tired a little, and when they fell into line my sense of euphoria and companionship all but disintegrated. Reunited with my solo journey, I refocused my sights.

Just 50 km from Kopa lay the shores of Lake Balkhash, a long, narrow body of water stretching around 600 km from east to west. A geographical curiosity of the lake, the world's third-largest inland sea without an outlet, is that the eastern half is saline, while the western half, which curves in a crescent shape to the south, is freshwater.

My plan was to ride west, parallel to the shoreline, where the moderating effect of the lake would buy me some time before the onset of extreme cold. The challenge of this route lay in the arid and uninhabited terrain. There were no permanent streams or rivers feeding the lake from the north, and the eastern half was too saline for livestock to drink. My only hope in the event there was no snowfall was to rely on getting water from a remote industry-serving railway that ran just north of the shore. At regular intervals there were control points and sidings with camps of rail workers known in Russian as *raz'ezds*.

As I headed south from Kopa, then west, tracks and roads petered out, giving way to wide, cracked clay pans, between which grew tough, gray

woody plants without foliage. Far to the north the escarpment of the uplands was just visible, but ahead the horizon was one finger thick—so flat
and deserted that nothing but Tigon with his tall pointy ears bridged it
with the sky.

The routines of travel that had carried me to Kopa brought reassurance
in such a wild setting, but on the evening of the second day I hadn't found
any water or pasture and made for the railway line and a raz'ezd known as
Zhaksybulak. During my time there it became clear that while I had left
more populated territories behind, I had also departed from communities
whose livelihood, like mine, was closely connected with the pursuit of
pasture.

The single-track railway the raz'ezds served carried a cargo of oil and
gas from the Caspian Sea in western Kazakhstan, much of which was
bound for Druzhba on the border with China. Zhaksybulak itself—the
largest siding I came across in the area, and the only one with any livestock and permanent residency—was a disorderly handful of huts clinging to the rail line, laden with litter, broken glass, and a couple of rusting
truck chassis. Most of the houses were either half-built or semi-demolished
shells, and the rail workers eked out a living in rooms they had been able
to improvise and close off to the elements with tarpaulins. Water
supplies—even for the token sheep and cow—were brought weekly by
train. Through an unbroken maelstrom of wind-whipped sand, dirt, and
salt came the rumbling, and screeching of giant steel trains with tanks
stained black with oil and grease. Long after they had been eclipsed by the
horizon, acrid diesel fumes carried on the wind. With my animals freshly
watered, I left as soon as I could.

The next five days—four riding and one resting—melted into one another. Two subtly different tones of gray offered the only contrast in a
landscape of fading monochrome: the sky, which remained overcast and
dim, and the featureless, color-drained steppe. There were no livestock,
and only morsels of grass and wormwood plant to be found. The lake
shoreline remained out of sight.

I rode a safe distance from the railway line but once a day made a trip
to look for water at the raz'ezds that were spaced along the line at 20 km

and sometimes 40 km intervals. Some raz'ezds had run out of water and the men had little or nothing to drink for themselves. Most were manned by only one or two workers.

At night I camped to the north, where there were tiny oases of grass, and retired to the tent, where the world was smaller and easier to comprehend. In Zhaksybulak stories of wolf sightings and attacks had abounded, so I began throwing firecrackers out the tent door before going to sleep as a precaution. One evening I tried to film myself with the firecrackers but forgot to open the tent door before I lit them. The result was a hole burned in the fly—an addition to a growing list of needed repairs.

Although I resented my dependence on the railway, I had nowhere else to turn when the horses tired and I clean ran out of grain. A day's ride short of a copper-mining hub called Sayak, I hesitantly approached a raz'ezd, two small buildings trackside.

In a room flooded with the stench of vodka and tobacco I found three men playing cards, heads down. At first they thought I might be a Russian illegally fishing the lake, but upon seeing my horses, they let loose with all manner of jubilant profanities and agreed to help.[3] I paid one of them to hitch a ride on a train to Sayak and bring back a sack of grain and some food supplies for me by evening.

Waiting a day amid the diesel stench, blackened earth, and scattered rubbish was not pleasant, but the only other possibility for resting the horses and getting supplies was to ride into Sayak myself—something I had been told to avoid at all costs. By all reports, this declining mining town was "full of bandits," unemployed "Oralmans"—Kazakhs who had recently emigrated from Mongolia, China, or elsewhere abroad—and competing Mafia groups.[4] More worrying for me were reports of the corrupt Sayak police. Apparently they were known to abduct people or arrest them on false grounds, drive them out onto a remote part of the steppe, steal their valuables, and leave them for dead. The police were said to be awaiting my arrival, and even though I suspected the rumor to be nothing more than scaremongering, I had managed to fly under the radar of the authorities until now and feared what they might make of my visa papers.[5]

After dark a sack of grain, some rice, and some canned meat were delivered. I settled into camp near the tracks, relieved that my time at the raz'ezd had passed without event. Just after tethering the horses, however, a special workers' train pulled in, and a group of around twenty men piled out. The workers, who had arrived from Sayak for a week of track maintenance, swaggered over to an empty dormitory hut, sniggering and swearing, smoking cigarettes. I was dragged into their smoke-filled den, where vodka was flowing and men sat on their bunks freely spitting onto the floor between drags.

One man with straw-like hair, pockmarked skin, and an unblinking stare poured me a glass. "Give me one of your horses! Or at least sell it to me cheaply! After all, what do you need three for?" When I refused, he backed off and replied in a gentler tone, "I have heard there are thieves in Sayak coming to steal your horses tonight, so be careful."

When I managed to extricate myself from the hut I found Tigon curled up by the door guarding my boots. He leaped up at me, paws on my chest, whining. I ran my hands along his snout, caressed his head behind the ears, and let him bury his moist nose in my coat.

It should have been obvious that I needed to stick close to my animals this night, but instead I took up an invitation for dinner inside the signal-control room with the engineers. This lapse of caution would very nearly prove the end of my journey.

I was partway through a slop of canned meat and fried potato when I stepped outside and heard a great thwack and muffled thump from the direction of my camp. Crouching, I could make out the silhouetted figure of someone scurrying away from Taskonir. As I ran toward him I tripped and fell over an object that proved to be my backpack. Even as I rushed to raise the alarm, the turn of events was becoming clear. The mystery figure had taken my backpack—which included my video camera, passport, and money—and leaped bareback on Taskonir for a brazen getaway. What he hadn't realized was that Taskonir was tethered on the lower front leg with a 20 m line. Taskonir had only made it to the end of the rope before he and his passenger somersaulted to earth.

It wasn't long before the would-be thief was dragged into the hut and revealed as the very same man who had warned me about thieves. Since our earlier meeting I had learned that he had been born in Mongolia and immigrated as a child to Kazakhstan, and was colloquially known as "the Mongol."

I had barely begun to make sense of these happenings when an engineer from the signal station took command. "You know what we do when there is a problem like this?" he announced. "There is just one solution." The men around him looked on, captivated. "To drink!"

They went back inside and raised toasts to anything they could think of. When their vodka ran out they demanded I hand over any alcohol I might have stowed away.

"Don't worry, Tim! Timokha! Tamerlane! Timurbek! This is the way we do it—this is the way we solve our problems. Don't be offended!" the men chanted.

Even the would-be thief, who was unapologetic, joined in for a drink.

I retired to the tent and packed so I could leave at the first hint of light, but the course of events still had a ways to run. At two in the morning Taskonir vanished, leading to a sortie of drunken men running clumsily through the dark on a desperate search. Someone tripped on an old wire and fell, and another face-planted on the train tracks. There were rumors that someone had *really* stolen the horse this time, and that it couldn't possibly have been the Mongol because he was asleep. But then, just as I was recovering my breath, the men wandered back, leading Taskonir. I tied the horses on short ropes for the rest of the night and lay in my sleeping bag on the ground among them.

At 6:00 A.M. I was up and saddling, and by sunrise I was ready to go. There was just one last issue to solve: Taskonir's hobbles were missing. I roused some men and told them to wake the Mongol. When he appeared looking sullen and disinterested, I was already sitting high up on the horse, so I was looking down on him.

"I don't care who stole my horse, but I need my hobbles!" I said sternly.

With a sigh he walked around to the rear of the hut and came back with them.

Other men came out, rubbing their eyes, to say goodbye as I set off into a fast trot. Tigon was already far ahead.

"Have a good journey! We hope you are not offended!"

⊟⊟

I KEPT MY eyes straight ahead for hours and didn't stop until the railway had been so long extinguished from view that I felt beyond its orbit. I felt as though we were setting ourselves adrift back into the embrace of the steppe. I didn't care if it meant drinking salt water for a whole month; I was no longer going to be seduced by the illusion of security the railway suggested. It was true what I had been told: "The most dangerous wolf of all is that which walks on two legs."

By evening my pace slowed to a walk, and the adrenaline ran dry. Safely beyond the gaze of human beings, I felt more able to contemplate what had passed. Given the repercussions that might have ensued if the horse thief had been successful, I couldn't shake a feeling of dread and anger. Simultaneously, however, the farther I made it from the raz'ezd, the more the personal offense faded, and I began to find something curiously endearing about the thief.

In a kind of honorable way, the Mongol had warned me of the theft—an unspoken acknowledgment that he liked my horses, and a backhanded compliment. Most interesting was his choice of horse. Had he wanted to steal the most valuable mount for resale, Ogonyok would have been his pick. Instead, he chose Taskonir—a horse invaluable for herding, but long in the tooth and comparatively bony. If the theft was partly born of an appreciation of Taskonir's qualities, I believed there was some degree of honor in that.

More broadly, in the context of nomad culture and history, it was clear that my tendency to associate horse theft with the communities of the railway was misplaced. Horse rustling was an art as old as horsemanship itself, glamorized in oral epics of the steppe, and very much a part of everyday nomad life. Kazakhs had explained to me time and time again that he who has the skill to steal horses and cattle and get away with it deserves those animals more than the owner. One had to respect the daring and heroics of such men.

What was more, in getting my horse back from the Mongol, I had engaged in a centuries-old custom called barimta, which means "that which is due to me." It dictated that he who has been stolen from has the right to steal back, and if he is good enough, he can confiscate the offender's entire herd or even his wife until the dispute is resolved. Over time I came to think that the evolving history of this custom said a lot about the nature of the Mongol and the theft.

Prior to the colonization of Kazakh land, barimta was adhered to as a way of resolving conflicts ranging from unpaid bride-prices to contested grazing rights. It was condoned by the tribal justice system known as adat and governed by strict guidelines, such as that the confiscation had to take place in daylight so that the avengers' skill had to be exceptional and therefore honorable.

Like nomadic life in general, barimta began to erode with the arrival of the Russians, who gradually supplanted it with their own model of law. In 1822 they criminalized barimta as horse and cattle theft, and in 1868 they decreed that all land previously used for livestock grazing would be taken over by the state. In a move born partly of rebellion, but mostly spurred by the need to keep order among themselves, Kazakhs continued to recognize barimta. The term, however became more synonymous with the brazen horse thefts that Kazakhs carried out against tsarist emissaries.[6] These skilled Kazakh horse rustlers passed into legend and were rarely handed over to Russian justice.

In light of the background of barimta, I felt that the Mongol had stolen Taskonir in rough keeping with the spirit of his ancestors—a thought that offered cold comfort, but was at least a way of coming to terms with the theft. In the future, I would have to accept that if I wasn't good enough to look after my horses, then the thief probably deserved them more than I did. Ultimately, I would also have to understand that as a foreigner, without the protections of a traditional nomad society or colonial law, I was very much on my own.

9

BALKHASH

A GOOD 40 km from the raz'ezd where I'd nearly lost Taskonir, I crested a rise and brought the horses to a standstill. It was near sunset, and a low ceiling of dark clouds pressed down on the earth, rendering the steppe a uniform black. This had been the norm in recent days, but now to the south, east, and west, where the land ordinarily petered out into a smudgy embrace with the horizon, it merged with the broad, silvery waters of Lake Balkhash.

From a height and distance such as this, as vast as the lake appeared, it was not hard to imagine it was but a mere puddle on the canvas of the Eurasian steppe, draining the snowmelt of Central Asia's Tien Shan farther south. It was a reminder that although it was November 30, nearly five months since I had climbed into the saddle, I had come little more than a fifth of the distance to the Danube. West of Lake Balkhash still lay the most challenging landscapes of my journey—the Betpak Dala ("starving steppe"), then the deserts surrounding the Aral Sea. Even then, I would only just be reaching the halfway point to Hungary.

As I let my eyes be drawn in to the sense of space and grandeur before me, the bigger picture melted away and I became absorbed in the details of the land immediately in front of us. A series of peninsulas, coves, and bays formed an intriguing corrugated look to the northern shoreline of Lake Balkhash, the scale and drama of which could be more accurately described as an ocean coastline. For the next week or so I hoped to forget about the attempted horse theft and lose myself in the shore's furrows. We had traveled about half the length of Balkash's saline eastern half along the railway, and from here my aim was to avoid human contact for as long as I could manage and somehow find enough fresh water to be self-sufficient. I hoped that would prepare me—physically and mentally—to carry on farther west as the real winter set in.

⁊⁊

ON THIS FIRST evening I camped on the highest hill I could find. Overnight it snowed heavily enough that by morning there was no need to find water. The next afternoon I felt my way down through gullies to the shore of the lake.

Close up, Lake Balkhash was even more spellbinding than from afar. When the sun came out, the water was a rich azure. Small swells arose and crashed onto veneers of ice that had formed around the lake edges. Soon, I surmised, both these vast bodies—the sea-like steppe and the lake itself—would fuse as one.

The period of on-and-off freezing—characterized by cold nights but warmish days—would prove a stroke of luck. There were polished pieces of relatively salt-free ice being washed up on the pebbly beach. There began a routine that would last for a couple of weeks—collecting ice during the day in plastic bags, and melting it in the evening for drinking water and dinner. The horses crunched on this ice as well, although they also began to drink water from the lake. It was a sign the lake was becoming less brackish the farther west we traveled.

As I rode, the evolving contours of the shoreline made for an engaging story. Flats grew into muscled hills, which in turn became stony ridges overlooking the lake. In places the earth below came to life with a smattering of red, green, yellow, and purple pebbles, but then these gave way to soft clay and patches of sand, where getting to the lakeshore meant fighting through marshes and tall reeds. The horses moved briskly, their pack boxes rattling rhythmically, hooves clipping the frost off plants. We trotted ten to twenty minutes each hour and set a fast walk in between.

At night when the dangers and fears seemed to crowd in, the growing sense of family with my animals provided comfort. The responsibility of being their leader and protector gave me more courage than I would have had alone. There was nothing better than falling asleep on a luxurious mattress of saddle blankets as the horses grazed around my tent. The sweet smell of horse sweat, hair, and leather permeated every waking moment.

Although my aim was to remain unseen, it wasn't possible to avoid people entirely. In places the railway hugged the shore, and I could see raz'ezds in the distance. There was also the odd mud hut camouflaged into the side of the hills, but the fishermen who inhabited them were just as reclusive and unwilling to be seen as I. I met only one of these men—a shriveled old Russian who came out to ask if I had vodka and if I was "migrating." Later I was told more about these poachers, and how the state authorities would sometimes send helicopters out to spot the illegal fishing shanties.

Especially in light of the scattered human presence, I relished the test of finding campsites hidden from prying eyes. The longer I evaded humans, the less likely it was that anyone would know to expect me, let alone look for or find me. It was rewarding to feel that only the land and my animals knew of my existence.

It was during a rest day, while I sheltered in the tent from flurries of snow and sleet, that I realized the wear and tear on my equipment had been creeping up on me. Much of my gear, which up until now I had considered new, was falling apart. My list of problems to solve, as I wrote it in my diary, went thus: *Trousers falling apart—winter hat needs sewing up—tent has another few holes (seems to be falling apart)—buckles broken on saddle—gloves need sewing up—hobbles need to be fixed—stirrup leathers almost knackered—zip on my jacket is going—tripod leg broken—stakes need straightening.* Oddly enough, perhaps, given the length of the journey that still stretched in front of me, I found it satisfying I had reached a stage of the journey when nothing was new and shiny and I had to persevere without the aid of the freshness with which I had begun. Some romantic part of me hoped all my foreign equipment would eventually fade away and I would be forced to borrow exclusively from the indigenous ways. Only then I could become part of the landscape like the nomads whom I so wanted to understand.

Eventually the steppe began to offer some more generous pasture. There were more signs of life, too. One frosty morning we came face-to-face with a herd of shaggy Bactrian camels. All three horses—which were from eastern Kazakhstan and therefore had never seen camels—reared, muscles tensing and nostrils flaring. I was riding Zhamba at the time and could feel his heart pounding through my lower legs. In a fraction of a second, I found myself a substantial distance from where we had been standing, holding on for life as the horses bolted away. Tigon, for his part, didn't help things when he began herding the whole group of camels toward us.

For the first time since leaving Kopa, I came across nomads' dome tombs. One in particular was at least 5 m high and made of well-preserved mud brick. Its entry was facing south, just like a yurt, and Tigon and I ate our lunch inside, huddled out of the wind. When I was moving again I scanned the surrounding area, imagining where camps might have been and herds might have grazed.

One week after we left the last raz'ezd, our bubble was finally broken. I was wakened at dawn by a whinnying from Ogonyok, and broke out of the tent. Two paces from the sleeping bag I stopped in my tracks: Ogonyok and Taskonir stood facing me with their ears back and hind legs flexed. Behind them in the half-light was the ghostly figure of a dark, wooly stallion. He snorted, demanding a confrontation. Beyond him, hidden among the shrubbery, were a hundred beady eyes and ears straight as nails. They were barrel-chested little horses with thick necks, coarse split manes, and brands on their hindquarters. Very Mongolian, I thought.

We all froze until Tigon came to his senses and sprinted over with the most aggressive bark he could muster. Foals, mares, and geldings broke into a gallop, and the steppe came to life with a thousand muffled thuds and the splintering of twigs. In their wake shrubs quivered, but even they soon returned to stillness.

It had been so long since I had seen another horse—more than two weeks—that I had forgotten the magic of it. In fact, the last two weeks had been the first time on the journey when the distant silhouette of a horseman hadn't been as common as the rising sun. I missed the cry of a herder, the rustle of a flock of sheep, and the movement of horses, all of which brought a sense of vitality to the steppe.

It was time to take a gamble with humans. Besides, the weather of late had been getting cold—around -10°C—and I was out of grain. And the next day was my twenty-sixth birthday.

⊞

FROM CAMP IT didn't take long to discover a kstau by following the converging trails of sheep and goats through tall tussocks of ak-shi, or white grass. Ever since coming across this grass the previous evening I'd known it was a good sign: a herdsman in western Mongolia had once told me that wherever ak-shi grew, Kazakh nomads have always lived. Sometimes towering taller than a rider in the saddle, it provided shelter for sheep and goats, survival food for horses, and an indispensable resource for nomads. Its woody husks became so thick and strong that the tallest blades were gathered, assembled in a mat, and placed upright between the collapsible lattice walls of the yurt and the insulating felt, acting as a natural screen to keep out flies and rodents when the felt was lifted up to let the cool air in. They were also used as drying trays and bird-proof covers for dried curd.

I sighted the kstau from the safety of the ak-shi, and it took some time before I mustered the courage to come out of hiding. Holding Tigon back and keeping his snout closed with my hand, I spied on the man who had his head down and was fixing an old motorcycle. Only after waiting for some herders in the distance to move out of view with their flocks of sheep and goats did I ride out into the open.

I was nearly on the man before he spun around and looked up at our caravan. I took the initiative.

"Who are you?" I asked. "Are you the owner? Do you have water? Do you have grain? Is there a trail from here to Balkhash? How far is the closest aul?"

Even as I spoke I could see Tigon out of the corner of my eye, sniffing around in reconnaissance. To my dismay when he pissed on things he did it crouching, like the puppy he still was, betraying his age and belying our fanciful cover as tough, hardened beings of the steppe.

The man, named Kuat, was the owner of this grazing station, and as he answered my questions ran his eyes meticulously over my horses. He began with the front hooves, then went up the legs to the mouth and across their backs to the rump before following the curves down from the hindquarters, finishing off with a peek underneath to confirm they were geldings and not stallions or mares. I was beginning to understand that you could read more about a person from his animals than his words.

There was a short silence thereafter, suggesting he was putting together the funny foreign equipment and my accent.

"So my dogs were not mistaken!" he said at last. "When they started barking last night we thought there were wolves. Your horses are hungry. I have some feed for them. Let's go drink tea."

Only inside the warm confines of his hut did I begin to relax. This was part of my plan to drop my guard cautiously, layer by layer. It became a protocol that I would adhere to religiously.

The first step was trusting the stranger enough to get out of my saddle. I kept in mind a saying that a Kazakh once told me: "When walking past the behind of a foreign horse, unless you have spoken first to its owner, keep walking."

If I felt comfortable after getting out of the saddle, I would risk unloading the animals and enter the home. Only over a cup of tea would I explain who I was and where I was headed. I also learned to monitor Tigon's reaction—if his tail shot down and he shied away from the host with a growl, it was better to move on. The ultimate shedding of defenses was unsaddling the horses, having some vodka with my host, and stripping down to thermal underwear for bed. To sleep without the hard handle of the knife on my belt digging into my hips—I never took my trousers off at camp on the steppe—was a luxury, but concurrently made me aware of being at the mercy of my hosts. I would then have no choice but to cave in to trust and exhaustion.

A couple of herders who worked for Kuat joined us for tea and bread. Although Kazakhs almost exclusively eat meat and dairy, bread and salt are considered sacred, able to draw guests from afar. Not eating or trying the bread shows disrespect.

As I cradled the tea and dipped the bread into some fresh *kaimak* (cream), we talked exclusively at first about pasture and the weather. This environment, with its soft sandy soil and vegetation, was a relative paradise and I recounted the harrowing land that I had been traveling through. They were impressed, but mostly intrigued to hear I had encountered their herd of horses. Had I seen the foals? Had I seen the stallion? What did I think about them?

With the second round of tea came the familiar questions: "Do you have parents? Where are your horses from? How did you find us?" And finally: "Where are you from?"

They tried to veil their excitement, but it was too much when I explained it was my birthday the next day. "Then it is decided. You must stay here to celebrate!"

I spent the rest of the day tinkering away with repairs and letting the adrenaline of the past two weeks turn to fatigue. Kuat, who had moved gracefully into his middle age with silver hair and was educated as an agriculturalist, had an authority born of life on the steppe, and I felt myself leaning toward trusting him. I knew it was risky, but I needed a rest, and so I accepted his invitation. It might have been an achievement to survive alone for some time, but not trusting in people wasn't sustainable.

At dawn the next morning I sat bolt upright, my recurring dream leaving a residue in my mind, and reached for the tent door. By the time I recalled where I was, I was fully awake, so I stepped outside to water the horses. Tigon, who was sleeping on a horse blanket next to my saddle, opened one eye briefly before tucking his nose further under his tail and pretending he hadn't seen me. I would have gone back to bed had I not noticed a shadowy figure coming out to the barn.

In the half-light Bazibek, a sixty-year-old herder, was limping bow-legged over to a camel. He had a gun slung over his shoulder and was wearing felt boots and a traditional fox-fur hat. His body looked as rigid and gaunt as an old skinny sheep, and wind had eroded his face, stranding his cheeks like broad boulders in a furrowed mess of landslips. For forty years straight he had worked as a chaban, and he set about saddling the camel, his motions sure as the rising sun, silent and unrushed. Age had worn away his agility, but everything he did, from fitting the felt blanket to tightening the girth and hanging the rifle from the front hump, was done with precision. I had the feeling he was trying not to wake the land. Even when he spoke to me he did so in a husky whisper. How was it that, despite its size and harshness, the land felt so tender at this time of day?

When the flock of sheep had been let out of a pen, Bazibek hauled himself into the saddle, and the camel rose. It was a dramatic transformation, he and the camel becoming one. Bazibek was now the eyes, the camel the legs, and in that moment the frailty of Bazibek's age vanished. As I was told by many, on the steppe men learned to ride before they could walk, and could still ride a stallion after they could no longer stand. Directing his sheep with a long pole and whip, Bazibek set off into the distance, calling rhythmically. Since the days were now so short, he would only step out of the saddle at dusk, when he returned.

Long after he had gone the look in his eyes stuck with me. There was a humble, faraway expression there that told something of the simplicity of the steppe. I had begun to feel it myself, out there all day—the steppe consumed and gently coaxed you into a motion and rhythm until you intuitively knew your place on this earth.

It was with this enchantment I returned to the hut for breakfast and Kuat said something that stirred me further: "Do you know that Genghis Khan and his men stayed here?"

I looked up at him, with his hair all awry and his mustache glistening wet above the steam pouring from his teacup. He looked a little nervous—perhaps it had taken courage for him to say it, as if it were a secret, or he was risking ridicule.

"Really? How do you know?" I asked.

"The old men know."

There was probably no written evidence to suggest the legend was true, but among a people for whom oral history had been the bedrock of knowledge, it was foolish to discard such legends. Within these stories was always an element of truth.

As I mulled over this conversation with Kuat in the coming days, I found several reasons to think it was possible that the area had borne the hoofprints of Mongols' horses. The ak-shi was a sign that the area was a relative oasis, suitable for a winter or summer camp, and I knew the region had long been home to nomads. And then there was the geographical location. It was here, at the very narrowest point of Lake Balkhash, that the fresh waters of the west flowed through the bottleneck into the saline eastern part. Because of the abundance of fresh water, this part of the lake would freeze over even early in the winter, and it would have been possible for an army to ride across the short stretch of ice to the southern shore.

Most important, the southern shore of the lake marked the northern border of the strategic Jeti-su or "Seven Rivers" region. The Jeti-su stretched from Lake Balkhash to the Tien Shan in the south; its extensive river systems traditionally supported a symbiotic mix of nomadic and more agrarian sedentary societies. From the Bronze Age to the present, aspiring empires—including those of the Usuns (a Turkic people in the third century BCE), the Huns, the Mongols, and Tamerlane—knew that whoever ruled the Jeti-su controlled a vast swath of Central Asia. This fact was not lost on the Russians, who in the middle of the nineteenth century established Almaty in the heart of the Jeti-su—it became Kazakhstan's largest city, and was the capital until Nazarbayev moved it to Astana in 1997.

The more I dwelled on it, the more I reasoned that this land just north of Lake Balkhash seemed like a logical retreat for armies between campaigns. It would have been a remote hinterland home to hardened nomads who had much in common with the Mongols, and ideal for grazing horses. In summer—the season for planning and grazing, not war—the lake would have offered natural protection from the south. In light of this, I wondered whether Kuat's herd of horses might have been the descendants of Mongol mounts. Still, it all seemed very farfetched, a romantic hope that I had stumbled on a piece of the nomad puzzle.

Weeks later I happened to be talking to Gansukh in Mongolia on the satellite phone and recounted the story, mentioning that the aul near Kuat's farm was known as Ortaderesin. In turn, he told me that *orta* in Mongolian means "tall," and *deres* is the Mongol term for ak-shi—something probably unbeknownst to most local Kazakhs, since *orta* is also a Kazakh word meaning "middle." Still, that piece of information made it seem all the more likely that this Mongolian hoofprint had withstood the test of time.

THE MEN AT Kuat's farm were ecstatic about the prospect of a birthday party and set about cleaning the hut in preparation. Kuat, meanwhile, agreed to drive me 50 km west to a market in the small copper-smelting city of Balkhash, and that night we returned in high spirits with delicacies such as fruit, salted fish, cake, salami, salad, the filled Russian dumplings called *pelmeni*, orange juice, and, of course, a few bottles of vodka.

As we pulled up at the farm, however, my spirits faded, for parked outside the hut was a military police vehicle. Word had clearly spread via the *uzun kulak* or "long-ear news" of the steppe. Kuat went silent.

Inside two inspectors stood in winter army garb. They ordered me over. "How can we understand your journey? What is your business here? Are you really Australian?"

I reached for my letter of introduction—which had been written in Russian on United Nations Development Programme/World Wildlife Foundation letterhead by Evegeniy Yurchenkov, who had given me invaluable assistance upon my arrival in Kazakhstan—hoping they wouldn't request my passport. I had never shown my "business" visa to officials, had not registered it, and wasn't sure it authorized my journey. Perhaps these men had a connection to the railway and the police in Sayak?

"We don't need papers. Just tell us, are you *really* from Australia?"

"Yes, I am from Australia, where kangaroos are from."

That was all they needed, and their expressions softened. "It's true! We have come to wish you a happy birthday!"

Like so many people I met during my travels, they had heard on the winds about my journey and wanted nothing more than to see me with their own eyes. My Australian saddle, in particular, was legendary, and I was more than happy to bring it in so they could look over it and try sitting in its deep leather seat. What's more, one of the men went out to the jeep and brought in a bag of barley.

"This is for you, a gift for turning twenty-six. My grandfather taught me that a palmful of this uncrushed grain is enough to keep a horse going when it is tired."[1]

After the police had gone, it was endearing to see the way the herders put on a proper feast with all the frills. They donned their finest for the occasion, including old creased dress pants, and combed their disheveled, unwashed hair. One of the young herders took on the role of tea pourer—something that was usually strictly for women.

In such a male-dominated environment there was a danger of falling into a pit of neglect and alcoholism, so it was admirable that they seemed to be consciously compensating for the absence of family. The men working here operated on shifts, returning periodically to homes in the aul. The exclusion of women was partly because of the paternal culture of the Kazakhs, in which men dominated physical herding work, and also because of Islamic influence, but mostly it was a legacy of Soviet collectivization. Nomadic life traditionally depended on family and kinship groups, and women were known to gallop alongside the men. Unlike in many parts of Muslim Central Asia, Kazakh women did not wear the veil, and the Koran was used selectively to support the role women play, as evidenced by a common saying taught to children: "To mother, to mother, to mother, and then to father." But collectivization meant not only that a sense of ownership was erased as herders became employees of the state, but also that farming was run divorced from the family unit.

The evening slid into night with the slosh of vodka and tea. The conversation meandered through quiet troughs of spiritual and political issues, boisterous highs of vulgar jokes, and chatter about horses. I marveled

at the setting of our celebration—it was the first time since an evening
with a chaban in the Altai that I was not dining at a conventional table
with chairs. Just as Kazakhs had always done in the yurt, we sat on cushions on the floor around a low table called a *dastarkhan*. What I couldn't
have known was that during my travels along Lake Balkhash I had crossed
an invisible line, beyond which the influence of Russian ways had always
been weaker. Although the dastarkhan had been an exception until now,
I would barely see another set of table and chairs for the remainder of my
journey in Kazakhstan.

FROM KUAT'S FARM the horses carried me swiftly across a landscape of
frost-encrusted sand and ak-shi. We skirted the city of Balkhash to the
north, then began following the arc of the lake as it turned to the southwest. My plan was to carry on along the shoreline for two weeks until I
reached the lake's westernmost point, at which stage I would head west
into the Betpak Dala.

Owing to the fresh waters of this end of Lake Balkhash and the scattered auls on its shores, I had speculated that the way ahead would pose
no problems in terms of water supply. As we began to head southward,
however, the conditions conspired to create new challenges.

A cold freeze fell on the land without any of the earlier ambiguity, and
the sheets of ice that had been timidly creeping out from the shore now
rapidly grew into vast expanses. At times when the sky was clear and the
wind stopped it was an exquisite sight—a polished turquoise slab of ice
meeting a distant glinting silver sea. Mostly, though, I was aware that as this
sealing over progressed, the moderating effect of the open water waned,
and the daytime temperature plummeted.

As always, Tigon's behavior was somewhat of a bellwether for these
changing conditions, especially when it came to getting up in the morning. He would rise from my sleeping bag when I had finished cooking
breakfast, and after wolfing down his porridge he would return to the
tent and pretend to lie dead. To get him out, I would first roll him off the

horse blankets, and he would lie on his back on the floor of the tent like a sack of bones, his neck bent at a right angle and his long legs crisscrossed in a tangle. After everything else had been packed up and it came to pulling down the tent, he would spring to life in fierce resistance. He refused to move of his own accord, so I would have to throw him out one end of the tent, only to have him sprint around to the other and leap back inside. Often the only solution was lifting the tent up and shaking him out, at which point he would go off and curl up in a ball until we were ready to go.

A day south of the city of Balkhash, I was confronted with more serious problems. While the water near the shore was frozen all the way to the bottom, there was still no snow on the ground. The only way to collect water for the horses was by tethering them to stakes onshore, walking out onto the ice, breaking a hole with my hand axe, and returning with pails. This process used much valuable daylight and was fraught with dangers. One day my thirsty horses broke free and went scuttling onto the ice. By now the metal studs on their shoes had worn down to nothing, and all tied up to one another, they skated uncontrollably out onto thinner ice, threatening to topple over.

Water issues came to a head one afternoon after the horses had gone thirsty for twenty-four hours. I detoured to an aul called Gulshat, where I found a well just as it was becoming dark. Zhamba was the first to drink, and by the time the third horse had finished he was shaking uncontrollably. You could see by his widening, despondent eyes that he was going into hypothermic shock, and soon Taskonir and Ogonyok started to rattle on their feet in the same way.

By nomad custom, it was sacrilege to water a horse in the cold immediately after a long ride—Kazakhs everywhere had taught me to restrain them for at least two hours before letting them eat or drink—but I felt there had been no option. I leaped back on Zhamba and took them off at a trot, continuing beyond darkness until they had recovered. If I had stopped and made camp any earlier, the horses could have been dead within hours.

As I rode onward, it was sad in a way to realize that the charm of Lake Balkhash was withering. This companion of mine that had offered a reprieve from winter would be sorely missed. At the same time, my window of opportunity to develop as a horseman in more forgiving conditions was fast passing. The snows of winter—the thinnest layer of which would make it possible for me to take the horses away from the lake, with no worries about water supply—could now not come quick enough.

10

WIFE STEALING AND OTHER LEGENDS OF TASARAL

It was December 17, and after more than 600 km and a month of riding along Lake Balkhash, I was three days' ride from its westernmost tip. The waters were now frozen as far as the eye could see, but the land was dark and empty—still no snow had fallen. If it did not come soon, then branching westward into the "starving steppe"—where there were no people or operating wells—was unthinkable.

Prolonged cold and dry conditions were known in Mongolian as *harin zud*, or "black zud," and were feared by nomads even more than deep snow cover and ice. Without snow or access to substantial underground water—which was rare on the arid steppe zones of Eurasia—livestock faced dehydration, then starvation in the early spring, when lack of snowmelt meant lean pastures.

My circumstances, of course, weren't that dire. I had just three horses and a dog, and in recent days had adjusted to the conditions by peeling off the scabs of ice that formed on my tent to melt for my own water supply. Public wells in the few auls scattered along the shoreline had sufficed for the horses. If it didn't snow, the worst scenario meant finding somewhere with a well to hole up for a while. By contrast, nomad graziers traditionally had thousands of animals to care for, and most did not have the luxury of a freshwater lake. The difficulties they faced—as did the Mongol armies and their tens of thousands of horses as they crossed these steppes— were beyond imagination.

Not long after breakfast I approached an aul called Tasaral, a gaggle of cigar-brown, blue, and white mud-brick homes barnacled onto the stony shoreline. Where the steely blue waters might have afforded a playground in summer, pressure ridges of ice were forming like frozen waves. Nearby, rusty old fishing boats rested at angles on their keels, their navigators retired to the indoors, where fires would now be chugging 24/7 until spring.

From the outside, where I sat hunched in the cold, this settled way of life beckoned with the immediate respite it offered from the rigors of nomad life. If nomadic pastoral existence was an ongoing process of adapting to the moods of the natural ecology, then a part of the legacy of the Soviet era was that people could now live with a greater sense of security against the fickle and uncontrollable trends of the weather.

From the interior of Tasaral, where I would stay for the next two nights, however, I was to discover a community that was, like me, precariously navigating through the midst of an awkward transition. Just as autumn had passed but winter hadn't arrived with life-giving snow, the old nomad ways and the Soviet system were history, and ordinary people had not yet settled on a cultural identity or an economic model to follow.

My host in Tasaral was an unmarried thirty-year-old man named Shashibek. He had approached me on the lakeside and offered to sell me grain, and when I arrived at his home he insisted I stay for the night. Since leaving Kopa, I had found good grazing to be scarce, and the horses had lost weight. I seized the opportunity.

"I can only stay if you can promise my horses lots of hay, for they are hungry," I said. And, leaving nothing to chance, I refused to unload the horses until Shashibek let me inspect his family's barn. I was in luck. Shashibek was the son of the local akim, and their treasure trove of fodder included bundles of reeds—the primary winter fodder of the region, which was cut from the lakeshore in summer—and bales of hay that had been trucked in. Additionally, Shashibek promised that my horses would receive three meals a day of the grain of my choice. Before leaving the barn I was plotting to stay more than one night.

It took only a cup of tea with Shashibek and his parents to learn of the unique geography and historic pattern of life in Tasaral. *Tas* meant "rock," and *aral* meant "island"—a reference to a long, broad island rising in dramatic cliffs far offshore. For centuries, first nomads and then the settled Kazakhs of the aul had been herding livestock over to the island in the spring when the ice was still thick enough. The livestock would be left to graze there until there was adequate ice in autumn for them to be returned for winter.

The community in Tasaral continued this tradition, but a quick stroll around the aul was enough to know that animal husbandry was no longer at the center of life. A slew of cheap tangled Chinese nets strung up at the back of homes bespoke of the thriving contraband fishing industry, which most people relied on. In the wake of the collapse of the Soviet Union, fishing Lake Balkhash's waters had helped fill the vacuum of regional unemployment, and it was common knowledge that inspectors routinely took bribes to supplement their poor wages—a practice that had led to profits for all, but also to rampant overfishing. Shashibek's father acknowledged that the current levels of fishing were unsustainable, but he explained that people had few other options, and in any case, Lake Balkhash was under other, more serious threats. The metallurgical plant in the city of Balkhash was known for its emissions of lead, zinc, and copper, which contaminated the lake, and the main tributary flowing into the lake, the Ili River, had long been dammed, with 89 percent of its flow diverted for agricultural irrigation and industry across the border in Xinjiang province, China. The lake's water levels had been in decline for decades, risking the desertification of its immediate surroundings—as had happened to the Aral Sea. This, Shashibek and his family recognized, would bring an end to life in Tasaral.

For the middle-aged and elderly, the realities of the bare-knuckle era of capitalism represented a stark break with the past. For Shashibek, like all of the younger generation, however, it was a reality that had dominated his formative years. My experience in Tasaral was, above all, a fleeting opportunity to join him in his own personal journey through these times.

The evening of my arrival in the aul coincided with the grand opening of the new village tavern. Shashibek and two of his childhood friends took me to a room in the back of a mud-brick grocery decorated with strings of colored lights and a makeshift bar. From a portable stereo a CD of contemporary Kazakh tunes played on repeat.

Vodka was on the pour even as we stepped in, and it wasn't long before my entourage moved on to Russian brandy. As the alcohol sank in, Shashibek's fleshy cheeks turned red, his groomed mustache began to twitch, and the seniority he had exuded earlier receded. He and his friends broke out of their huddle and approached the only other group in the place— three or four girls on the dance floor—with rather imbecilic dance moves. One by one the girls, all of whom knew the men, rolled their eyes and slinked away. Sometimes Shashibek, giggling childishly, propelled me forward into the group of girls, but mostly I hung back, feeling a little embarrassed and out of place. I could see no signs of the evening finishing early, and so I kept throwing back the brandy handed to me. The party came to an end with my vomiting during the stumble home.

In the mist of a collective hangover the next morning, the male bonding session continued with a duck hunting expedition. All four of us squeezed into a Moskvich, a small Soviet-era car, and set off onto the steppe with a rifle pointed out the window, stereo blaring. The three Kazakhs— one of whom was a hunting inspector—took turns taking pot shots as we covered our ears. After scaring away the ducks and moving on to gunning down flocks of sparrow-sized birds—which were to be fed to the dogs—the highlight was when the Moskvich fell through the frozen crust of a salt marsh. We spent an hour digging it out, eventually pushing it free to wild yahoos of delight.

On the way back to the aul I sank back into the seat of the clattering car, cradling bleeding bird carcasses in my lap and watching the tangle of fishnets and boats grow on the horizon. Only a couple of generations ago, a hunt at this time of year—as still happens among Kazakhs in western Mongolia—would have been an event of significant prestige and celebration. In the late autumn, around the first winter snows, men of the community would have gathered on their horses, decked out in fox-fur hats, sheepskin coats, and ornate belts and whips, with a trained eagle at hand or perhaps a tazi dog by their side. It wouldn't have been uncommon for a grandfather, father, and son to take part in the hunt together—it was an opportunity for skills to be shared across generations.

Later Shashibek's neighbor was proud to unveil evidence of this past— his great-grandfather's saddle, which was more than a century old and had been hidden from the Bolsheviks at the height of the purges in the late 1920s. Covered with hundreds of intricate motifs engraved into a silver veneer, it was complete with stirrups carved from the antlers of an Argali sheep and silver-plated girth straps.

Just like this uncouth style of hunting, however, the saddle hinted at how strangely alien the old ways had become. It had been plunked unceremoniously on the floor of the house, wiped of dust, then awkwardly held up by Shashibek's neighbor with unaccustomed hands. It may have been testament to the deep sense of connection to the horse that its original owner had possessed, but this connection—unlike the saddle itself— had not survived to the present.

Even as Shashibek tore up the dirt doing burnout turns on the outskirts of the aul, a part of me could not help but feel dismay at the behavior on show, particularly by the son of a family to whom the community looked for leadership. On the other hand, the tide of history Shashibek faced as he forged his path and identity as a young Kazakh man could not be understated.

The forces eroding Kazakh culture had been multiple and complex. The seventy-year Soviet regime had not only dispossessed the Kazakhs materially and brought about the end to the traditional way of life but also cultivated an environment in which, in order to survive, let alone prosper, many Kazakhs had had little choice but to turn their backs on traditions and beliefs associated with nomadism and integrate into Soviet society.

In the wake of collectivization, dramatic transformation of the ethnic landscape coupled with unprecedented urbanization had had an incalculable impact on Kazakh society. The migration of foreigners to Kazakhstan—such as the 1 million people from European Russia resettled during the Virgin Lands Scheme—meant that by 1959 Kazakhs constituted just 30 percent of the population [1] In the fast-developing towns and cities, where there were more opportunities to be found than in auls, Kazakhs found themselves not only in the minority but with nomadic traditions largely incompatible with urban life.

The corrosive effects that these changing demographics would have on Kazakh culture were not necessarily intentional, but Soviet authorities concurrently painted traditional culture as "backward" and "nationalistic"—and therefore counterrevolutionary—and sought to supplant it with Russian culture and values under the rubric of "internationalism."

The decline of the Kazakh language and the uptake of Russian is an example of how this doctrine played out with long-term effect. As early as 1949 Russian became the official tongue for all party meetings, and in the 1950s it was the mandatory language for university entrance examinations. According to research undertaken by Dave Bhavna for his book *Kazakhstan: Ethnicity, Language and Power*, even speaking Kazakh in public became socially frowned upon, as "it could invite allegations of nationalism and tribalism."

Within a generation of the Bolshevik revolution, the Kazakhs found that the language that had carried the heritage of their ancestors for centuries had become largely useless and even disadvantageous—without Russian-language skills, one could simply not climb the social or political ladder.[2]

In the present era of independence and "nationalism" into which Shashibek had been born, the climate had somewhat turned around. In the 1990s the Kazakh language was given official status alongside Russian, and as non-indigenous citizens emigrated, the population of Kazakhstan dropped by more than two million, leaving Kazakhs in the majority. Even as a sense of cultural identity and empowerment was emerging, however, a deep-set stigma of backwardness and disadvantage remained associated with traditional culture. Moreover, the fractious divide between rural and urban Kazakhs cultivated in Soviet times had calcified. The urban, russified life represented privilege, opportunity, wealth, and prestige, while to those in the towns and cities, the auls, where Kazakh was the predominant language, represented poor living standards and a relic of the past from which they had moved on. As I would later discover, there were Kazakhs in remote areas, particularly in the south and west, who could not speak Russian at all, and many Kazakhs in the cities who did not have any handle on their native tongue.

In Tasaral, nomadism was no longer a viable way of life, and many traditions associated with it had been lost, never to be reclaimed. In a society grappling with what appeared to be insurmountable hurdles to cultural revival, however, auls such as Tasaral were still a relative stronghold of indigenous language, knowledge, and culture where the old ways hadn't been completely displaced by the new. In this sense, it wasn't the degradation of Kazakh culture that came to define Shashibek and Tasaral for me, but the resilience of the people in maintaining pride in their heritage and, despite the odds, keeping the flicker of tradition alive.

ALL DAY WHILE hunting, Shashibek's friends had been discussing wife stealing. "It's time for Shashibek to get hitched! His mother needs someone to talk to in the evenings! Who is going to cook for his poor parents when they are old?" they had teased.

As the youngest son, Shashibek was bound by tradition to inherit the family home and take care of his parents. The wife of the youngest son was also traditionally responsible for all the housework. Having an unmarried thirty-year-old son, especially one who was the son of the akim, generated some sympathy for his mother and father.

I had of course dismissed the talk as empty ranting, but by dusk the plotting to steal a wife had turned serious. A Tasaral girl whom Shashibek was courting would be invited to meet me—the "Australian bait"—and someone would be sent to pick her up by car. Shashibek's home was a trap, where Shashibek's relatives and friends were gathering to watch him ask for her hand in marriage. The process was part of a tradition in which men could kidnap their desired future wife, with or without her agreement or prior knowledge. Shashibek and his friends joked about one woman whom they said had been stolen from America and was the sister of the boxer Mike Tyson—a tribute to her feistiness. Another woman had been stolen from Mongolia: "Here we have a real Mongolian girl! Look at her, she is so wild!" they said, pointing.

In a nomadic aul, abduction involved luring the girl from another community, or simply kidnapping her by horse. Once she was at the kidnapper's family home, a messenger would be sent to the parents, who would then send their oldest son and his wife, or oldest daughter and her husband. Across the steppe's nomad societies it had always been essential to marry someone who was not related along the paternal line for at least seven generations back.[3] Once it had been established that this was indeed the case and the girl had freely agreed to marry, then began the fierce negotiations for a kalym—a bride-price. This ordinarily involved livestock paid by the groom's family to the bride's, and it could be the cause of much contention, since an unpaid kalym was seen as grounds to wage reprisals including the use of barimta. Only once partial payment of the bride-price had been made did the groom have the right to begin discreet visits to the bride. From the bride's family a dowry was also expected, but this was negotiated later and usually paid in the form of a yurt.

These rituals had been a mainstay of nomadic society, but in the late 1920s and 1930s, as Kazakhs were collectivized, the paying of a bride-price had been specifically outlawed and used as a pretext to accuse families of being kulaks or *bai*—wealthy peasants who hoarded wealth rather than hand it over to the authorities. Regardless of whether a bride-price had been negotiated or not, in some cases merely having a married daughter had been enough evidence in itself to brand a family as an "enemy of the state," with the men sent to prison, their children denied schooling, and animals confiscated. As a result, ceremonies for betrothal and marriage in the aul went underground or were canceled altogether.

This was, needless to say, not the case today in Tasaral.

At eleven that evening the plan swung into action. Along with twenty or thirty of Shashibek's relatives and friends, I hid in another room as the girl entered the home. We gave her time to talk with Shashibek before breaking out and forming a huddle around them. It wasn't long before it was intimated that she had accepted Shashibek's proposal, and a woman stepped forward to place a white scarf on her head—a symbol that she had been embraced as part of the family. Then came a stampede as fistfuls of confectionery were showered on the couple and everyone fought for a turn to shake their hands. The old women were the most frenetic, fighting their way to the front amidst both tears and laughter. Children, meanwhile, raced to pocket chocolates and other sweets that had fallen to the floor.

I was nearly run down by the rush of people, and by the time I had collected myself, they had moved into another room, where the bride-to-be, a pretty girl who looked no older than eighteen or nineteen, was sitting with Shashibek on a *shumudrak*, a special settee-cum-bed adorned with curtains. As the realization of what was transpiring hit her, she alternated between tucking her hair behind her ears and drawing her hand over her mouth. Had she been expecting this? Did she love Shashibek? It was hard to tell, and I didn't get to ask her. Later in my journey, in southern Kazakhstan, I had the opportunity to speak with two young newly wedded women who had become betrothed through the process of kidnapping. Both of them had hardly known their husbands, and one of them had been taken 300 km by car to the groom's herding station before her parents were informed. They explained that they had had the right to say no but had willingly agreed, and they maintained they lived happy married lives. If they later decided to leave, they had a right to separate, known as *kizdi alip kashu*.

Back in Tasaral, the intensity of celebration ascended with each step of the ritual, and when the signal was given, the bride-to-be stood up and led the crowd to the entrance of the house, where a special collection of twigs called a *baiyalish* was set alight. Cheering went up as she poured oil onto the leaping flames in a custom meant to bring warmth and luck into the home. Back inside, vodka bottles were decapitated with a symphony of cracking seals.

Things toned down again when the girl's older sister and her husband arrived to negotiate with Shashibek's relatives. While most people were asked to leave the room, including Shashibek and his new fiancée, I was allowed to stay.

In modern Kazakhstan, kidnapping was said to be more theater and symbolic ceremony than anything else, of course—technically, bride kidnapping was illegal—and when I later told the stories about what had transpired in Tasaral and other places to city Kazakhs in Almaty, they looked at me angrily. "You are wrong! We live in a civilized Kazakhstan now! That does not exist!"

Yet, based on the dark, angry look of the bride's brother-in-law and the uncontrolled sobbing of her sister, the wife steal was clearly anything but a staged event. Each person present said his or her piece gravely, followed by a toast. The emotions on display by the bride's family were apparently to be interpreted not as a disagreement, but as the grief of a family preparing to let go. Although I wasn't privy to the details since they spoke in Kazakh, a kalym was agreed upon, and planning for the wedding got under way—a celebration that, if it resembled even remotely what I had witnessed in Tansyk, promised to be of epic scale, lasting a full three days.

During the planning I was invited to give a toast of my own, and it dawned on me that I was being treated like an honored guest that they had long planned to be part of the events. Perhaps the theater of the kidnap was no less real than the role-playing of my journey—at some point it became much more than symbolic homage to ancient convention or nostalgic cravings for the past.

Indeed, that night as the vodka hit like a tremor from the gut, the actual and the acted, history and the present, seem to marry into one. The nomad life might have gone, but an opportunity to forge identity anew had been born. Customs carried through from history might have been juxtaposed in the chaos of modern times but were still every bit authentic.

11

THE STARVING STEPPE

UNBEKNOWN TO SHASHIBEK, his wife-to-be, and the other revelers who had partied into the early hours, a stealthy freeze had moved in under the cover of darkness. As I rode out at dawn, the ground underfoot felt as hard and cold as steel, and a sprinkling of snow, light as dust, brought a dull glow to the steppe. It was a promising development, given that in just 100 km I planned to turn west into the Betpak Dala, the "starving steppe," where I would need to rely on snow for hydration.

For the first day out of Tasaral the temperature hovered around −25°C. A headwind whipped up a pall of serrating snow. To meet the shift in conditions required yet another adjustment of my gear and riding routines. I pulled on all but my thickest down jacket and donned a balaclava and a pair of crude ski goggles I had picked up in a market. Even with thick mittens, my fingers quickly grew numb when gripping the rein, and so I held the reins one handed, alternating hands every few minutes. Fortunately, I had grown accustomed to the lead rope from the packhorses being threaded through a carabiner on my saddle, over my right leg, and under my butt, enabling me to ride with one hand free. Tigon delighted in chasing foxes and hares, but when he stopped his paws swiftly became painfully cold.

For three days we traveled south from Tasaral, settling into our new winterized routine. Just as I rode through an ever-changing terrain of hills and salt pans, so did my emotions go through highs and lows. When in the saddle and moving forward, I felt like I was floating, gunning toward the empty horizon as if in a dream, but when one or another of the saddles loosened and needed time-consuming refitting, frustration set in. Aset's saddle was still a constant hassle, and its narrow gullet had begun to irritate Taskonir's wither.

At night the tent offered more psychological warmth than real heat, and in the mornings the journey felt like a game of survival. To utilize daylight meant working by flashlight for two or three hours before the sun brought relief. The inner tent would be laden with hoarfrost, and ordinarily simple tasks such as pulling stakes and tent pegs out of the frozen earth became epic.

It was one of these mornings, as I lay in the cocoon of my sleeping bag, that I made a phone call to Kathrin in Germany. She was working eighteen-hour days in her teaching job and was boarding in the basement of a home near the city of Karlsruhe. I caught her, she told me, as she was stepping out of the shower. I imagined her standing there in a towel with her wet hair, and it reminded me of the cozy ritual of drying off and slipping into fresh clothing. She felt very far away.

It was about this time that a vision of the end of my journey crept into my mind, where it lingered for many months. When it was all over in Hungary, I imagined, I would pack Kathrin's little Opel station wagon with my green boxes and saddles. I could see myself closing the trunk, climbing into the passenger seat, and taking a deep breath. Then we would drive out, first into Austria and then Germany, and only with the steppe far behind would stories about my journey begin to trickle out.

The irony of contact with Kathrin, as with others in the outside world, was that while having the satellite phone was a luxury, even a godsend, it sometimes made the feeling of being alone and remote more acute. At the same time the phone could all too easily become a crutch—allowing me to vent and share feelings in moments of challenge that I would have otherwise had to overcome alone.

⯎

ON THE THIRD day from Tasaral I was faced with a dilemma. I had reached the westernmost point of Lake Balkhash, from where I planned to head west into the steppe, but a 40 cm rip had appeared in my tent. The fabric was so threadbare that if a storm came, the winds would probably tear it apart. It was foolish to go on until I had fixed it, but sewing the fragile material would be possible only if I could first patch it with gaffer tape—but that kind of tape wouldn't adhere in the extreme cold.

Erring on the side of caution, I headed into the raz'ezd of Kashkanteniz. It was the first time I had approached people on the railway since the attempted horse theft, and although this was a different line—the Almaty-to-Astana railway—my earlier dark impressions of its culture were reaffirmed. I moved from house to house looking for a place to stay but was met with glaring looks of aggression. Most of the workers kept stores of reeds and some hay but refused to sell even when offered a high price.

"No one knows how long winter will be. If I give you one bale, where will I get another?" a woman yelled.

By the time darkness fell, it was too late to ride out into the steppe, and I was hypothermic. A young railway worker let me inside his shack, which lay a stone's throw from the rail tracks. He convinced a family to take my horses in—for which I paid $30—and I stayed up late fixing the tent. But then all night I lay awake with asthma triggered by cigarette smoke, listening to trains bearing down on us, shaking the mud-brick walls as they passed. Tigon was an unwelcome guest and had to fend for himself—I hoped he had found a warm hayloft somewhere.

In the darkness of the next morning, while I was preparing the horses, Taskonir took a bite out of my hand. When I pulled back my gloves, the skin between the first and second knuckles came off like a sheath, leaving a raw, bloody ring. I stared back at Taskonir in bewilderment, struggling not to cry.

It was −28°C as I caught my last glimpses of Lake Balkhash and left the raz'ezd. The lake's blue waters were long gone. The ice had turned black, strangled in a web of frost. A week ago it might have been sad to say good-bye to this friend of mine, whose moods I had ridden out for more than a month, but now I felt no remorse.

From here to the west stretched the Betpak Dala. It was an immense swath of steppe stretching from Lake Balkhash toward the sands near the Aral Sea and as far south as the Chu River. Renowned as a desert of ex-tremes, with little water, it was empty even by Kazakh standards—a re-minder of the origin of its name, the "starving steppe." My aim was to trek 220 km as the crow flew across its southeast corner to a village on the Chu called Ulanbel. This probably equated to 300 km or more by horse.

Even as I set the compass west and climbed up a snow-encrusted slope, I could feel the cold and remoteness ratchet up the stakes. As if the earth had run out of breath, the wind died, and in the intense stillness, spar-kling ice crystals fluttered to ground like dead butterflies snapped frozen in flight. Ice rings formed around the horse's nostrils and clouds of frozen breath blew back onto their necks and flanks, spraying them white. The few pieces of hair that dangled out from my balaclava turned into icicles, and with every inhaled breath my nose hairs became needles. Even my eyelashes gathered frost, fusing together until I pried them apart and put on the goggles.

Soon there were no sounds, no trails, no people. Over the sea of pearly white, awash with frozen troughs and crests, I watched the sun creep into the empty sky, a pale, sickly yolk. In fact, I felt, it wasn't the sun at all, but earth, Australia perhaps. I was riding on an icy planet, drifting far away, flung out of orbit.

Later, as the sun dipped away, there came a phenomenon I had never seen. The sun squeezed vertically into an elliptical shape from which rose a golden column far into the sky. I could only assume that it was related to the particles of ice in the air.

There was much to think and digest, but little time for my mind to drift. One slip could mean trouble. My greatest fear had long been that one of the horses would lose its balance, sending me falling off, and that I would break a leg and be abandoned by the horses. Since there were no longer any functioning studs on my horses' shoes, this now seemed like a distinct possibility. As a precaution, I carried hot tea, my satellite phone, and a down jacket in my backpack, but when Ogonyok fell to his knees on an icy salt pan, I decided it was safer to get off and walk.

I carried on until sunlight had nearly vanished, then raced to make camp. The cold fell hard, and after unloading, my first priority was Tigon, who was whimpering inconsolably. I wrapped him in a spare horse blanket and zipped him inside my canvas duffle bag. Later, when the tent was up, I opened the bag a little way and dangled a piece of salted pig fat over it. Tigon's jaws swiftly snapped up the offering, after which he didn't stir until dinner was on the boil, at which point the bag began hopping toward the stove.

While I set up camp, a process that included driving in stakes, tying tethers, and barricading the side of my tent with the plastic boxes, it was vital to have the horses secured. To prevent them from eating snow initially—it was crucial to let the horses cool down before rehydrating—and stop them from running away, I had devised a system where I would make a rein from their lead ropes, then tie this to their saddles so that they couldn't dip their heads. The horses would then be tied alongside each other lengthways, facing in opposite directions, so that for them to wander off would involve near impossible coordination. Over the last couple of weeks I had noticed that after two hours of standing like this, their grumpy and impatient mood transformed into one of calm and composure. They had learned that this was an opportunity to rest and that patience was rewarded with a serving of grain.

When dinner was nearly ready I untied them and took off their saddles. Their bodies were as still as statues encrusted in ice, but under the blankets their backs were warm and dry. It had become routine when my hands were numb to place them under the saddle until they came back to life. As Aset had advised, I left the bottom blanket on this night, and folded it out so it covered the horses from wither to rump. This wasn't to warm them but to reduce the shock as their backs, heated and sweaty, were exposed to the cold.

The tasks at camp were unending, and with everything that needed to be done—packing tomorrow's lunch, eating half of the stodgy pot of canned meat and pasta (the other half was Tigon's) before it froze to the bottom, checking the maps, and marking my camp with GPS—there was little time to sit and absorb. One luxurious exception was feeding the horses. The mere rustle of a grain bag brought whickering from all three as they raced to the end of their tethers. This was the only moment of the day that lent itself to some affection, and although I spent twenty-four hours with my animals, it was also my only opportunity to truly acknowledge them. In the darkness I could tell them individually by smell and feel. I rubbed their necks and felt through their manes, under their hairy chins, and along their wooly bellies. Part of the routine involved lifting the blanket and feeling around for any problems. Apart from the sensitive spot on Taskonir's withers, their backs were clean.

By the time I finished feeding the horses, my feet were numb. I leaped inside the tent, where Tigon had been warming my sleeping bag, and took off my boots. To prevent moisture being absorbed and freezing in them, I wore large plastic bags over my outer socks, and a smaller bag between them and my thermal socks. As I took the bags off and shook them out, the pooled sweat instantly turned to ice. It took an hour for my feet to warm up in the sleeping bag. Tigon was covered in frost even though we were inside the tent. I tried running my hand down his bony spine, but he growled. Although I had grown to lean on him emotionally, I had hardly had a chance to show him much warmth. I felt guilty—how could I have alienated the one little creature who had stuck loyally with me through the tumults of the last eight weeks?

Before I pulled the drawstring of my sleeping bag tight I doused his paws in vodka—a technique to help prevent frostbite—and let him snuggle inside my down jacket. As he drifted off to sleep I had little doubt that he was thinking, *Well, thank God Tim is protecting me from the wolves.* I too was convinced I was safe in his hands, so we were at least able to get some sleep.

It seemed nonetheless as though I had barely slept when I woke at six o'clock, three hours before sunrise and at the peak of the cold. My body remained tense, and as I felt around my sleeping bag I realized my sweat had formed frozen clumps in the down. This was bad news, since down loses its insulating quality when wet. Once up, I shivered into my jacket and stepped out to check on the horses. Almost at once my feet turned to stone, and I spent the next twenty minutes jogging around the tent.

The horses, by comparison, didn't seem to be suffering—and for good reason. Descendants of horses that had survived natural selection over thousands of years, they were equipped with a physiology uniquely adapted to the extremes of the steppe. For example, their bodies had the ability to cut off the blood supply to their hooves in extreme cold to conserve heat. Their hairs, lifted slightly away from the body by special muscles under the skin, also gave them the ability to regulate heat loss. Later, in Ukraine and Russia, where people had a more Western approach to horses, I was told that leaving horses in the open without winter blankets, as nomads did, was unimaginably cruel. I came to think that this view was based on one of several misconceptions that many Westerners hold in relation to the natural horse and therefore the culture of horsemanship on the steppe. Horses in Europe, after all, are blanketed largely to prevent the horse from growing a long winter coat, which is considered unsightly. And if a horse has been blanketed from a young age, the muscles under the skin that control the movement of the hair and thus regulate heat are not able to develop. The horses are therefore unable to keep themselves warm, the need for blankets being a human-induced one. Indigenous to the steppes, my horses had never known blankets, let alone stables, so there was nothing more natural than for them to be standing in the open.

Ahead of me like every morning lay the laborious task of brushing the horses, folding the blankets, saddling, cooking, and packing, a sequence rarely completed in less than three hours. Sliding my hands into textured rubber mitts and brushing the horses was not my favorite chore, but not to brush was sacrilege, since removing sweat, dust, and other matter was crucial for preventing saddle sores.

Getting everything done was a race against sunrise and required all my concentration. That morning, when I tied the last knot in Ogonyok's load, my feet were still numb and my balaclava an ice mask. Although my ther-mometer had broken, I later learned that a couple of days' journey to the north, the temperature had been below −40°C.

Before climbing into the saddle I unfolded the map and pulled my GPS out to double-check the bearing toward Ulanbel. The GPS refused to turn on. Then, when finally the screen flickered to life, none of the saved coor-dinates were there. The screen flickered a little more, then went blank. Until now the GPS hadn't been of great use, but in such a featureless envi-ronment, with the prospect of blizzards and a map with a scale of 1:500,000 that had been made for airline pilots, the prospect of relying exclusively on a compass was worrying.[1]

I tried to stay calm, but the predicament was undeniable. It was the twenty-third of December, just a couple of days beyond the solstice, which usually marked the beginning of the coldest period of winter. Ahead of me lay the loneliest section of my journey to date, and I had to get through it with a fragile tent, a frozen sleeping bag, a dodgy pack saddle, numb feet, and a damaged GPS.

No matter how positive I tried to be, the odds seemed to have closed in. The situation also made me think of a different milestone, which I had dismissed until now as unimportant. From the age of eighteen I had spent most Christmases abroad and never paid much attention to the holiday's significance—and, in truth, had come to think of Christmas as a hollow, commercialized convention best avoided. Now, however, I realized that in my juvenility I had missed the point: Christmas was about relishing the company of loved ones. The thought of being alone and freezing on the "starving steppe" on a day when my family was celebrating together was too much.

I opened up all my maps to see if there was anything remotely closer than Ulanbel. On my large tour map of Kazakhstan there was one dot on the "starving steppe," marked "Akbakai." Although it wasn't on my more detailed chart, there were some roads that converged on the same approximate area, which was about 75 km to the west. These road markings often represented nothing more than faded wheel tracks, and the absence of any marked aul made me think that perhaps Akbakai was an abandoned military base. Then again, it was my only hope. If I was good enough, I could cover the distance in two days and arrive on Christmas Eve.

It was a relief to get moving. Hooves squeaked and snow exploded in plumes. The sky was clear and the air eerily calm, with the snow cover little more than fetlock deep. We moved up the salt pan valley as it narrowed and rose through uplands. My aim was to follow it to a plateau, then beyond to a cluster of hills and small mountains where I hoped to find Akbakai.

Higher up, the valley split into a maze of shallow ravines choked with ak-shi, and in places dotted with thickets of a stumpy steppe tree known as saksaul. The danger of wolves began to prey on my mind. Midwinter was their breeding season—the time when they were apparently at their hungriest and the males hunted in packs. I had been promised by Kazakh herders that wolves would follow me unseen, possibly for days, before choosing their moment to attack. It was commonly said that a pack could take down a full-grown horse or camel. Stories about attacks on humans were also abundant—there was "a lady in the next aul who last year was killed," or "the boy who went to herd his sheep and never came home." One of the most common wolf stories was of an attack on a woman and her daughter who had been waiting at a bus stop on a lonely road in winter. The woman had saved her daughter by lifting her onto the roof of the bus stop. All that was found of the mother were her valenki, still filled with the lower part of her legs. The story bears a striking resemblance to one recounted by German explorer Albert von Le Coq, who, in the early twentieth century, was told a story about a girl who had run away from her older husband into the steppe of western China, and "all that was found later were blood-stained fragments of her clothing and her long top-boots with her legs still inside."[2]

I later met a Kazakh journalist who had spent months researching stories of wolf attacks on humans. After following hundreds of leads, he had been unable to find firm evidence that any had actually happened. It was always "another aul," "another time," and there was no official record of anyone having been eaten by wolves. Whatever the truth, all I had right now were the stories, and in the face of this cold and empty land my earlier skepticism seemed foolhardy.

Just after lunch, when the pale sun was limping toward the horizon, I found myself in the shadowy crevice of a gorge. Ogonyok's load had come loose, and I leaped off to reload, paranoid about an ambush by wolves. I felt like I was testing my luck to be riding out here alone, and I knew deep down that I shouldn't have been on the "starving steppe" in winter—the nomads who traditionally might have lived here in spring or summer would have long retreated to warmer, low-lying areas.

We continued on, and by early afternoon the horses had gathered more sweat-frost than I had ever seen. I was thankful I'd trained them to ride with a halter and rope rein instead of with a bridle and bit. Bitless riding, part of a modern trend of "natural horsemanship" in the Western world, had once been practiced widely on the steppe. Genghis Khan forbade the use of bits while armies were on the move. Not only was it beneficial because of the damage a cold bit could do to a horse's mouth, but the horses could eat and drink freely whenever there was an opportunity. This approach is voiced by the Kazakh saying "Only in an emergency should a young *dzhigit* [warrior] enter the water in his boots, or should a horse be allowed to drink in its bridle."

It was essential to cover at least half the distance to Akbakai if I was to make it by Christmas Eve, but in my rush I took several wrong turns up narrow, winding ravines and had to backtrack to the main valley. Feeling rushed, I pushed beyond nightfall under moonlight, willing the horses into a trot.

Tigon was soon exhausted. At one stage when I halted to check the map, he must have curled up under a grass tussock in the snow, thinking we had stopped for camp. I continued on without realizing he had been left behind—that is, until I heard a desperate whimper ring out through the frozen night air. He was sprinting to catch up.

By the time I made camp the temperature had fallen further and the snow glowed an ethereal blue. I struggled to hammer the tent pegs in, and when I inserted the tent poles they broke through the fabric sleeves.

My camping stove refused to ignite, and I spent half an hour pulling it apart and cleaning it—a task involving bare fingers.

There was a voice inside my head reminding me that as long as I took care and didn't rush or pin my hopes on Akbakai, then everything would be okay. Stupid decisions such as this—making camp long after dark and trotting blindly over snowy terrain—could prove disastrous. Yet I couldn't break my growing obsession with finding company for Christmas Day. Akbakai, I fantasized, would be an aul where the akim would welcome me in and I would take refuge in the embrace of a family. I imagined sitting around a table telling stories about my travels, in the security of a warm home bathed with the golden light of a fireplace.

I slept lightly, afraid that at any moment a storm would roll in from the mountains and knock down my damaged tent, or, worse, that I would wake to find the horses under attack by wolves.

At dawn we set off at a trot and rose to a plateau where the fragile calm was broken by raking winds. A great, hazy, white emptiness flowed down from all sides. There were no features, shadows, or depth to give any scale at all—the world had been distilled to pale blue, white, and the rumble of wind. Destinations and landmarks didn't seem to exist, the geography more a landscape of changing moods. Usually this emptiness instilled a sense of freedom, but now it brought dread. I tried to be conservative and plan for the event that Akbakai either didn't exist or was abandoned. Even if it was somewhere out there, my compass bearing had to be only marginally off target and I could pass it without knowing.

It was just as the sun was gliding into my line of vision that I caught sight of something through my monocular that gave me hope—a tower. The horses were tired, struggling to lift their hooves through the snow. I egged them on with the promise of hay and shelter.

For the next two hours there were times when I was sure Akbakai was just a derelict ghost town, then others when I thought I could see a tendril of smoke. I could make out strange buildings unlike any I had seen in farming auls, which made me think it might be, as I had suspected, an abandoned Soviet military base.

When Ogonyok's load came loose after dark, I lost my cool and let out a string of curses. The voice of common sense was still there and told me to stop rushing, but the intoxicating vision of hot tea and company possessed me.

⊞

I BEGAN TO stir from my stupor as we limped through some twisted scrap metal on the deserted outskirts. I was stiff as wood. The horses hung their heads in fatigue. As wind filled my ears, Tigon's whimpering rose in pitch. We had made it to Akbakai, but I'd forgotten that no one was waiting for us.

12

THE PLACE THAT GOD FORGOT

THE ONLY SIGN of life I could find on the edge of Akbakai in the failing light of Christmas Eve was the shadowy figure of a man hunched over a pile of firewood. Maksim, as he was known, suspected that I was a lost Russian geologist at best, and at worst an escaped prisoner on the run. After much pleading, he reluctantly led me to a half-built mud-brick shack. I tied the horses in the windowless end of the structure, then, together with Tigon, climbed into a small adjoining room. Inside, the flickering of a coal stove offered a fragmented picture of two old spring beds, mattresses, and cardboard-matted floor. Vitka and Grisha, the Russian laborers living here, were too inebriated to speak, but details didn't matter. I was out of the wind, I was warm, and I was not alone.

Christmas morning brought a more sobering reality. Wakened by a couple of puppies licking my face, I pried my eyes open to a panorama of dog shit, piles of empty vodka bottles, and a frying pan filled with ossified potato sediment and congealed fat. Lying under a pile of rags on the other bed, Vitka and Grisha were dead to the world but alive with the stench of body odor, tobacco, and alcohol. They were truck drivers from southern Kazakhstan who had been stranded in Akbakai since being caught drunk at the wheel and losing their licenses two years earlier.

Eventually they were stirred by their own snoring, and when they learned who I was, they cried: "Australian! We understand that today is your Christmas. By all means we will have a celebration tonight. A treat!"

When it was light enough I left the hut to search for hay and grain. Akbakai was not the herding community I had hoped for. The streets were littered with frozen clumps of rubbish, and lined with rubble and mangled machinery wreckage. Homes were a medley of mud-brick houses barricaded with tall fences. Some appeared to be semi-underground. There were few signs of animal shelters, and I only had to look to the edge of town to know why.

To the west and south heavy trucks labored through dirty, blackened snow. Beyond them the trapezoid shape of mine shaft headframes cast eerie silhouettes against the sky. Akbakai was a gold-mining town, and the livability of the environment had been an afterthought. Built on a range of rocky hills, the town had no natural water supplies, nor was water provided by the government. The handful of people who kept a milking cow were fiercely protective of fodder and water—both were precious resources shipped in from far away.

After hours of fruitless searching, I pried some concessions out of the local hunting inspector. He let me climb up his ice-encrusted water tank to fill pails for my horses, and agreed to sell me hay to last twenty-four hours—but no more than that.

I returned to the mud hut in the evening hungry and stiff as wood. Grisha and Vitka were rolling drunk. They had caught a couple of street pigeons earlier that day and had boiled them up for dinner.

"Everything will be fine! Sit down, lie back, have a vodka, a cup of tea, we will find you a wife . . . and you can use your horses as a bride-price!" they chanted.

I capitulated—on account of the vodka, that is—then watched as Grisha and Vitka argued, stumbled, and fought into the early hours. Both had dirt-ingrained skin, rotten yellow teeth, and untamed mustaches that grew animated by the candlelight of the hut. When they tired, they fell together onto a single bed and told of their tragic personal histories. Grisha's wife was as "honest as they come"—a quality proven by the fact that when she "butchered a man with a carving knife," she stayed with her victim and called the police. She was due for release from prison in five years. Vitka, on the other hand, had been deeply affected by the death of his only son, who had been hit by a car at age twelve. His daughter had run away to Russia and cut all ties.

To survive in Akbakai—a town they described to me as "the place that God forgot"—Vitka and Grisha worked odd laboring jobs, including felling saksaul trees on the steppe to sell as firewood.[1] The money they earned was spent on vodka.

When Vitka and Grisha passed out I lay awake listening to the wind, unable to sleep. On the far side of the wall behind me the horses had finished their hay and were standing hungry. When finally the vodka swept me under, I clung to fleeting visions of home and being close to my siblings, mother, and father.

I HAD URGED the horses on to Akbakai determined to find refuge with a family and a barn full of hay, but come the early hours of December 26—Boxing Day—that vision was in tatters. But things were about to get a lot more difficult.

My plan had been to stay two or three days in Akbakai, but when I woke to pack, Taskonir was holding his back left leg in the air. It was an abscess in his hoof—most likely the result of a stone bruise suffered during our rushed ride to Akbakai. He could barely walk, and the Australian vet, Sheila, warned via satellite phone that it would be many days before I could expect it to heal. The nearest village west from Akbakai, Ulanbel, was another five days across uninhabited steppe. Carrying on was not an option, yet with no feed for the horses and a precarious refuge with Vitka and Grisha, it was hard to see how I could cope here for any length of time.

I knew that the next few days were going to be tricky. What I could never have imagined, however, was that the abscess was to be the first of many hold-ups and failed attempts at leaving Akbakai. It would, in fact, be three and a half months before I was able to ride out of there, and while my personal struggle was uppermost in my mind at the beginning of my stay—and became a low point of my journey to Hungary—what emerged over time was that my troubles were merely reflective of circumstances in town immeasurably more difficult than my own. Through the many people I met—both those who helped me and those who hindered me—I came to see a dismal picture of social dislocation, survival, and corruption in this remote gold-mining society in the middle of the "starving steppe."

For two days I scrounged for fodder and water, to little avail. Neither the town's administrator or anyone else I met would so much as invite me past the front door for a cup of tea. When I approached Maksim—who was the owner of the mud hut where Vitka and Grisha lodged—for help, he retorted angrily, "What makes you think anyone should help you! You are better off selling your horses for meat before they are too skinny!" Traditions of nomad hospitality found in auls didn't widely function in Akbakai—most people simply didn't have the means.

Like many others, Maksim had come here lured by the promise of work but found himself unemployed and stranded far from his hometown. He lived in a derelict apartment block where he had rigged up a woodstove in a room on the third floor. To support his wife and two children, he had turned the basement of the building into a makeshift workshop where he made furniture to order out of scrap wood. Without a network of relatives or friends, it was hard to imagine what fallback he had if this venture failed.

This kind of scenario was unusual in the herding-based auls of modern Kazakhstan and would have been unthinkable for nomads in pre-Soviet times. A tradition called ata-balasy, which means "the joining of grandfather's sons into one tribe or family," was the bedrock of nomadic existence, and in many communities it is still only by banding together in wide circles of kin that it is possible to overcome the chaos of post-Soviet Kazakhstan and support those fallen on hard times.

Maksim's predicament was symptomatic of the widespread Soviet pol-

icy to develop entire towns and cities around a single industry or, in Akbakai's case, mineral resource. These monogorods, or "monocities," emerged
largely in isolated environs that were unsuitable for agriculture, and drew
on migrant workers from across the country. For Kazakhs, monogorods
subsequently created even greater displacement from traditional lands and
breakdown of traditional kinship structures than did farming collectives.

During the Soviet era, state-funded social welfare became the back-
bone of monogorods, substituting for the traditional safety net of family—
but this also made them particularly vulnerable to the economic collapse
of the 1990s. The failure of the state-run companies that held monopolies in
these one-industry towns caused mass unemployment, and residents had
neither an alternative economy to turn to nor a network of kin for support.

Three days after Christmas, Taskonir's leg was worse, the wind had
picked up to gale force, and clouds were marching in from the north and
east. Come what may, though, I had decided that anything was better than
staying in Akbakai. After saddling up, I went inside the mud hut to say
goodbye to Vitka and Grisha. They were sad to see me go and worried what
would become of me. It was in the throes of this farewell that my fortunes
changed.

Stumbling into our hovel came a short, squat man wearing thick,
crooked glasses that magnified his eyes and pinched his red nose. I took
the opportunity to slump back silently in the darkness and study him.
From the weathered texture of his face I would have guessed he was in his
sixties, but I knew in this harsh environment it probably meant he was a
good ten years younger. His voice was deep and husky, and as he spoke,
his defrosting mustache wiggled.

Curiosity eventually got the better of him. "Who is he?" he asked,
pointing at me.

"We have a guest from Australia," Grisha related. "He came here to us
by horse . . . from Mongolia."

The man stepped back, straightened his glasses, then leaned forward into
the narrow shaft of light in front of the window. "Come to my home!" he
exclaimed. "Why freeze here? I'll give you a sack of wheat to help you on
your way!"

As I left the hut to take the horses to the man's home, Grisha and Vitka were excited for me. According to them, Baitak was a "millionaire" and a "king." I would surely be safe in his hands. Viewed later on with the benefit of a full stomach and grain for the horses, however, their description seemed like a bit of an exaggeration. His house was an underground one-room hut surrounded by a fence made of flattened drums that had once held sodium cyanide. He didn't own a car, had no washing facilities, and the toilet was a long drop full to the brim with frozen shit and just a tarpaulin to protect one from the elements. His water supplies were trucked in, like everyone else's, and the much talked-about cafe and bar he owned was a coal-heated hut that was within shouting distance of his house and backed onto a mountain of rubble.

At the time, though, to me everything about Baitak's empire shone. My first meal with him was a memorable example—I was presented with a series of fried eggs, and each time I chased the yellow from the plate, it would be replaced with another. Tigon ate buckets of stale bread and milk, until his little belly bulged out to twice its normal size and he sprawled out royally on the floor.

The true meaning of Baitak's wealth became clear over the weeks and months to come as my well-being and that of my animals came to gravitate around him. As one of the most established people in town—he had been in Akbakai since 1976, when mining operations were in their infancy—he had unique authority and knowledge. Above all, though, I think Baitak's status as a "king" was a measure of his generous heart, for certainly that is what would ultimately save my life, and those of Tigon and my horses.

After our meal, Baitak inspected Taskonir and shook his head. He knew I was in trouble, but he also knew what to do. He co-owned a fledgling kstau 6 km out of town—the only of its kind anywhere near Akbakai—where cattle were kept. "You can ride there and stay until your horse heals and the weather improves. Tell the herder there, Madagol, that he can feed your horses with my hay."

There were times in my journey when I felt like I was a captain, firmly in command, and steering my caravan on a course of my choosing. There were other times, however, when I simply had to let go of the reins and accept that the journey—or, in this case, Baitak—would guide me.

TO REACH THE kstau, which was hidden in a valley between two knobby ridges, took two hours, by which time Taskonir was reluctant to move at all. In the midst of a windstorm I was greeted by Madagol—a gruff, wiry old fellow with tightly coiled graying hair and heavy, callused hands. He invited me in with a fusillade of curses regarding the weather.

"Wind is the worst thing in Akbakai! When it blows on the third day, you know it will blow for seven, and when it blows on the eighth day, it will blow for fourteen . . . after that it will blow for a month. It's not like that where we come from!"

Madagol was from Moiynkum—a regional center 250 km south of Akbakai—and had come with his wife to work as a chaban. Their new home was a shabbily constructed hut with such thin brick walls that despite a coal stove that burned 24/7 it was still below freezing indoors. When I entered I removed my coat and hat, but hurriedly I put them back on. Curled up on a bed under a mountain of blankets, Madagol's wife sat looking frail and utterly miserable.

Later I came to appreciate how terribly isolating it must have been for Madagol's wife. Although the town was not far away, few braved the weather to visit in winter. The main contact she enjoyed with the outside world was when Madagol rode a horse into town to sell milk and buy bread every second or third day. When the blizzards set in, there were some periods when they were completely cut off.

For me, the shortcomings of the hut were nevertheless a mere detail, and in fact the isolation was a godsend. The vet, Sheila, had suggested the abscess would pass within a week. All I had to do was sit tight.

It was, of course, wishful thinking to believe my journey was back on track.

After my first night in Madagol's hut, a man known as Abdrakhman—a friend of Baitak who owned shares in the kstau—came barreling down in his old Russian four-wheel-drive vehicle and hauled me back to Akbakai, exclaiming, "My daughter's birthday is tomorrow night. You will be an honored guest! We are chaining you to our home until the new year!"

Abdrakhman was a relative newcomer to Akbakai, and my presence was a drawing card for strengthening his network of friends. As the guest of honor, I was expected to raise a toast to the stream of guests visiting his home. In the coming days I fell into a whirlwind of feasts and drinking, culminating with a New Year's Eve dance in the snow to Kazakh, Russian, and Uzbek music, while Chinese firecrackers flew around like rockets, rebounding dangerously off the walls of the house. For me, as for the other revelers—including explosives experts, traders in contraband gold, and miners—it was a fleeting opportunity to forget about the realities of Akbakai.

The celebration was brought to an end by the onset of severe frost, and come New Year's morning there was a price to pay. I woke in a cold sweat and by afternoon was lapsing in and out of fever. Abdrakhman was exhausted and bedridden. He decided it was high time for me to leave.

In this way I once again found myself derailed and taking refuge with Baitak. He took me in without question and for three days insisted I sleep on the only bed in his home while he, his wife, and their son slept on the floor.

I intended to stay for one night, but as the flu took hold, this drew out to two weeks. In the beginning I was conscious of losing precious time, and concerned about how Madagol was coping with my horses and Tigon. At Baitak's insistence, though, I surrendered to the inevitable, and spent days lying disoriented while his wife, Rosa, fussed over me. As I lay there hour after hour, the underground hut felt like a ship berth. Far above there was the faint raking of wind. Only on rare excursions into the elements to relieve myself did I become aware the weather was closing in. A blizzard was gathering, and as the town battened down, visitors to Baitak's home dried up. Such was the isolating effect of the cold and snow that although Abdrakhman's house was only five minutes' walk away, as were Vitka and Grisha's hut and the lone apartment block, I never saw the alcoholics or Maksim ever again, and only met with Abdrakhman long after I had recovered. I could only begin to imagine what it was like for Madagol and his wife in the drafty hut at the kstau.

About a week into my sickness, Baitak too fell ill, and from that point on we lay side by side in our sickbeds, waited on by Rosa. We spent hours discussing politics, the contrasting realities of the Western world and Kazakhstan, all things nomad- and horse-related, and of course life in Akbakai. It was challenging to relate to Baitak and Rosa how I lived in Australia. Given that I had three horses and didn't appear to have a job, they assumed I was so comfortably rich that money was not an issue.

The reason for my journey was a topic on which Baitak and I could understand each other better. Baitak had grown up in the foothills of the Tien Shan Mountains near Almaty. He reminisced about how he and his friends used to catch the collective farm's horses from the herd and gallop bareback until they fell off. Although he no longer rode, he owned a herd of thirty horses that roamed the steppe around Akbakai. This was a source of great pride, and once every two weeks he set off by motorcycle to look for them. Later, when we had recovered from the flu, he pulled out two old saddles from a rusty trunk. "Not to have a saddle would mean becoming an orphan in my own land. Not to own horses would death," he said.

His respect for the nomad past and his understanding of my predicament delineated a significant difference between him and the majority in Akbakai who were severed from the land and more focused on trying to make money. Over time I decided that some of Baitak's wisdom must have been inherited from his father, who had been born in 1893, married a girl thirty-one years his junior, and survived the era of collectivization as a simple shepherd.

When Baitak and I finally were on the road to recovery, we regularly dined in his cafe. As breakfast, lunch, and dinner drifted into one another, it gave me a valuable opportunity to gather a broader picture of life in Akbakai.

Judging from the clientele, there were two types of locals. The first were pale, beaten-looking men who would arrive to eat and drink vodka after their grueling work in the mines. These were professional miners, some of whom were bused in from afar for fifteen-day shifts. Their work, by Western standards, was poorly paid and dangerous. Twelve people had apparently died in the mine shafts this year—a "very good" result, according to Baitak. Then there were those people, largely the permanent residents, who either had been established long before the Soviet era came crashing down or, like modern-day prospectors, had come seeking riches.

When I related my thoughts to Baitak, he described Akbakai residents somewhat differently. "There are two kinds of thieves in Akbakai: those aboveground, and those below."

It hadn't been obvious to me initially, but I came to see that there was an altogether "other" economy in Akbakai. Many of the "aboveground" thieves were workers in the processing plant who stole ore from the production line and sold it to locals to supplement their poor wages. It was standard practice for them to pay off their bosses and the security guards to get the material out of the plant. People who didn't work at the plant could also get ore and tailing debris by paying off security guards at night, and for this reason there was a raft of unemployed people from faraway regions who had come to try their luck.

Baitak pointed out that the real profits were being made not aboveground but by men who risked their lives below. Within the ranks of residents in Akbakai were a breed of men willing to rappel as far down as 400 m into disused shafts. According to Baitak, there were whole teams of skilled workers who put down the ropes and ladders and set up living quarters in the shafts. They had beds, kitchens, and even entire slaughtered cows down there, he said. Later on in the winter evidence of this came to light when twenty-eight illegal miners were discovered by police in a single shaft. One, it was said, fell to his death upon seeing the police near the exit.

Over the course of my stay I came to realize that almost everybody I met—except Madagol, Vitka, and Grisha—was involved in stealing ore and tailings in one way or another and processing it in crude backyard labs. I once walked in on Abdrakhman refining gold amalgam in a frying pan—a poisonous method involving the use of mercury, but one commonly used in most households in town. Abdrakhman was hoping to make a fortune before retiring to his hometown, Moiynkum. Several times in Madagol's cattle shelter I also encountered young men pulverizing ore in a metal tube and mixing it with sodium cyanide. It was part of what they called "secret business." At the end of the supply chain were traders who bought contraband gold for 1,000 tenge (about $8) per gram and then took it to Kyrgyzstan to sell on the black market.

Baitak estimated that 50 percent of the residents—most likely including himself—were actively involved in the contraband economy. Despite this, there was good reason to keep the activities hidden. Being caught by the police meant paying large bribes to avoid jail. The twenty-eight miners arrested that winter reportedly paid a collective $20,000 so that they could return to work. This made the post of police chief in Akbakai a very profitable one, and it was rumored that getting the job involved paying $10,000 to regional superiors for a two-to-three-year term.

As the scale of the operation and the complicity at every level dawned on me, I realized it was not possible to make an honest living in Akbakai and prosper. Perhaps, as might have been the case in other monogorods, the contraband economy was merely substituting for the breakdown of Soviet-era social security. At the very least, it was clear that unemployed and disadvantaged locals had little choice but to engage in this business and often had to take out loans at exorbitant rates to pay for bribes. Many of them were on the edge of survival, including one Russian family I came to know who could not feed themselves on their small share of the gold market and were forced to eat dogs to get by. They bred puppies exclusively for this purpose, eating them when they were still young, and leaving just one or two to mature from each litter.

The microcosm of corruption in Akbakai painted a bleak picture for Kazakhstan as a whole. Simple, everyday things such as getting a driver's license, a university degree, or even a seat on a train routinely involved paying a bribe. For those wanting a loan, the bank would approve the financing only if a cash-in-hand commission, known in Russian as an *otkat*—usually a percentage of the loan—was agreed upon. Everything, from securing a job to having enemies killed, was possible given the right price. A police officer in southern Kazakhstan later explained that in his region, as long as you didn't kill someone within your own family, you could pay off the police to have them overlook it, or pay an extra fee and have the police do the murdering themselves.

All of these examples of corruption were trivial in the bigger picture of Kazakhstan, which was ranked by the International Monetary Fund in 2005, the year I was there, as one of the world's corruption hot spots, alongside Angola, Libya, Bolivia, Kenya, and Pakistan. Among Kazakhs it was widely known that the president, Nursultan Nazarbayev, and his extended family controlled all of the key sectors of government and the economy, including national security, taxation, the media, and the oil, sugar, alcohol, and entertainment industries. Less well known—since it was hushed up in the Kazakh media—was that Nazarbayev had made headlines around the world when he was implicated in a foreign bribery case involving American merchant banker James H. Giffen. Giffen, who worked on behalf of oil companies vying for access to the vast reserves on the Caspian Sea, was charged with channeling $78 million to Nazarbayev.[2] This was heralded as the largest bribery case in history against an American citizen.

Kazakhs were typically cynical when I brought this up. "Seventy-eight million?" one man told me. "That is just kopeks for Nazarbayev!"

Most Kazakhs I met nevertheless had a high opinion of the president and believed it was "those around him" who were "corrupt and conniving." Even then, Kazakhs who were disillusioned with Nazarbayev often commented: "At least Nazarbayev and his family have done all their stealing and are now giving back to the public. If we vote in a new president, then his family will spend the next ten years stealing for themselves before they start to help us!"

Politics and graft in Kazakhstan were beyond my comprehension and the scope of my journey. Baitak urged me not to even attempt to understand the system. He wanted me to focus on recovering from the flu and protecting my horses. "At this time of year the hunger begins, and one horse can provide food for a family for months. Every year, two or three horses will be stolen from my herd. This is normal. However I am afraid that your horses may be stolen and eaten as well."

During my illness, Madagol had run out of hay for my horses and had released them into the steppe. There was no other way for them to graze and have a chance at surviving the winter.

⊞

MOST OF MY stay in Akbakai was removed from any real experience of traditional steppe life. There were, however, some customs I was lucky to observe under the wing of Baitak.

After we both recovered from the flu, Baitak informed me there was a special occasion I needed to witness before leaving. It was *sogym*, the winter slaughter of animals—and not just any *sogym*, but the most sacred of all, the slaughter of a horse.[3]

On a relatively mild mid-January morning, Abdrakhman, Rosa, and others gathered at Madagol's hut armed with knives and axes. The horse in question was an eleven-year-old gelding that had been fattened on a diet of wheat, barley, and hay. "The fatter the horse, the better the *kazy*," explained Baitak. On many occasions I'd enjoyed kazy, the prized national Kazakh dish of horsemeat sausage made from the meat and yellowy fat that runs down from the spine along the ribs to the stomach. This meat and fat are cut into strips and stuffed into intestines with a mixture of garlic and salt before being boiled.

Specialists can tell at a glance whether a horse is "one finger," "two fingers" or "three fingers" fat for the purposes of kazy. I had become accustomed to Kazakhs routinely approaching me and prodding the ribs of my horses, specifically quantifying their fat. Ogonyok was always judged two or three fingers—a reminder that traveling with a fat horse through Kazakhstan was fraught with danger.

After the horse was led out of a corral, things swiftly got under way. At first the gelding's legs were bound together. When the horse lost balance and fell onto its side, the men hurried to roll it upside down.

Sensing my apprehension, Baitak talked me through it. "We have different horses for riding, racing, milk, and meat. But whatever the case, you won't find any horse dying of old age in Kazakhstan. It is sacrilege to let such precious meat go to waste—a single horse can keep a family alive for winter. More than that, to let a horse rot provides no dignity for the horse—it is like abandoning your animal, disowning it. And another thing, a horseman here will never slaughter his own favorite mount—it will be symbolically given or sold to someone else for the task. I could never imagine putting the knife to my own horse."

I stood back and watched the men heave the horse's head over a chopping block. Madagol cupped his hands in prayer. I focused on the horse.

At first the horse's eyes were wide. He labored to look back at the men who held him down. His nostrils flared, sending frozen breath shooting into the air. But then he stopped struggling and his eyes panned skyward.

Madagol cut back and forward with a long knife. I wanted to look away but felt cowardly. A gasping sound was followed by gurgling as a fountain of blood surged, filling a specially placed basin. Then it was all over. The unmoving head was flipped backward, hanging on by threads of skin and bone. Blood rushed back to my head and my heartbeat slowed. The men relaxed too, stepping in with knives and axes. The horse had gone.

Before long Madagol's wife brought a vodka bottle down to the men. Madagol drank first, followed by Baitak, then the others. Within a couple of hours the various cuts of meat were being sorted into hessian sacks. We sat around a table dining on kurdak, a traditional dish made of fried innards, including heart, liver, and kidneys.

Most of the horsemeat would be shared with people less fortunate than Baitak, including Madagol and Baitak's relations in the city. This was a nomad tradition known as sybaga, when the prosperous wing of a family shares the meat and milk from its herds with less successful kin. Sybaga also requires that the most respected and honored guests be given the best from the table.

At a visceral level, there was no denying I had disagreed with the horse slaughter. I'd grown to love my horses and could not imagine putting them to the knife. And yet as I sat chewing on freshly fried liver and watching the swelling happiness in the eyes of Baitak, Madagol, and others, I was overcome by the miracle of life on the steppe—that the morsels of grass the land offers can be turned into life-giving fat and muscle. Partaking of the flesh of the horse was a crucial part of the horse worship that had sustained nomads from the beginning of time. In full knowledge that their animals were traditionally the only link to survival, these people could appreciate the value of meat more than most of us could conceive of doing.

The celebration continued for two days, after which I prepared to leave. By this stage I had become so much a part of the family that the prospect of departure saddened me. Even Madagol, who seemed to have his reservations about me, had warmed somewhat. This was partly because I had let on that Australia had about half a million wild horses roaming in the outback. He had been dreaming of mustering a herd and bringing them home to sell for meat.

"That Indian Ocean, is it a shallow or deep lake?" he asked one night.

WHEN THE DAY came for my departure, Baitak was furiously opposed to my decision. Madagol, for his part, was angry that I would not cave in to his requests: "What do you need a dog for? Leave him here!" he demanded. Likewise he asked for my horses, ropes, clips and saddles.

Baitak's gripe with me was because Ulanbel, my next stop five days away, was a village renowned for its criminals. Moreover, this was precisely the time of year when wolves hunted in packs. He was afraid for my safety and concerned that I was rushing and being reckless.

It was nevertheless a relief to be alone again when I rode out from Madagol's kstau. I made good progress following little gullies and valleys, picking out features on the horizon and setting new bearings from there. By the time I made camp the mountains surrounding Akbakai were a blip on the horizon. But then came another blow. The seal on my fuel bottle split, and before I could begin cooking, the gas had all leaked out onto the snow. Furthermore, upon unsaddling I discovered that the sore spot on Taskonir's withers had once again swollen to the size it had been three weeks earlier. By morning a blizzard had come in, and the abscess in Taskonir's foot was back with a vengeance.

I packed up and turned back east, knowing it was the end of winter riding.

Upon my return to Akbakai I resolved to travel back to Oskemen, in eastern Kazakhstan, where I intended to pick up my second Canadian packsaddle—which had been mailed from Mongolia—and tackle visa registration issues before returning better prepared. Madagol was over the moon to receive advance pay to look after my horses, and Baitak was relieved to hear of my new plan. Within a couple of days I was on my way in a taxi, loaded up with 50 kg of raw horsemeat that I was to deliver to Baitak's relatives in Almaty before heading on to Oskemen.

I planned to be away from Akbakai for two weeks, but things became complicated. In Oskemen, where I was staying with Evegeniy Yurchenkov and his family (who had given me invaluable support on my arrival in Kazakhstan), I was summoned by the local immigration service for not registering my visa. They were aghast that I had traveled through so much territory—much of it close to sensitive border and military zones. I was either to be fined or deported, they decided (though this was eventually avoided with the help of a national TV correspondent who ran a story about me).

When I finally returned to Akbakai, toward the end of February, I found that winter had taken a heavy toll. The temperature there had stayed around −30°C for a month. It had, in fact, been one of the coldest winters in living memory, with a low of −52°C recorded near Oskemen, far to the northeast. In southern Kazakhstan there had been unusually high snowfall, and as Aset had predicted for times of zud, there were reports of horses that were practically naked after surviving the winter by eating their own hair.

Although I had arranged for wheat to be taxied out to Akbakai from the town of Chu, my horses had largely gone without fodder or shelter, fending for themselves on the steppe. Baitak and Madagol had lost track of the horses at one stage, and only after a week of searching discovered them in a gully sheltering from the wind. It wasn't long after this episode that Madagol had fallen off the roof of his animal shelter and snapped his leg in several places. His son had since taken over responsibility of the kstau. Madagol lay in traction in a hospital in Moiynkum.

Something I had already sensed from Oskemen was that the winter had not been kind to Tigon. One night I had been haunted by a dream in which Tigon was looking at me with big sad eyes. He was covered in grease and muck, trapped in a dark place, looking frightened. Upon my arrival Baitak and Rosa relayed the bad news. While on a visit with Madagol into town, Tigon had vanished for some time, and was feared eaten. One of the mines had gone bankrupt, and some of the hungry, unemployed workers were known to be hunting dogs. While Baitak searched for Tigon, his own pet dog had disappeared without trace. Eventually Baitak had heard a rumor that Tigon was being held by a Russian dog eater named Petrovich.

"If that Australian's dog doesn't come back, I'll know it was you. Don't you dare eat him!" Baitak had told him. Seven days later Tigon had been found locked away in an old mining shed. He had been badly beaten and was covered in grease and muck.

"No one thought he would survive, so I arranged immediately for him to spend several hours in a sauna, then fed him raw eggs and vodka," Baitak told me. When I was reunited with Tigon he was all skin and bone and barely moving.

It took another three weeks before Tigon could walk, and during this time I was invited by CuChullaine O'Reilly of the Long Riders Guild to join what he described as an unprecedented international gathering of equestrian explorers in London. There I was to be made a fellow of the Royal Geographic Society.[4] Although I was initially opposed to the idea of going, I couldn't go back out on the steppe while Tigon was still sick, and my great-uncle and -aunt, John and Alison Kearney, offered financial support to buy tickets. I decided it was an opportunity I shouldn't refuse, particularly because I would have the chance to see Kathrin for a couple of days.

So I was more removed from my journey than ever by the time I arrived back in Akbakai at the end of March. What had begun as a two-day stopover for Christmas had become more than three months, and with the misery of midwinter fresh in my mind, I doubted I could pull through to Hungary. Even if I could, I wondered whether I would ever find a trace of the nomad spirit again.

Baitak, however—to whom, in hindsight, I owe my life, or at the very least the lives of Tigon and my horses—says he never once doubted that I would make it to Hungary.

13

OTAMAL

BY THE END of March, as the days began to draw long, there were signs winter had capitulated. Across northeast Kazakhstan the frost was broken by slush and rain, and in the south the snow was retreating to the high slopes of the Tien Shan. Some brave girls in Almaty were baring their legs, which, a Russian once told me, explained the high incidence of car crashes by male drivers near bus stops in spring.

The repressive hold that winter had on political life had also been broken. Neighboring Kyrgyzstan had just erupted in what would become known as the Tulip Revolution, making world headlines. The deposed president, Askar Akayev, accused of corruption and electoral fraud, had fled to exile in Moscow. To many Russians, and Russian-leaning Kazakhs in particular, this seemed to be part of a grand conspiracy of "color" revolutions that they assumed had been funded by America following the Orange Revolution that had swept Ukraine in the autumn and winter months and the Rose Revolution in Georgia a year earlier. It was all the talk on the street, at the markets, and on buses in the city, especially among pensioners who reveled in any whiff of news that could lift them from the drudgery of winter. The spring air seemed to be brimming with possibilities.

What would happen next? Was this the beginning of a greater rebellion across Central Asia? It was an election year in Kazakhstan, and Nazarbayev was reportedly paranoid about the sentiment of discontent spilling across the border. Word was that as soon as the Tulip Revolution had begun in Bishkek, Nazarbayev had ordered security forces to move south and be ready to quash any unrest. Spring was a dangerous time, as people no longer had to concentrate on surviving winter and their fervor was yet to be snuffed out by the heat of summer.

When I arrived back in Akbakai, people were emerging from their homes, pale, gaunt, and broken-looking, counting the costs of winter. In the wake of the snowmelt, the surrounding steppe had become a morass of impenetrable swampland, although I was told it would soon rise in a sea of red and yellow tulips.

I spent several days tweaking my equipment, gathering my animals from Madagol, and preparing them for travel, and during this time the steppe dried out enough to be navigable. With a new packsaddle, a healthy-looking Tigon, and a little extra weight on my own frame, I figured my window of opportunity had arrived.

It was with a sense of disbelief, then, on April 4—the day earmarked for my fourth attempt to depart Akbakai—that I stumbled out of Baitak's hut into a predawn blizzard. The thermometer read −15°C and by the time I had watered the horses I was chilled to the bone. So confident that I had seen the last of the cold, I had left my winter clothing behind in the city.

I didn't bother saddling the horses, and instead decided to return to bed. Baitak saw me come back in. "So Akbakai is still holding you here? It is you we blame for this weather. Only that man in the sky knows what is best for you, and he is keeping you in Akbakai for a reason. You have done the right thing."

Baitak had warned me about this seasonal phenomena, known by no-mads as otamal. It was a period of sudden cold that usually occurred in mid-March, just as it appeared the weather had turned the corner. Ani-mals that had grown thin through winter could be polished off, and many people were known to perish, too, if caught unawares.[1] Spring,

Baitak told me, was the season of greatest weakness and vulnerability for all living things.

For me there was a larger message in all of this, summed up in a saying often repeated to me by Baitak and others: "If you ever have to rush in life, rush slowly." On the steppe, time was measured by the seasons, the weather, the availability of grass, and, most important, the condition of one's animals. To think I could hurry the seasons was as foolish as rushing with horses.

⌘

TWO DAYS AFTER the failed departure attempt, the sky had been blown clean and the sun glinted off the frozen streets of Akbakai. After a meal of horsehead, Baitak, Rosa, and Abdrakhman escorted me out of town for a departure ceremony. Baitak's farewell toast was simple: "I suggest you stay away from young people, and stick close to the elders."

Bundled up in an old woolen vest and buttonless coat that Baitak had given me to see me through the remaining cold, I hauled myself up into the saddle, whistled for Tigon, and hunched forward into the wind. When some time later that I took a peek over my shoulder the steppe was empty.[2]

Ahead of me now stretched nearly 150 km of the Betpak Dala to the aul of Ulanbel. In the wake of winter this formerly frozen wilderness had become a waterless desert, and to get through I hoped to find puddles of remaining snowmelt.

For the first three days we hugged the edge of brown silty salt flats, passing in and out of cloud shadows that wobbled and rippled over the land's undulations. Hills no more than bumps were akin to mountains in this exposed, flat land. They emerged from the earth in front of us, passed by our flanks, and then with time shriveled away behind.

Despite the cold and the ragged, ice-charred appearance of the earth— its many plants crushed and flattened by the snow—there were early signs of spring: yellow wrens jumping toward the tent door and V-forma-tions of geese cutting the sky. What captured me most were the shoots of grass emerging beneath tough desert plants. Resilient enough to defy the odds of winter, here was the miracle sustaining life itself. The horses were electrified by the sight and spent much of their free time trying to reach the new growth, often succeeding only in scratching their noses on the tough, brittle plants above.

Tigon, for his part, was beside himself with excitement. The snow was nearly gone, so his paws didn't freeze, yet it wasn't too warm, which meant he could run forever and barely had to let his tongue out to cool down. He galloped about, digging, chasing, and sniffing, often running parallel with us on distant ridges. Periodically he returned to my caravan to check in and give the horses a lick on the face. Zhamba and Ogonyok didn't seem to mind this, but Taskonir, being the hardened old grump he was, usually snapped back and warned Tigon with a hoof pounded into the dirt. Tigon couldn't understand this unfriendliness and would peer up at me all concerned, his amber eyes aglow and his tail between his legs.

On the fourth day the temperature had risen and the remaining snow from the otamal had melted. Dust devils hurled across the flats, sometimes hitting us with a cloud of dust and sand. I became stuck in a series of salt bogs and was forced to retreat. The horses were thirsty, and the absence of sturdy ground made the going slow.

Late in the evening I put my compass away and followed a large bird of prey instead. It took me up into red rocky ridges, from where I could look down on never-ending salt flats to the south and at rising steppe to the north, where jagged little mountains cut the horizon. I reveled in the feeling that as the horizons were expanding, my own world was shrinking to the intimate family circle of animals I had known previously.

When I reached the top of the ridge the bird took off a little farther. Not only did it lead me straight to a set of old wheel tracks heading west, but it was now perched on one of two large round piles of rocks and earth. They were the unmistakable sign of ancient nomad graves.

Before moving on I dismounted and stood for some time. I couldn't help but wonder what it would have been like to make this same journey a hundred years ago. I had little doubt that in early times I could have made my way right across the steppe from aul to aul, directed by people who, from the saddle, knew every corner of their land. To some degree I had experienced this in Mongolia, where even in the most hostile of country it was rare that a yurt or a rider couldn't be seen somewhere on the horizon and approached for advice. I felt as though I was treading through the graveyard not only of the individuals who lay before me but an entire people and their way of life.[3]

After leaving the graves I found some snowmelt pooled in a rocky gully and the following afternoon reached the perimeter of the Betpak Dala. To the south, the plateau I had been on dropped away to a sprawling plain. A myriad of lakes and marshes and the Chu River glinted in the sun, and beyond them lay the burning red sand of the Moiynkum Desert.

We camped on the edge of this plateau, with the water tower and homes of Ulanbel on the horizon. At dinnertime the horses crowded around to pinch food from my pot, and Tigon barked indignantly at them to steer clear of what he thought was rightly his. I felt proud and relieved. If I could make it to Ulanbel, then maybe Hungary was possible.

⸎

EVERYONE I HAD spoken to in Akbakai warned that in Ulanbel not only would my horses be stolen, but I would be "stripped naked and left with nothing."

Abdrakhman had shaken his head ominously on the day of my departure. "Timurbek! Be careful! You won't find any Baitaks in Ulanbel!"

For such a small, isolated aul, it didn't seem credible that it could be full of bandits, yet there was a reason for its reputation. As recently as the year 2000, the Betpak Dala had been home to a unique migratory species of antelope known as saiga. Believed to be related to fauna from the era of the mammoth, and a living genetic link between antelope and sheep, the saiga was renowned for its speed, said to be around 95 kph. In Akbakai many had described to me how until the late 1990s Ulanbel had been swamped by hundreds of thousands of the animals as they swept through during annual migrations. There were apparently so many you could almost catch them by hand in the streets, people said.

For years now, though, in the middle of a region once called the "Serengeti of Central Asia," barely a single saiga had been sighted. The sad reality was that the collapse of the economy and of the rule of law in the 1990s had triggered an explosion in poaching, particularly of the male saiga, the horns of which are used to make cold and flu remedies in China. The estimated 800,000 saiga living on the steppes of Kazakhstan and southern Russia in 1990 were said to have dwindled to less than 40,000—almost none of which lived on the Betpak Dala.

The genocide of the Betpak Dala's saiga population had been partly coordinated from Ulanbel. Conveniently isolated from central authorities, it had had become renowned as a hotbed for traders, poachers, and contraband dealers. Nowadays—or so Baitak had heard—things had settled down because the poachers had run out of saiga to shoot. Baitak therefore reasoned that my horses would be in even greater danger of being stolen by "bored," "out-of-work" criminals.

With knowledge of this state of affairs weighing on my mind, I nervously crossed the Chu River to the southern banks where the aul lay. The bridge did not bode well—halfway across I had to dismount and lead the horses around holes big enough for a car to fall through. Safely on the far side, and still on foot, however, I was overwhelmed by an entirely different world. There were stone huts and fences, and mud-brick homes rising from wide, sandy streets. Cows wandered lazily about, a motorbike could be heard starting up somewhere, and there was even an old man with a few token teeth leading his donkey and cart to the river. I could hardly remember a place so positively blooming with life.

There was admittedly little time to indulge in a sense of reverie. No sooner had I reached the main street than a man came rushing from his home dressed in a green silky gown and fur hat. He stood at a distance, hands on hips:

"As-salam aleikum! Sell me your black horse! I like your black horse!"

"No! I need my horse! I will not sell!" I said, clambering back up into the saddle.

As the man drew near, Tigon sniffed at his crotch, and he raised his hands in fright. I came to my senses. The man's greeting to me had been a compliment, I realized, and in any case, the man's plump belly, rosy cheeks, and distinctive Kazakh mustache hardly presented a picture of intimidation. Five minutes later, I was in his family home drinking tea.

Temir, as he introduced himself, was adamant that I stay the night and proceeded to tell me that the name *Ulanbel* meant "red hillside" in Mongolian, which referenced the long sandy ridge seen to the south in the Moiynkum Desert. The aul had previously been home to a sheep farm collective that peaked at about 60,000 head but which had since been dissolved. About 10,000 sheep remained among private individuals. The herders who once had worked for the collective had turned their skills to poaching saiga, fishing, and digging up rock to be sold for the making of fences, homes, and animal pens.

The rumors I had heard in Akbakai about saiga seemed to be true. Temir asked me with a hopeful look whether I had seen any during my ride. I replied that I had not, and he shook his head sadly. Even now, with the saiga on the very brink, there were apparently instances of the odd kill, and locals were still trading in the horns they could find scattered out on the steppe.

Given what I had already learned about the pillaging of Kazakhstan's resources in Tasaral and Akbakai, this was really more of the same, but when Temir began to tell me about nomads and how they lived in the desert nearby, my ears perked up.

"You are in luck, Tim. Word is they are on the move, and will be coming through Ulanbel tomorrow on their way to the Betpak Dala."

JUST AFTER LUNCH the following day the idleness of the aul was broken by a wildfire of barking. A great cloud of sand and dust billowed in from the southern horizon like a main sail. Tigon, who had already joined a rabble army of local dogs, charged off in hysteria, his tail pointed sky high.

By the time I made it to the bridge I had been hit by the wafting aroma of livestock. What had been a desolate road angling into the aul from the desert was now throbbing with a tangle of five hundred sheep and goats, fifty horses, twenty shaggy camels, and a few donkeys. Ahead of them, breaking through a bow wave of dust, grunted a Russian truck full to bursting with belongings, and behind it a motorcycle with a sidecar brimming with wide-eyed toddlers. Bringing the group up from the rear were several men, one of them an old gray-bearded man who wore a purple fox-fur hat and sat astride a gray horse.

Upon reaching the bridge, the leaders in the truck lay down planks and boards to cover the holes. After a brief pause to let the animals drink, the whole caravan then rumbled over to the northern bank. Within half an hour the caravan had come and gone, and the dust had settled as if they had never been.

Eager to know more, I paid Temir's son to follow the caravan by motor-bike to where they were planning to stop for camp. Tigon came with us, sprinting behind, leaving his own plumes of dust and sand.

What had been a silent steppe the previous day now bustled with movement. Toddlers played with baby goats in the back of the truck while large pieces of brown felt were unfurled and a team effort got under way to build a yurt. There were fifteen or so members of the extended family group to be accommodated between the yurt and a rusty old wagon that had been towed in by the truck.

First the collapsible lattice walls were put up, then the many roof poles to support the circular ring at the apex of the ceiling. After the felt had been pulled on, a young boy was sent scrambling up to the top to make adjustments. The silver-bearded elder directed with stern but soft commands.

When the yurt was erect the women set about decorating the insides with felt carpets and wall hangings. Outside, fencing for pens was set up, and a trench dug around the yurt. As proof that the pens were necessary, I was shown two horses with shredded rumps—the victims of a wolf attack.

By dark, the yurt was furnished, sheep were settling into their pens in a chorus of snorts, farts, and snuffles, and freshly slaughtered lamb sizzled on an open fire. In the midst of this camp scene, which had once been universal across the steppe, men came to earth with sighs of relief. I rested among them, savoring every detail.

One of the eldest men turned to me and grinned.

"You realize that the 'starving steppe' isn't really that hungry? There is good grass out here, and our animals always come back fat. It's just that you have to know when and how." His eyes were lit up, as if he were describing a feast.

I asked him to go on. He requested a pen and paper, so I handed him my diary, and in the light cast by the glow of the coals he drew a basic map.

"Every winter we live in the Moiynkum Desert. The soil is sandy and soft, there is little snow, and it is much warmer than other places." He sketched an east-west-running stretch of land that lay between the westerly flowing Chu River in the north and the Karatau Mountains in the south.

"Then just before the ticks come to life in the spring we pack up and leave. If we stay too late, the animals suffer from the ticks, and the grass won't have time to recover for the next winter. Our next camp is here, on the northern banks of the Chu River. As you can see, there are reeds to be eaten on the riverbanks, and grass is beginning to grow. We will stay here until the lambs and kids have strengthened. But eventually this river runs dry in the summer and the pasture gets burned by the sun. In just a few weeks, the grass will be long enough in the Betpak Dala, so we can go there."

At the peak of summer, the family would continue north nearly as far as the city of Zhezkazgan. There, in uplands that provided cooler weather and winds that kept the mosquitoes away, they would mingle with other nomad families who had migrated from other regions. Timing the return south was crucial—too late and there was the risk of getting trapped by blizzards, too early and the winter pastures would not sustain the herds until spring. By the time they reached the Moiynkum Desert for winter they would have completed a round trip of around 600 km.

The man finished his sketch. "This is my land, and that of my ancestors, the Naiman tribe, and we have camped in the same places for generations," he said. The completed map was an oval shape running from north to south bordered by the traditional lands of other tribes who had their own migratory routes. At the northern and southern ends the winter and summer stopping places overlapped with those of their neighbors. It was here families had the opportunity to socialize with other tribes and clans. Summer in particular was a time of festivity when horse races were arranged, feasts held, and courtship took place.

A piece of saksaul wood was rolled over, and a swarm of sparks spat into the sky like bees disturbed from a hive.

There had been times on my journey when it was tempting to imagine Kazakhstan as one great big swath of steppe and the nomads as living somewhat free-wandering, isolated lives. Now, however, I began to picture a sophisticated map of traditional grazing lands, stretching from the Caspian Sea to the Altai, the Kyzylkum Desert to Siberia. Each had clearly been home to generations of nomads, who, like this family's ancestors, had developed a unique migratory pattern according to the local ecology and who were connected to other groups by adjoining camps.

There was no official map, of course, and in the near absence of nomads in present times I must have unwittingly crossed many boundaries during my journey to date. But Kazakhs had never relied on fences or maps. Instead they had known their territory, history, and likewise their identity through detailed knowledge of ancestry, known as shezire.

I was already familiar with one important element of shezire—that before choosing a marriage partner it was a requirement to know the details of seven generations of the paternal line, for it was taboo to marry anyone within those lines. This information had been passed on through the centuries via epic poems that wove together a riddle of names, stories of land, and important historical events.[4] In the present day, as I witnessed in many Kazakh homes, it had survived in the form of family tree diagrams.

Also at the core of shezire was knowledge of clan, tribe, and juz (union of tribes)—three circles of allegiance that I had always found somewhat difficult to understand but which in the context of this family's ancestral grazing land was easier to grasp.

This family was part of the Orta Juz—the horde that traditionally lives in the north and east of Kazakhstan.[5] Within the Orta Juz they were Naimans—a tribe descended from the Naimans of Mongolia, whose defeat near Kharkhorin by Genghis Khan heralded the founding of the Mongol Empire. First and foremost, though, this man was of the Baganali clan.

"This here is Baganali land. We are the most honest clan. But see that woman over there?" the man said, pointing to a woman turning the frying lamb. "Don't trust her, because she is Tama!" There was much laughter.

"And when you get into an aul, Timurbek, be sure to find out which clan lives there. Then when you arrive and they ask who you are, you should tell them that you are one of them. They will take you in like a brother . . . but when you get down to the Karatau Mountains, don't tell them you are a Buzhban, because they are wild people!" There was more laughter.

For me, a foreigner, shezire would prove to be an icebreaker, just as the man advised, but had I been a Kazakh wandering the steppe, it would have been a much more integral part of greeting strangers. By asking, "What clan do you come from?" even today two Kazakhs can quickly gauge one another's geographical homeland, common ancestors, enemies, and living relations. It was becoming clear to me that shezire was much like a passport and a map combined, allowing people to understand who they were, the land to which they belonged, and even whom they could marry.

Tigon crept closer to the fire and sat straight-backed, licking his chops, his paws shifting restlessly. He sensed, as did I, that the lamb was almost ready to eat.

I had all but become absorbed by the man's story, but as hunger lifted my eyes beyond the glow of the fire, the distant lights of Ulanbel were a reminder that in a nation where nomadic life had been the norm for thousands of years, this family found themselves on the periphery of society.[6]

One of the men, who had been listening to the discussion, leaned in and said, "Life here was much better before this capitalism came! Back in those times we were all out herding. I used to be in charge of more than ten thousand animals! We had reliable wells, and everyone was employed, not like today. There were whole auls of yurts on the Betpak Dala until that idiot Gorbachev came along."

Until now I had overlooked the fact that arid land such as this—unsuitable for conventional farming or cultivation—had been grazed by animals from Soviet stock-breeding collectives, following the same migratory routes as their predecessors. Wells and concrete feeding troughs had been maintained every 20 km, even through the "starving steppe." In this way, Soviet doctrine had married successfully in part with traditional knowledge.

Come the collapse of the Soviet era, this surviving nomadic existence had abruptly halted, and I could see more clearly how things had unraveled. Most fundamental to the crisis was that with so few livestock remaining, the pasture in the immediate surrounds of auls and towns was adequate for them to graze on all year round. There was now no reason to migrate to the traditional seasonal pastures—a trend confirmed the following day in Ulanbel by people who spoke with bitterness and envy about the nomadic family I had met.

In fact, in Ulanbel one could find any number of hardened men playing dombras and singing melancholy songs. Crippled by nostalgia, they seemed to believe that the modern era was a temporary stage and that ultimately they would return to the life of the ancestors in the future. I began to see many of these sedentary Kazakhs as dormant nomads waiting for the day they had enough animals to justify a return to the steppe.

It must have been nearing midnight by the time Temir's son pointed nervously to his watch. The man with whom I had been speaking tried to persuade me to stay: "Timurbek! Maybe you could even travel with us into the 'starving steppe.' We could find you a Kazakh wife!"

If only I could. But then again, my animals were waiting, and the mild spring conditions beckoned with promise for travel in the coming weeks. I climbed onto the back of the motorbike and clung on for life as we crashed through the darkness.

⌗

A DAY'S RIDE west from Ulanbel I made camp by a lake flooded with overflow from the Chu River. Ducks whispered high across an orange sky, smaller birds darted acrobatically among reeds, and a pair of white swans milled at a safe distance from shore. As my mash of rice and canned meat boiled I watched the horses rubbing their sweaty backs in the sand. Taskonir went first, digging with his front hooves before falling to his knees and attempting to roll over. It took him more than a couple of tries before he managed to get up onto the ridge of his back where he thrashed about, his unkempt mane mopping up the sand. Once he had gone down, the other two followed. When they had all gotten up and shaken off, they, like me, stood gazing to the west.

For the next 200 km I planned to follow the Chu River as far as possible on its westerly course between the Moiynkum Desert and the Betpak Dala. Like many watercourses in Central Asia, it started off with great promise from the Tien Shan Mountains of Kyrgyzstan but withered as it flowed inland, finally disappearing ungraciously in a series of salt lakes and thirsty flats. Every year in spring, however, fresh snowmelt flushed through its system, bringing a fleeting abundance of life. For the first time on my journey this thin green line suggested the kind of reprieve I had only dreamed of previously: ready access to water for days on end and the prospect of plentiful grazing.

That first night out of Ulanbel I slept in the tent without a warm hat—the first time in six months—and rose in the morning feeling light and clearheaded. By sunrise I was in the saddle, and knew at once I was in for a good day. With a slight press into Zhamba's side we were moving forward across the sandy earth. I held the reins lightly in one hand and let the other go lax, twisting my torso at times to take in the full panorama. Following a series of horse tracks, we crossed empty flats, then threaded our way between tall desert bushes. There was always water to our right and grazing to our left. By lunch we had covered 20 km, by dinner more than 40 km.

The following day I was unwilling to lose the gathering sense of momentum and took a wide berth around an aul called Shyganak before hugging the shoreline of salt lakes. In the evening I descended to floodplains and brought the horses to a slow walk among a carpet of orange and red tulips that were backlit by the low sun. Between them crawled an engrossing sight—hundreds upon hundreds of tortoises. There were so many it was nearly impossible not to tread on them, and indeed, in coming days we encountered many corpses of those unfortunate ones crushed by horses and motorbikes. Tigon was fascinated at first by the plodding tortoises but soon decided they didn't play fair when they receded into their shells. Later, at our camp, he growled when they crossed by the tent through his territory, but invariably let them shuffle on.

That evening, as I sat glowing with the visions and feelings of our ride, I sensed that tortoises and wildflowers were not the only life unharnessed by spring. Tigon's ears rose suddenly to attention, and the horses went stiff and tall.

As I stood and turned, I locked eyes with a chestnut stallion standing resplendent in his shiny spring coat, tail raised like a war banner and ears speared forward. At first I watched, captivated, as he snorted, pawed at the earth, and marked his territory with droppings. But then he pranced forward, and my mind began to race. Spring was renowned as a time of chaos and conflict for horse herds, as maturing mares were expelled from the family and stallions fought for mating partners. I'd heard stories of competing stallions fighting to the death.

The stallion began circling, his focus bearing down on my horses, which stood defenseless in their hobbles. Tigon leaped to defend them, but the stallion charged anyway. All I could think to do was run between the stallion and the horses, taking aim with rocks and sticks. When finally a rock landed between the stallion's eyes, he retreated for a minute or two, but then came charging in again.

This routine went on until midnight, at which point I managed to chase him beyond camp. At dawn, he was back again, and just as I became absorbed in cooking porridge he took his opportunity.

When I looked up, a blur of mane, tail, and teeth was bearing down on Ogonyok. Ogonyok turned to run, but the stallion mounted him from behind, dug his teeth in, and dragged them along his spine from head to tail. Ogonyok reached the end of the tether that was tied to his front leg and somersaulted to earth. Almost at the same time, the stallion came crashing over the top, and the metal stake torpedoed overhead. It wasn't over yet, though. As Tigon took up the fight, the stallion caught him in the bushes and bit down on his back before flinging him through the air. Only after Tigon limped into my tent did the stallion recede to the bushes in the dunes. When the dust had settled I brushed Ogonyok down and uncovered two bloodied fang tracks from neck to rump. I cleaned the wounds and resolved to carry rocks in my pocket—a tactic that proved crucial for the remainder of my journey.

The stallion was not the only spring danger that seemed to have blossomed overnight. Even as I packed to leave, I noticed dozens of small bugs jumping aboard my boots and crawling up my chaps. They were ticks, and on inspection the horses had swollen specimens the size of grapes hanging off their chests, the sheaths of their penises, and under the tail around their anuses. It was dangerous work to pluck them off, especially from Ogonyok, who was sensitive at the best of times. In the process many ticks exploded, and by the time I had finished, dark oozing blood, thick as sap, had congealed with molting horsehair and stuck like glue to my hands.

It was a relief to eventually climb into the saddle and pick up the momentum of the previous day. Yet while the coming days would not turn out to be quite as eventful as the past twelve hours, it was clear that my encounters with the stallion and with the ticks were part of the many rhythms of spring I would have to learn to take in stride.

A WEEK'S RIDE west from Ulanbel we approached an aul called Tasty—a cluster of adobe houses on a peninsula of land that jutted out into a bend of the river. It was evening, and as I drew close, herders were returning for the night with sheep and cattle from all directions.

I decided to wait it out hidden among twisted desert shrubs before unpacking in darkness and making camp, but a herder spotted me with his binoculars and invited me to his home. The following day, while the herder's children took my horses out to graze, I joined him at a gathering of the aul's elders.

In the cool confines of a mud-brick house with whitewashed walls hung with rugs I squeezed in on the floor along a dastarkhan. Opposite sat men with faces as old and gnarly as camel-gnawn desert bushes. Most had patchy gray whiskers and wore traditional Kazakh hats. Women wore silky vests and were wrapped up in white head scarves. Most understood Russian, but few could speak it fluently.

On the table between us sat a freshly boiled camel's head surrounded by mountains of baursak (the deep-fried dough Mongolians call boortsog) and plates of the national dish, beshbarmak.

"C'mon, Tim, eat!" the old men demanded.

Using the communal knife to cut meat from the cheek of the camel was one thing, but I was yet to master the eating of beshbarmak. The name means "five fingers," and it is a dish of meat and boiled squares of pastry often cooked with wild onion.[7] The technique of eating it involves scooping up the meat and angling it into the mouth so that the fat doesn't spill. When I tried, the hot fat and meat burned my fingers, and I sucked on my fingers to cool them. As I shoveled the food down, pieces inevitably dropped to the floor, and the elders laughed.

After the meal I lay anchored to the floor by my full belly watching the chiseled old faces and listening to the guttural sounds of Kazakh. Russian influence hadn't penetrated here as deeply as it had further to the north and east, and I sensed that these people were closer to the nomad past—a trend confirmed that night in my host's home.

Serik, as he was called, led me to his one-month-old baby boy, who lay in an old crib sucking on a piece of sheep tail fat.[8] As I bent over and smiled Serik gripped my arm and gently pulled me back. In silence we left the room. Once out in the kitchen he told me, "We Kazakhs believe that for the first forty days a baby has not been fully born and released by God to us, and must be protected from bad spirits, especially the evil eye of Zyn, which is like the devil. We would not usually show our baby to strangers during this time, only close relatives. We think you will bring good luck to our baby, but you should not look into his eyes."

I had often wondered why babies I had seen in Kazakhstan had black dots, usually from charcoal, on their forehead, and thanks to my host I now understood. "We make those dots to draw the attention of onlookers away from the baby's eyes. You would not even know yourself if you had the evil eye—don't be offended."

Traditionally, Kazakhs used all manner of techniques to keep bad spirits from harming the young. One involved giving the baby an unpleasant name that would make people laugh and therefore distract evil spirits.[9] An amulet called a *tumar* was also worn, traditionally filled with a sample of the baby's own feces, although nowadays with a prayer from the Koran. There was even a tradition known as *satyp alu* (buying a child), in which parents gave the baby away to an old woman dressed like a witch, and then went to her home dressed in rags to beg for a baby. The baby would be delivered through the door headfirst, as in birth, to ensure a long life and that he or she would eventually die while standing—traditionally considered honorable. In return, the parents would gift the old woman with several sheep, firewood, and a kettle.

FROM TASTY THERE remained just 40 km of riding along the Chu River to the town of Zhuantobe. During the two days it took me to get there, I never quite found my rhythm again.

Leaving Tasty was awkward after I discovered that my headlamp and watch were missing—it turned out they had been stolen by Serik's children. Then, just half a day from the aul, Tigon was hit by one of the first cars he had seen in his short life. At the time we had been forced onto the shoulder of a road to avoid floodwaters and had been transfixed by a solitary Lada hurtling in from the west. After the impact Tigon lay bleeding and unconscious. I was sure he would not survive, but the very next vehicle to arrive was a motorbike carrying the veterinarian from Zhuantobe. Tigon regained consciousness, and on inspection had a broken rib and concussion. The vet arranged for Tigon to be taken to Zhuantobe, where he would be looked after until my arrival.

When I reached the town I was greeted by a throng of barefoot children eager to lead the way to Tigon. I found him lying like a prince in the shade of an outhouse. He had been dining on bowls of fresh milk, meat scraps, and his favorite, eggs.

After two days Tigon was on his feet again, but it was clear that both spring and the respite of the Chu were over. The heat had arrived, and not far west of Zhuantobe the river came to a finish, spilling into a series of salt lakes and swamps. My immediate route lay to the southwest across 120 km of the Moiynkum Desert to the Karatau Mountains.

In what would prove a taste of the conditions and landscapes of central and western Kazakhstan in coming months, we covered this next leg in two long, hot days. At first I was guided by a local man and his friend on a motorcycle, but halfway across their fuel ran low, and we discovered that the artesian bores once used by nomads had been closed off—rumor had it that the water table had recently been poisoned by operations at a Canadian-financed uranium mine.

The last 60 km were the thirstiest to date for my little family of animals. I pushed them on across the shadeless steppe and desert until finally the olive-green ridge of the Karatau Mountains emerged from the dusty horizon. Beyond them lay the Syr Darya River, which I hoped would be my next lifeline, carrying me deep into central Kazakhstan.

Just at dusk we came to a gorge between the Moiynkum and the mountain ridge, at the bottom of which lay a cluster of adobe homes—an aul called Karatau. I hurried down and caught the last herder on his way home for the night. I didn't have to say a word before he led the way to a trough and invited me in.

14

SHIPS OF THE DESERT

IN THE LATE autumn of 1219 Genghis Khan rode along the freezing banks of the Syr Darya leading somewhere between 90,000 and 200,000 men and probably at least twice as many horses. He was drawing close to battle after the long journey from Mongolia, and one can only imagine that the cold air would have lifted the energy and alertness of his mount.

In Genghis's sights was the city of Otrar, which lay on the northern banks of the river, and beyond it Samarkand and Bukhara, at the heart of the powerful empire of Khwarezm.[1] A year earlier, Inalchuk, the governor of Otrar, had enraged the Mongol leader by executing a 450-man merchant caravan from Mongolia. The sultan of Khwarezm, Muhammad II, had added insult to injury when he beheaded an ambassador sent by Genghis to offer a peace agreement.

This was more than enough to invite the wrath of Genghis, and what lay in store was not just a hot-blooded act of retaliation but a carefully planned campaign to conquer all of Central Asia. It is well known that Genghis used a vast network of spies and diplomats to gather information prior to attack, and a mobile corps of Chinese engineers who built sophisticated catapults, battering rams, and siege engines. What is sometimes understated is that as a nomad, Genghis was also well aware that success of any campaign depended as much on timing, taking into account the seasons and the health of his animals, as it did on technology and intelligence. His early life growing up on the edge of survival had taught him to fear and respect Tengri, the eternal blue sky, over any living enemy.

Knowing that the journey from Mongolia to Otrar and beyond was going to be particularly hard on his horses, he had ordered that no one was to go hunting of his own accord, and use of horses was strictly minimized. Traveling in autumn with the object of conquering through winter was a crucial part of his strategy. That way he could avoid the heat of summer, with its increased risk of saddle sores, and because of dew on the ground there would be more pasture and less need for water. As rivers froze over in late autumn and winter, his army could also cross rivers at will.

Come the scorching heat of summer in 1220, Genghis Khan's timing had proven nothing short of genius, and it is little wonder he believed his aspirations to conquer the world were vindicated by Tengri. Otrar had been destroyed and its governor, Inalchuk, executed by molten silver poured in his eyes and ears. Following an unprecedented trek across the Kyzylkum Desert, a section of his army had also surprised the holy city of Bukhara, and after subduing the garrison, Genghis had entered the city and proclaimed to the ruling class that he had been sent by God to punish them for their sins. Samarkand was the next to fall before Genghis and his army retreated to the hills to rest and graze their animals for the summer. Sultan Muhammad II, meanwhile, was fleeing for his life, with a detachment of the Mongol army hunting him down. After an epic game of cat-and-mouse, Muhammad was eventually cornered on a remote islet on the coast of the Caspian Sea, where he died of exhaustion and pneumonia in the winter of 1220–21.

At the age of fifty-seven, having already conquered much of China and Turkestan, Genghis was now the ruler of an empire that stretched from Persia to Peking. Although his success in China to date had already proven his prowess, it was this crushing victory over the once powerful

Khwarezm Empire that set a precedent for the brilliance and terror that would characterize Mongol conquests in the future.

By contrast with Genghis Khan's first major foray into Central Asia, my approach to the Syr Darya was not going well. Two days' ride west from the aul of Karatau, I woke at midday slumped against a twisted tree root and listened to blood throbbing through my ears. The sun burned a rosette through my eyelids and pressed down on my cheeks like an iron. During my snooze the sliver of shade under the poplar tree had moved and the horses likewise had shifted, their bums facing the west, heads propped forward in the shade. Tigon had dug himself into a fresh hole for the third or fourth time and lay panting with his tongue out on the dirt and his eyes reduced to slits.

I felt lethargic and dizzy, so it took me some time to pull myself away from the tree trunk and reach for the battered plastic soft drink bottle that held my drinking water. Earlier I'd been lucky to find a well next to an abandoned winter hut and managed to lower my collapsible bucket 20 m to the water using tether ropes. As I pulled the bucket up it had broken away from the ropes, but I had managed to retrieve water by lowering this drink bottle, and had watered the horses from my cooking pots.

As this hot, algae-filled water now flushed out the dry bed of my throat, the stench of dry manure rose through my nostrils. It was a smell that would have been a comforting symbol of family and togetherness in the winter and early spring when there might have been hundreds of cattle, sheep, and horses milling about this tree, the only one I'd seen in two days. Now, though, the lingering fragrance of livestock was a sharp reminder that the people had moved away to the safety of summer pastures and I was alone under the tree.

The sickly feeling that I was traveling against the grain of the seasons had, in truth, been building ever since I'd met the nomads of the Betpak Dala some weeks ago. I'd tried to ignore it, but in recent days it had become unavoidable. Since I'd left the aul of Karatau, the land had been dotted with empty huts with boarded-up windows and abandoned yards. Horizons had crawled with nothing but heat mirage and billowing clouds of fine manure particles. The only people I had seen were a family who had just migrated from the Moiynkum Desert and were headed for the high pastures of the Karatau Mountains. They'd invited me to watch the final spring ritual for the year, camel shearing, and looked at me gravely when they understood my route. "Soon the flies will be here," they told me. "Down on the Syr Darya, where you are going, they will be even worse. If you leave your horse tied up for half an hour there, it will be dead."

The flies hadn't yet come, but although it was still only late April the temperature was reaching 30°C by nine o'clock in the morning and what pasture I could find was sun-fried and hollow. To avoid the heat—and decrease the risk of saddle sores that it posed—I had begun breaking the riding into two sessions, leaving before sunrise, then riding until mid-morning before unsaddling and finding shade, then doing more distance close to dusk. The conditions might have felt endurable had relief been in sight within days or even weeks, but everything I was now experiencing—the heat, isolation, and lack of water and grass—were merely precursors of what I could expect in coming months.

The ultimate goal of this leg of my journey was to navigate about 2,000 km through Kazakhstan's arid center and west to the Caspian Sea—a vast, sparsely populated region of open deserts and salt flats that lies midway between Mongolia and Hungary at the heart of the Eurasian steppe. It was here that Friar Carpini recorded the most harrowing leg of his journey from Europe to Mongolia, writing that it was so dry "many men die from thirst," and that he "found many skulls and bones about in heaps over the ground."

My original plan had been to make this traverse in the winter and spring, when the slightly warmer winter temperatures (at least slightly warmer than those found in the north) and a thin layer of snow would have been an advantage over a more northerly route. The holdups in Akbakai, however, had left me on course for one of the driest parts of the country at the hottest time of year—a prospect that any nomad, and certainly Genghis Khan, surely would have done all he could to avoid.

The big consolation in all of this—and one that would become my motivation in the months ahead—was that beyond the fiery core of the Eurasian steppe lay the relatively mild climate of the Caspian region and geographical Europe, where water and pasture promised to become pro-gressively more abundant. In the short term, I simply had to accept that things were only going to get harder.

⊞

LATE IN THE afternoon, when the sun's heat waned, I lifted from slum-ber under the tree and rode on, determined to remain positive.

To tackle the trek ahead, I had broken my planned route into three stages, each of which I estimated would take a month. The first—and I reasoned the easiest—would be to drop south to the Syr Darya River and follow it about 500 km to the point where it spills into the Aral Sea. From there I would break away and track northwest around the northeast tip of the Aral Sea's old shoreline and continue as far as the Zhem River (known in Russia as the Emba). The final phase would be southwest along this minor—and partly seasonal—watercourse, which I hoped would see me through the western deserts to within range of the Caspian Sea. It was a very indirect route, at the mercy of where water lay, but if all went ac-cording to plan, I would cross the Ural River—into geographical Europe— and be entering Russia come autumn.

It took several more days of riding through abandoned pasturage be-fore I crossed through the Karatau ridge and began my descent to the Syr Darya. Viewed from a distance, the river appeared just as it did on my map: an improbable belt of water and leathery green vegetation that flows some 2,212 km from the Tien Shan down through Uzbekistan and Ka-zakhstan, snaking its way northwest through mustard-yellow desert to-ward the Aral Sea. In an otherwise inhospitable landscape, it was a fabled artery dotted with ancient towns and cities that have played theater to the aspirations of conquerors ranging from Alexander the Great to Genghis Khan and later Tamerlane.[2] In more recent times the Soviets had har-nessed the Syr Darya—in tandem with its sister river, the Amu Darya—to fuel a massive expansion of the cotton industry in Uzbekistan. The conse-quence of these developments was that while irrigated crops in the desert of the upper reaches had bloomed, further downstream both the Syr

Darya and the Amu Darya had slowed to a relative dribble. As predicted in 1959 when the water was diverted, the Aral Sea, which relies on the two rivers as its primary feeders, had now shrunk to around 10–20 percent of its original size—and was still receding.

It was not far west of the town of Shieli—about 100 km west of the ruins of Otrar—that I reached the riverbank and began the long journey west.

Initially the river environment offered reprieve. For the first two days I waded through a cluster of crop-farming communities where irrigation canals—predominantly for rice, corn, and cabbage—brought plentiful water and greenery. When navigating through the labyrinth of canals slowed my progress, I crossed to the less populated southern banks via a makeshift pontoon bridge—the last 15 m of which could be crossed only by laying down horse blankets and felt pads on a narrow ramp made from a grid of reinforcement wire welded to pipes.

Once on the far side I moved with a hint of rhythm along desert tracks. A typical day involved rising at 4:00 A.M., at which hour there were the whispers of a cool breeze. In the early morning the horses moved with purpose, their hooves shuffling quietly through sand. As the sky grew from purple to shades of crimson, I could see the glassy surface of canals and auls nestled among sand dunes with yurts set up outside permanent mud-brick homes. The Syr Darya forms both the eastern and northern boundary of the Kyzylkum Desert, and now and then I caught glimpses of this undulating landscape of tired-looking shrubbery and sand that angles away endlessly southward into the heart of Central Asia.

During the day it was suffocatingly hot, and I did my best to retreat to the shade of bushes and wait it out. The evenings, by contrast, were pleasant, particularly in the dusty, sun-baked auls. At dusk young children— already with dark summer tans—played about on the sandy streets, and old women sat on benches, chatting in their long, colorful gowns and scarves. Outdoor, dung-fired stoves and traditional samovars came to life, the bittersweet aroma of the smoke mingling with the smell of camels, which, naked and gray-skinned after recently being clipped, wandered freely through the streets. On my way through I was often offered fermented drinking yogurt, *airan*, which left a tangy flavor that lingered well into the next day.

In the scheme of things, this relatively smooth passage was nonetheless a fleeting one. After little more than a week, canals became less frequent and vegetation along the banks gave way to shadeless plains of clay and sand. Simultaneously, auls became rare, the days longer and hotter, and then, as I had been warned, the flies came.

My first encounter was one stifling morning as I attempted to descend the muddy banks of the river. The sludge was so thick there was a risk of the horses becoming bogged and so I had improvised a new bucket for carrying water to and fro. No sooner had I dismounted, tied the horses, and returned with the first pail, than a swarm descended. These weren't light, pesky mosquitoes, but meaty, gray, large-winged critters, and within minutes, each horse had trickles of blood running from their spines, down their rumps, ribs, and necks. I went about swatting as many as I could, but as numbers steadily built, I abandoned the river and rode out as quickly as possible. The river that brought life into the desert was, from now on, also to be a curse for me.

For the next three weeks—the time it took me to reach the old Russian fort of Kazalinsk (which Kazakh-speakers called Kazaly), near the river mouth—the trend of harshening conditions continued. Returning to the northern bank, I watched the silty brown water grow sluggish and the land fade to pale yellow. I adjusted my routine, starting earlier—usually by 3:00 A.M.—and spent more of the day attempting to escape the sun.

Every day during this period was different yet also somehow the same—a characteristic I found to be true everywhere in the desert during summer, when there were no crisp edges to the horizon, to days, or even to thoughts. It was also true, however, that there were two or three standout exceptions that punctuated the course of my journey along the Syr Darya.

Already by the time we had reached the Syr Darya, Zhamba, the fifteen-year-old horse that I had acquired in the foothills of the Altai, was looking underweight and weary. He had worked most of his years as a carthorse and his spirit was broken. Externally he exhibited large scars from all the haul-age, and through his sad, submissive eyes emanated a melancholy soul. I'd known that sooner or later I would have to retire him.

While camped on the outskirts of the city of Kyzylorda I arranged to sell Zhamba to a man who agreed to keep him as a riding horse for his grandchildren. At dawn the next morning I went to the local livestock market to find a replacement. Among the hundred or so mounts brought in by herders from afar, I chose a rather gangling but strong-looking bay stallion. He was not an ideal choice given that it was still spring (and stallions were still in a very aggressive mood), but that was the only option in a region where castrations were apparently seldom practiced.

Three days' ride from Kyzylorda I left Zhamba with the buyer's relatives in an aul called Akkum and rode on racked with guilt. I felt like I had betrayed Zhamba by abandoning him in a place where the intensity of heat would have been foreign to him, a horse from the mountains and steppe of eastern Kazakhstan. Yet to take him further into summer would have been a death sentence for him.

In the scheme of my trip, it was not the first or last time I would be haunted by the decision to leave a horse behind, and although Taskonir and Ogonyok proved reliable, the new stallion was just one of several trades before I happened upon a good long-term third mount.

Apart from Kyzylorda, there was one other large center I passed along the Syr Darya: the city of Baikonur. A fenced-off cluster of apartment blocks on the northern banks, it lay in the same anonymous desert country that I was becoming accustomed to, although it had long risen from obscurity to international renown. In the 1950s, the featureless desert just north of the Syr Darya, about 200 km east of the Aral Sea, had been chosen as the launch site for the Soviet Union's space program. From here in 1961, the young Russian cosmonaut Yuri Gagarin was sent into orbit, becoming the first man in space. Today, the cosmodrome remained the nucleus of Russia's space program, catering to an array of scientific, military, and, increasingly, commercial missions. With the impending retirement of the U.S. space shuttle fleet, it also had a crucial role in servicing the International Space Station.

The city of Baikonur itself—built exclusively to service the cosmodrome—

lay on territory leased to the Russian government. A permit was required to enter the city, and inside, it was said, Russian roubles were the official currency.

Unable to ride through Baikonur, I took a northern route between the cosmodrome and the city. I began early but got caught out in the heat navigating through vast stretches of junk metal, some of which consisted of hundreds of thousands of empty steel cans. I passed satellite dish installations and crossed the northbound rails that are still used to transport the rockets to the launch pad. Above, a large, unusually shaped plane circled. There was something surreal about it all.

It was a matter of national pride that Kazakhstan continued to play an important role in the history of space exploration. In fact, the large map of Kazakhstan I consulted daily was emblazoned with a picture of the rocket launch pad. I had come to think of it as a symbol of a world ever more interconnected via satellite and Internet—an unlikely icon in a country of almost inconceivable open wilderness.

I took shelter that night with a herding family on the periphery of Baikonur. The young man who hosted me in his simple mud hut explained that in Soviet times no one had been informed about the rocket launches. His parents had apparently watched in terror from their yurts as the first rockets were shot skyward. Nowadays rockets had become a routine sight but remained part of an unfathomable, incongruous world of little relevance to most herders.

JUST SHY OF Kazalinsk I broke away from the Syr Darya and began the trek northwest around the northern tip of the remnants of the Aral Sea.

It was the end of May, and even as prospects of fresh water promised to be fewer and farther between, the temperatures were on the climb. To beat the heat and avoid dehydration I began saddling the horses at sunset with the aim of riding through the night and finding shelter by sunup. This routine, which would see me through the next two months of my journey, was fraught with its own difficulties and risks.

During my final camp along the banks of the Syr Darya, it became clear that one of the main issues of night riding was that getting rest during the day was virtually impossible. Although I had learned to insulate the tent with horse blankets and pads, laying them over the top, the interior still became so baking hot that it left me in a state of semi-delirium, feeling as if my blood were cooking in my veins. Keeping an eye on the horses was crucial, and at this particular camp a stallion that had pursued us earlier in the morning remained on the attack. Every time I felt a hint of sleep pulling me under, I found myself having to reach for the nearest stick and go charging off again.[3]

When the sun went down, my spirits lifted and I set out with conviction, but the lack of sleep soon took its toll and my body surrendered to weariness. In the hours that followed it was only the constant task of keeping a lookout for Tigon that kept me awake. He spent his time roaming far and wide, only homing back in every half hour or so. His black coat was nearly invisible in the night and kept me guessing.

When gray-blue light did bleed back into the landscape I was nevertheless half asleep and only vaguely aware of my surroundings. It was a dangerous state of mind to be in, especially this morning, as I found myself crossing empty canals via crude bridges made with parallel ramps of narrow, wheel-width steel.

Faced with such obstacles, I would have ordinarily led each horse individually on foot, but in my somewhat detached state I tried to cross without dismounting. Halfway across the bridge, I felt Taskonir's lead rope pull out of my hand. As I turned from my perch on the new stallion, Ogonyok—who was tied to Taskonir from behind—reared up, then planted his front hooves wide apart in an effort to reverse away from the bridge. Taskonir was pulled off balance, and I heard the scuffle of hooves on steel, then a visceral crunch as he fell between the two bridge ramps. Fortunately, the plastic pack boxes were wide enough to prevent him falling all the way through, but now he was wedged between the ramps, one leg caught up on the bridge, the other three dangling over the drop to the empty canal below. Ogonyok, still tied to Taskonir's pack saddle, was pulled forward by the short lead rope and now teetered on the edge of the bank, theatening to fall in on top of Taskonir at any moment.

I rushed back to untie Ogonyok, then cut Taskonir's girth strap and ropes. As 450 kg of horse went tumbling down, I shut my eyes. No sooner had I reopened them, however, than Taskonir darted out of the canal— saved by the soft canal bed. I couldn't believe how foolish I'd been, or lucky I was to escape with little more than some scratches and bruising on Taskonir's back left leg.

When I left the bridge my little caravan was shaken up and facing the kind of predicament I had endeavored to avoid. Although I had managed 38 km as the crow flies that night—a very good distance—the delay meant I was marooned in the open in temperatures pushing 40°C. It took another two or three hours to reach water and shade in the next aul, by which time the horses were caked in salt stains from all the sweat and looking shriveled and strung out. Come nightfall, when the whole cycle of night riding began again, I had once again barely rested. At this rate, it was difficult to see how I might make it as far as the Caspian Sea without coming to grief. And yet finding a more sustainable routine was a conun- drum—it was dangerous to ride sleep-deprived at night, but suicide to move through the heat of day.

Three more hard but less eventful night rides brought me to Aralkum, a small community that lay just east of the Aral Sea's original shoreline and one day south of the former fishing port of Aralsk. Invited in by Dauletbas, a retired train station manager who now made a living rearing camels, I accepted—it was an opportunity to take stock for a couple of days, while also coming to learn more about the Aral Sea.

Due to the diversion of the Amu Darya and Syr Darya for irrigation, the Aral Sea was a "sea" in name only. What had once been the fourth- largest inland sea of its kind, providing one-sixth of the Soviet Union's fish supplies, was now a series of deserts and unconnected lakes—one in the north fed by the Syr Darya, and a puddle in the south fed by the Amu Darya that was said to have split into three different lakes, the largest of which was already fast evaporating into a saline swamp.

During an excursion to Aralsk, Dauletbas accompanied me to the old waterfront where as children he and his friends used to jump into the cooling waters from the pier. Nowadays the harbor was nothing more than a graveyard of rusting ships sinking in the sand. The shoreline had receded by as much as 100 km, leaving most of the fishing fleet stranded in the desert and many of the forty thousand people who had once worked in the fishing industry unemployed.[4]

West of Aralkum we drove over the old seabed, which was little more than a shell-encrusted plain, and visited an aul where mud huts and corrals were under siege by wind-driven banks of sand. In a region where pasture was already very thin on the ground and life particularly marginal, the retreat of the sea had led to creeping desertification and more extreme summers and winters. Compounding these problems, the ever-dropping sea level had caused a dramatic increase in salinity in the remaining waters, which had killed off much of the lake's vegetation and aquatic life. Frequent windstorms, which once had brought a moderating sea breeze in summer, now whipped up clouds of salt, sand, and toxic chemicals—largely pesticide and fertilizer runoff from the cotton fields of Uzbekistan that had collected on the seabed. These toxic clouds, according to many I spoke to, had caused an epidemic of respiratory, liver, and kidney disease.[5]

It had been a calculated decision by Soviet authorities to doom the Aral Sea, and the upshot was that while the Kazakhs of the Aral Sea region had watched their health decline and their livelihoods disintegrate in the space of a generation, Uzbekistan had become one of the world's largest exporters of cotton. And if the Soviet authorities could not have cared less that up to 75 percent of the diverted water was lost to evaporation and seepage in open and largely unlined canals, there was perhaps even less political will from the now independent Uzbekistan to invest in solving the problem.[6]

It took two days of travel from Aralkum before the northern tip of the old Aral Sea passed behind. Ahead lay around 400 km of steppe and desert to the river Zhem. It was a stretch of particularly arid terrain renowned for claiming the lives of Russian and Cossack soldiers in what had gone down in history as one of imperial Russia's most humiliating military failures in Central Asia.

The campaign in question—still spoken about by Kazakhs of the region—was an 1839 expedition of five thousand men, untold numbers of horses, and some ten thousand camels that had set out from Orenburg in southern Russia with a mission to free Russian slaves from Khiva, deep in Turkestan.[7] The army general charged with leading the campaign, Alexander Perovsky, had planned a route through the Kazakh steppes to the Aral Sea, from where he would carry on through the Kyzylkum Desert. Before departure he was said to have proclaimed that "in two months with God's help we shall be in Khiva!"

Perovsky led his troops out in early winter, wisely choosing to avoid summer because of the heat and scarcity of water—there were limited wells right across the region, some possibly more than a day's march apart. Not long into the expedition, however, it became clear he had underestimated the Kazakh steppe (then known as the Kirghiz steppe). The expedition was hit by repeated snowstorms, and come February 1840 the column was forced to retreat, having barely made it halfway to Khiva. During the return, wolves attacked the column—attracted by the rotting flesh of camels that had succumbed to the harsh conditions—and soldiers fell victim to exposure, scurvy, and even snow blindness. By the time the expedition hobbled back into Orenburg, seven months after departure, fewer than fifteen hundred camels remained alive and more than a thousand men had perished, all without the army having reached enemy territory.

To me the tragedy said less about the nature of the landscape or even the incompetence of the Russian soldiers than it did about the skills and hardiness of the nomads who had carved out a livelihood in the region, not to mention the Mongols, who six centuries earlier than Perovsky had used the same region as part of a thoroughfare to Europe. The fact that Carpini, a portly friar from Europe, and later William of Rubruck had traveled through these regions so quickly and made it out alive points to the efficiency and skill of their Mongolian entourage.

In the present day the Moscow–Tashkent train line blazes a trail northwest from Aralsk to Orenburg over some of the very terrain where

Perovsky had failed. In the absence of nomads and the desert wells they once maintained, I had the luxury of relying on remote railway auls and sidings along its path for water. Even so, it proved a particularly challenging stretch of terrain.

During a month of travel that took me through to July, I would pass through a landscape of sand dunes, clay flats, and barren uplands with negligible shade. Unlike the Syr Darya, with its army of flies, such were the heat and the dryness that the pale, bleached clay and white sandy earth appeared sterilized of life. I rode exclusively at night, and learned that it was crucial to find water and shade by 8:30 A.M., at which time the great molten orb had well and truly returned over the horizon. When I did get caught out, my long-sleeved shirt, and my saddle became hot to the touch, and the horses' sweat dried off as quickly as it beaded. Tigon began a routine that would endure for the rest of the summer—sprinting ahead and furiously digging holes in which he would lie for a few minutes until I caught up. When this didn't help he whined endlessly, his paws burning on the sand and his tongue out, forever wanting water.

Since the only water to be found was in auls, I stayed with families and did not camp, although, somewhat ironically, I did not come to know the people very well. Typically I would stumble into a community feeling spaced-out and groggy and ask for somewhere to rest. My arrival was usually greeted with fanfare, but I could rarely last more than a cup of tea before passing out. The horses would be set free to find whatever grass was available in the vicinity of the aul. Sometimes I would be woken up by the family to be told that the horses had come to the front door of the house looking for their owner. The heat was so oppressive that the horses could do nothing but search out the slightest sliver of shade.

Then, just as everyone was preparing to roll out their mattresses on the floor of the mud huts—or, as was the case in many places, simply out under the stars—I would reemerge, saddle up, and ride on. It was a feeling of acute isolation that I knew would never leave me—moving while the rest of the world slept.

There was, on the other hand, a kind of dreamlike quality to this period of my journey that a part of me truly enjoyed. Although I was following the same path as the railway, I rode far away from it for most of the time, navigating by matching my compass bearing with star formations and following them until the sky faded to blue. At times I rode through auls under the rising moon, discreetly pushing the horses through the sand, disturbing little more than a few camels and dogs. It wasn't possible to remain awake right through the night; I regularly napped in the saddle, and woke to discover that the horses had taken me astray. At other times I dismounted and slept on the earth. Even rocks could appear as a comfortable mattress when weariness had gotten the better of me. Sunrise was a sublime time of the day, when it felt as if I were riding the waves across the steppe. Once the sun was up, however, the long hours of the doldrums would begin.

Despite being very much immersed in the landscape and occupied by the challenges of summer, I was by no means impervious to goings-on beyond the scheme of my journey. At some point during the past few weeks Kathrin had discovered that she was suffering from Cushing's syndrome, a deadly disease caused by a brain tumor that produces an elevated release of cortisol into the body. For months Kathrin had been suffering from horrendous symptoms, including rapid weight gain, back pain, and unusual mood swings. It had taken some time before a doctor had discovered the tumor, but he had told her that if it was left untreated, it would be fatal. Just as I was heading through this hottest part of the Kazakh desert, Kathrin was preparing to undergo brain surgery in Germany. I knew that in this region to leave the horses and dog would almost guarantee I would never see them again, and so I did not consider it an option to abandon the journey and travel to Germany. Kathrin did not try to persuade me to leave my journey behind, either, and was very understanding, although I imagine it must have been hurtful that I did not offer to come.

At the same time that Kathrin was preparing for surgery, on the other side of the world, in Cairns, Australia, my longtime friend Cordell Scaife and his partner, Cara Poulton, were readying to fly to Kazakhstan to join me for the month-long trek along the Zhem River. I had often spoken with Cordell—whom I had met at age of nineteen during my six-month stint at Australian National University—about the idea of his coming for one stage of the journey or another, and I was thrilled he could join me. Ironically, though, it meant that while I could look forward to the close-ness of a friend during a stint of galling isolation, Kathrin was alone to deal with a far greater struggle.

Fortunately, Kathrin's surgery, which she underwent not long after Cordell and Cara's arrival, would prove successful, and she would be on the road to recovery by the time I was nearing the Caspian Sea.

CORDELL AND CARA joined me at the railway siding of Kopmula, little more than a week's journey short of the Zhem River. There we went about purchasing two extra horses and a pack camel that I hoped would reduce the burden on my mounts.

Two weeks later we were camped above the meandering Zhem. It was a shallow band of ale-brown water carving out a sunken gorge through wind-whipped hills dotted with dust-coated bushes and wormwood. Far-ther on, the river split into multiple channels among the curves and rip-ples of sand dunes.

From where we were, a day's ride from the junction of the river and the Moscow–Tashkent railway, the Zhem flowed some 600 km southwest through desert country to the Caspian Sea. At various points downstream it apparently dried up and went underground—particularly during the sum-mer. I had also been warned that it was so brackish that only livestock could drink its waters. It had been a wet spring with heavy snowmelt farther north, though, and some had also suggested the river would keep flowing till August. My aim was to follow the river for a month as far as the oil town of Kulsary, 100 km from the Caspian.

Although we set out along the Zhem with the same night-riding rou-tine I had followed since departing the Syr Darya, with water close at hand, we were not reliant on auls and could make camp along the river-bank to see out the heat of day. During the hottest hours, when the tem-perature breached 40°C, we rolled out of the tents and lay in the river's shallows. While the sun beat from above, I kept my head down, entranced by multicolored pebbles that shifted beneath the current and minnows that nibbled at my toes. Running as it did through the desert, the Zhem was a miraculous watercourse that the camel and horses also relished. They spent hours in the middle of the river, taking swipes at fresh green reeds and overhanging bushes. Even Tigon joined in, curling up in the water with only his nose and two tall ears poking skyward above the waterline.

When darkness fell, we became accustomed to feeling our way up the bank and onto the open plains, where the horses were adept at tapping into animal tracks that took us on efficient, direct routes, sometimes far away from the wide, arcing bends of the river but ultimately leading back to water. Harvette, as we had named our camel, brought a welcome new cadence and character to these long hours of riding. A seven-year-old female sporting the distinctive double humps of the Bactrian breed, she had a stoic rhythm and a sense of labored care to her every movement that made her very unlike the moody, short-tempered horses.[8] In camp, she was always in the mix, forever foraging around my kit bags. It was not uncommon to see her sucking on my sauce bottle or getting into other food—on one occasion she devoured an entire watermelon. When we slept, she often wandered a fair distance from camp, and it was quite some task to locate her and bring her back.

There was another shift in the nature of the journey that was evident in the early days along the Zhem. For two months I had been absorbed with the task of surviving summer. There had been precious little opportunity to get a real feel for the people, particularly while following the railway. Now, however, far from the economy of any main thoroughfare, and more accustomed to the rigors of summer travel (and greatly helped by Cara and Cordell), I could turn my attention to the nomad heritage of the region.

For some weeks I had been in the lands of the Kishi Juz, or the Junior Horde, a group of Kazakh tribes renowned as a hardened warrior people of the desert. Their territory stretches from the Aral Sea to the Caspian

Sea, and from Russia's southern border as far south as Turkmenistan. In the past, tribes of the Kishi Juz had wintered over in the deep south between the Caspian and the Aral, then migrated north to cooler climes for the summer.

For the first week and a half we passed typical examples of Soviet-era collectives that had brought together former nomads into settled communities. There were also permanent summer stations where families ran large herds of camel and sheep. At such a station beyond an aul called Zharkamys I inadvertently stumbled on an intriguing clue as to the fate of nomadic culture in the region.

While I lay in the family's mud hut nibbling on boiled lamb scalp, my eyes caught sight of a familiar curved piece of timber among a row of slats laid into the ceiling. It was a roof pole from the frame of a yurt—and an old one at that. I mentioned this to the herder of the house, and he looked at me sadly.

In this region of Aktubinsk Oblast, he explained, after the collapse of the Soviet Union, many herders, believing that independence and capitalism would usher in a new era of modernity, had hacked up their yurts—mostly family heirlooms from before collectivization—and used the frames for everything from firewood to building corrals. By the time they realized they would not be liberated from a life on the land, they were without yurts or the skills to make them. Now many herders who moved between seasonal camps made do in summer with rusty old wagons that were like tinderboxes in the heat.

It was hard to know how credible the herder's story was, but just two days downstream from the family's station—nearing the border between Aktubinsk Oblast and Western Kazakhstan Oblast—we entered remote country where the rhythms of nomadic life had certainly not faded.

At sunrise we rode out onto an elevated plain of powder-dry steppe looking for water. Long before we saw the river, there came a billowing plume of dust and the distinctive rumble of sheep and goats. After some time, the unmistakable figure of a man on the back of a camel came into view. Sitting wedged between the two humps, he wore a long scarf under his hat, and with a whip in hand, he rocked back and forth, pushing a sea of goats and sheep out to pasture. The gap between us rapidly shrank until the man was leaning down from his giant animal with a handshake, imploring us to return with him to his home.

The summer camp from which the herder had appeared was a sight to behold. We were led through a huddle of around two hundred camels in various states of leisure. Some sat on their haunches asleep, while babies frolicked on shaky stick-like legs and two or three bulls sauntered about, their front thighs thick as tree trunks, and humps the size of small refrigerators swaying to and fro. There was something dinosaur-like about their power and grace.

In the center of the huddle lay the camp itself—animal pens, a rusty old wagon, and an underground hut dug into the top of the riverbank. The camp overlooked the shallow waters of the Zhem and, beyond it, sweeping sand dunes and crusty plains. As I would witness during the remainder of the journey to Kulsary, many Kazakhs of the region spent summer squirreled away underground during the day, and the cooler nights sleeping in a yurt or simply on mattresses under the stars. All the work, which primarily involved milking camels, was done at dawn and dusk.

After unsaddling, we were led to a young woman who stood barely as high as the camel's back legs, her own right leg bent up to support a milk bucket on her thigh. While she milked, her infant daughter, who had barely learned to walk, stumbled about among the camels, unfazed as a couple of particularly gigantic specimens edged closer and gently sniffed at her hair.

When the milking was done, the full pails were whisked away for the production of cream, yogurt, dried curd, and fermented camel milk, known as shubat. Two teenage boys who had been lying in wait for the last camel to be freed mounted their horses and roused the herd with shouts and whistles.

As the boys and their horses worked like a tugboat, pushing and pulling at the vast herd, the camels rose reluctantly to their feet, then moved to the edge of the riverbank—a precipice where the steppe dropped away in a rather dramatic bank of eroding clay and sand. Only when the animals were bunched up did the first camels take the plunge. It began as a trickle—a few camels clambering down to the water—but soon became a torrent. Legs flew, saggy lips wobbled, the earth trembled, the sky filled with dust, and one by one they leaped into the river.

The boys continued after them, whistling and charging, urging on the lazier ones at the rear. From back up on the bank I watched as the herd crossed the river to the far side, where they rapidly shrank to nothing more than faint specks in a land of empty horizons.

Back at camp, the temperature was cranking toward 40°C, and what had been a hive of activity was now a picture of desolation. Hot wind gusted from the west, picking up dried dung from the empty pens and tossing it viciously through the air. A couple of dogs lay under the rusty wagon. Nothing moved. Tigon stuck close to my horses, which were standing still in the river below.

We were invited down some clay steps into the underground hut, where the glare and exposure gave way to darkness and intimacy. For some time we sat propped up on cushions, gulping down fresh bowls of fatty camel milk in the dark. But then our host, a man named Murat Guanshbai, lit a candle and the world reexpanded a little, revealing a room padded with felt mats and wall hangings and featuring shelves cut into the clay for the display of ornaments.

Murat was as exotic as his surrounds. He had a square, open face with a short flat nose, and his almond eyes were protected by bushy, overhanging eyebrows. Unlike most Kazakhs' hair, his was thick and curly as steel wool, and his jaw was masked with stubble. Murat and his family were Kozha, one of the tribes that composed the Kishi Juz. The Kozha were known as the descendants of Bedouin missionaries to Kazakhstan some thousand years ago.

More important for Murat than his tribal background, however, were his nomadic roots. Although he had an education in veterinary science, he had chosen to carry on the tradition of his family as camel herders. In fact, his family were herders of some local renown, owning somewhere in the order of five hundred camels—no small number, given that a large camel could fetch in excess of $1,500 at market. With a herd this size, it was crucial to migrate with the seasons, and Murat's family had five different camps. Soon he would move with his family to the August camp, which lay far away from the riverbank to the west.

I got along well with Murat, and he seemed to genuinely care about his animals. In light of this I decided to offer him the stallion that I had bought in Kyzylorda. My stallion was a tall, slender horse that many had offered to buy from me along the way because his build was seen as good for racing. Unfortunately, these same characteristics made him unsuitable for long-distance travel. In recent weeks he had been unwell, suffering diarrhea, and although I had wormed him and fed him more grain than the others, he had lost considerable weight. Murat promised me one of his horses in exchange—a quiet, fat little horse of Mongolian proportions—and made an additional offer that seemed like a godsend at the time, but which I would later regret.

I'd long planned to say farewell to Cordell and Cara in Kulsary before carrying on alone toward Russia. The horses, however, were in desperate need of a rest, and it had come to my attention that I would need to apply for a Russian visa in Almaty well in advance of reaching the border. I had decided to look for a place near Kulsary to leave the horses for the month of August. Upon hearing this, Murat warned that it was even hotter in Kulsary, and there would be no fodder for my horses in the area. He proposed instead that upon our arrival in Kulsary—where an uncle of his would host us—he would send a truck to bring my horses back here for grazing until September. All I would have to do is pay the costs. What I could never have foreseen was that Murat's plan would fall through, and so I would become trapped not only in a region without fodder, but the middle of an urban oil town with nowhere to go.

That was in the future, though, and for now I was intoxicated by the majesty of Murat's camp, where for two days more I drank in every detail, from the sound of the camels moving back under moonlight to the sensation of lying down under the stars at night and waking with not a drop of dew under an eternally blue and cloudless sky. There was a completeness, an intertwining of nature, animal, and man, that could not be replicated in an environment compartmentalized by walls and fences, and it reinvigorated Cordell, Cara, and me for the remainder of the journey together.

FROM MURAT'S CAMP, there lay just 150 km to Kulsary. One day south of Murat's we met with his father, Guanshbai, and decided to sell him our little camel, Harvette. From there, the land became flatter, the pasture—as Murat had forewarned—grew thin and the ground metamorphosed into white clay pans with nothing but salt bush. The temperature climbed over 50°C, and the water became brackish—but still fresh enough to drink. There were times when we were so exhausted by the struggle to keep cool during the day that we'd saddle up the horses at night but then fall asleep until after midnight; when we finally woke, we gave up and unsaddled. It didn't really matter, though, for the end of my journey with my Australian friends was drawing near, and we had experienced the essence of steppe life that we had come for.

On July 27 we packed up for our last day of riding along the Zhem. I was thinking happily that my horses were about to be trucked back to paradise for a month of grazing. For the next month I could also look forward to some time away from the punishing routine of night riding, and come the cool of September, when I planned to return, my horses would be fat and rested. Never again, I thought, would I have to deal with the heat of the Kazakh summer.

15

THE OIL ROAD

SINCE DEPARTING AKBAKAI in April, my journey had taken me four months across the unbroken steppe of central and eastern Kazakhstan. During that time, the challenges of each and every day had been defined by the rhythms of summer, when daylight was cheap and the cool hours of night precious. On the outskirts of the oil town of Kulsary, 100 km short of the Caspian Sea, however, the steppe abruptly began to break up. The open desert and saltpans on the flanks of the River Zhem that had so infused in me a feeling of inner peace gave way to mangled earth that had been bulldozed into a maze of mounds and ridges. Then came twisted, rusty pieces of steel, shattered glass, and burned-out cars. On the asphalt road leading into the center, heavy trucks and SUVs hurtled past at unchecked speed, spraying gravel and leaving us in a wake of dust and fumes. The brave, indomitable Taskonir trembled.

I'd long known about the oil economy of western Kazakhstan, and in the past few weeks we'd glimpsed something of the industry—permanent gas flares on the horizon, the odd truck—but nothing on this scale.

Tanbai, the relative of Murat who had agreed to host us until the truck came to pick the horses up, met us on a street corner. As we came to a halt, he flicked his cigarette to the ground and looked us over.

"Where are your cars?" he asked, concerned. It turned out that Tanbai had mistakenly understood from Murat by phone that we were wealthy tourists traveling by jeep.

Tanbai begrudgingly led us to his house in the center of town, where we tied up the horses and took shelter from the heat. No sooner had we sat down for tea and bread than Tanbai's twenty-year-old son, also named Murat, shuffled in next to me and leaned over with a new Nokia phone. With his parents across the table, he covertly displayed a porn clip, and then a gruesome video of an American soldier having his head severed by Taliban. Oblivious to this, Tanbai said to us with pride: "My son can speak English, you know. He is studying to be an engineer, and is already working for an American oil company."

In the light of morning it was clear that in the world in which the younger Murat had grown up, horses, the turn of the seasons, and grass held little currency. Tanbai earned a modest living as a bus driver and mechanic, and their simple mud-brick home was hedged in by new two-story townhouses. Pointing to the house opposite, which had a brand-new black Toyota Land Cruiser parked behind the gates, Tanbai said of his neighbor, "He supplies concrete for the oil companies." Indicating another house, and then a third, he added, "And that one over there is a local politician . . . Him, his son is working for an oilfield."

A drive through the town of just over forty thousand people revealed mansions at all stages of hasty construction, most of which backed onto potholed dirt streets where camels wandered haplessly in the heat and piles of rubbish sat uncollected. There was little infrastructure for water or sewage—even the more luxurious homes had pit toilets in their yards. On the edge of town water tankers were lined up, ready 24/7 to deliver water at a rate of $200 for 3,000 litres.

In the past, the vast, sterile desert on the northeast shoulder of the Caspian Sea—at the center of which lay Kulsary—had been renowned for its warrior tribes, who kept their land impenetrable to invading armies. Nowadays, the mishmash urban landscape was the hallmark of a region in the throes of an oil boom, which had attracted a relative invasion of multinational oil companies. The scale and pace of economic transformation were difficult to fathom. Little more than an hour's drive south lay the Tengiz oilfield, which was built over the sixth-largest oil bubble on the planet and tapped by a joint venture between the Kazakh government and American-based Chevron. Tengiz was the single biggest contributor to the government's coffers, and combined with the Kashagan field in the nearby Caspian Sea—the second-largest known oil reserve in the world, and at the time of its discovery in the year 2000 the biggest find in thirty years—it placed Kazakhstan in a position to become one of the world's biggest oil exporters.[1]

The oil reserves of western Kazakhstan set the country's economy apart from many of its resource-poor Central Asian neighbors and had helped steer the country into a relatively prosperous and stable post-Soviet independence. Yet for all the potential and promise that oil brought, there were signs that the industry was a source of social division and corruption. In the early days of the boom, the president, Nursultan Nazarbayev, had been implicated in a scandal when it was revealed that billions of dollars in proceeds from a 1996 agreement between Mobil and the government were hidden away in Swiss bank accounts—and that $500 million of it had inexplicably vanished.[2] At the other end of the spectrum, the many herders and unemployed rural folk I had met in recent weeks were locked out of the oil economy and could only look on as their traditional livestock economy was pushed further to the fringes.

It is true that the oil industry offered lucrative opportunities for many regional Kazakhs, as evidenced by the pace of development in Kulsary. The corruption and lack of trickle-down wealth, however, contributed to a common perception that most of the oil money was being funneled to the east, where it ended up either in the pockets of officials or at the president's political disposal. Even among those workers employed at the coal face, there were recurring tensions over unsafe conditions and discrepancies of pay compared to that of foreign workers. There were instances when this had boiled over into violent rioting at the Tengiz field.[3]

Aside from this, there was also the view that foreign companies such as Chevron were taking more than their fair share of the nation's riches. "Back when the deals were made, Kazakhstan was desperate for money and the Americans paid too little," said Tanbai as we pulled up to the central market. "We were cheated. We didn't know the real value. Kazakhstan is a country surrounded by wolves on all sides—the Russians, Chinese, Turks, and of course the Americans!"

By the time we made it back to Tanbai's home it was 40°C, and the horses stood tied and sweating in the shade-less yard. I had paid for a water truck to fill Tanbai's tank, and hay was on its way, but Tanbai was unhappy about the growing pile of manure. In a town where I had long imagined that I could spend some time recuperating, it was becoming clear that while the most challenging terrain of Kazakhstan might have been behind me, my journey—like Kulsary—was at an awkward intersection between a life dominated by the natural elements and one in which survival would increasingly require navigation through the thickets of trouble brought on by industry, bureaucracy, and the every-man-for-himself attitude of the oil economy. Somewhat symbolic of this, my route from Kulsary to the Russian border—500 km of desert, punctuated by the central oil city of Atyrau—lay alongside the $2.2 billion oil pipeline that now pumped crude to the west as far as the Black Sea throughout the very untamed land once trodden by Mongol warriors and Silk Road traders.

BEFORE I COULD ride out of Kulsary I needed to travel 3,000 km to Almaty to apply for a Russian visa. To do this would first involve arranging for the horses and dog to be transported to Murat's farm for a month of grazing and finding buyers for Cordell's horse and the short, fat horse I had acquired from Murat. As a replacement for my third mount, I had settled on a gray horse named Kok, which Cara had been riding.[4]

In the end the agreement with Murat did not work out, and so instead I left the animals under the watch of a herding family in a nearby aul, Karagai. It was a community set in a mustard-yellow dustbowl with no grass to be spoken of. A herder there named Albek offered to buy Cordell's horse and assured me that, for a price, he could take the other horses out to graze at a summer pasture. Albek's elderly father promised to guard Tigon.

Five weeks later, I returned from Almaty pessimistic about my chances of finding the horses alive. I had been away longer than anticipated, and the only correspondence I'd received from Karagai was that the horses remained in the aul—they had not been taken out to summer pastures for grazing as agreed. Problems I had encountered in Almaty contributed to my gloomy outlook. The Russian embassy had refused my visa application. After much waiting I had mailed my passport to a travel agency in Finland instead—a risky move, since by law I had to carry my passport at all times.[5]

When I jumped out of a buckled old Russian jeep and landed my backpack in the dust and sand of Karagai, it appeared my worst fears had been realized. I found Taskonir tied up at the back of a corral with his head hanging and ribs resembling the corrugations I had just driven over to get to Karagai. The other two horses were missing, and the only person to be found at Albek's home was an emaciated shadow of a man who reached out to me from the doorstep for balance, then crashed drunkenly into the dirt.

After a tip-off from a neighbor, I was directed on foot east of the aul, where I found men cutting up two freshly slaughtered horses. They weren't mine, but the men knew who I was and waved me on further. I found Albek and a friend of his in the midst of a gallop—they were riding none other than Kok and Ogonyok, and explained that my horses had been entered in a *baiga*—a horse race—that was to be held the next day!

Back in the aul, the removal of saddles and blankets revealed fresh sores. Albek shrugged sheepishly and admitted that the 300 kg of grain I had left with his family had vanished within a couple of weeks—this, he explained, was why the horses were skinnier than when I had left them.

Albek's elderly mother tried to lighten my spirits: "Those sores are in memory of us! You will never forget us!"

Although I was angry, I was genuinely grateful that the horses were alive. I paid Albek the promised $300 and thanked him. Any mistakes were forgiven when I found Tigon. I spotted him from a distance dug into the sand under a wooden platform-cum-deck near Albek's house. On top of the platform, sitting cross-legged and guarding Tigon, was Albek's father. As I approached, Tigon's dusty ears sprang to life and his tail flopped about uncertainly. When I was nearer he sprinted to the end of his lead and leaped up with his paws on my chest. The old man straightened out his chicken bone legs, a smile opened up between his hollow, sun-blackened cheeks, and he rose to embrace me. "See! Everyone thought I was mad. They were sure you would never come back, but I didn't forget you!"

Departure from Karagai was one of the more vivid farewells of my Kazakh journey. Albek's father had gotten hold of a pink plastic gem-encrusted hair band and wore it over his bald scalp from ear to ear. As I saddled up to leave, he rose from a blanket on his platform, resplendent in this headwear, holding out a glass of vodka. As I went to accept, he pulled the glass back and fell back on the dirt in laughter.

"Whatever you do, don't rush!" he said, his eyes rolling as he slipped into another world.

The aul passed by in a series of wafts of dry dung until it had been eclipsed by the horizon and I was breathing in fresh, clear air. Then came silence and the empty steppe.

It occurred to me that the openness was like a big blank canvas, and being here after the turbulence of the past month allowed me to rebuild my picture of the world from the tiniest details. I closed my eyes, felt the swaying of the saddle and waited for the first sensations to bleed back in. It came as the sound of the horses brushing gently against the wormwood plants. Then came the feeling of the breeze lightly cooling the sweat on my back, and when I opened my eyes, I saw the saksaul trees coming and going like driftwood floating aimlessly by on the ocean.

After a short ride I made an early camp on the Zhem River. Tigon ran circles in the sand, pausing momentarily at times to come in close, roll onto his back, and demand a pat on the belly. The horses rested their necks on one another. Ogonyok let out long, breezy farts that tailed off lazily. Taskonir's condition was bad—he was all skin and bone—but at least he now looked at ease. I let my clothes drop to the ground and lay in the ankle-deep water watching the pink moon rise like a lamp into the sky.

In the morning I had ridden only a short distance when I slumped from the saddle with a banging in my skull and my stomach writhing—probably a consequence of the vast quantities of horsemeat I had consumed the previous day in Karagai. I managed little more than 13 km before heading for a herder's hut, where I feigned interest in finding water for the animals and swiftly collapsed on the floor inside. For the next three days I lay in a fever. I ate almost nothing but even so made frequent sojourns to relieve my stomach and bowels. At first I made an effort to do it discreetly, but eventually I let go of all pride.

I stayed a week in all, but only as I began to regain strength was I able to get to know my hosts and through them the curious farming arrangement they were part of. Aigul was a twenty-year-old woman with an open, round face, long brown hair, and a mischievous smile. The rigors of life on the steppe hadn't yet taken away the beauty of her youth, although her hands were wrinkled and callused, and the skin on her cheeks was freckled and dark from a lifetime of sun. During the day she brought me water and tea and in between chores scrutinized my photo album. She knew very little Russian. When her husband, Bulat, returned from herding each evening she would shrink away into the background and avoid eye contact. Bulat was a strong, handsome man in his late twenties with a thick mop of hair and light green eyes.

From a distance, the herding station that Aigul and Bulat managed, with its large herds of camels, horses, sheep, and goats, appeared like a traditional nomad camp. All was not as it seemed, though. The hut was neither a summer domain or a winter one but a permanent base, and Bulat and Aigul were not indigenous to the area but hired farmhands from neighboring Uzbekistan.[6] The owners of the farm and livestock were Kazakh businessmen from Kulsary who had taken out a forty-nine-year lease on the land.

"Kazakhs won't do this work—it's too little money. But for us, well, there is no work back home," explained Bulat, who spoke fairly coherently in Russian. I had heard about this type of farming from many Kazakhs, who complained the government was offering long-term land leases affordable only to city businessmen who didn't have skills or interest in animal husbandry.

This explained some of the glaring oddities of life at the hut. Every meal was a bland serving of rice or pasta mixed with a bouillon cube and onion. "Our employer won't let us slaughter sheep—we have to buy our own food. Meat is too expensive for us," they told me, as excuse for the fact that they had no meat to offer.

Their horse tack was as appalling as their food. Bulat's saddle was a crude construction of plastic and steel that left a permanent sore on his horse's back. Without investment from his employer in decent equipment, and no sense of personal ownership of work, there was little incentive for Bulat to take pride in herding. It was a pattern I had witnessed time and again in Kazakhstan, suggesting that the capitalist master had no more interest in the well-being of people and their animals than did the Communist predecessor.

The true nature of this style of steppe farming became clear the day before I departed. A Toyota Prado hurtling across the steppe signaled the arrival of the owners. They were two burly men dressed in city clothes and seemed to have come out for a bit of fun. For an hour or so they roared back and forth in pursuit of a terrified herd of horses, tooting the horn and flashing their lights. When the horses began to tire, a lasso was dangled out a passenger window and the vehicle closed in on a fat specimen. After being caught—and nearly strangled—the horse was bound by the legs, pushed upside down, and hauled up an old door used as a ramp into the back of a waiting van. For good measure it was kicked a few times before the doors were closed.

In a land where nomads had been perfecting horsemanship for at least 5,500 years, it was a saddening image that stuck with me.

⁜

OVER THE NEXT 500 km to the Russian border I took a direct route across the desert to the Volga River. It was a hard and gritty ride, characterized on one hand by the haunting beauty of the desert and on the other by the disruption brought by the oil industry.

In what proved a full month of travel, I spent the first two weeks picking my way through a morass of salt lakes, flats, and bogs known in Russian as *solonchak*. Following a web of narrow ridges I watched from the saddle as glassy shallow pools of water, glittering white crusts, and chalky plains unfolded, interspersed by carpets of yellow, pink and green plants. From this washed-out palette thousands of birds would lift in the distance like giant swarms of mosquitoes.

In the evenings we all rejoiced in the simplicity of our campsites—the horses rolling on their backs on the brittle, sun-bleached grass, and Tigon curling up asleep next to the tent. It was mid-September, and although the sky was pale and clear, the oppressiveness of summer had gone, meaning that for the first time since May, I was able to ride long hours through the day, and enjoy unbroken sleeps at night.

The downside of the barren landscape was that there was no fresh water to be found, and so I was forced to stray daily to local railway sidings and auls built around small-scale oil-extraction sites. These visits were invariably depressing, and when I rode out to reenter the open land I tried to leave the memories of them behind. Nonetheless, I couldn't stop my mind from filling with a tangle of thoughts. The nomadic life that had defined the people for eternity had clearly been pushed so far to the margins by oil, by the Soviets, and by the new era of capitalism that it was no longer on the radar. The more I stewed over what I had witnessed, the more the image of Kazakhstan as a land of hundreds of interlocking grazing territories, within which each nomad clan had its unique pattern of seasonal migration, began to crumble. In place of this a very different picture emerged. If the farm that Aigul and Bulat managed was the model of the future, then it was not difficult to imagine the rise of corporate-run farms that could one day carve up the land with fences. If this happened, then herders and nomads could be evicted from their ancestral lands and either be replaced by cheap imported labor or be forced into employment and lose the very independence that was the heart of nomadic existence.

The halfway mark to the Russian border from Kulsary was the city of Atyrau, the oil capital of western Kazakhstan, built on the banks of the

Ural River (a river historically better known by its Kazakh name, Yaik). Atyrau also represented the gateway out of geographical Asia into Europe.

After some preliminary work on veterinary documents for the border, I rode west, following the oil pipeline across flats and marshes on the northern fringe of the Caspian Sea. Next to me flowed untold riches on the way to powering the engine of economies in faraway countries. To me, what mattered was there were very few edible plants or grass for the horses. The only advantage of the oil pipeline for me was that every 20 km there were huts made of reeds and mud manned by security guards who were paid a pittance to patrol their stretch of pipe. Here I was usually able to find water and some advice about the terrain ahead.

Only a couple of days out of Atyrau my cooking stove broke and I went for the next eleven days without hot meals. The only comforting thoughts I could find lay in the nature of the harsh land around me. With such thin pickings of grass and limited fresh water, this kind of land would never be suitable for fixed farming. There were surely only two choices for land users of the future—abandon such steppe or return to some form of nomadic herding to utilize what little pasture there was.

My journey from Atyrau to the Russian border was broken by one unexpected discovery. Just beyond the aul of Isatai the land spread out into a sea of wavy sand dunes speckled with tussocks of grass and other desert plants. I had reached the southern edge of a desert known as the Naryn Kum. At a railway siding a gray-bearded herder took me in and spoke with passion about the land he had grown up in.

"I was raised as a nomad way out there in the dunes," he said, pointing to the north. "When I was young all nomads wintered over in the dunes and then migrated to the Caspian coast for summer. I didn't see a Russian until I was eighteen years old! In my day the best musicians in the area would turn up and volunteer for a wedding, not only looking for pay, like nowadays." There were few people who still lived in the Naryn Kum. According to rumor, this was partly because oil and gas exploration had destroyed many natural springs.

In the evening I retired to his home, and he brought out a remarkable-looking saddle blanket loosely woven with horsehair. "This is called a kyl terlek," he told me. "My father's father taught me how to make it, and he was taught by his father. We make them by cutting off the tails and manes of three horses in early winter when the horses no longer need to swish away the flies. In all my life using a kyl terlek, I have never had a sore on my horse . . . even in the heat of summer!"

I fondled it carefully, the significance beginning to dawn on me. In this blanket was a genius I could now appreciate.

"In the past, all Kazakhs used a kyl terlek. It drains away the sweat, allows air in, and is the most natural fiber available. When crossing a river, or in the rain, unlike wool felt, this blanket doesn't stay wet for long, and is never heavy!" he said.

Throughout my journey, I'd been asked whether I had ever seen or heard of a mysterious saddle blanket made from horsehair. No one had seemed to know how to make it, although everyone, from Kazakhs on the Betpak Dala to Mongolians in the central Khangai Mountains, knew that a horsehair blanket was the best option for long distance travel.

I had always wondered how campaigning Mongolian armies were able to swim across rivers with their horses, then get back on and keep riding. Although there were known methods the Mongols used, such as bundling clothes and saddles into a buoyant sack of leather that was tied to the horse's tail and towed across the water (such as is described by Carpini), it was inevitable that their saddle blankets would have often become wet in this process. And, as any nomad of the steppe knows today, a soaked felt saddle blanket remains wet for days and can rub a horse's back raw within hours. A kyl terlek, on the other hand, would drain almost instantly, allowing horsemen to continue without detriment to the horses. Could this kyl terlek—a term that coincidentally approximately means "summer deel for horse" in Mongolian—have been one of the Mongolian nomads' secrets to their long campaigns?[7]

It was a long bow to draw, but later when I informed CuChullaine O'Reilly of the Long Riders Guild about it, he was overcome with excitement. Only months earlier he had received a report from Swedish long rider and adventurer Michael Strandberg, who had made the same observations about horsehair blankets made by indigenous Siberians for

Yakutian ponies. Had the horsehair blanket once been used throughout Central Asia and the steppes of Eurasia? If so, why had the knowledge disappeared?

卍卐

FROM THE NARYN Kum I dropped down onto flats near the town of Ganushkino. There, on the verge of the Volga River's vast delta, the Kazakh steppe I had known for so long came to an end.

A year earlier, and more than 4,000 km to the east from here, I had set out from the Altai with Ruslan and my new troupe of horses. With winter bearing down and the colossal steppe of Kazakhstan yawning, I'd been overwhelmed by the bare nature of the landscape, which seemed to have been scoured clean through sheer exposure. Since then I'd become accustomed to the arid, sharply continental climate of the Kazakh steppe, where the air was dry enough to parch the throat and clouds evaporated before they had a chance to germinate. Now I was descending into a warm breeze that brought thick, humid air. The smell of wetlands was all around, and the sky carried clouds in full bloom.

As gulls, ducks, and swans tracked above, the horses dipped their heads, stealing mouthfuls of luminous green grass. Tigon porpoised through reeds near the edge of a stream, and as if to mark the milestone finally cocked his back leg to urinate on a grass tussock instead of squatting on all fours.

In the scheme of things we had not yet technically reached the end of the arid steppe zone—that still lay ahead, about 300 km to the west of the Volga—but the natural riches of the delta signaled that the bulk of the harsh center of the Eurasian steppe was nevertheless behind us. From here onward to Hungary the conditions promised to grow milder and more fertile.

The next day, only a short distance from the border with Russia, I left the horses in the care of a man named Muftagali and took a taxi back to Atyrau to finalize my veterinary documents. Initially I thought things were looking up—my passport had arrived with the Russian visa, and I met with the director of the local Ministry of Agriculture, Kosibek Erzgalev, who promised to help. After a week, however, the permits were not yet ready, and being in the city forced me to confront issues that I had been conveniently avoiding while in the saddle.

In a city where the oil boom was giving rise to flashy new hotels and apartment blocks, my daily budget of $10 was looking particularly feeble. The cheapest accommodation I could find—an old Soviet-era studio apartment plagued by mosquitoes—was $250 a week. Recent repairs to my video camera had cost $487, my Russian visa had been $229, and I was accumulating a daily debt for the keeping of my horses. At this rate, even if I could pull my horses through as far as the Danube, my budget would not stretch that far.

Beyond my financial worries, though, there was a greater anxiety that had been welling up in me for months, and which was now impossible to ignore. In an Internet cafe I read an email from Kathrin with a sense of dread: *Why is it that I feel sick in the pit of my stomach and hollow after our phone calls?* she wrote.

After saying goodbye to Kathrin in Mongolia, I had long clung to a dream of reuniting with her in Hungary and spending some weeks getting to know her again. The journey would be behind me, and I could be present in a way that I hadn't been, even since before I left Australia.

In recent months, though, it was a dream that had faded, and the truth was that underneath I had always harbored some sense of unease about remaining with Kathrin. It would always be challenging to maintain a serious long-distance relationship such as ours by relying on satellite phone connections, but it also felt incongruous with the very nature of my journey. There was a tinge of irony that the very shared attribute that had brought us together—passion for travel—was also the thing drawing me away from her.

As time had gone on and the journey had become more uncertain and drawn out, the feeling of unease in me had grown, and in the process it had become abundantly clear that keeping our relationship alive was not among my priorities—that much had become obvious when Kathrin had been admitted for brain surgery and I remained riding through the desert instead of abandoning my journey to be with her.[8]

There was another feeling that had grown, too, though, albeit a selfish one—I had come to feel that I did not want or need any fixed horizons. I was happy to be dedicated to my journey and immersed in the experience. Not only could I not envisage life after Hungary—at this stage I couldn't even imagine getting there—I simply didn't want to.

After one of many sleepless nights I called Kathrin and told her that I wanted to break up. It was a difficult and painful conversation, and I was riddled with a feeling of guilt that I had entered into a relationship promising more than I could have given.

I spent most of my remaining time in Atyrau shuffling between the Ministry of Agriculture and an Internet cafe where I traded emails with Kathrin. Being unable to see each other in person must have been so much harder for Kathrin, especially in the midst of her recovery from surgery, and also because she had already waited so long. To add to the feelings of being apart, Kathrin planned to spend her upcoming school vacation in a remote village in northern Italy where there was no Internet or phone. We would each have to deal with everything in isolation, and in the circumstances I desperately wanted to get back out on the horses, where I hoped the sense of movement, the feeling of progress, and the company of my animals would make the pain easier to deal with.

⊞

AFTER TWO WEEKS in the city, I was able to pick up my veterinary permits, and I returned to the border. Although the Ministry of Agriculture was adamant that I had the right documents, riding horses into Russia was an untested thing, and I was nervous.

Nevertheless, things at first appeared to go smoothly. Not far beyond Muftagali's aul, Kuegen, I passed through a police post just before the border, where my only issue was that Ogonyok ate the roses from the post's one and only flowerpot. At the border, the presence of a familiar veterinary official from Atyrau put me at ease. "What took you so long?" he said. He arranged for the processing of my documents, took me to lunch, and then escorted me through immigration.

The customs officer showed no concerns. "Now, what model horse do you have? What year is its release?" he joked, waving me through.

Come afternoon I had left Kazakhstan, been ferried across a branch of the Volga River on a barge, and was approaching Russia. Tigon led from the front, bristling with optimism.

At first the Russian border personnel were friendly. I was led through to the customs inspection bay, where an officer called out in jest, "You know we will have to take the wheels off to check for narcotics!" The inspections were all over in a few minutes, and then all that lay before us was a simple boom gate leading into Russia.

It was just as the guards began to wave me through that my luck changed. From an office in a shipping container marked "Vet Control and Transport on the Border," a woman who appeared to have none of the joviality of her colleagues came my way. I broke the ice with a handshake and a smile, but as the horses edged closer her eyes widened, and the shaking of her head, which had begun hesitantly, became vigorous and full of conviction.

"I don't know what to do! I am in shock! My God, what problem has fallen on me tonight?" she cried.

I followed her to the shipping container, where she sat under a framed portrait of Vladimir Putin and made a phone call.

"I have a Hungarian traveling from Mongolia on Mongolian horses without documents!" she yelled. There was no opportunity for me to intervene and correct her misapprehensions. I could hear the reply that came down over the line from her superiors in Astrakhan: "What a nightmare!"

The woman hung up and regained some composure. "I must impound your horses! I cannot grant you permission to pass!"

I reassured her that I had all the right papers and that she had misunderstood my story, but she wasn't listening, and several hours later I knew I was in serious trouble. The only official means to export live horses from Kazakhstan to Russia was to process them for sporting events or as meat. Even if I could overcome this issue, there was a crucial document I didn't have: a transit permit from Moscow that would allow me to follow a strict route through Russia to Ukraine.

I called my contacts in Russia—Anna Lushchekina of the Russian Academy of Sciences in Moscow, and her friend and colleague Liudmilla Kiseleva in Astrakhan—but to no avail. According to the vet official I had two choices: "You can leave your horses and dog impounded with us, and go alone into Russia . . . or you can go back to Kazakhstan, where you came from." It was nearing midnight by the time I gave up and rode back into the no-man's-land between the two borders. The Kazakh border would not reopen until eight o'clock the following morning, and so I found a grassy hollow and made camp.

Come morning I was confronted with a fresh shift of Kazakh immigration, veterinary, and customs officials who accused me of horse rustling and illegal export of the horses. An eight-hour stand-off ensued, resolved only by negotiations between customs and the head of the Ministry of Agriculture in Atyrau. After this I dove back into the core of the problems from the day before.

❖

MY HORSES WERE again left in Muftagali's care, and within twenty-four hours I had returned to my purgatory in Atyrau, where I was warned that to get transit permits from Moscow could entail a two-month wait. Given that my visa was only valid for six more weeks and I no longer had the funds to pay for rent, my situation was all the more tenuous. Additionally, unlike any other time on my journey, there would be no sympathetic ear from Kathrin—even if she was prepared to listen, she was in Italy and unreachable.

I got through the first week or so consumed by my frustration at the bureaucracy, which at least fueled my determination to beat the system. I spent hours each day at the Ministry of Agriculture learning about the laws and protocols, sending faxes to Moscow and Astana. Soon I was fluent in the kind of bureaucratic jargon used by the staff. During the daytime I was spurred on by the feeling that I was actively doing something about my situation. Each evening when the ministry closed its doors, however, I felt helpless and lonely.

As the days wore on, it seemed that my internal battle between clinging to optimism and being tempted to fall into dejection was mirrored in
the city around me. Everywhere I looked burgeoning wealth from oil that
spoke of a bright future collided with sectors of the economy that had
been left behind. The Ministry of Agriculture was clearly not part of the
economic boom—it was situated in a gloomy building cast among other
Soviet-era structures, all in a state of decay. Staff wages were pitiful, and
many had to come up with other ways of earning money to support their
families. By contrast, the city center showcased upmarket apartment com-
plexes and new office buildings. The city square had recently been rebuilt,
and opposing it was a newly constructed mosque of palatial proportions. All
around, billboards boasted advertisements by mining companies, banks,
and investment groups. Among these the face of President Nazarbayev was
unavoidable. A presidential election had been announced for December,
and his lavish campaign was in full swing. "Forward with Nazarbayev!" his
slogan read, as if claiming credit for all the visible affluence.

Two weeks passed, the miniature budget I had allowed myself for rent
had run out, and there was still no whisper about permits. I had nowhere
to go.

Then, as I was sitting in a cheap cafe having lunch, a young man
dressed in stylish designer clothes approached and introduced himself in
English. "I was just curious to know why a Westerner would be eating in
this kind of cheap place and wearing such bad, worn clothes. I thought
you were reaching out for communication with people, so I thought
I would come to talk," he said.

Azamat, as he was known, was my age and worked for a local oil firm.
We exchanged stories for a couple of hours and I learned that he was a
devout Muslim, and yet almost exclusively spoke in Russian.

"I feel ashamed that there are Kazakhs who do not understand Russian
language. I love Russia. I can't understand that there would be people interested in Kazakh culture," he said.

It was a curious perspective that I had observed in other cities like Almaty, but which I had never heard being articulated. For Azamat, Russian
culture represented modernity and sophistication, while nomadic life was

as alien as it would have been to a city dweller anywhere in the world. "I think you are the only man still wanting to be a nomad in my country! Why would you want to leave your home and come here?" he said, a little aghast.

While he could not quite identify with my journey, he was fascinated and could see I was in trouble. His aunt owned the cafe, and so he made a generous offer: "You are welcome to eat for free here as often as you like for as long as you need!" The only condition was that I would meet with him so he could practice his English. Later that evening he turned up at my rented apartment with a solution for my accommodation. Azamat's friend Dauren was a soft-spoken man who worked in security at Tengiz-Chevroil's head office.[9] He had just bought a new apartment near the city center. "It's unfurnished, and you will be alone, but you are welcome to stay," he said.

In the coming weeks my friendship with Dauren and Azamat not only gave me immeasurable comfort and support but provided an absorbing insight into the multiple realities of Atyrau. On occasion Dauren invited me to visit him at work in Tengiz-Chevroil's headquarters. A modern office block fronted by immaculate green lawns ticking twenty-four hours a day with sprinklers, it was an environment far removed from the brutality of Kulsary. Opposite the headquarters lay a secure living compound for Western workers that boasted row upon row of two-story cottages complete with double garages. The only life on its dust-free streets appeared to be security guards and company vehicles shuffling workers safely to and from the compound. Through Dauren's contacts I was invited inside to spend an evening with a Canadian engineer and his family. Over dinner the sense of insulation from the outside world was complete. We sat at a table using knife and fork and dined on broccoli shipped frozen from Canada. Afterward we drank beer on the couch in front of a wide-screen TV. At one stage the engineer's son came tiptoeing down the stairs in his pajamas to ask about a problem with his homework.

Back at Dauren's office, the reality of the oil business was less masked. During my first visit, he was irritated and stressed. "They've just found a murder victim at one of the Tengiz accommodation villages . . . and there has been another terror threat against the compound here in the city," he complained.

Violence among Kazakh workers at Tengiz was an ongoing problem, and there were some elements within Kazakh society, particularly of the Muslim faith, who were ideologically opposed to Western companies working on Kazakh soil. Kazakh security guards working outside the gates of the Atyrau compound were frequently threatened for working for the Americans and sometimes warned of potential bomb attacks.

Although Dauren worked in the oil industry, he was nevertheless sympathetic to many of the concerns of his fellow countrymen. "The oil industry is destroying our natural environment," he told me. "Bribes are paid to government agencies to cover up bad practices. The air is so bad at Tengiz that westerners are not given permission to work there for more than a year before they are sent home . . . but Kazakh workers stay there for years on end."

His views about President Nazarbayev and the looming election were equally cynical. "Nazarbayev considers himself the father of Kazakhstan. His political party is the Kazakhstan brand. The only true opposition is in exile in London, and Nazarbayev has a monopoly on the media. Yes, we will have a democratic election . . . but do you think that the government doesn't take note of which party people vote for? Anyone working for the state who chooses to vote for the opposition will lose their job."

When the election was over, Nazarbayev would prove to have won around 99 percent of the vote. Given this iron grip on power and his popularity, I wondered why he had bothered spending so many millions campaigning.

⊞

AFTER MORE THAN five weeks in Atyrau, I had a greater understanding of this urban society, but I had little to celebrate in terms of a breakthrough for crossing into Russia. With two weeks left on my Kazakh visa, a permit had been faxed through from Moscow but was quickly followed by a qualifying phone call from the border: "If Australian Tim Cope arrives on horseback we will turn him back. The permit only allows him to transport his horses and dog by truck or train through Russia."

My only success in Atyrau had been to convince the head of customs for western Kazakhstan to guarantee smooth passage out of the country. Technically, to send Kazakh horses abroad required a wild-animal export license, but to overcome this he had ordered his assistant to classify my horses as "house pets."

Now, with just five days remaining on my Kazakh visa, I lay on the floor of Dauren's apartment with the small of my back knotted up. It was Wednesday, December 7, my twenty-seventh birthday, and I felt more like sixty.

If, by the end of the working week, Moscow hadn't issued a new permit specifically allowing me to *ride* horses across the border and through Russia, then all hope was lost. I would have to give away my animals, but I didn't have the money to buy new horses in Russia. It was surely the end of my journey.

Friday, December 9, permit or no, would be my last day at the agricultural ministry. Like every day, I was there starting at eight in the morning, on the fax and the phone. By lunchtime there was no permit and my frustration was boiling over. I refused to let Kosibek's secretary leave on her lunch break. "Please, let's just call Moscow one last time," I begged. "If we don't get it now, then we will never get it."

She looked at me with a small smile, trying to keep the tears out of her eyes. Like everyone else in the office—which was labeled, in English, "Exsperts Room"—she had battled my problem every day for six weeks. Everyone from Kosibek down had given it their all.

"Tim, I'm sorry, we have done everything we can."

I reluctantly exited the office, and she locked the door on her way out to lunch.

I had a miserable last meal at Azamat's aunt's café. Azamat had remained upbeat and believed I would get the permit somehow, and now I had to disappoint him. The many meals his aunt had provided me had all been in vain. I called Muftagali in Kuegen and explained we would need to find new owners for the horses. Then I spoke with Dauren and promised to be moved out within a day.

Finally I made my way back to the ministry. I needed to say goodbye to Kosibek and the other staff who had put their hearts into helping me.

As I reentered the building I noticed something odd. Lunch hour was not yet finished, but the door to the "Exsperts Room" was ajar. I pushed it open, and there, looking pale and sunken, was Kosibek's secretary. She looked up at me, and though there were tears in my eyes, I approached to console her. She whispered something.

"What?" I asked.

"I got it." She held up a fresh fax in her trembling fingers: *This is to certify that in addition to the permit of the 29th of November Australian traveler Tim Cope can transport his three horses by riding them. His one dog can be carried by its four legs.*

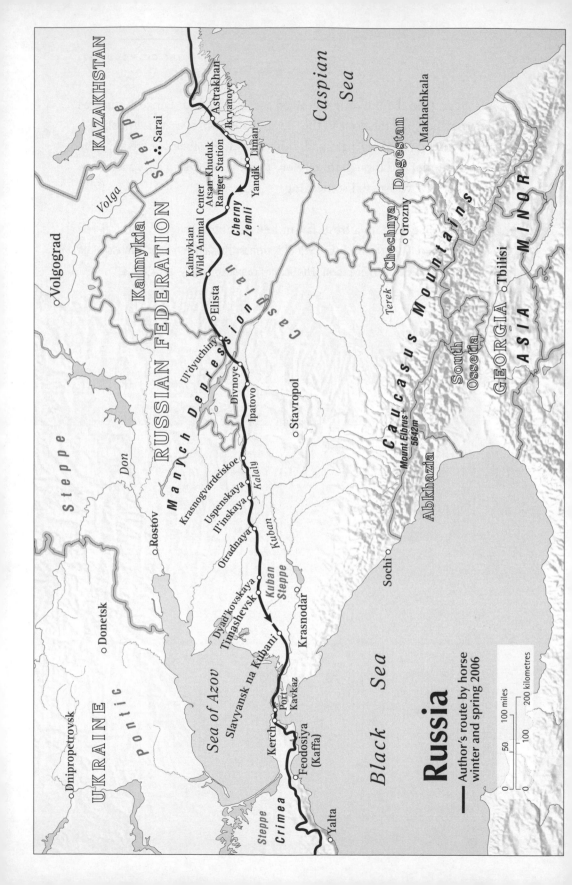

KAZAKHSTAN

Steppe

Volga

Sarai

Astrakhan

Ikryanoye

Liman

Yandik

Atsan Khuduk
Ranger Station

Kalmykian
Wild Animal Center

*Cherny
Zemli*

*Caspian
Sea*

Makhachkala

Dagestan

KALMYKIA

RUSSIAN FEDERATION

Volgograd

Elista

Ul'dyuchiny

Manych Depression

Caspian Depression

Divnoye

Ipatovo

Stavropol

Terek

Chechnya
Grozny

Caucasus Mountains

South
Ossetia

GEORGIA
Tbilisi

ASIA MINOR

Mount Elbrus +
5642m

ABKHAZIA

Steppe

Don

Rostov

Krasnogvardeiskoe

Uspenskaya

Il'inskaya

Kalaly

Otradnaya

Kuban

*Kuban
Steppe*

Krasnodar

Sochi

Pontic

UKRAINE

Dnipropetrovsk

Donetsk

Dyad'kovskaya

Timashevsk

Slavyansk na Kubani

Sea of Azov

Port
Kavkaz

Kerch

Feodosiya
(Kaffa)

*Steppe
Crimea*

Yalta

*Black
Sea*

Russia

— Author's route by horse
winter and spring 2006

50   100 miles
0
0   100   200 kilometres

16

LOST HORDES IN EUROPE

When in the steppe I stand alone
With far horizons clear to view,
Ambrosia on the breezes blown
And skies above me crystal blue,
I sense my own true human height
And in eternity delight.

The obstacles to all my dreams
Now shrink, appear absurd, inept,
And nothing either is or seems
Except myself, these birds, this steppe . . .
What joy it is to feel all round
Wide open space that knows no bound!

—Unknown Kalmyk poet

ON A BLUSTERY morning, when sleet and snow clogged the air and wind careened across the freezing waters of the Volga delta, I found myself once again at the Kazakh border post. The same workers who had given me such a hard time on the way back from my failed crossing were on duty.

"You cannot export the horses—you do not have the necessary permit. These are commercial export!" the official in charge told me.

I'd anticipated this and had a plan. I used the public phone booth to call the head of customs in Atyrau, who was waiting and ready. No sooner had I replaced the handset than the official in charge at the border post took a call and turned pale. Shortly he came cowering apologetically: "Don't worry, everything will be done."

Later that evening, with just a matter of hours remaining on my Kazakh visa, I rode through and made camp in no-man's-land. Come morning the visa had expired and there was no way back.

This time around the Russian officials proved friendlier than their Kazakh counterparts, and within a couple of hours I sailed under the boom gate into freedom. Tigon led the way, chest puffed out, tugging hard on his lead, tail pointed high "like a pistol," as the guards joked.

Once through, I refrained from looking over my shoulder and covered as much distance as possible before dark. Only from the safety of camp did I dare pull out my satellite phone to break the news to my family. It was the thirteenth of December, my father's fifty-fifth birthday, and I could claim to be inside Russia.

For the next couple of days I was paranoid about still being within the web of influence of the border officials, and so I kept up a brisk pace. I seldom stopped during the day and hid my camp at night. It was only after I had crossed a few channels of the Volga that I began to relax. Liberated from the impasse, it was a luxury not only to be with my family of animals but to once again lift my sights to new horizons.

In the scheme of my overall journey, the Kazakh-Russian border was just the second of four international borders to be navigated on the way to the Danube, but it was a milestone greater than all the others. With time I would come to see that the Kazakh-Russian border demarcated two

Ruslan descends from a peak in the Altai Mountains of Eastern Kazakhstan—the starting point for my year-long crossing of the country to the Volga delta on the Caspian Sea.

Nurkhan (far left) on newly purchased Taskonir, Ruslan (second from left) on Ogonyok, and friends, not far from Pugachevo, Eastern Kazakhstan.

Aset with his disabled son, Guanz, who is trying out my Australian saddle on Taskonir. Zhana Zhol, Eastern Kazakhstan.

Aset's mother-in-law—witness to the collectivization of Kazakh nomads and survivor of the resulting famine, believed to have wiped out 1.7-2.2 million Kazakhs between 1930 and 1933.

Aset leads off into a brewing *buran* (winter storm) a day before we took shelter in Kindikti, with a young Tigon in tow.

(Left) Tigon's first winter—he was desperate to get his paws off the snow. (Right) Bakgetbek, our host in Kindikti, is an Oralman—an expatriate Kazakh born in the Xinjiang Province in China—whose family has since returned to Kazakhstan.

Aul of Kindikti, Eastern Kazakhstan.

The barren land along the north of Lake Balkhash. No snow, but freezing conditions.

Portrait of a Kazakh *chaban* (herder) near Ayagoz.

The *chaban* Bazibek and his camel near Ortaderesin, Lake Balkhash.

Lonely Kazakh grave on the north shore of Lake Balkhash—the kind that Aset advised me to sleep in so that the "old men" of the steppe would protect me.

Riding out onto the Betpak Dala (the Starving Steppe). I'm riding Zhamba, with Ogonyok and Taskonir in tow.

Self-portrait on the Betpak Dala, two days before Christmas. Temperature was dropping below –22°F.

Getting porridge cooking in camp on the Betpak Dala. Tigon is out of sight, curled up in my sleeping bag.

The grim gold-mining town of Akbakai on the Betpak Dala, where I was forced to hole up for the better part of three months.

Grisha and Vitka, the Russian alcholics who took me in on Christmas Eve 2004 in Akbakai.

Baitak—the man to whom I owe the lives of my horses and Tigon, and the journey itself.

Spring has arrived. Children hold some freshly picked tulips next to their woolly camel near Tasty on the Chu River, Kazakhstan.

Taskonir shares my oatmeal porridge in one of my first camps on the Syr Darya River. Note the green spring grass.

A Kazakh woman from the family in Zhuantobe that nursed Tigon back to health after his run-in with a car.

Chilikti, a typical aul of adobe huts, a few days ride north of the Aral Sea.

After a long night ride I take refuge from the heat on the floor of a family's mud-hut, somewhere north of the Aral Sea.

Tigon and I often took naps during my night-riding routine. Here on the banks of the Zhem River, there is fortunately some shade to be found.

I film Murat Guanshbai's vast herd of camels being herded across the Zhem River.

A nomad greeting not far shy of Kulsary, Western Kazakhstan. In this region, people traditionally take cover in underground homes in the daytime heat and sleep in their yurts at night.

Bulat—the Karakalpak herder-for-hire—at the ranch near Kulsary where I fell ill with food poisoning.

Nomad child amid the camel herd.

broadly different cultural spheres of the Eurasian steppe—and therefore split the experience of my journey into two distinct halves.

In the east were Mongolia and Kazakhstan—both countries deeply affected by the Soviet era and, before that, the Russian Empire (Kazakhstan to a much larger degree), but nonetheless self-ruling, sovereign nations where nomadic culture remained predominant. Even Kazakhs and Mongols who lived in cities were only a couple of generations at most removed from the saddle.

In the western portion of the steppe, from the Russian border to the Danube, the nomadic way of life had long since faded out. Hungarians had abandoned their nomadic way of life even before the Mongols' appearance in the thirteenth century, and the so-called Pontic and Caspian steppes—encompassing the grasslands stretching from the Volga to north of the Black Sea—which had been a historical stronghold of nomad culture and a key to Mongol rule in Europe, had been subjugated long ago by the Russian Empire and was now incorporated into modern Russia and Ukraine. The many steppe peoples that lay ahead of me, including Kalmyks, Cossacks, Crimean Tatars, and even the Hutsuls of the Carpathians, formed ethnic minorities with only limited autonomy. Most of them had been singled out under Stalin, and some had shared the experience of mass deportation to Siberia and Central Asia. In post-Soviet times they were experiencing cultural revival—in the Crimean Tatars' case, return from exile—and their lands were in varying states of stability.

The first of these formerly nomadic nations was one I had anticipated with particular intrigue. The Caspian steppe, which has at its heart the rich pasturelands of the lower Volga, had once been ruled by the Kalmyks, an ethnically Mongol people of the Oirat confederation of tribes, whose arrival in the region in the early seventeenth century heralded the last migration of a nomadic people from Asia to Europe. In 1771 there had been a catastrophic attempt by Kalmyks to flee en masse back to Mongolia to escape oppression under the Russian Empire. Almost two-thirds of those who set out had perished on the very Kazakh steppes through which I had ridden in the last twelve months.

The first I had known about the Kalmyks came from Oirat Mongols in western Mongolia who had claimed to be descended from Kalmyks who survived the exodus. "Thousands of kilometres from here in Russia near the Caspian Sea, you will meet our relatives who never came back. They are our Mongol brothers and sisters, and they are still stuck in Europe," they had told me.

What remained of the once powerful Kalmyk khanate was a small, semi-autonomous republic known as Kalmykia, situated to the west of the Volga River and nowadays renowned as the only Buddhist republic in geographical Europe. Legend had it that Kalmyks there were descendants of those unable to cross the partially frozen Volga in the mild winter of 1770–71.[1] Whether coincidence or not, the name *Kalmyk* originates from a Turkic root word that roughly means "to remain." I'd been waiting to lay eyes on the fabled steppe of Kalmykia for what seemed an eternity, but even now, when it lay less than two weeks of travel in front of me, it was premature to set my sights on it. Before reaching the Kalmyk steppe, I first needed to cross through the labyrinth of bridges and towns that are dotted along the braided channels of the Volga River delta.

Crossing the main channel in particular proved difficult. The only bridge lay smack in the middle of Astrakhan, a Russian outpost city founded in the sixteenth century by Ivan the Terrible. The historic fortress walls that are still a feature of the old city center served as a reminder that for centuries it had come under attack by nomadic horsemen. In the modern era, though, Astrakhan was a bustling metropolis of more than half a million, and on horseback it was my turn to be terrorized. A marathon day saw us weaving a dangerous path through a sea of trucks, trams, and cars. At times when we were forced onto narrow sidewalks, there were hordes of pedestrians and lethal, ill-fitting manhole covers to deal with.

Upon reaching the far side of the city after dark, my horses were so spooked that no sooner had I dismounted to make camp than they bolted, still packed and saddled. I was left with nothing but my thermos, video camera, and satellite phone.

Local police and emergency services came to my aid, but after a fruitless all-night search we retired empty-handed to the police station. It was only due to the intuition of a policeman of Kazakh descent that my journey was rescued. At 6:00 A.M. I was awakened by shouting and opened my eyes to see him leaning over me, his machine gun slung over his shoulder. "Wake up! You have to get in the car! I have had a dream that I went fishing and caught three fish—a brown, a gray, and a red one, the same color as your horses. I just know we are going to find your horses this time!"

An hour later we came across a long trail of equipment leading to my horses. It was a remarkable sight as the policeman, machine gun and all, strode over to Ogonyok and planted a kiss on his nose.

AFTER PULLING MY caravan back together I spent a week riding from Astrakhan south along the banks of the Volga through a tangle of fishing villages. When the Volga's waters began to freeze I crossed the last bridge and turned west, leaving the web of roads, towns, bridges, and traffic behind.

I was now on the western fringes of the Volga delta, and as I rode through a landscape of marshes, lakes, and broad flanks of open pastureland, my thoughts returned to the Kalmyks. It was precisely this combination of reed beds, open land, and low-lying pastures irrigated by spring overflow that had drawn the Kalmyks' forefathers to the Caspian steppe. Those early pioneers had been war-hardened Oirat Mongols, who, like waves of nomads before them, had been prompted by conflict in their Inner Asian homeland to pick up and ride out across the steppe in search of new beginnings.

More specifically, the powerful empire ruled by the Oirats, known as Zhungaria, had begun to decline by the turn of the seventeenth century, and one Oirat tribe, the Torghuts, had sent scouts west to locate a refuge for their people.[2] As early as 1608, encampments on the vanguard of this mass migration were spotted along the Zhem River. By the 1640s Kalmyks had driven out the nomadic Nogais from the Caspian steppe and established their own khanate, the center of which was located around the Lower Volga.[3] In Zhungaria their Oirat brethren would mount a resurgence and hold power until the mid-eighteenth century, but the Oirats who had migrated to the Caspian steppe generally became known as the Kalmyks.

For the better part of the next century the Kalmyks utilized the unique river ecology and pasturelands of the Caspian steppe and more or less lived by the traditional nomadic patterns that had long defined life in the region. They lived in yurts, roamed seasonally with their livestock, and indulged in the age-old nomad pastime of raiding their neighbors. Horse rustling and slave trading were important parts of the Kalmyk economy, and Russian captives in particular could be sold at lucrative prices in the markets of Khiva, or returned to Russia for ransom. Unable to pacify or control the Kalmyks, the Russian tsar took advantage of their fearsome cavalry skills, hiring them to defend Russia against the Ottoman Empire.[4]

By the mid-eighteenth century the Kalmyks' fortunes had well and truly turned. For thousands of years, nomads had enjoyed military dominance as horseback archers of unmatched prowess, but the Kalmyks had arrived on the Caspian steppe at a time when the advent of cannons and muskets was eroding this supremacy. More generally, the seventeenth and eighteenth centuries were an era that marked the demise of nomads and the emergence of powerful sedentary societies on the fringes of the Eurasian steppe—namely, those of China and Russia.

As Russia's might grew, the tsar's demands on the Kalmyk cavalry's services increased, and southward colonization pushed into the lush pastures of the lower Volga. Traditional Kalmyk grazing lands were turned into hayfields and put to the plow, driving the Kalmyks to less fertile steppe. By 1740 the number of livestock kept by the Kalmyks had declined dramatically, and around ten thousand Kalmyk "tents" (families) were without enough animals for subsistence. To survive, Kalmyks resorted to more frequent raids, sold their children as slaves, and even took up fishing.

It was these oppressive conditions that, in 1771, gave rise to the exodus of Kalmyks back to their roots in Asia—after which the Kalmyk khanate was all but absorbed by the Russian Empire.

More than two centuries on, in January 2006, it was hard to imagine that very much remained of this once fiercely reputed people—particularly because the descendants of those who stayed behind at the time of the exodus had since been deported en masse to Siberia by Stalin during World War II. And yet, as I approached the modern border of Kalmykia, there were signs suggesting that the pattern of tension and conflict between Kalmyks and their neighbors was an ongoing one.

It was late on New Year's Day when I reached Liman, a sleepy village on the very edge of the Volga delta where marked roads came to an end and a series of marshes and lakes gave way to wild, waterless steppe. This kind of unique intersection of environments had no doubt been a pillar of the local nomadic economy, but it also had long attracted settling farmers, and nowadays lay outside Kalmyk territory.

Through my friend Anna Lushchekina, a local Russian man, Anatoliy Khludnev, had agreed to guide me through the Stepnoi nature reserve to Kalmykia itself. Anatoliy, a retired lieutenant colonel who nowadays worked as the director of the reserve, was quick to point out the issues of his region: "The land here has long been disputed between Kalmykia and Astrakhan Oblast, and there is still no agreement as to where the official border lies."

Still, the border dispute was trivial in the scheme of things. A wider problem, or at least the issue of the day, was the friction between Kalmyks and the growing Chechen population. "Chechens who are fleeing their own country on resettlement programs are taking over. They are the new settlers of the Kalmyk steppe," Anatoliy complained.

Racked by conflict and unemployment, Chechnya lay little more than 100 km from Kalmykia's southern border. In the past decade thousands had migrated here seeking work and a safer life. According to Anatoliy, their presence had scared many Russians into moving out of the area. "It's not too bad for us, I guess, though," he reflected. "We have all of Russia to go to if we want. The Kalmyks, on the other hand, have little elsewhere if they want to be among their own. I don't blame them for getting into conflict with the Chechens."

Anatoliy may well have been projecting some of the prevailing preju-dices against Chechens, but violence between Chechen migrants and Kalmyks in the area had recently made headlines. In August, in the village of Yandik, not far from Liman, a Kalmyk girl had been shot dead by Chechens. In retaliation a crowd of five hundred mourning Kalmyks re-turning from the funeral had rioted through the village, torching homes and forcing the Chechens to flee. The situation had threatened to spread into a wider ethnic conflict until the Russian army was brought in to ease tensions. The peacekeeping force had rolled out a week before my arrival.

Things had apparently settled down for the time being, and the plan was for Anatoliy to escort me from Liman through Yandik, then across 70 km of wild steppe known as Cherny Zemli, or "Black Lands," that straddle the disputed border region.[5] Anatoliy explained that he would lead the way in the patrol vehicle and stand guard at night. He would take his gun in case we ran into wolves or poachers.

On a freezing morning when curtains of light snow raked the land I packed a week's supply of food and set off out of town. Half an hour later there was a distinct air of unease as I followed Anatoliy through Yandik. Many houses lay in burned ruins, the streets were largely deserted, and those people I did see peeked out shyly from half-opened doorways. At the far end of the village I rode past the cemetery, pausing briefly by the fresh grave of the murdered Kalmyk girl.

For three days from Yandik I followed Anatoliy through a landscape of wild, frostbitten grasslands. Our route followed a centuries-old trail once used by merchants to ferry fish from the Volga across the steppes to more temperate Stavropol. By day Anatoliy told tales about the grueling journeys of these merchants, who had come under constant attack from Kalmyk brigands. By night, as the temperature plummeted to around −20°C, Anatoliy was less cheerful. He tried to sleep in his vehicle but was forced to repeatedly restart the engine to keep warm.

The only people we met along the way were a couple of old shepherds who worked for a Chechen sheep farmer.[6] One of them was a Volga Tatar who had spent the best part of his days in prison. In colorful language he warned me about the dangers of Kalmyks, and told a running joke: "What could possibly be worse than a drunk Kalmyk? Only a drunk Kalmyk woman, of course!"

On our third morning we entered the nature reserve. The sun was creeping into a solid blue sky, sending an orange light angling across a still sea of pale, bleached grass. It was the seventh of January, and although there was no snow cover, evidence of winter could be seen in the form of frozen shallow ponds that sparkled like silvery discs embedded in the land.

As frost gathered around my sheepskin hat and the horses moved briskly across the frozen sandy soil, I couldn't help but think it might have been a morning like this on January 5, 1771, when the Kalmyks had embarked on their exodus back to their origins in Zhungaria. On that day Ubashi Khan, the Kalmyks' young leader, had set out east from the Volga to lead an estimated thirty thousand nomad families, somewhere between 150,000 and 200,000 individuals, with their untold camel caravans and probably more than a million head of livestock.[7]

For those who departed, it was the beginning of an epic journey that would prove to be a tragedy of extraordinary scale. Traveling a route similar to the reverse of the one I had followed across the Kazakh steppe, they had to deal with the inherent environmental challenges, compounded by attacks waged by Kazakhs who took the opportunity to settle old scores. When finally the Kalmyks arrived on the Ili River in what is today Xinjiang province in China, around a hundred thousand men, women, and children—as many as 75 percent of those who had started off—had perished.

For those Kalmyks who survived, dreams of refuge in Zhungaria were swiftly quashed. Little more than a decade earlier, the Qing dynasty had embarked on a campaign to exterminate the Oirats, with some historians suggesting that as little as 7 percent of the population had survived. Ubashi and his people were dispersed throughout Xinjiang, and in the words of historian Michael Khodarkovsky, "the Kalmyks had escaped Russian tentacles only to be ensnared in Chinese ones."

AT AN ABANDONED hut we had a late lunch and decided to part ways. We had, by now, crossed an invisible line into Kalmykia, and besides, Anatoliy was short on fuel.

"See this trail here?" Anatoliy said, pointing to a vague line of ruts and hollows that was more sketch than road. "If you follow it and keep your compass between 270 and 290 degrees, then you should come to a hut called Atsan Khuduk—it's manned, and the caretaker there should be expecting you."

After watching his four-wheel-drive vehicle shrink back the way we had come, I sat still in the saddle long enough for the sound of the engine to peter out and a sense of aloneness to bite. When I turned and pulled away, silence was replaced by the swishing of sixteen legs—Tigon included—brushing through frozen grass.

For the next three hours I rode with urgency, wanting to reach the hut as soon as possible. The sun sank into a smudge of black cloud, the shape and texture of the land faded into pastel grays, and the cold drew in like a noose. I called Tigon in close and kept an eye on my compass. When the moon rose, and my caravan cast dim shadows across the frosted grass, my transition to an older world felt complete. I slowed to a walk, snuggled deep into my winter coat, and opened the bell on Taskonir's neck—something I always did at night in case the horses broke free (so I would be able to hear where they had gone) and in this case, also because it as was an old steppe tradition along courier and trading routes to have a horsebell to warn rest stations of the approach of a horseman. After traveling nearly 40 km into the cold of evening, I was beginning to worry I had missed the hut, but around 11:00 P.M. three dark shapes emerged from the moonlit steppe. From one came the faint flicker of an oil lamp.

I was greeted by an old man reeking of vodka who introduced himself in Russian as the caretaker. Word hadn't reached Atsan Khuduk—a station for rangers and scientific researchers—about the special permission I had received to ride through the reserve, but it didn't worry him. I was led inside to a mattress, where my body withered, my vision blurred, and I collapsed into sleep.

Some time later I woke to another world. I heard banter and heavy footsteps and opened my eyes to a group of four or five men clambering into the hut, dusting off the frost from their army fatigue coats. The dull flicker from the lamp caught the profile of broad, chapped red cheeks with skin drawn taut over the bone. The men's eyes were long and slender, and when they spoke I was astonished to hear the familiar sounds of Mongolian.

I joined the group around a wooden table, where Mongolian salty milk tea was on the pour, and with the last remaining battery power in my laptop showed video footage of Oirat Mongols whom I had met in the far west of Mongolia fourteen months earlier. The men leaned in and listened intently:

"They speak a purer Oirat dialect than we do, and clearer than Oirats we have met from China! You know what we say about those who went back to Asia: 'Tasarsan makh'n, usersen tsus'n'—it translates to 'Split flesh and spilled blood' and means 'We are one people with you.' But how was Kazakhstan? What was it like to ride where our ancestors perished?"

As I sat there sharing stories about the steppe, with the salty tea warming my insides, it was as if Kazakhstan had merely been a bridge between these two disparate nomadic Mongolian societies. One could almost be convinced that these men were nomads who had just returned from a wolf hunt. Symbolic of modern-day Kalmykia, however, the men were Kalmyk scientists and rangers who had come back from a fox count as part of a biology study. One of them was the deputy director of the Cherny Zemli reserve, Boris Ubushaeva—a professor whom I would later see dressed in a suit and tie at a university in Kalmykia's capital, Elista. Impressed by my journey, he promised to take me out to see the very reason the reserve had been founded.

In the morning we left the hut when the sky was still dark and a residual glint of stars remained. It was an hour later, as we crested a subtle swell of sand, that the professor told me to crouch down. In the still conditions the faint twitching of a grass tussock had been enough to betray the presence of an animal, and as I focused closer a shaggy creature the same pale color of the grass darted away.

By the time the professor had handed me the binoculars a whole swath of grassland before us shimmered to life and a flock of these creatures lifted like startled sparrows. The animals possessed goat-sized bodies draped in a thick winter coat and were scuttling along on twig-like legs. They were saiga.

Since first learning about the saiga on the Betpak Dala in Kazakhstan, I had heard untold numbers of stories about these enigmatic antelopes of the Eurasian steppe, which could migrate hundreds of kilometres in a single day and which as recently as 1990 had numbered around 800,000. But the herds of the Cherny Zemli were the first I had seen on my travels. "We have around eighteen thousand saiga left on the Black Lands," the professor explained. "Our efforts to catch poachers are working, but saiga are nomadic, and when they leave the boundaries of our reserve we have no jurisdiction, and often they never return . . . In 1998, during a cold winter, around a hundred thousand saiga migrated south into the Republic of Dagestan, and only a few came back. They say that the snow in Dagestan was painted red by the slaughter."

A short way past my first sighting, we startled another herd, this time much closer to us. Not more than 100 m ahead stood a male saiga. His horns, set above bulbous eyes, struck me first. Backlit by the sun, they rose with a slight inward curve and a ribbed texture, looking like a set of glowing amber pincers. Below this spectacle hung a long curved nose that functioned to filter out dust and heat the winter air during inhalation. The head and trunk were so large and heavy-looking it seemed his matchstick legs might give way. So peculiar were the features that it was not hard to believe this was a surviving ice age species that had once coexisted alongside the likes of the mammoth and the saber-toothed tiger.

When the male and his herd sprinted away, I was left mesmerized, yet also aware of how the empty steppe that I had ridden through in the past twelve months had been lacking in saiga. I understood that the saiga's presence, like the magic of a horseman set against the sky, had been a quintessential part of steppe life.

Back in the hut, where we warmed up with more tea, the professor turned to me thoughtfully. "In the past we Kalmyks used to hunt saiga in our everyday lives. In fact, hunting saiga was how we honed our skills for battle. The key tactic for getting a saiga was to feign retreat, then lure the animals into an ambush—the very technique used so well by Genghis Khan. Ever since the exodus of our brothers back to Asia, however, it has been Kalmykia itself under ambush."

Like the saiga's once vast habitat, Kalmyk land had contracted to a small island of steppe where nomadic life was nearly impossible. Not only this, but Kalmyks had faced cultural extinction during World War II, when they were accused of sympathizing with the Nazis and deported to Siberia. More than a third had died in the cattle wagons en route, and, unprepared for the terrible conditions of the Siberian winter, thousands more had perished on arrival. In their absence the Republic of Kalmykia had been dissolved and Kalmyk livestock wiped out so comprehensively that the Kalmyk horse became virtually extinct and the fat-tailed sheep would never again graze the Kalmyk steppe.[8] It was only in 1957 that Kalmyks had been allowed to return from exile and had begun to rebuild a sense of their homeland.

A product of this turbulent history, the professor's life story mirrored that of untold thousands of his compatriots. He had been born in Siberia and studied at a university in the city, never having experienced or witnessed the traditional way of life of his ancestors. "We can no longer live as nomads, and for the saiga it's a similar story—they have been decimated and no longer run free across the steppes. Nevertheless, we have not lost everything and we know that the Kalmyk steppe without saiga would be like tea without milk—very poor indeed. To protect the saiga we need to preserve our culture, and draw on modern science as well as our heritage."

Over the coming days and weeks, the sentiments expressed by the professor were repeated by many Kalmyks I met. The plight of the saiga had become a metaphor for the fate of the nation. The efforts to bring the four-legged nomad back from the brink reflected a broader struggle to revive all facets of Kalmyk heritage and culture.

JUST THREE DAYS' ride beyond the wardens' hut, I had traversed half the territory of Kalmykia, yet in that time encountered just one Kalmyk family living out on the steppe—a former schoolteacher and his wife who had decided to try cattle and sheep farming for a living.

In a land so reduced in width, it was perhaps inevitable that like the modern-day culture of the Kalmyks, my journey through Kalmykia was destined to be more spiritual and academic than a physical one. Fifty kilometres shy of the capital, Elista, I was welcomed at the Kalmykian Wild Animal Center by a Kalmyk professor of biology, Yuri, who had been charged with the task of breeding saiga in captivity. Dr. Anna Lushchekina, who had flown from Moscow, was also there to meet me. She headed a UNESCO project, "Human and Biosphere," in the pre-Caspian region and was responsible for much of the effort to preserve the saiga. For the next week, Anna and Yuri became my chaperones, introducing me to the many faces of modern Kalmykia. With the horses resting at Yuri's farm, most of that time was spent in Elista, where I would come to understand that the revival of Kalmyk culture was being promoted not on the steppe by horseback nomads but from the urban environment of the capital.

From a distance Elista appeared like any other Soviet city—a drab series of dilapidated apartment blocks and ramshackle homes barnacled to the bare, snow-dusted slopes of a valley. Up close, however, the unique eastern identity was hard to miss.

The city's main park was dominated by a giant wooden archway decorated with impressions of saiga, wolves, and mounted horsemen gazing over the city. On the central square a statue of Lenin had been moved aside to make way for a Buddhist prayer wheel housed beneath a towering pagoda. On the street the Russian language seemed to be predominant, but there were places where only Kalmyk could be heard. A cheap Kalmyk eatery was one of these, where Kalmyks of all ages congregated to dine on nomad food including boortsog, Mongolian milk tea, and an assortment of mutton dishes.

These may have been rather anecdotal examples of ways in which Kalmyk culture was being reasserted, but as Anna guided me around it became clear they were signs of a wider groundswell of cultural reclamation driven by a dedicated and diverse group of individuals.

At the Kalmyk Institute of Humanitarian Studies I was introduced to a young Kalmyk woman, Kermen Batireva, who was writing her doctoral dissertation on traditional Kalmyk costume. She gave me a tour of a museum that displayed original Kalmyk yurts, horse tack, and Buddhist art. In the same institution where she studied I came to know the eighty-one-year-old librarian, Praskovi Erdnievni. Standing not much higher than her desk, this pint-sized woman had single-handedly been gathering written resources about the Kalmyks for more than fifty years. Her stories of lugging suitcases of books from as far afield as Moscow at a time when there were no paved roads to Elista and many of those who were returning from exile lived in tents were legendary. When she was unable to take books back to Elista, she had copied them by hand or on a typewriter.

There were many other individuals who, with characteristic pride and vigor, were pursuing one aspect or another of Kalmyk culture. Two in particular, however, came to take on particular significance for me.

Stepping out of his office in the newly opened monastery, known as the Golden Temple, Erdne Ombadykow did not look anything like what I had imagined. The fresh-faced thirty-three-year-old who wore a chic suit and tie and spoke English with an American accent was the supreme lama of the Kalmyks, recognized by the Dalai Lama as the reincarnation of the Buddhist saint Telo Rinpoche.

"My father was born here in Kalmykia, and my mother was born in a refugee camp in Yugoslavia, but I grew up in Philadelphia. I didn't see my homeland until I was nineteen years old," he said softly.

At the age of seven, Erdne had decided he wanted to become a monk. His parents supported his wishes and sent him to India, where he was to live and study in a monastery for thirteen years. It was in 1991, as part of a delegation with the Dalai Lama, that Erdne had first been to Kalmykia. The following year he returned to live in Elista, elected as the first supreme lama of the Kalmyks since the Bolshevik revolution.

"The task to revive Buddhism here was so challenging that in the first two years it drove me to despair. When the Communists destroyed the monasteries in Kalmykia, they didn't leave one brick at the site—everything was rooted out. When my people returned from exile in Siberia, we started from zero, both materially and culturally."

As I stood with Erdne on the top floor gazing down at a golden Buddha 9 m high, I could see that those early days were a far cry from the present.

The monastery, at 63 m tall, dominated the skyline just west of the city center and was now considered to be the largest in all of Europe. On December 1, 2004, little more than a year before I visited, the Dalai Lama had consecrated the building site—an old Soviet metal factory—and only a month before my arrival the temple had opened to the public.

I couldn't help thinking that the significance of this temple, and the thirty-three others across Kalmykia that Erdne had overseen the building of in recent years, went beyond a mere revival. Ever since the Kalmyks' arrival on the Caspian steppe, maintaining a connection with Tibet had symbolized self-determination in the shadow of the Russian Empire. In the early years a lama from Tibet had been sent to Kalmykia to be the spiritual leader, and until the mid-eighteenth century pilgrimages from Kalmykia to Tibet were common. These pilgrimages ended due to the increasing dangers of crossing through hostile Kazakh territory and control by Russian authorities who saw links to Tibet as a threat to their own supremacy. In the present day, Moscow was no doubt keeping a close eye on developments in Kalmykia. In a move that perhaps reflected suspicion about growing independence in Kalmykia and other republics of the Russian federation, Russian president Vladimir Putin had recently revoked the right for citizens to elect their provincial governor or president, bringing control of all republics directly under Moscow.

With Erdne I toured the monastery from top to bottom, marveling at the impressive construction. But by the time we had returned to Erdne's office it struck me that there was an absence of reference to the nomadic way of life. I pressed him on his thoughts.

"Just because the world is modernizing, it doesn't mean we should forget our past," he replied, "but it's also true that it's unrealistic to think we can return to being nomads." Because he had grown up without a connection to horses, the steppe, or a lifestyle of herding livestock, it was, perhaps, understandably difficult for him to identify with the nomad culture of his ancestors.

In a relatively luxurious house on the other side of the city, I met another Kalmyk who was perhaps equally as influential in reviving Kalmyk culture, but whose philosophy was strongly at odds with Erdne's. Okna

Tsahan Zam (who also used the Russian name Vladimir Karuev) greeted me in a deel and colorful Mongolian winter boots. His hair was trimmed to a crew cut halfway back along his skull, and at the back plaited into a ponytail that dangled as far as his bottom

"As Kalmykians, the earth is our mother, Gazar Eej; the sky is our father, Tengri Etseg; and traditionally, where it was good for horses, we lived, and where our animals went we followed. Buddhism is not our faith—it was introduced after we arrived on the Caspian—so we must look to our more ancient nomad heritage and belief in Tengri for strength and inspiration," he told.

Okna was a renowned musician and singer whose traditional songs about life on the steppe, combining throat singing with contemporary music, had topped the pop charts in Mongolia and captivated live audiences in Europe. But he hadn't always lived this way.

"I graduated in Moscow as a nuclear engineer and worked for years at a nuclear plant. In my twenties, I suffered a personal crisis. To heal myself I turned to my culture, and my heritage, and began reciting the prose of our national epic, Zhungar," he said. He opened a bottle of vodka, poured a shot, then dipped his ring finger in the liquid three times, rubbing a little on his forehead, sprinkling a bit over me, and throwing the rest in the air. "If people know their history, their traditions, they understand the value of experience that our people have collected over thousands of years. When we know who we are, our place in the world, and why we exist, we are happy and have a purpose in life!"

After the customary three shots, Okna offered to sing for me, and for the next half hour I sat engrossed by his deep, gravelly voice and the haunting otherworldly harmonics of throat singing.

As we made our goodbyes, he said to me, a little somberly, "I used to believe in politics, but I had a falling-out with the president. I am not happy here in Russia. Even now we Kalmyks are feeling the pressure, the suffocation of Moscow. It's time for another mass exodus, which I will lead . . . What do you think—maybe Australia next time?" he chuckled. "Anyway, may the sun always shine on your horses."

When my week in Elista was over I returned to the Kalmykian Wild

Animal Center, where the city gave way to empty, snow-blanketed steppe, but my mind continued to churn with the color and intensity of all I had witnessed. I'd swum in euphoria at the thought that Kalmyks were meshing the realities of modern life with wisdom from the past. The passion of the people I had met made me reflect that Kalmyks seemed to be more conscious of the value of their heritage than Mongolian nomads, who still lived the very traditional lives that Kalmyks pined for. But I wondered: was the romantic, nostalgic view of nomadic life held by many Kalmyks possible only for a people who were an educated, urbanized generation removed from the horse and the yurt? How far could the revival go in this modern world?

In a vast fenced enclosure at the saiga farm I spent a day battling snow and wind to film the saiga that roamed within. They came to feed at special troughs and kept a wary eye on me at all times. At one stage saiga were caught and hustled into a barn for blood sampling. Under Yuri's supervision, the blood was put into test tubes, spun on centrifuges, and whisked away.

It occurred to me that, like the saiga at the Wild Animal Center, Kalmyk culture was fenced in and under the microscope of intellectuals. This guaranteed preservation, but how would it be for future generations of Kalmyks who would be born, like these saiga, into relative captivity?

THE SEASON'S FIRST blizzards had only just begun to set in, but the saiga farm was destined to mark the end of my winter ride. Unfortunately, the six-week delay on the border meant I had just days remaining on my Russian visa—not nearly enough to cross southern Russia to its borders on the Azov and Black Sea. I had no option but to leave the horses behind and travel to Ukraine to apply for a new visa.

Yuri, who had a hardened team of workers at the saiga farm, was eternally helpful. On the condition I pay for hay and grain, he offered to put the horses under the watch of his workers for the time I was away. So on January 17 I boarded a Crimea-bound bus, waved goodbye to Anna and Yuri, and promised to return within a month.

17

COSSACK BORDERLANDS

On a freezing evening in early March 2006 I was back on the horses and riding into a headwind with a Kalmyk man named Anir. Reawakening to life in the saddle after the winter break, I was acutely aware of the fine mist particles turning my cheeks numb and the sound of long, brittle grass fracturing beneath the horses' hooves. We had departed the Kalmykian Wild Animal Center three days earlier and, just as it had been during the first few days of spring in Kazakhstan a year earlier, my body felt a little stiff, the horses were wound up, and I was seeing the land afresh.

Framed between Taskonir's ears, the ridge we'd been following for most of the day angled southwest, turreted every so often with the silhouetted domes of ancient kurgans, mounds of earth and stones raised over graves that probably dated back to Scythian nomads.[1] Further on, the ridge gave way to empty plains where the sun was nestling into a golden haze. Empty and uncluttered, it was the kind of vista that could easily be mistaken for the steppe of central Mongolia, where I had begun two years ago. In fact, it was the kind of landscape that had defined most days of the journey since. It was difficult to imagine, then, that within the next twenty-four hours, it would pass behind.

Not long before descending from the ridge, Anir took me to a lone tree. Covered in prayer flags and ribbons, it had been planted on the grave of a lama. Following Anir, I led the horses around it in a clockwise fashion three times. Anir threw vodka into the air. "You might think the hardest part of the journey is behind you, but it is only beginning. Ahead are towns, fields, and roads—down there not even a wolf would find cover, and I don't know where you will camp. This is for good luck."

Forty kilometres ahead lay the Manych Depression, a system of rivers and lakes that in ancient times connected the Sea of Azov with the Caspian Sea. A historical crossroads of Asia Minor and Europe, it nowadays forms the southern border of Kalmykia and the northern reaches of Stavropol Krai that lie in the forelands of the Caucasus.

Significantly for me, the Manych represented the end of the arid and somewhat wild belt of steppe that stretches from Mongolia to Kalmykia. Beyond the Manych I could expect arable and more populated steppe.

The immediate leg of my journey lay along a corridor between the restive Caucasus and the uplands of southern Russia. Stretching west beyond the Manych as far as the Azov Sea, it once was a highly sought-after nomad hinterland that the Russian Empire had since fought hard for and plowed up under Stalin.

From the holy tree we pushed beyond darkness. Our aim was to reach Stavropol Krai, from where Anir would return home. To get there involved crossing the Manych via an artificial embankment controlled by a police checkpoint. In theory, this should have been a rudimentary procedure. In practice, things had become complicated in recent times.

On my return to Russia in late February, I had learned that Kok, my hardy gray packhorse from central Kazakhstan, had stepped on a 12 cm rusty nail that lodged deep into his hoof. It had gone unnoticed for many days before being removed. When I arrived he was sitting on his haunches, unable to stand on the injured limb. Sheila in Australia advised me that if the infection had reached the bone, he would probably never recover; if he did, it might take six months. I treated him for two weeks to no avail before deciding to leave him behind.

Losing Kok not only meant I needed to find a new packhorse but also complicated the fine line I had to tread with the Russian veterinary and quarantine authorities. Technically I had to remain in transit with the Kazakh horses and have them inspected in every province en route. Recently I had also learned that officially stationing my horses at the Wild Animal Center over winter required the center to apply for a permit—something neither the director of the center, Yuri, nor myself had been aware of. Even so, the fate of Kok might have been easily explained to authorities but for one further complication—the head of the provincial veterinary authorities in Elista apparently held a grudge against Yuri and had heard on the winds that Yuri was harboring my horses. In my absence, inspectors had visited the center but Yuri had managed in the nick of time to have the horses ridden away and hidden; he told the inspectors I had passed through in the winter, had long exited Kalmykia, and never stopped at the center. If the truth was discovered, the ramifications for Yuri could be significant, and so to help me get out of Kalmykia unnoticed he had agreed to supply a replacement horse—a fine-featured chestnut gelding I had named Utebai. Utebai would travel on the existing papers of the fallen Kok.

At around 11:00 P.M. we rendezvoused with Yuri by the edge of the still-frozen waters of the Manych. He had transported Utebai in the back of a truck, and now he opened the back gate. Already terrified by the ride, poor Utebai nearly fell out before we slapped a packsaddle on him and got under way.

Yuri had earlier made an audacious plan to guide me below the embankment out of sight of police, but the tangle of crushed-up ice pushed up against the edge made this impossible. There was nothing we could do but try riding straight through.

As I approached the boom gate under the glare of floodlights an armed policeman strode into the middle of the road. I came to a halt at the point where I was looking directly down at him, then offered a handshake. There was a moment of silence as the cold, unblinking man looked on. At this crossing in particular, Yuri had warned, they routinely checked the transit papers of live animals, particularly because of the prevalence of rustling.

Gradually, however, the policeman's face melted into a smile.

"Hello, Genghis Khan! Welcome!"

WHEN DAWN BROKE Anir and Yuri had gone, and like my new horse, I watched nervously as the sun illuminated a new world.

Somewhere during our crossing in the night, the unbridled steppe had given way to fields, canals, and endless lines of poplar trees. I rode through lingering mist on the outskirts of the town of Divnoye, passing residents emerging to till their backyard plots. Out in the larger fields a horse and cart rattled its way along a lane, and an old Soviet tractor pushed through plowed earth. They were scenes reminiscent of an ancient cradle of agrarian society, yet the history of the area belied this picture of settled life.

For most of the last few thousand years the land that stretched ahead to the Azov Sea had been rich, open grasslands, home to nomadic societies. Wave after wave of horseback peoples who inhabited the region had benefited from trade and from close cultural and political ties with their northerly Slavic neighbors. History, however—Russian history in particular—has overwhelmingly remembered them for using the strategic nature of their territory to exploit the southern underbelly of Slavic lands. Violent raids, which often involved taking Slavic peasants into slavery, had in part led to Russia's obsession in recent centuries with subduing the region.

The pattern of nomads penetrating Slavic lands from the south was no better demonstrated than by the Mongols when they made their first appearance on European soil in 1223. What has since become known as one of the most remarkable military campaigns in history—and which ended with the humiliation of Russia's armies—began as nothing more than a manhunt. Following the Mongol defeat of the Khwarezm Empire in Central Asia, Genghis Khan had sent twenty thousand soldiers under the guidance of generals Jebe and Subodei to hunt down the deposed Khwarezm leader, Muhammad II. I have recounted this episode earlier, but after pursuing him west to the Caspian Sea, where he died, the generals were granted permission from Genghis to return to Central Asia via the Caucasus along the north Caspian coast. There began their foray into Europe.

After conquering armies twice their size en route and plundering vast regions of Iraq-Ajemi, Azerbaijan, and Georgia, this roving band of hardened nomad warriors crossed the high passes of the Caucasus and rode down onto the steppe between the Caspian Sea and the Azov Sea. At the time the region was under the rule of nomads known as Kipchaks—a powerful Turkic people who at times held sway from Siberia and Central Asia to the Balkans, and who would feature prominently in the expansion of the Mongol Empire. After persuading the Kipchaks to honor the brotherhood between Mongols and Turks, Jebe and Subodei turned on them and pursued their fleeing armies northwest into Slavic lands.

Although the Kipchaks were not allies of the Russians, one of the Kipchak khans, Kotian, was the father-in-law of Prince Mstislav of Galich—the ruler of one of the most important princedoms of Russia. Afraid that if the Mongols conquered the Kipchak Empire they would invade his own land, Mstislav enlisted the support of several princedoms, including powerful Kiev (whose prince was also named Mstislav), to fight the Mongols.

In an attempt to halt the Mongol advance, a Russian army of around thirty thousand was assembled on the banks of the Dnieper River. The Mongols melted away into retreat in what must have appeared as a sign of capitulation but which was a classic nomad tactic—the likes of which Herodotus had described more than a thousand years earlier. Lured into a sustained pursuit for nine days, the Russians were weakened by the rigors of travel and taken far beyond their borders. When Mstislav of Galich became overconfident and crossed the Little Kalka River ahead of the main Russian army, the Mongols seized their chance.

Prince Mstislav of Kiev could only look on as the Mongols turned on Mstislav of Galich's soldiers, who were no match for the Mongols in the open, marshy terrain. Realizing that retreat for his own army would be fatal, Mstislav of Kiev fortified himself on a hill and offered surrender on the grounds that his army be allowed to return home. When their weapons were put down, however, the army was slaughtered, and the bodies of Mstislav of Kiev and his fellow princes were crushed beneath planks of wood upon which the Mongols feasted and celebrated victory.

Little more than a decade later the Mongols, under Subodei, would return to subjugate Russia in its entirety and use the Pontic and Caspian steppes (also simply known as the Pontic-Caspian steppe) as a base from which the Golden Horde would rule over Russia for 240 years.[2] After this initial invasion, however—a sort of reconnaissance sojourn—the Mongols retreated as abruptly as they had appeared. Riding east via the Caspian and Aral Seas through what is modern-day Kazakhstan, they rejoined the main Mongol army in 1224. In a paltry two or three years the small, disciplined detachment had traveled at least 10,000 km, conquered armies at will, and created a reputation of invincibility that would endure for centuries.[3]

It was humbling to reflect that in roughly the same time it had taken Jebe and Subodei to achieve this military expedition from Asia to Europe and back, I had barely managed to reach Russia in one piece. In fact, before my first day of riding beyond the Manych Depression was out, I was feeling more depleted than at almost any other time on my journey.

Little more than 30 km from the checkpoint, I fell ill with a high fever. For the next three days I lay in the care of a Dagestani farmer, drifting in and out of sleep, haunted by a dream in which Kok appeared with his two front legs chopped off. He stood on the bloody stumps with terror in his eyes, searching for his family. I had imagined arriving in these settled lands infused with the courage of the big wide steppe, but without Kok I felt exposed and vulnerable. Utebai was a small, weak horse unsuitable for travel and sooner or later I would have to find a replacement.

Uncertainty was creeping up on me from another quarter, too. As a foreigner, I was required to receive official registration to account for every day of my stay in Russia. The hotel in Elista registered me for the days I had been there, but beyond that I had no fixed address or host. This hadn't been an issue in the Kalmyk countryside, but I was now in provinces closer to the unstable republics of Ingushetia, Chechnya, Dagestan, and Ossetia. The ongoing insurgency in Chechnya, raw memories of the

Beslan school hostage tragedy, and recently foiled terrorist plots had created a heightened atmosphere of suspicion. I had experienced an indicator of this during my bus trip from the Crimea to Elista, during which I'd been ordered out for document checks eleven times. Almost every intersection in Stavropol and Krasnodar Krais— *krai* is a term that is the equivalent of oblast but historically used for territory on Russia's frontier—were manned by heavily equipped police, some even with light tanks. Because I was a foreigner riding three horses (one of which was not the same one listed on the papers I was carrying), carrying a satellite phone and GPS (technology that also required a permit), and traveling on an unregistered visa, things felt a little precarious.

After recovering from the fever, I set off gingerly. Fixing a westerly course and trying to avoid unwanted attention, I began by resisting any attempt to conform to the reality of fields, roads, and villages and took direct routes via compass. But it wasn't long before the hidden dangers of this environment were revealed. In the deep, soft soil of plowed fields, the horses tired fast, and I became hemmed in by a web of irrigation canals. While trying to jump across one such canal Taskonir fell up to his chest in muddy water and spooked the other horses. As I tried to calm them down Tigon ran off chasing a hare and did not return. An hour of searching led me to a railway track where he was tangled dangerously by the collar.

The next evening I thought my luck had changed when I crested a hill to find myself looking down at a green sea of virgin spring pasture. It was sweet, thick, grass—the kind I could only have dreamed of in the arid steppes of Kazakhstan and Kalmykia. I found a hidden hollow for my camp and the horses ate until morning and their stomachs were as tight as drums.

In the morning, I had only just emerged from the tent when a Russian jeep came barreling down on us. The driver was on his feet before the engine cut out. "So, you think you've found some good pasture?"

I nodded. The man angrily explained I had destroyed his autumn-sown barley—there were apparently hefty fines for such "vandalism." I couldn't bring myself to apologize and instead explained it was one the first fields

I had seen since leaving Mongolia. But the man didn't leave until I had tied the horses to a row of trees on the edge of the field. As he drove off he shot me a venomous look and left me with these words: "I hope you *do* keep grazing fields. Soon the mouse and rat poison will kill your animals anyway."

Over the coming days remnants of open pasturage became increasingly rare, and just as Anir had warned, the only grazing to be found was among the single-file rows of trees so narrow I could barely fit a tent on them. I could no longer afford to let the horses graze free, and tethering ropes had to be especially short. Afraid that Tigon, who loved catching mice and rats, might be poisoned, he too was permanently tied. I put him on a long leash and let him guide from the front of the caravan.

As I rode I cast my eyes sadly over Taskonir. With his coarse, tangled mane, stormy eyes, and untamed spirit, he was a living descendant of wild horses that had only ever known the freedom of open steppe. I felt guilty for bringing him to a land where he did not belong.

A WEEK BEYOND the Manych I passed the town of Krasnogvardeiskoe and crossed out of Stavropol Krai into Krasnodar. I was now about 400 km from the Azov Sea and had arrived on the Kuban—the most fertile and heavily cultivated steppe in southern Russia.

Given the intensity of farming onward from here, I expected conditions to grow more difficult. Instead, I found respite by following a series of rivers that flowed on an east-west line—some draining eastward into the Manych Depression, and others westward to the Azov Sea. I was able to locate pasture along the banks and enjoyed the cover of reeds. Most of all, I took heart that I had reached the home of the Kuban Cossacks—the legendary horseback warriors of Russia's frontier who had evolved on the very kind of crossroads of sedentary and nomadic society that I now rode through.

The most accepted version of Cossack origins holds that they were lawless Tatar bandits who began to fill the power vacuum left behind on the steppe after the disintegration of the Mongol Empire. Living in unclaimed borderlands between the Turkish, Russian, and Polish empires, the borderlands that were once so important for the Golden Horde, they were joined by Russians and Poles and emerged in the fourteenth century as a loose federation of military societies. Although Cossacks came to adopt the Russian language and Orthodox Christianity, their oft-worn Asiatic-style forelock on a shaved head, known as a *khokhol*, was a symbol of their unique place on the crossroads between the perceived "wild" East and "civilized" Europe.

Most Cossacks fought for whoever paid them, and so their alliances changed like the seasons. The free Cossacks—those not registered as soldiers in service to the tsar—commonly made raids on both Ottoman and Russian territory, and the ruler of one often asked the other to curb the attacks. Ivan the Terrible's reply in 1549 to the Turkish sultan was typical of such exchanges: "The Cossacks of the Don are not my subjects, and they go to war or live in peace without my knowledge."

At the end of the eighteenth century Russia moved to expand its empire and defeated the Cossack armies, after which Cossacks served the tsar and went on to become the imperial army's most feared cavalrymen, playing crucial roles in Russo-Turkish wars and the colonizing of Central Asia and Siberia.[4]

The Cossacks' dogged, independent spirit nevertheless endured, leading to a series of uprisings. In the twentieth century they had fought for the Whites and the Reds, the Nazis and the Soviets, and consequently Stalin considered them unreliable, if not traitorous. Cossack Nazi collaborators repatriated after World War II were infamously executed en masse in what Nikolai Tolstoy (a distant descendant of Leo Tolstoy) labeled the "secret betrayal." They also were singled out for repressive measures during collectivization.

In the post-Soviet era these harms had been publicly acknowledged, and Cossacks were reportedly reestablishing their culture. This was something I had long hoped to witness, not least now, because I was desperate to believe that some spirited fight for freedom still existed in a land that had submitted to the plow.

⁙

TEN KILOMETRES SHY of the town of Uspenskaya I happened on a rich meadow along the banks of the Kalaly River. Hidden from roads and almost entirely encircled by reeds, it seemed an ideal place for a rest day.

I had only just unloaded the horses, however, when the sound of Soviet-era motorbikes—a model found universally in former Soviet states called a Ural—thrust rudely from behind the reeds, passengers in sidecars bouncing about wildly. It was too late to pack up and move, and my spirits sank as I contemplated a long, sleepless night.

One of the drivers nearly drove into me before he stopped. As his mop of curly ginger hair settled, he barked at me, "What the fuck are you up to?" Hugged by a much-darned woolen sweater, he hauled his heavy gut up against gravity and stood with hands on hips. With his sights trained on me, I told my story rather pleadingly.

"Fuck off. Did you fuckin' hear that, boys? Mongolia to Hungary. Fuck me!" he replied.

Two other men who had tumbled out of the motorcycle sidecar stood a breath away. They had hulking, fat shoulders, and their faces were sunburned landscapes of freckles and unruly stubble.

It turned out that I was apparently guilty of making camp in their private fishing hideout. A deflated rubber raft was bundled out of a sidecar and pumped up by hand. Meanwhile, a picnic of salami, cucumber, vodka, and beer was laid out, and two more motorbikes came roaring to the scene.

One of the newcomers was a mountain of a man with a face as broad as a wheat field and green eyes the size of eggs. His gargantuan head swam in an even bigger wobbling chin, and like the others he had chipped teeth and mismatched clothes. Bellowing expletives, he settled next to me, rested his head against my saddle, then tore the cap off a beer bottle with his teeth, saying, "This is the most important part. You know the saying: beer without vodka is like throwing money to the winds!"

The food and alcohol consumed, my new friends unpacked a pile of fishing nets and set about the main business of the evening. They had only just managed to paddle out from the reeds, though, when the large man received a call on his cell.

"Boys! Police! Quick! Let's get the fuck out of here!"

The raft was deflated in seconds, and everything was stuffed into side-cars before the bikes were push-started in a scramble of legs. As they tore away they yelled at me in no uncertain terms: "Don't say a word or else! As soon as those fuckin' police have gone, we'll be back with more vodka!"

Fifteen minutes later the headlights of a Russian police jeep jittered across the uneven land in the falling darkness until the reeds around my camp were lit up like an amphitheater. Three policemen stepped out stiffly. "You haven't seen any poachers around here, have you? On motorbikes?"

A skinny, pale officer with a wiry mustache butted in. "You know these damn Cossacks—you have to be careful. Remember, you are on the Kuban now."

The jeep had only just taken off when the roar of motorbikes came to life and I was assaulted with backslaps and wild shrieks of thanks. They had managed to collect wood in the meantime and went about establishing a roaring campfire.

When the nets were set, we bundled up in my horse blankets and lay on the earth roasting salami and preserved pig fat on sticks. Vodka and pure spirits flowed, and by the flickering light the cracked-tooth smiles and tough but boyish faces took on an air of celebration. They talked rude, freewheeling talk about women, fishing, and fights, creatively describing everything using variations of just a few obscene words.

Listening to the ebb and flow of the stories, I sank into my coat, relishing the feeling of pig fat warming my belly. Tigon sat among us all, one of the gang. For the first time since crossing the Manych two weeks ago I was not alone; it was nice to feel a sense of camaraderie.

For a time the conversation petered out, then the large man poked the coals and looked at me. "You know, we are Cossacks after all. We have to live free! Stalin turned our land into fields, took away our horses. Brave men became wheat farmers and tractor drivers! Now we're not even allowed to fish without permission!" In the pained expression that spread across his face, you could tell he was trying to appreciate the identity of his people, something he would never have the luxury of knowing as anything but legend.

Cossacks had been targeted by Stalin not just because of their split loyalties, but because they lived on the most fertile land of the Soviet Union. Stalin relied on grain production in the Kuban and other Cossack territories in Ukraine to fund his push for industrialization. During collectivization, hundreds of thousands of Cossacks were accused of sabotaging the grain procurement campaign and were either executed, exiled to Siberia, or sent to forced labor camps.[5] Another policy that aided Stalin in his long-term assault on the Cossacks was that private ownership of horses was declared illegal. When the Nazis advanced into Russia, horses and cattle were herded away from the Kuban and never replaced. With the Cossacks horseless, their land depopulated, and their militaries outlawed, any hope of a return to the former life was snuffed out when the Kuban was set upon by a large-scale project of irrigation and cultivation.

Nowadays Cossacks, like these poachers, were free to revive their culture but the overwhelming reality was that the grinding process of industrialization had long rendered the horseback way of life redundant. And this is now what these young men faced.

One of them who had been quiet until now spoke up. "Have you seen the wild dogs yet? You should be carrying a gun—they are even more dangerous than wolves."

At the very thought of these wild predators, the man's eyes were full of hope and expectation. It seemed to me he wasn't so much frightened by the idea of wild dogs as he was proud of them. The idea excited me, too, to think that somewhere in this land there was a wild spirit that carried on even if the wolf was long gone.

At some point during the night one of the fishermen traveled into the village, then at about 3:00 A.M. returned in a car with more friends. As the beat-up old Lada lurched drunkenly to a halt, eight or nine bodies were disgorged in a wave of cigarette smoke, techno music, and the stench of vodka and beer. The fisherman at the wheel grinned. "We have a gift for you, Timofei!" Reaching into his pocket, he pulled out three small purple packages, which he held up to the headlights. They read: "Contained: 1 condom. Fish flavored." A robust-looking girl stepped out of the car with a giggle. I was told to take her to my tent.

At the time my temper was frayed—the car had spooked the horses, and Ogonyok and Taskonir had managed to rip out their tethering stakes; I had narrowly managed to hold on to them—and I declined. They seemed quite offended, and later on I couldn't help but feel bad for rejecting their offer so emphatically.

Traditionally the free life of a Cossack—who was obliged to serve in the army until the age of forty—was incompatible with marriage. Until the eighteenth century, most Cossack men were single, and even when the domestic family unit was adopted with the influx of Russian settlers, it was custom for married men to walk some distance in front of their wives and children in public places. This was to symbolize the uncertainty that Cossack men lived under, since they could be sent away to war for many years at any time. Women had to be prepared to carry on raising the family without a husband, and to some degree it was acceptable for them to be unfaithful while their husbands were away. Many young Cossacks I later met spoke proudly of their grandfathers, who had been known to have many mistresses. Like the romanticized version of their forebears, it naturally followed in their eyes that my life as a single wandering horseman should entail a love interest—or at least a visit to a prostitute—at every watering hole from Mongolia to Hungary.

THE FISHERMEN HAD deflated their raft and taken away the nets by dawn, leaving me with the condoms for "another time." I continued along the Kalaly River for a day until it began to curve north, then cut across to another watercourse that flowed west toward the sea. Confident the Cossacks wouldn't turn me in to the police, I relished the prospect of riding through the long, trailing Cossack villages that clung to the banks of the rivers.

Known as *khutors*—a Ukrainian term used by Cossacks to describe new settlements—they were built by the original Black Sea settlers who arrived from Ukraine in the late eighteenth century. Khutors consisted of single rows of timber and mud-brick houses and were traditionally not large enough to warrant a church. It comforted me that in the modern era most didn't have police or administration representatives, either.

Bypassed by major roads, these khutors seemed to belong to a bygone era. Each house had a healthy plot of land and a run of chickens, pigs, and the odd goat. As firewood was scarce, most families also had mountains of dried corncobs out front—the staple source of fuel on the Kuban. Babushkas bent permanently at the hip worked the earth, and old men rowed leaky flat-bottomed fishing boats into sleepy waters. The clop and rattle of a horse and cart sometimes rose and faded along the single, unsealed streets.

Initially I had hoped I could slip in and out of these settlements inconspicuously, but even the dead would have been woken by the wave of barking dogs and honking geese that preceded me when traveling the length of a khutor. The longest was 15 km but had a population of less than 1,000. The kerfuffle gave people time to ready themselves to greet me with jars of homemade vodka and preserved cucumbers, peppers, tomatoes, jams, honey, juice, pears, and *salo* (pork fat). The key to getting past was having at least one shot of vodka, although under duress this often became three. On one occasion I was told that if I wanted to become a genuine Cossack, I would have to drink a giant bottle of home-brewed vodka, known as *samohon*[6] and then "jump over a fence." It was a drinking culture that reminded me of a description I'd read in Leo Tolstoy's short novel *The Cossacks*:

"All Cossacks make their own wine, and drunkenness isn't so much a tendency common to all as it is a ritual, the non-fulfillment of which would be considered apostasy."

Within two days I had accumulated so much heavy produce that the offerings had become a serious danger to the packhorses. When I explained this, the gift bearers always glared back indignantly. More than once I was told, "If I have given it to you, you must take it! You know the saying: 'When they give, take. When they kill, run.'"

The fanfare in khutors sometimes delayed me long enough for Cossack men to dress up and greet me on the street in traditional regalia. Near Il'inskaya, a stanitsa (a town larger than a khutor, big enough to have a church), one such man stepped proudly into my path in a black Astrakhan hat, a golden embroidered cloak fitted with bullets in the chest pockets, and a whip and antique dagger on the belt. His near-royal refinement was strongly at odds with the uncouthness of the poachers I'd met a few days before.

"Welcome, Cossack! I am the ataman of the Il'inskaya Cossacks. Where are you migrating to?" he said, shaking my hand. "As ataman, I am the leader of the Cossacks here and responsible for getting young people enlisted in the Kuban Cossack army. But my job is also to instil the spirit of freedom, fairness, and independence that was crushed in the Soviet era."

I asked the ataman what relation he felt to the nomadic people of the steppe.

"Like nomads, we could always pack up and leave wherever we needed. In old times, like for nomads, the steppe gave us all we needed—horses, wild game, and fish." He cast his eyes over my gear and the horses with a look of envy. "I consider that Genghis Khan was a Cossack by definition. Although we did not live in yurts, we adopted the best of nomad custom: most important, their horses and horsemanship. We have a saying: 'Only a bullet can catch a Cossack rider.'"

As I rode on there was no doubt in my mind that Cossacks genuinely identified with my journey and were conscious of their history as great horsemen. I took great heart from this and was beginning to lose my fear of authorities. Nothing, however, could hide the fact that the essential ingredient of their past—horses—had disappeared. I felt the absence of the equine at every move. Most village atamans I met stepped out of cars or traveled on foot, and no one thought to offer me fodder—a meaningful gift for a nomad. The few horses I did encounter had never been saddled. Famous don breeds that had once been ridden into war were now used for pulling carts. When I passed them on the road they shied at the sight of my caravan and sometimes bolted off the edge of the road, the driver hanging on for dear life.

In another telling sign of the absence of horses, in all my time on the Kuban steppe only one family ever invited me to stay. Very few had horses or the facilities to keep them overnight, and those who did didn't believe they had room or feed for three extras. Whenever I asked if there was somewhere I could lodge, I would be directed to a collective farm beyond the village. These ranches were depressing Soviet relics, many of which had been converted into piggeries and almost exclusively manned by poor men who lived in the village and worked out at the farm on irregular shifts. As it had elsewhere in the Soviet Union, collectivization had clearly driven a wedge between farming and family life. Horses had subsequently become associated with state farms and were no longer treasured family members.

Beyond Il'inskaya, the freshness instilled by the winter break wore off. My body began to ache, and the accumulated lack of sleep took its toll. At the first sign of hunger my mood would crumble. The horses felt heavy themselves, and during breaks they kept their heads down. Even Tigon was exhausted. He had learned that the most important thing while on the lead was keeping well out of reach of Taskonir, for whenever Taskonir caught up he would take a nip at Tigon's hind legs to remind him who was boss. Several times Tigon's lead became dangerously tangled in the horse's legs. The worst torment was when the front horse happened to step on the lead at a trot. It nearly strangled poor Tigon, who, pinned down and trampled by the caravan, was spat out the end in somersaults. How he came out of these scrapes without serious injury was beyond me.

Then came the rains. The lanes and tracks turned to sticky black mud—a telling sign that I was riding through *chernozem*, or "black soil"— the fertile soils that stretch from the Kuban across the southern steppe of Ukraine, forming the breadbasket of Russia and the former Soviet Union. It was so sought after for its richness that, legend has it, when the Nazis advanced through southern Ukraine and Russia they took soil back to Germany by the shipload.

As mud, however, this precious soil balled up under the horse's hooves until they slipped and fell. I resolved to walk, but within minutes the buildup on my boots turned them into heavy clogs. The slightest tug from the horses on the lead rope toppled me into the mud. I walked the better part of three days, descending into a quagmire of filth. The horses were still losing their winter hair, and the shed hair combined with the mud to stick fast to my clothes, my skin, and my sleeping bag. But the dirtier and more desperate for hospitality I became, the less likely it was that anyone would let me in.

And then one night, while I was setting up camp in the pouring rain beyond a ramshackle khutor, a local drunk stumbled upon my muddy patch of earth and twisted the knife. "How dare you camp here on the Kuban, you foreigner! If I tell my friends about it, they will come in the night, take your horses to the meat factory, and drown you in the river for the crayfish to eat!" I swore at him darkly, and he stumbled away. But the look I caught in his eye meant that I slept the night in my filthy riding clothes and with my axe by my side.

Out of grain and low on food the following night, I was forced to camp on a narrow strip of grass next to freshly plowed earth. Despite tying the horses on short tethers, they managed to get out and roll in it. By morning they were all plastered in black grime.

As I sat there with my porridge, a thought dawned on me. I'd become the picture of a down-and-out, homeless wanderer that many westerners and Russians mistakenly associate with the word nomad. My condition reminded me of when I had been in Siberia at age twenty-one, riding a bicycle to Beijing. I had been living on a budget of $2 a day, had a single change of clothes, and hadn't shaved in more than four months. A village woman, who looked at me in horror, explained the word bomzh, which usually referred to a homeless bum, to me this way: "Well, Tim, bomzh . . . it's basically you, only without your bicycle."

How ironic, I thought, that this same mud that caked us all, the pride of the Kuban, had spawned the end of the nomad era and the downfall of the free Cossack way of life. Stalin had never trusted Cossacks and had needed grain to pay for his dreams of industrialization, and plowing up the chernozem had been a valid pretext to solve both problems. I understood it now: to dispossess a nomad, you take away his horse and plow up his land. Horseless and coaxed into a life between four walls, the once brave warrior becomes toothless and redundant in the space of a generation.

On a lighter note, as I noticed the tattered fabric hanging around my legs, I sadly concluded that the trousers I had been wearing since day one in Mongolia were close to the end of their own road.

18

THE TIMASHEVSK MAFIA

BEYOND THE STANITSA of Dyad'kovskaya, the rain came down in sheets. I slipped behind a row of trees and headed down a narrow track into some deserted wheat fields. Protected by the hood of my jacket, I kept my head bowed and considered my circumstances.

I was now only 250 km from the Kerch Strait, which lay between Russia and the Crimean peninsula in Ukraine, but before leaving Russia I needed to find a replacement for Utebai and start the process of getting my horses approved for passage through customs. To do either of these would require a miracle. Horses were a scarcity on the Kuban, and no one would ever agree to trade for a wimp like Utebai. In my filthy, disheveled state of late, it was also true that I would struggle to convince a shopkeeper to sell me a loaf of bread, let alone a border guard to give me entry into another country.

But when I lifted my eyes, columns of light peeled away the gloom, and it seemed my prayers had been answered.

The unruly beard of the man before me caught my eye at first, then his tall, burnished velvet hat and long black robes. He lifted a small broom from a bucket of water, flicking drops from high above his head into the field. Then he turned to me.

"We've come here to bless the wheat fields with holy water! Where are you going?"

He was the priest of Dyad'kovskaya, and he explained that since ancient times it had been the role of the Orthodox Church to bless every wheat field of the parish in the spring. As I went on my way, he showered my caravan with holy water.

It was only a few minutes later that proof of his friends in higher places materialized. Accustomed to noisy Russian jeeps and Ladas, I'd failed to notice the purr of a new four-wheel-drive Range Rover until it was right up alongside me. Tigon took a sniff, then retreated. As a tinted window slid down silently, a man who was polished but not as elegant as his car grinned out at me from the leather interior.

"So, fellow traveler, partisan, Kazakh, Cossack—how can I help you?"

I wiped mud and rain from my eyes and peered down as he stepped out and swaggered up to me. Standing only little taller than he was wide, he was adorned with flawlessly buffed shoes, a black jacket, sunglasses, and a silky tie in red, green, and white, the colors of the Krasnodar provincial flag. This was crowned with silver-streaked curly hair and a handlebar mustache. He might have been the second apparition in as many minutes, but there was no doubting it: this man was no priest.

"My friend! You do not know me, but soon, I think, we will be friends. I am Nikolai Vladimorivich Luti: ataman of this region, owner of ten thousand hectares of crops, and employer of eight hundred workers."

I stammered out my story. Luti, as he liked to be called, looked at me thoughtfully. Finally he said, "Thirty kilometres away at my friend's farm you will have all the services you need. Go there tonight, and tomorrow we will consider your problem. If we can find a new horse for you, we will."

Rain streamed down as I hightailed it through fields and villages.

Flocks of geese parted, avenues of dogs erupted, and goats tied on short chains nearly strangled themselves in panic as my caravan thundered by. It grew dark and cold, and my body ached, but sometimes I had to let the reins go—I had, after all, been promised hot food and a wash.

It was well into the night when I pulled up alongside a throng of Soviet harvesting equipment, peeled myself out of the saddle, and hobbled inside a cavernous machinery shed. There, under floodlights on a plastic table, lay a tub of freshly roasted meats, fruit, and salads, surrounded by a forest of vodka bottles. Around this table sat Luti and three other men, all clearly ravenous.

As I sank thankfully into a chair, Luti introduced himself as the "big farmer," and Sascha Chaika—the owner of the farm where we had arrived—as the "little farmer." Luti then rose with a glass of vodka and puffed out his chest. "I want you to know that you have fallen in with simple people. It's Easter, and although we are observing fasting, Cossacks were always allowed to eat meat and drink alcohol when on the road . . . and, well, we are on the road!"

The vodka had barely hit our guts before we swooped down on the food. Sauce exploded from the corners of our mouths, oil ran down our arms, and soon all that remained were empty disposable plates and a "tablecloth" of oily newspaper. Our attention then turned to drink, and soon the shed was filled with a cacophony of laughter, man-to-man talk, and heated arguments that were resolved by more drinking. It wasn't until the vodka ran out that the calm of night reclaimed the wheat field and the shed grew cold, then dark and silent.

In the morning came a message through Chaika that Luti would agree to see me again only *after* I had had a wash. Luti had booked me a hotel in Timashevsk for a night, and sure enough I soon found myself with rivers of black and brown mud flowing off me in a luxurious bathtub. Luti had suggested that a little love was in order as part of this "recovery package," and although I had turned the offer down, I had half expected to find a woman waiting in my room when I arrived.

Clean and sober the next morning, I knew it was time to face the challenge of finding a new horse and eking a way into the tangle of bureaucracy so I could leave the country with my animals. Luti was not fazed by this challenge. Timashevsk, he said, was the perfect base from which to organize everything.

Over the next six weeks, my problems would indeed be solved, but in this farming center on the main road between Krasnodar and Moscow, my time among the circle of Luti's friends and acquaintances would offer me an intriguing portrait of a society in which the void created by the collapse of the Soviet Union had been filled by endemic corruption. Partly in an effort to cope with the eternal uncertainty this created, but also as a celebration of the unregulated times they were living in, people had adopted a carefree approach to life and had a remarkable propensity to enjoy the moment—albeit with alcohol (and, in the case of Luti's men, the liberal use of prostitutes) at its core.

Much of my journey from Mongolia to Hungary was an external one, dealing with the elements and the horses. But here in Timashevsk, challenged by this culture, I would experience a chapter that would prove to reveal as much about me—and perhaps my naiveté—as it did about those around me.

卐

THE FIRST PRIORITY was finding a place for my horses, and it wasn't long before Luti had made a few calls and come up with a solution: "I have the perfect place! My friend owns a scrap metal plant in town." When he noticed my blank stare, he added, "You will thank me for this, I promise!"

Later that day my blank look turned to one of extreme apprehension as I led my horses toward a run-down industrial building from which came violent booms and the screeching of metal. It looked and sounded more like a glue factory than a stable. I felt Taskonir tremble as we entered and navigated through a mess of twisted car wrecks and mangled steel. A man wearing grease-covered overalls waved urgently at me to stop as a crane swung a full-size truck through an arc just 5 m ahead of me. The truck was dumped in a huge steel bin with a deafening clang, then set upon by a gang of men wielding crowbars and sledge hammers.

Metal recycling had thrived in southern Russia since the 1990s, and plants like this had become processing facilities for the dismantling of seventy years of Soviet machinery. The metal business was also known to have a close affiliation with the Mafia. I was beginning to wonder just who my benefactor was when a blond woman in a figure-hugging dress and high heels emerged from an office and picked her way toward me through the dust and debris. She led me toward some stables in a corner of the recycling yard that I'd overlooked.

There, I met the owner of the plant and Luti's friend, Igor Maluti—a man who was half Tatar, half Cossack, almost 2 m tall, and bearing shoulders as wide as a draft horse's. Stooped forward, veins flaring at his temples, he wrenched rather than shook my hand while declaring that his life was devoted to the love of three things: horses, pigeons, and women. As I would soon learn, he was determined to introduce me to all three as soon as possible.

His horses were expensive breeds ranging from English thoroughbreds to ponies. He never rode them, but he made sure they were given the finest food, and he had the Gypsy stable master wash them weekly with special horse shampoo. "They are food for my soul," he explained in his coarse, dry voice.

Next he drove me to see his wife and mistresses, one after another, to whom he brought gifts and money. On the way home we came to a screeching halt on a bridge. Luti leaped out and managed to catch a pigeon from the ledge with his bare hands.

"Don't you see? Pigeons are freedom, intelligence, and peace," he said, canoodling with the bird, which he held against his powerful chest.

While I sensed that he could be brutal and cruel in different circumstances, there was a directness and honesty in Igor that I warmed to. Flexing his powerful hands over the steering wheel, pigeon tucked under his arm, he turned to me with a sigh and said, "Of course, Tim, to live your free life is my dream." He turned back to the road, and I saw the folds in his trunk-thick neck smooth out. There was a sad look in his eyes. "But alas, your life is not my destiny."

The hidden genius in leaving the horses with Igor was revealed later. The Gypsy stable master was an expert at bringing horses back to health. He professed to know when to feed and water them, and how much was needed to make a horse gain strength and weight. By the time I left, the horses were being prepared for the first shampooing of their lives.

On the other side of town Tigon and I moved into an industrial site of our own. Owned by Luti, it was a huge yard fenced in by concrete and barbed wire that contained a tile-making factory and a transit facility for gas and diesel.

My new home was located in a ramshackle security guard's hut, where I was given a room filled with old tires, car parts, and tools, and decorated with flaking stickers of naked women. In moving in, I had dispossessed Luti's head mechanic of his love shack.

To assist in finding a new horse and getting veterinary papers in order, Luti granted me two drivers. One was his loyal assistant, Aleksei, and the other was Edik. The two couldn't have been a more curious contrast. Aleksei was a tall handsome womanizer from Dagestan, who wore white leather dress shoes and a suit. His hobbies were women, vodka, smoking, cards, and more women, generally in that order. Edik, on the other hand, was a family man who worked as a tractor driver and wore nothing more glamorous than a pair of cheap Chinese-made sandals and threadbare track pants. Aleksei, or "Lokha," as he was known for short, took charge of finding me a new horse, while it was decided that Edik would look after my veterinary affairs.

Field trips with Lokha began well. We narrowed the horse search down to a farm 20 km out of town, owned by a proud Cossack named Nikolai Bandirinka. The stables of this onetime secretary of the local Communist Party was home to more than one hundred stud horses—the jewels of which were twenty prize stallions from lines famous for dressage, show jumping, and racing.

Although Nikolai generally did not keep workhorses, he did by chance presently have one: a four-year-old palomino stallion named Sokol, whose name meant "magpie." Sokol was about fifteen hands, broad and strong, with a flowing blond mane and an inquisitive nature. Although he had lived his whole life in a stable and had never been ridden, I liked him at once. There was only one problem: it was spring and Kok was a fully-fledged stallion. Luti offered to pay half of the $1,000 to buy the horse, and Nikolai agreed to organize a castration. The deal was agreed to, vaccinations administered, and blood samples taken.

Solving the issue of my veterinary and customs papers with Edik proved more complex. To get exit permits from Russia I needed cooperation from all levels of bureaucracy, including the regional Timashevsk veterinary and transport authorities, the provincial laboratory, the veterinary department in Krasnodar, federal authorities in Moscow, and the equivalents of all of these in Ukraine. Naturally, this had never been done before by a horseback traveler here, and so I faced the same labyrinth of red tape and confusion I had experienced on the Kazakh border. Edik explained that locals would never go through with such a torturous process—it was far easier to pay bribes. Because I was a foreigner, though, this was tricky territory, since no official wanted to be held accountable for making an error in relation to my case.

I persisted, and after establishing reliable contacts a semblance of routine developed to my life in Timashevsk. Two or three days per week I was ferried by Edik between the local veterinary department, the horses, and the laboratory in Krasnodar—there were twelve different diseases to be tested for, and for those tests that could not be done in Krasnodar, blood samples were couriered to labs in Moscow. Most days I also visited Luti in his office to fill him in on my progress. He sat in an executive chair, smoking imperiously, as he listened to my latest account. While there were fits of angry phone calls and times when Lokha was being ordered to do this and that, they were interspersed with long periods of silence during which he sat contemplatively, the one small window casting light onto his speckles of silver hair. "Tim," he would say at last, pulling a rolled-up $100 bill from his top pocket, "take some pocket money and go and buy yourself some cigarettes or something!"

On days in between the expeditions to Krasnodar, Lokha took me to Nikolai's farm to train Sokol, whom I had already renamed Kok. The new Kok, as it turned out, was not only unridden but had never even been tied to a fence nor been fitted with a halter, saddle, crupper, or girth strap. Unaware of this initially, the first time I tied him to a fence he panicked, reared, and ended up hanging by his throat with the rope wrapped around his neck. I had four weeks to get him ready to take his place in the caravan.

Using "approach and retreat" methods that the Watsons had taught me in Australia, I gradually accustomed Kok to my touch until I could rub him all over and he would stand still. The next step was to familiarize him with a girth strap. After initially taking it well, he let fly one afternoon with a fit of bucking and pig rooting, rearing up and punching his front hooves into the air. I had little experience with stallions, and he had a power and will that frightened me.

During the second week of training, Kok underwent castration. With his legs bound and Nikolai standing on his neck, his testicles were clamped and then twisted around until they sheared off. As Kok struggled in agony, Nikolai laid a fist into his nose to distract him from the pain. I went home feeling sick.

Despite also witnessing the castration, Lokha was unconcerned and had other things on his mind. The trips to Bandirinka's farm doubled as reconnaissance missions to find venues for the infamous weekends of debauchery he shared with his boss. Earlier that day he had discovered a suitable sauna retreat nearby and couldn't wait to get back to Timashevsk to share the news with Luti. "Oh, Tim. What more could you ask to relax? A good sauna, sex, drink, and sleep!" he said, one hand moving restlessly over the steering wheel, the other deftly pinching a cigarette. He and Luti were regularly sampling prostitutes, and conversations with Lokha generally orbited around this subject.

He had already invited me along for the weekend and, unhappy that I had declined, turned to me. "What are you resisting for? You can have your pick of the women, eighteen-year-olds, twenties, younger, whatever you please!" His pointy leather shoe drove downward on the accelerator, and we swerved out around a truck and zoomed ahead.

I was having difficulty coming to terms with the fact that Lokha, who indulged so openly with prostitutes, was also a family man with a wife and children. My discomfort with the subject surely reflected my upbringing in Australia, but in truth, I'd also never felt completely at home in a culture of masculinity in its more extreme forms. As a result, there was a part of me that felt out of place with the company I was keeping.

Whatever the reason for my feelings, the awkwardness with which I reacted to Lokha's offers frustrated him. This boiled over one day when I was explaining my deep reservations about a suggestion from Lokha that I should try to export Sokol to Ukraine on Kok's passport. "This is Russia!" Lokha expostulated. "This is the way things are done here! Listen to me and you will get your horses through without trouble! You should quit worrying and have some fun with some girls while the offer stands! Sometimes you think too much!"

A month went by, Sokol's wound healed, the air in Timashevsk grew thick and warm, and all around the wheat and barley crops began to bulge. Lokha raved about the coming summer, which would be filled with a good harvest, barbecues, drinking, and romance. Quite apart from getting the horses ready for the border, I found every minute of my day occupied. The industrial base that had become my home was a thoroughfare for workers, mostly drunken, who all had stories to tell.

Take, for instance, the security guard who worked night shifts from the shack where I slept. He was a balding man in his fifties, whom they all called Lisi, "Baldy." Security watch for Lisi meant a night away from his wife, drinking a bottle of vodka and having sex with a string of women in the hut's kitchen. All night he could be heard laughing hysterically as the level of vodka in the bottle went steadily down, then groaning and creaking as he made love on the tea table. One night I caught a glimpse of his lover storming out after a fight, pulling her dress on as she ran barefoot into the murky hues of the pre-dawn hours. Having let her go, he broke into my room, pulled me up by the arms, and, drawing his face close to mine, showered me with spittle as he said, "C'mon, Tim! What are you waiting for? Let's go to the highway!" When I protested sleepily and asked why, he shook me in a rage. "To get prostitutes, of course!"

I wasn't the only one who had to endure these tirades, although I was probably the only one who found them the least bit curious. Sharing the hut with me was Yura, an illegal immigrant from Georgia who worked at the tile factory. His passport and visa had long expired; afraid of what might happen at the border, he hadn't been home to see his family for four years. His situation had recently become more tenuous because of the deteriorating relations between Russia and Georgia. The nightly TV news was filled with stories condemning Georgia's president, Mikheil Saakashvili, who was drumming up support for Georgia to join NATO. Moscow had just banned all imports of Georgian wine, cut off diplomatic relations, and halted cross-border postal services. During the dead of winter a mysterious explosion on the gas pipeline had left the population of Georgia's capital, Tbilsi, freezing, and Georgia had accused Russia of sabotage. Georgians such as Yura who lived and worked illegally in Russia found themselves the focus of unwanted attention from authorities.

Yura's story would have resonated among hundreds of thousands of illegal immigrants in Russia who had come from former Soviet republics to work but were stuck with expired documents and cut off from family with no support or legal protections. Like everything in Russia, citizenship could be bought at a price, but few could afford the going rate, which apparently was around $5,000.

To make matters more complicated, Yura's girlfriend—a girl from a nearby village—had become pregnant, and he was doing his best to set up his shoebox of a single room as a family home. Yura was philosophical. "Life is different for everyone. For some it's easy, for others hard; some are rich, some are poor. At least when you are poor you have nothing to fear. If you are rich, the law means nothing—but for that, people will try to kill you," he said.

He often spoke of his dream to set up a car detailing business, raise a family, build a home in Timashevsk and live with a sense of normalcy. Every night when I came home he would greet me with his round, boyish face, some Georgian wine, and stories about his home on the Black Sea coast. On weekends he would lie on his humble little sofa bed with his girlfriend and watch TV programs ranging from *Who Wants to Be a Million-aire?* to the Russian version of *Big Brother*—shows that portrayed a life in Moscow that might have well been on another planet.

As days stretched into weeks in Timashevsk, it seemed that no matter whom I talked to, if they weren't being strangled by bureaucracy or in the thrall of prostitution, then they were certainly tangled in corruption, voluntarily or otherwise.

Chaika—the farmer who had hosted my arrival feast—said to me one day with a jaded look, "A couple of months ago the state prosecutor turned up to my farm and told me that I had broken some environmental laws. He offered me a choice, saying, 'If you want to take me to court, then you are more than welcome. But I can guarantee that you will lose, because I am the court! The fine will be three hundred thousand roubles'—about $10,000. 'But if you want, you can pay me thirty thousand roubles now and I will forget about it.' "

Chaika's muscular old body moved restlessly in the chair. One could sense the honest toil that had made up a good part of his life. Unlike Luti, whose transition from a collective farm director to big farmer was murky, he had built his farm up from scratch with hard work. He took a sip of his tea and continued. "So what am I supposed to do? If I don't pay, then he is sure to bankrupt me and sell off the machinery cheaply to his friends." Chaika, like so many other Russians, accepted as a given that the law was largely a tool for those in power to extract bribes and provide a pretext for convicting anyone the authorities pleased.

My only time out from the intense swirl of events and people in Timashevsk was when I was alone with Sokol. After three weeks of circle work inside the compound at Bandarinka's, I had finally been game enough to ride him. On the first attempt he bucked me clear and bolted back to the stables, but gradually he learned to trust me. During rides along a river out back of the farm I could feel his body bristling with wound-up energy as he moved nervously along, pausing and sniffing at flowers, grass, puddles, and trees. Unlike any other horse I had ridden, he had no problem negotiating fences, gates, tractors, even wire and steel, yet he was petrified of birds, the river, and the reeds that rustled in the wind. He was most at ease in his stable and around the roar of farm trucks. This couldn't have been more contrary to horses of the steppe, which were petrified of anything remotely unnatural. His behavior, like that of the people in Timashevsk, were simply a reaction to the world into which they had been born.

After nearly six weeks in Timashevsk, the feeling of tranquility and effervescence that I had had right after my arrival had faded. The constant battle with bureaucracy, on one hand, and the flagrant disregard for law, on the other, mingled with the culture of masculinity among my companions, had worn me down. One evening over a drink with Luti and Lokha my spirits bottomed out. They had been discussing Luti's only son, who was set to be married in just a couple of weeks' time. With a look of resignation Luti took a deep drag of his cigarette and eyeballed first Lokha, then me. "Yes, no matter how you look at it, it's true. Wives over time inevitably become just friends, partners. You are yet to learn this, Tim, but it is a true fact."

I returned that night alone to the grimy mechanic's shack where everything was imbued with the stench of alcohol and diesel. I felt as far away from the steppe as I had ever been on my trip. It was time to get back in the saddle and move on—a luxury that people living here did not have.

The next morning I had a meeting with the priest of Dyad'kovskaya, whom I had originally met in the fields all those weeks before. The derelict state of his church seemed symbolic of the spiritual condition of the people I'd been meeting. In fact, the church where he held services was an abandoned Soviet-era school hall where cardboard posters of saints, Mary, and Jesus Christ were stuck to the wall with Scotch tape. Although in his grandfather's day there had been three churches and a thriving attendance, his regulars at the Sunday service amounted to three old pensioners.

"The original churches were torn down by the Bolsheviks, and my church has become a three-day church," he said philosophically. "The only time people come to church is for baptism, marriage, and death. Money is the problem—if only people like Luti could give more generously, then I might be able to resurrect a sense of spirit in the local community.

"You see, Tim," he continued, "we are still suffering the destruction of the Soviet era. Modern-day Cossacks grew up as nonbelievers, and everything connected to ethics, morals, and spirituality takes a long time to resurrect. This is how I think of it: A wound on the body heals fast. A wound in the spirit might take ten years to heal. But if a wound is in the spirit of an entire people, it can take a hundred years. And what we experienced during the Soviet revolution wasn't just a wound—it was a killing blow, a death of the soul and spirit. I would like to think that Russia could again be great in more than just the size of its territory, but at the moment it doesn't seem to be the case."

I came away from my talk with the priest with my faith in the ability of people to transcend their social and political realities anything but restored. The truth was that the deeply penetrating corruption and the coping mechanisms of alcohol and prostitutes had personally affected me. It wasn't that any of this was unique to Timashevsk, of course; in fact, they were realities that I had witnessed throughout my horseback travels. At this stage of the journey, though, two years after setting out, I felt less able to step back into the role of an observer and more a part of society. Particularly because I was traveling by horse, I depended on the generosity and goodwill of people of all walks of life, and so I was both a victim and beneficiary of corruption. This left me feeling conflicted.

On the upside, the priest had got me thinking. Within the context of the upheaval of the twentieth century, there was a sense of cohesion among Luti's men—a genuine care for one another—that had endured through these times and was perhaps incorruptible. Some, like Luti, could to some degree create their own rules. But even then, whether it was Luti, Edik, or Yura, they were all people eking out their precarious lives the only way they knew and casting aside worries about the morrow they could not control. It was an attitude I could no doubt benefit volumes from.

WHEN FINALLY MY documents were in order, I gave Utebai to Igor Maluti at the metal recycling factory, who in turn donated him to a local riding school for children. Bandirinka gave me a royal send-off, dressed up in Cossack gear on one of his stallions, and Luti paid a visit to congratulate me on getting everything done.

Two weeks after departing, I found myself riding through the crisp air of morning watching the sun splinter through fractured clouds, turning the reeds by the roadside a luminous green. On the horizon I could see ships floating idly on the silky gray sheen of the Azov Sea.

I was a few kilometres shy of the ferry port of Kavkaz, where, if all went well, I was hoping to catch a ferry with my horses out of Russia and across the narrow Kerch Strait to Crimea. But I was under no illusions about my chances of getting through customs and immigration. Among other things, my unregistered visa remained an unresolved issue, and to reach the border I would have to pass through a police checkpoint.

As the boom gate, police cars, and a watchtower crept into view, I had the terrible feeling that my whole journey was about to unravel. When I reached the border crossing, the guards failed to appear, and I thought for a moment they might let me pass. But then a door opened and a large man sauntered out, machine gun dangling loosely against his belly. "Tie them up and come inside!" he ordered.

My passport was taken away by the superior officer, who went to run a check on their computer. He returned shaking his head. "What are we going to do with this lawbreaker?" he said, looking at his colleague. He was referring to the lack of the required registrations that would cover each day of my stay.

I started to explain the circumstances that had prevented me from getting the proper documentation, but after a while the boss pulled me aside. "Look, I'll tell you what to do. You see that registration date from the hotel in Elista that expired more than two months ago? Take this pen and put in today's date." He paused awkwardly. "Usually, for permission to write that, it would cost you eight hundred roubles . . ."

I pretended not to understand the hint, scribbled down the date, and carried on into immigration, where the veterinary officers were waiting. They were impressed with the thoroughness of my paperwork and told me, laughing, that it was the first time, to their knowledge, that anyone had completed all the required tests.

The last obstacle before boarding the ferry for Crimea was customs. Just as I pulled into the inspection bay, Ogonyok disgorged a gigantic turd. The junior officers laughed but their superior did not see the humor. "You are not leaving Russia until you clean that crap up!" he yelled.

"Okay, okay. But I'm not going to shift it with my bare hands. You will have to find me a shovel," I replied, disembarking from the saddle.

While he sent some officers off in search of a shovel, most of the customs people on duty came out to look at the spectacle. Meanwhile, I went inside to be processed and breezed through the screening post to have my passport stamped. Back outside, nobody had found a shovel, and the boat was due to leave. Within minutes I was casting off into the Kerch Strait leaving behind the cluster of officials still gathered around Ogonyok's parting present.

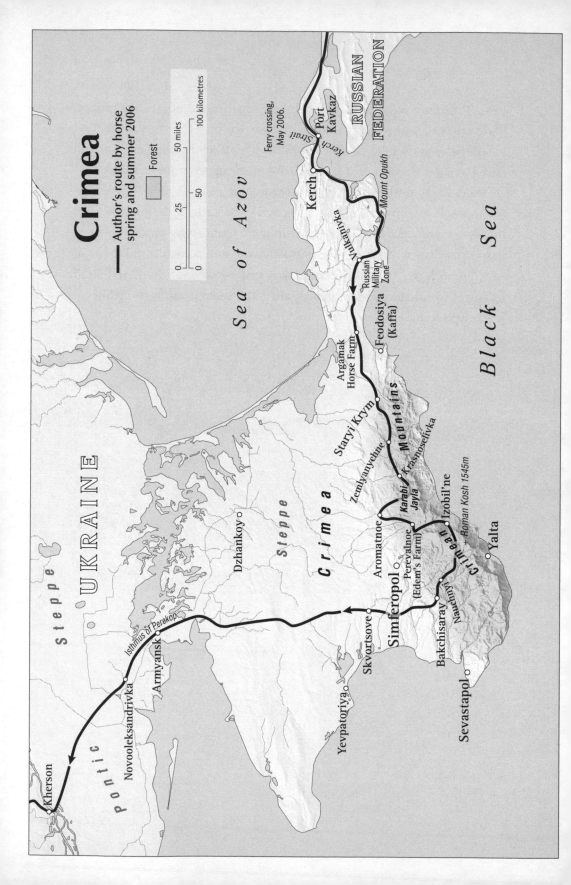

Crimea

— Author's route by horse
spring and summer 2006

Forest

0   25   50 miles
0   50   100 kilometres

UKRAINE

Steppe

Pontic Steppe

Kherson

Novooleksandrivka

Armyansk

Isthmus of Perekop

Yevpatoriya

Dzhankoy

Skvortsove

Simferopol

Crimea

Steppe

Aromatnoe

Perevalnoe
(Edem's Farm)

Bakchisaray

Nauchnyi

Sevastapol

Izobil'ne

Crimean

Roman Kosh 1545m

Yalta

Krasnoselivka

Karabi
Jayla

Zemlyanychne

Mountains

Staryi Krym

Argamak
Horse Farm

Feodosiya
(Kaffa)

Russian
Military
Zone

Vulkanivka

Mount Opukh

Kerch

Port
Kavkaz

Kerch Strait

Ferry crossing,
May 2006.

**RUSSIAN
FEDERATION**

Sea of Azov

Black   Sea

19

WHERE TWO WORLDS MEET

A SHADOW SWOOPED from the solitary cloud in the sky, and the whole sleepy mountain in front of us dimmed to olive green. As the salty breeze gusted, my sweat cooled and Ogonyok's wild ginger mane flew in all directions.

From the saddle I watched Tigon's tail and ears cut through the tall swaying grass like dorsal fins. He'd been on long-ranging missions all day, drifting back at times to check in, looking up at me with his tongue lolling about and his amber eyes alight. It wasn't long before he reached the crest of the hill and stopped, ears bent forward, the sleek shaft of his snout fishing for scents on the breeze.

As the cloud shadow peeled back toward us I, too, was soon surveying the view. From a foreground of waist-high grass, red poppies, and white chamomile, the steppe dropped away in a sea of green, gleaming with the same vitality as my horses' spring coats. Directly below, a narrow sandy isthmus cut a straight line to the west between the sea and a series of pinkish salt lakes. Immediately to our north, smooth, rounded peaks reached down to the lakes and surrendered to a plain beyond them.

By the time we'd descended to the beach, the wind had eased and the sun was losing heat and gaining color. I stepped stiffly down and walked along the ridge atop the isthmus. A pyramid-shaped hill was casting a flawless reflection in the lake, and as I shifted my gaze to the sea, a dark shadow shattered its glassy veneer. A school of dolphins surfaced, their shiny torsos rising and dipping effortlessly as they cruised along the shore.

By nightfall banks of dark cloud hung heavily over the sea. I pegged the horses out and watched as they buried their heads in the grass, feeding like a pack of hungry lions. Over dinner the western sky faded from peach to deep blue, then black. Tigon and I lay on my canvas duffle bag. I meant to write in my diary and study some Russian, but I woke at midnight with rain falling on my face. I'd managed to pen one line: *We're in horse heaven.*

TWO WEEKS EARLIER, I had sailed away from the cultivated lands of Krasnodar Krai in Russia and landed in the port city of Kerch. In making the half-hour crossing of the Kerch Strait, we had reached Crimea—a peninsula of historic renown that bulges southward via a bottleneck from the Ukrainian mainland into the Black Sea, forming a distinctive shape resembling a wide-bottomed vase. The dry steppe interior of Crimea, cut off from the coast in the southwest by a band of forested mountains, had long been a favored home for nomads.

Since my arrival I'd been looking forward to this moment when our little family could once again range free on unplowed grassland. Getting here had not been elegant. For three days from Kerch I had tracked along the southeast coast joined by a Ukrainian man, Giorgi. On the first day we'd been interrogated by the border patrol, Giorgi's stallion had bucked him off, and finally we had been pursued by a runaway foal; when the foal's owner tracked us down he accused Giorgi of stealing it.

On the second day we came to a dead end at a fenced-off military zone. We spent the evening camped at a Ukrainian outpost where an officer made us dinner and explained that it was from this base a rocket had accidentally been fired in October 2001 and infamously blown up an airliner en route from Tel Aviv to Russia. On the third day both Giorgi and Buran were limping and turned for home.

Now, finally alone, I sank into thoughts about the Crimean land around me—the same setting that in 1223 must have induced in the battle-weary Mongol army a feeling of jubilation. During Subodei and Jebe's remarkable campaign through Central Asia and the Caucasus that culminated with defeat of Russia, they and their men had spent time in Crimea, where they had no doubt taken the opportunity to rest and fatten their horses. Somewhere in these lush grasslands the night would have been filled with revelry and the sounds of thousands of weary horses being set free to graze. As nomads whose moods, like mine, fluctuated with those of their horses, the sheer abundance of grass must have left a deep impression, and one can only imagine the tales they brought home to the harsher climes of Central Asia.

There was something more significant than pasture that had attracted the Mongols to Crimea, though, and which made this peninsula so unique. As nomads had known for millennia, the true wealth of Crimea lay in the strategic port cities on its coast where the Eurasian steppe greets the Black Sea. For the largely landlocked societies of the steppe, the coast provided unique access to trade, communication, and plunder.

Long before the arrival of Subodei and Jebe, a historical trend had been established whereby nomads of Crimea's steppe interior both coexisted and clashed with the sedentary societies of the coast. Kerch had even been built on the ruins of the ancient city of Panticapaeum, the sixth-century BCE capital of a kingdom known as Bosphoria, which itself had been a fusion of Scythian nomads and Greek traders.[1]

The history of Crimea subsequently read like an almanac of both nomadic and European empires. The steppe interior had been ruled by Scythians, Sarmatians, Huns, Khazars, and Kipchaks, and the coast had passed through the hands of Romans, Bulgars, Goths, Byzantine Greeks, Venetians, and finally Genoese. The appearance of the Mongols in Crimea in 1223 was fleeting, but when the Mongols returned on their full-fledged conquest of

Russia, Crimea would become a pivotal outpost of the Mongol Empire for well over a century.

In the morning I woke to a sky flooded with stormy gray. Rain eased down, gently brushing the poppies and chamomile flowers on its way to earth. I packed unrushed, marveling at how the petals righted themselves with a shudder after every drop. When the sun broke through we rode—or, rather, waded—on.

Visions of Mongols and Scythian horsemen had sunk in overnight, and without signs of the modern world, I savored the feeling that I had become part of a continuum of nomad history. We had only traveled a very short way, however, before the hulking shape of Soviet barns broke the spell.

Since the fracturing of the Mongol Empire, Crimea had weathered many winds of change. A Tatar of Mongol descent, Hajji Giray, had founded the Crimean Khanate on the steppe in the fifteenth century, and the Otto-man Turks had replaced the Genoese as rulers of the coast.[2] In the eighteenth century, the Russian Empire expelled the Ottomans and forced the Tatars to submit to their rule. In the nineteenth century, Crimea was the stage for another struggle when the Russians fought a bitter war with the British and French. Next to arrive were the Nazis, subjecting the earth to the tread of angry tanks and laying siege to Sevastopol. When Crimea was reclaimed by the Soviets, the Tatars were accused as traitors and deported by Stalin en masse to Central Asia and Siberia. In 1954 Crimea was gifted to the Soviet state of Ukraine, finally emerging in 1990 as a semi-autonomous republic of an independent and democratic Ukraine.

Only fifteen years had passed since the collapse of the Soviet empire, but already the barns in front of us lay like lonely shipwrecks, overgrown with chest-high weeds and roofs folding in. The empty corrals that had once sheltered hundreds of sheep and cattle were filled with nothing but breeze. Like so many empires before them, the Soviets had come and gone.

No sooner had the barn been eclipsed by the horizon than the figure of a horseman came charging toward us across the grassy plain. His whip flew in a frenzy on the left rump, then over his shoulder to the right, in Central Asian style. It was moments before his short black stallion stood in front of me, foaming at the bit, sweat-drenched chest convulsing.

Sitting straight-backed in his tattered saddle, this rider had all the confidence and authority of a custodian of this land. "Where are you going?"

I looked into his sun-blackened face but could barely make out his eyes, hidden in the shadow of a shabby baseball cap. As I began to answer he softened, and we rode on together for some time.

Rinat was born in Tashkent and had moved here in 1990, but soon after his arrival he had been imprisoned. He had been released three years ago. It was sad to see his proud sense of authority wither away as he recounted his story.

"There are three Russian men in my village who attacked me because I am Tatar. Finally they beat me so badly I decided to knife one of them I wanted to get him in the butt but got him in the stomach." He looked away and spat. "It doesn't bother me now. I don't drink, I don't smoke. I have my cows and my sheep—I'm happy. Regarding those Russians—well, God sees everything from above."

Rinat was the first Crimean Tatar I'd ever met, and, as it turned out, the only one I ever saw on horseback. The Crimean Tatars had only been allowed to return from exile in Central Asia beginning in 1989, just before the end of the Soviet era. What I would learn in time was that Rinat's story reflected a broader conflict between local Russians and returning Tatars that belied the calm of this peaceful landscape. It was a conflict that echoed the pattern of Crimea's complex history as a place of hostility and cooperation between nomads and sedentary society—a history that would ultimately dominate my stay in Crimea.

Before Rinat rode away he pointed to the distant radio towers of a Russian military exclusion zone. "That's where my mother was born. Her village was there. God willing, I will see my true homeland again, but I doubt that will happen. The Russians won't let me."

THAT EVENING, A flotilla of Soviet apartment blocks on the horizon signaled the historic port of Feodosiya—a city with intriguing links to the curbing of the Mongol expansion and the eventual decline of the Mongol Empire.

Formerly known as Kaffa, the city had been an important slave trading post, through which the Genoese exported Slavic and Kipchak prisoners to the slave army of the Egyptian sultan. The Mongols benefited from this trade by demanding tribute from the Genoese, but what the Mongols could not have foreseen was that these Kipchak slaves—who were nomads with a wealth of experience in the tactics of Mongol warfare—would rise to become a powerful military caste in Egypt known as the Mamluks. In time the Mamluks would inflict the first serious defeats on the Mongol army, permanently halting Mongol advances into the Middle East and tarnishing their image of invincibility.[3]

The rise of the Mamluks is not the only historical event for which Kaffa became an unlikely catalyst. Although Mongol authorities had allowed the lucrative slave trading to continue during their reign, on occasion they had also sacked Kaffa and other Genoese cities in an attempt to shut it down. In 1345 a Mongol army had been preparing for one such attack when the plague reached the Golden Horde capital, Sarai, on the lower Volga. The plague decimated the Mongol armies and forced them to withdraw. According to one report, Yanibeg, the khan of the Golden Horde, ordered the dead bodies of the soldiers to be catapulted over the high fortress walls surrounding Kaffa. This tactic is unlikely to have succeeded in transmitting the plague, but it is believed the disease nevertheless spread from the Mongol camp into the city, and then via ships from Kaffa to Constantinople and on to Africa and Europe. Not only did the plague wipe out at least a third of Europeans, more than half of China's population, and twelve million Africans, but some experts, including anthropologist Jack Weatherford, argue that it contributed to the disintegration of the Mongol Empire.

By the time the plague hit in the fourteenth century, however, it must be acknowledged that the Mongol Empire had already begun to break down. Genghis Khan had established a remarkably robust system of rule and conquer that would outlive him by generations, but his heirs were racked by division. During the latter half of the thirteenth century, the four khanates of the Mongol Empire—the Golden Horde, the Chaghatai khanate, the Ilkhanate, and the Yuan dynasty—were well on the path to being independent states. In the 1260s, in fact, the Ilkhanate fought a war with the Golden Horde, and in the east, Khubilai battled with his brother Arikboke for succession to the throne of the grand khan.[4]

Nonetheless, even if the plague wasn't responsible for the fall of the Mongol Empire, then it certainly accelerated its demise. Ever since Genghis Khan proclaimed himself "the ruler of all those who live in felt tents," the empire had relied on an efficient network of trade and communication routes. This not only provided military advantage but also helped prevent vassal states from revolting by keeping the people happy with stability and thriving economies. Just as this complex network could carry a messenger or Silk Road trader from Mongolia to Europe without affray, it equally aided the passage of the plague. Just like a global pandemic would do today, the plague paralyzed the flow of trade, isolating cities and countries, and eventually entire continents. Mongolian aristocracies found themselves with depleted militaries, unable to procure the same kind of taxes that had funded the empire, and more outnumbered by subjects than ever before.

By the end of the fourteenth century, Mongolians in Asia had returned to a nomadic lifestyle in their homeland or were absorbed or killed by the rebelling Chinese. In Persia, the last Mongol successors to the Ilkhanate had vanished. The Golden Horde would hold together for much longer than elsewhere, but ultimately Mongols here became part of fractious Turkic nations, such as the Crimean khanate, which eventually fell to Ottoman and Russian rule.

COMPARED TO LAYING siege to a city of slave traders, my designs on Feodosiya were more routine. The main obstacle of my journey through Crimea was a set of rugged, densely forested mountains, which I would have to traverse as far as the old Tatar capital, Bakchisaray. To do this I would need someone to guide me. I also required a farrier—my horses had gone barefoot for the last eighteen months, but with the rocky terrain of the mountains, they needed to be shod. I'd been given the name of a Russian lady named Ira who ran a horse farm called Argamak near Feodosiya. She had promised not only to help with the challenges of the mountains but also to show me around the city.

I found Ira's sprawl of stables and yards in the open steppe about 20 km shy of Feodosiya. Locating Ira proved another matter. A wafer-thin woman with stringy, meatless arms, and a look of grit in her eyes stepped from a stable, and when I told her whom I was looking for, she said, "You must be Tim! Wait here."

Half an hour passed before the woman appeared again and led me to a muddy yard strewn with horse tack, empty vodka bottles, and half-eaten cucumbers. It was then I noticed a leg dangling out of a car door. I followed it up to a mop of curly blond hair slumped forward on the steering wheel.

Just then a burly man with balding white hair and an unruly beard approached. "Ira! You have a guest!" he shouted. The man swayed on his feet, hands fumbling with the buttons of his shirt, which was open down to the last sunburned rib. His name was Max, he explained, and it was Ira's birthday.

The foot dangling from the car wiggled. Then the car door swung violently open and the woman who had been collapsed against the steering wheel staggered into life. "It's very . . . very nice to meet you," she slurred.

Ira may have been blind drunk, but after steadying herself against me she charged past and ran her hands up and down the legs of my horses.

"Yep, sure thing, we will shoe them," she said, sitting down in the dust.

My stay with Ira was meant to be brief, but as had happened so many times before on my journey, I became engrossed by the goings-on of the place, and a sequence of events—namely, a misfortunate mishap with Tigon—saw me delayed for much longer.

The first evening was a precursor of how I would spend most of my time with Ira and her friend Max. I'd had my first shot of vodka even before my backpack and chaps were off, and we fell into a conversation that orbited around all things horse.

Ira had a background in equestrian sport and had moved out onto the steppe in the 1990s to pursue her dream of running a stud farm. Max, on the other hand, was a grazier whose father was a descendant of Bash-kirian nomads in Siberia; he had set up a farm on neighboring land. By virtue of their divergent approaches to life on the steppe, they were of very different schools of thought when it came to horsemanship—Ira kept her horses in stables, while Max believed in the virtues of a fence-free life. It was a point of endless baiting.

"Fancy cooping her horses up like this in this glorious steppe!" Max told.

"Well, with thieves like you around, what choice do I have?" Ira tossed back.

Despite their differences—and their passion for horses, which to me embodied the spirit of nomads—they were united on one front: neither of them was fond of my interest in traditional steppe cultures, particularly when it came to Crimean Tatars.

Ira said to me, "Tim, Crimean Tatars are not to be trusted. They are not like you and me. The only reason they are coming back to Crimea is to steal our land and make lots of money. I watched a Tatar on horseback once—he was so cruel to the horse, no style at all. Never again will I invite a Tatar onto my property!" Over the coming days—and, as it turned out, weeks—I learned to avoid the subject.

On the third morning of my stay Max came charging into the farm. "Have you heard the news? Those damn Americans are here! Their NATO ship arrived in Feodosiya port last night! We are rallying as many boys as possible. We are not letting them ashore!" This bluster served as a thin veil for the real reason Max had blazed in: his wife had kicked him out, and he was hoping to sleep in Ira's barn for a week. But as Ira and I soon discovered, the ship had certainly caused a stir in Feodosiya.

After catching a ride into the city we stepped into the mayhem. Several hundred protestors waving flags and banners were heaving forward to the gates of the port. An elderly man leading them chanted slogans through a megaphone: "We know you Americans! You are not taking our land, now get out!" It was a simplistic assertion of a deeply complex conflict.

Although the Crimea had been gifted to Ukraine in 1954, it had been a Russian stronghold ever since 1783, when Catherine II defeated the

Ottomans. Even after the breakup of the Soviet Union, when Ukraine gained independence, the vast majority of the Crimean population remained Russian, with few cultural links to Ukraine. Critical to the issue was that Russia had always had its Black Sea naval fleet based in the strategic port of Sevastopol. Russia had signed an agreement with Ukraine to allow the fleet to remain stationed there until 2017, with the assumption that the lease would be extended. Viktor Yushchenko, however, the pro-Western leader swept to power on the tide of the Orange Revolution, had promised to make it his mission to break with Russian imperialism and join NATO. Not only were Russians facing the prospect of the fleet being expelled, but Yushchenko had refused to make Russian the second official language for Ukraine. So while Yushchenko and his prime minister, Yulia Tymoshenko, enjoyed popular support in mainland Ukraine, particularly in the west of the country, in Crimea they were detested.

After we battled our way through the crowd, the sounds of the protest faded as Ira and I took a walk along the esplanade in the shade of regal trees. We then turned into the old quarter of town. Competing with tsarist and Soviet-era architecture was a fourteenth-century stone church, built no doubt with the riches of the slave labor trade. Further on we pushed uphill through tiers of old stone homes with terra-cotta-tiled roofs until we reached a labyrinth of paths that took us to an old rampart. I climbed to the top, from where the protest and the ship had shrunken to mere details. In the hills around the old quarter, remnants of stone walls ran along the edges like vertebrae wearing through the earth. Out at sea the water was calm and glassy.

It seemed that through the millennia some things here had not changed. Whether threats of invasion came from the Mongols or NATO, Crimea remained a flash point in the geopolitical landscape. To bear witness to this land by horse felt like a way of bridging the past and the present day. And my adventure in Crimea had only just begun.[5]

IT WAS UPON returning with Ira from Feodosiya I learned of news that crushed hopes of carrying on to the mountains any time soon. Tigon had run off after being violently kicked by a visitor to Ira's farm. I found the dog lying semiconscious under some bushes and spent the ensuing night holding him in my arms. In the morning a veterinarian concluded he had internal bleeding and swollen kidneys.

It was two days before Tigon began to eat again, and three weeks before we could contemplate riding on. By that time the rich green of the steppe had waned to yellow, the days were unbearably hot, and mosquitoes were descending like fog at night. It was a seasonal transition that once would have signaled to nomads of the Crimea that it was time to escape the heat and migrate to the cool alpine meadows of the mountains.

I had long put the word out that I was looking for a guide, but most shied away when they considered the route. There were no Tatars in the area with knowledge of the mountains anymore, and the tracks in the forested approaches to the high plains were overgrown. The only man willing to try was Seryoga, a Russian friend of Ira's.

"The only thing to keep in mind is that Seryoga likes to drink," Ira warned.

On the day before my departure, I watched with anticipation as my companion-to-be arrived driving a horse and cart. From a distance his heavyset frame, weathered face, and tawny, sun-bleached hair cut a handsome figure. As he pulled in with a series of whistles and commands, though, my eyes were drawn to his disfigured upper lip.

"This is my trophy from an accident a few years ago, when I was even younger and even more stupid!" he said, pointing apologetically to his toothless upper mouth. "I was drunk and fell off my horse at a full gallop on the pavement!"

We spent the afternoon shoeing. Seryoga was particularly impressed with Taskonir. The walls of the horse's hooves were so hard that when he tried hammering nails in, they bent and had to be pulled out. "That's what you call a no-problem horse," Seryoga exclaimed. "You could have boiled a cup of tea in his hooves and then ridden another ten thousand kilometres without shoes!"

We agreed that such naturally hardened hooves would have been a big advantage for the Mongols when they rode into Europe. Their European counterparts, riding on large, hay-fed horses, would have been hampered by the need to constantly maintain their horses' hooves and shoes.

The next day we began our journey to the mountains in a fashion I came to learn was true to Seryoga's character. Overnight Seryoga had shared four or five bottles of vodka with Ira and had not slept. Nevertheless, we rode eight hours straight in the heat, which at its maximum reached 38°C. Seryoga was bareback on his bony old mare, Zera, and wore nothing but a pair of cavalry jodhpurs and a rope tied around his waist. His lean, muscled torso was red with sunburn, and he smoked tobacco rolled in pieces of newspaper, stubbing them out one by one on the soles of his cheap Chinese-made running shoes.

Late in the day we reached the forested foothills of the Crimean mountains and rode on to Seryoga's parents' home in the town of Staryi Krym. "Give me two days here, Tim. I have some things to sort out, then I will be able to come with you," Seryoga promised. Two days soon became three, and then this grew to a whole week. Although I had initially counted on Seryoga only as a guide to see me through the mountains—where mostly I hoped to learn about Tatar heritage—he became a story in himself.

Seryoga saw the journey with me as an opportunity to quit his job as a forest ranger, and each morning he would walk an hour into town with the intention of handing in his letter of resignation. On the way, however, he would buy a couple of bottles of beer. With each bottle his mood would turn, and ultimately he never reached the forestry department offices.

On the eighth day, when I was on the verge of leaving alone, he picked himself up and promised I had to wait just one more day. That morning he walked 20 km to the coast to shoe a dozen horses at a trail-riding farm—they were poorly trained animals that no farrier would touch. He stumbled home after dark, nursing terribly inflamed cuts and gouges across his wrists and palms, but reassured me, "Don't worry, nothing could be harmful to my body! Tomorrow morning, we leave!"

We were joined for dinner by two local prostitutes who were a mother-and-daughter combination—they had heard on the grapevine that Seryoga had earned some money. Later on Seryoga vanished with them to a local bar, and finally the following morning he turned up ready to go.

"Let's go, Tim!" he yelled triumphantly.

The morning air was cool as we packed and finally rode out among a mob of mooing cattle on their way to pasture. A babushka wielding a stick hobbled after them. "I'll moo you if you don't move, you bunch of bitches!'" she called affectionately.

When we left the village behind and entered the forest, I rode behind Seryoga, enjoying the sense of protection the dense canopy of oak, ash, and beech provided. The sun drifted down in slender cascades, fragrant leaves tumbled, and red deer flashed through the undergrowth. Every now and then a gust of wind creaked through the trees, reaching us as a soft breath of air.

For centuries, the forests of the Crimean mountains had been home to one of the three distinct subgroups of Crimean Tatars, the Tatas. The Tatas were renowned for their European features, believed to be inherited from Goths who had inhabited the same area in Crimea for well over a thousand years. The Tatas differed from their Tatar brothers on the steppe, known as the Nogais, who were descendants of a long line of steppe nomads, the Kipchaks. The Nogais in turn differed from the Tatars on the coast, known as the Yaliboyu, who lived as traders and fishermen. The existence of these distinct identities went largely unacknowledged by Russians, including Seryoga and Ira, who believed that Tatars had only ever inhabited the steppe regions.

I kept my thoughts to myself while Seryoga smoked in silence, gently tapping Zera's rump. Whenever he spoke it was about his beloved mare. "Oh, Zera, my love!" he would say with a heavy lisp. "We don't need anyone else, do we? Just you and me . . . you should see her pulling carts of timber up and down the mountain. She is one courageous lady."

By evening we were lost, and for the next three days we pushed on along winding trails laden with fallen trees, with little clue as to where we were. The slopes grew steep, giving way to gullies that twisted and turned, choked with ferns and cascading streams. At one point we stumbled into a small sunlit meadow where a stone memorial to Soviet partisan fighters stood masked in moss and grass.

"It was in these forests that the Soviet partisan heroes lived during the

Great Patriotic War," Seryoga said reflectively. As I looked at him sitting on his sheepskin saddle blanket, wearing khaki jodhpurs, chaps, and a commando vest, it wasn't hard to picture the partisans he spoke about. For almost three years they had famously fought against the Nazi occupation of Crimea until the Red Army retook the peninsula in 1944.

From a word etched into the memorial stone, we were able to locate ourselves on the map. As I remounted to leave, Seryoga remained standing there. His expression had turned to one of bitterness. "But those traitor Crimean Tatars, Tim, they fought against us, the partisans. If you speak with the old-timers here, you will hear the truth of what they did. They slaughtered innocent women and children—anyone, in fact, who was supporting these brave partisans."

In my short time in Crimea, I had learned that this was a point of contention. Stalin had ordered the blanket deportation of Tatars to Central Asia and Siberia on the basis that they had collaborated with the Nazis. Word-of-mouth stories about violence meted out by Tatars abounded, yet modern-day evidence suggests that only a minority of Tatars ever sided with the Nazis. According to what I had read, a large percentage of partisans were in fact Tatar but changed their last names to Russian versions during the war to avoid suspicion. I wanted to point out to Seryoga that even those who did fight for the Nazis should perhaps be forgiven; after all, between the Bolshevik revolution and 1941 the Soviets had banned Islam and murdered, starved, or deported around 160,000 Tatars—about half the Tatar population at the time. Could anyone really blame some of the Tatars for choosing not to fight on behalf of the Soviets? I said nothing, however.

Sensing my sympathy for the Crimean Tatars despite my silence, Seryoga continued. "I know one good Tatar, but mostly, Tim, they are bad people . . . It's not for nothing they were deported by Stalin, you know."

IT TOOK A full week to reach the steep forested slopes just below the high alpine plateau. By this stage Seryoga had run out of cigarettes and we were down to the last scraps of food.

Just as we were preparing to retreat down the mountain—we were once again lost—the sun speared through the trees uphill from us and we walked, blinking, onto the Karabi Jayla. The largest alpine plateau of the Crimean Mountains, the Karabi was a place so renowned for its pasture that nomads once traveled here from as far as Moldavia to fatten their sheep and cattle. Echoing the important role this high pasture played in nomad life of the region, *jayla* is a Crimean Tatar word with Turkic roots, similar to the Kazakh term *jalau*, meaning "summer place" or "summer pasture."

We rode on to where the plateau fell away in dramatic cliffs to the Black Sea about 1,000 m below. In camp I gazed out over broad grassy slopes, imagining huddles of yurts and the fragrant smell of burning dung. In the seventeenth century, European travelers Guillaume le Vasseur de Beauplan and Pierre Chevalier had painted a picture of a nomadic culture here that was essentially unchanged since the time of Genghis Khan. The Crimean Tatars lived in felt tents, were feared horseback archers, and, according to the Europeans' observations, rode small unshod horses, described by both as "ugly"—although Chevalier qualified this by saying that "nature hath very well repaired their ugliness by their swiftness."[6]

Russian occupation of Crimea in the eighteenth century saw Tatars making migrations of a different kind—primarily across the sea for refuge in Turkey. Suspected as collaborators with the Turks, a hundred thousand fled during the annexation in 1783, and even more in the 1860s in the aftermath of the Crimean War. Many drowned during the risky sea crossings.

Come the twentieth century, in 1944 any Tatars who had remained and survived Soviet persecution were shipped away by train across the vast ocean of steppe to Central Asia. According to some, the very last camels—descendants of those used by Crimean Tatar nomads on migrations—were herded out of Crimea in 1941 during the Nazi invasion.

I was lifted from my thoughts by Seryoga. "If we have run out of cigarettes and vodka, and we have almost no food, there is nothing for me to do but sleep!" He crawled inside the tent, covered himself with a horse blanket, and collapsed.

When he woke I offered him dried curd, peanuts, and dried meat that had been floating about in the bottom of my pack boxes for over a year.

We picked some wild herbs for tea and went to bed immediately to mask our hunger.

By the time we got moving the following day, Seryoga had sobered up. The heaviness that surrounded him had evaporated and he seemed to have lost years from his face. "If I don't come all the way to Hungary," he said, "which I would like to do, please promise me one thing: if you aren't able to get the horses over the border, let me know and I'll be sure to travel there and ride them back. Don't think about giving that Taskonir to anyone else!"

I agreed, and for the next couple of days we rode on in high spirits. I felt that we had become good friends. For a short time I even began to believe that he might come with me as far as Hungary, but his positive state of mind lasted only until we descended to the village of Aromatnoe for food. There Zera pulled up lame and Seryoga was back on the booze.

The next morning he hugged me goodbye and began the long walk home.

20

THE RETURN OF THE CRIMEAN TATARS

Crimea, Crimea, Mother Crimea,
We did not forget our name,
We did not, Mother Crimea,
Exchange our isle for another's.

—Rustem Ali, *Crimea* (1992)[1]

AFTER LEAVING AROMATNOE I rode for nine hours over a pass before reaching the village of Perevalnoe. There, against Seryoga's advice, I had prearranged to meet with a Crimean Tatar farmer named Edem.

Given the animosity expressed to me about Tatars, I was all the more curious to meet Edem and learn firsthand about the Tatars' return to the Crimea.[2] Not so secretly, I was already partial to the cause of these once nomadic people, and I had spent much of the past few weeks pondering the underlying reasons for the hostile attitudes.

The vilification of Tatars seemed cruel to me given the tragic circumstances of their exile. On May 18, 1944, without warning, around 191,000 Tatars had been escorted by soldiers from their homes and deported in livestock train cars to Siberia and Central Asia. Many died during the harrowing journey, their bodies, according to witnesses' accounts, often hauled out on the order of guards and left in open graves by the tracks in the deserts of Central Asia. The survivors of those chilling events—for whom the trauma was still raw—had waited all their lives to return from exile.

Ostensibly, the antipathy harbored by Russians stemmed from the Tatars' alleged collaboration with Nazis.[3] I'd decided, however, that attitudes probably reflected a deeper, more enduring prejudice, hints of which had been explicit in Stalin's strategy. When Stalin deported the Crimean Tatars he had labeled them not only traitors but descendants of Mongol invaders. Soviet authorities had even falsely reasoned that Crimean Tatars were Mongol in origin and therefore belonged in Central Asia. After deportation the category "Crimean Tatar" was removed from the official encyclopedia of the Soviet Union's peoples, and evidence of their history in Crimea—including cemeteries, literature, and even place names—was erased. The homes, livestock, orchards, and grain stores they had left behind were seized, and unlike other deported peoples such as Kalmyks and Chechens who were allowed to return to their homes in 1957, Crimean Tatars were forbidden to return to Crimea until 1989.

In associating Crimean Tatars with Mongolians, Stalin not only justified indefinite exile but preyed on Russian hostility toward Crimean Tatars that dates to the founding of their khanate in the fifteenth century—a hostility that, in all fairness, is worthy of consideration. Like a series of nomadic powers before them, the Crimean Tatars had been renowned for riding up through Russia's southern borders to take captives for trading as slaves through the port of Kaffa (present-day Feodosiya). Slave trading was in fact at the core of the Crimean khanate's economy, and in 1571 during one raid alone Tatars managed to burn Moscow to the ground and take up to 150,000 Slavs into captivity.

Many historians point out that hostilities between nomads and Slavs have been overemphasized. Evidence suggests that nomads and Slavs often inter-married, engaged in mutually beneficial trade, and struck military alliances. Nonetheless, the historic propensity for Crimean Tatars to inflict terror on the Russian people is undeniable, and something I was perhaps guilty of not paying enough attention to in my broader evaluation of nomad society.

In the last two centuries, of course, Russians had come to dominate Crimea and decisively reversed the trend of predatory steppe empires. Even so, the exploits of the Tatars had somewhat understandably, left a deep scar on the Russian psyche. The very term *Tatar* could still rouse heated emotion, and the return of the Tatars had incited fears of a modern invasion. As I would discover in coming weeks this had created a tinder-box of ethnic tension and triggered a dangerous cycle of revenge.

For the last hour of the ride to Perevalnoe I felt my way down the mountains in the dark, relieved when a chorus of snarling dogs signaled my arrival at Edem's farm. The outline of men conversing in a Turkic tongue grew out of the darkness. Then a floodlight flicked on and I was met with a steel-gripped handshake.

"I'm Edem. Now c'mon, what are you sitting there for? It's time to rest and feed your horses!" the man said in flawless Russian.

In a rusty old worker's cabin I sat sipping tea with Edem and six of his employees who had recently migrated from Uzbekistan. Under dim light cast by a bulb shrouded in a haze of mosquitoes, the men ranged from a sun-blackened teenager with Russian features to a bandy-legged elder with deep-set eyes and a large Turkic nose, whose dark, freckled face had been sculpted far more by the harsh Central Asian sun than it could ever be now by the coastal climate of Crimea.

Edem himself was thickly built and balding with blue eyes, a narrow pinched nose, and a fine, pale mustache—classic features of his Tata ori-gins. He sat wearing leather sandals and an immaculate white shirt un-buttoned to the belly, exhibiting both the air of an aristocrat and the machismo of a worker. He had been in Crimea for twenty-five years and, like many of his generation born in exile, had moved to Crimea to pave the way for his mother, who had been deported as a child.

We had barely finished the tea when there came the roar of a truck grinding up the driveway. I went out and watched it come to a halt next to a half-constructed building before a bevy of women climbed down from the back laden with mops and brushes. The workers unloaded a bed, dresser, mirror, and mattress, while the driver personally carried a pot of hot plov (pilaf) to Edem.

Only after Edem and I had finished eating did I understand the goings-on. "Tim, you can move your things in now. I have been building this hotel for two years . . . and I want you to be the first guest!" Edem said.

In the light of morning I was able to get a better picture of where I had landed. Edem's hotel and farmyards were built into the slope above the village of Perevalnoe. Below, on the valley floor, the main road to the resort city of Yalta snaked its way toward the coast. Somewhere down there Edem had apparently built himself a two-story family mansion. In the other direction mountain slopes angled up in ramps of rock and craggy trees to alpine pastures. The teenager from the night before was high above, whistling and calling as he pushed a herd of sheep into cooler, thinner air.

After breakfast, when the yards were empty and the rising sun had taken the crisp edge off the morning, Edem and I sat in the shade with a cup of tea. To become this established as a Tatar in Crimea was a remarkable achievement requiring strong conviction—a fact not lost on Edem.

"For Tatars who are returning now, life is hard, but it is a fairy tale compared to what it was like for us earlier," he said, casting his gaze up to the high slopes. Edem had first tried to migrate in 1981—when it was still illegal for Tatars to live and work in Crimea. This discriminatory law had been enforced by denying Tatars a propiska, a residence permit, without which registration was not possible and employment prohibited.

"At first when I arrived from Uzbekistan in Semfiropol," the modern capital of Crimea, "I slept at the train station while I looked for a job. I was a communications expert and was offered work in the coastal city of Sudak. When my employer discovered I was a Tatar the police pursued me and I was beaten up and arrested. Eventually I managed to escape to the Ukraine," Edem explained.

Brutalization was a common experience of Tatars in those times and combined with the prospect of exile and imprisonment to create an atmosphere of desperation. Some returning Tatars had resorted to extreme measures to assert their right to live in Crimea, including acts of self-immolation. The most notorious case had occurred three years before Edem's arrival in 1978, when a Tatar named Musa Mahmut had doused himself in gasoline and lit a match as officers arrived to arrest him. He later died in the hospital and had come to be seen as a martyr for Tatars making the bold decision to migrate to Crimea. In fact, in the 1980s and 1990s many Tatars modeled their strategy on Mahmut's, keeping gasoline and matches at hand as a means to prevent eviction from lands and homes they were reoccupying. This proved effective—but it also drew great contempt from Russians.

Edem had been more fortunate than many others. "After one year in Ukraine I had gathered enough money to buy a car and drove back to Crimea. I was lucky to avoid authorities—with my blue eyes and fair hair, few people suspected me. Eventually I made friends with a city councilor in Kerch. He was one of the few Russians I have ever met who believed discrimination against Tatars was wrong, and he agreed to help me get a propiska. I remember when the lady at the registration desk noticed that I was a Tatar. She said, 'We can't register him!' but my friend yelled at her, 'Just do it!' "

This kind gesture had not been without consequences. Soon after Edem received the propiska, he was arrested and the Russian councilor was imprisoned. Nevertheless, Edem managed to escape following these events, and from that point on managed to find refuge in the Crimean mountains. Living up on the high plains I had ridden through, he had avoided the authorities for the better part of a decade, coming down "once in 1985 to get married to a Tatar girl." Only in 1989 was he given legal status, and he immediately began arranging for his mother and other relatives to migrate.

Nowadays, of course, Tatars had the right to return and were technically entitled to housing and land as compensation. Edem lamented, however, that Russian attitudes had not changed. In fact, he felt they might be growing worse. "These people who live in the homes that our fathers built, who eat the food of the trees that our fathers planted, drink water from the wells that were dug by our forefathers, of course they are not all that happy to see us again because it reminds them of what was done to us."

Edem was accustomed to insults from Russians and internalized most of his frustration. What he found most injurious these days was that his elderly mother, who had been the only survivor among her siblings during deportation, had to date been denied access to the home she had grown up in. "All she wants is to drink from the well that her grandfather dug himself, but the Russian occupants won't let her past the front gate."

I spent a week under Edem's wing, during which time I learned that while the struggle for early arrivals such as Edem was largely over, for many of those who had come later the battle had only begun. On the grassy flats by the Yalta road I visited one of hundreds of land claim sites established across Crimea. For four months Tatars had been living in an army mess tent, preparing to take the land by force. Surrounding the tent were hundreds of stacks of yellow bricks spread out over a large area. Each stack represented an individual family claim. The people here were waiting for a signal from Tatar leaders, at which point, according to the plan, building would begin at all sites across Crimea, and the numbers would be too vast for the authorities to contain. Inside the tent I spoke with aggrieved Tatars who complained that although the Ukrainian government had promised to provide homes, the program of resettlement had collapsed back in 1996, and of the 270,000 returned Tatars, more than half still had no land or housing of their own.

I had also been told the Russian side of the story: that the Tatars who were making claims already owned homes elsewhere, and after taking this coveted land they would build a house and flip it for profit. Edem had admitted that some of these Tatars were in fact abusing the system.

Whatever the truth, though, despite efforts by the Soviet regime to erase the identity of Crimean Tatars, it was clear that the Tatars' passion for their homeland remained stubbornly alive. Tatars such as Edem had even been prepared to risk life and limb to return. Perhaps it was this dedication that troubled Russians most, because it challenged the premise they had been sold that these people were not deeply connected to the Crimea, that they belonged somewhere in the savage East. The status quo reminded me of a phrase in Tolstoy's short novel *Hadj Murat*: "He [Tsar Nicholas] had done much harm to the Poles and to explain this it was necessary to believe that all Poles were scoundrels. Nicholas considered that to be so and hated the Poles in proportion to the harm he had done them."

Before leaving Edem's, I spent one day in the Crimean capital, Semfiropol, where I met with the deputy minister of culture of Crimea, Ismet Zaatov. Ismet put me in contact with leaders of the *mejlis*, the independent Tatar government, which in turn offered me the support of the Tatar community wherever I might need it. The most important connection he arranged was with the director of Tatar TV, Islyam Kishveye.

In an office at the back of the Tatar TV studio in Semfiropol—which Islyam later claimed was bugged by Russian and Ukrainian secret services— Islyam played me a video he had recently recorded in the old Crimean capital, Bakchisaray. It was there, he said, that the front-line battle was now being fought by Tatars.

Islyam skipped forward to footage of a wall of burly Russian men steaming toward a group of Tatar protestors. As they collided, the crowd exploded in fistfights. Some men were knocked to the ground and kicked, while others were chased away and beaten. Islyam had been attacked, too, and as his camera jerked from side to side there were flashes of bloodied faces and sounds of hysterical, wailing women.

At one point he paused the video on the image of a man with a shaven scalp in a gray suit. He had just moved in to kick a Tatar man who lay on the asphalt. "This is Medvedev," Islyam said. "He is the director of the market where this whole battle is taking place. He has hired these thugs that you can see now."

I didn't yet understand the reasons for the conflict I had seen, but I couldn't wait to get back to my horses and on to Bakchisaray.

⌗

FROM EDEM'S FARM I rode for three days along mountain and forest trails. It was the peak of summer, my third on the steppe, and a part of me was mentally weary and comforted by the thought it would be my last in the saddle. The mosquitoes stressed the horses, and the heat increased the risk of saddle sores. Additionally, I was beginning to feel claustrophobic in Crimea. In wider spaces, people bearing historical grudges with each other were separated by the muting qualities of distance. Here, trapped on such a small, sought-after chunk of land, cultures, layers of competing histories, and even environments were compressed, and I found myself bandied from one to another. There was no let-up, and ahead of me, things were only about to get more intense.

In the evening of my third day out from Edem's farm a Russian horseman led me as far as the edge of the forest, where oaks gave way to an old Tatar walnut orchard. Pressing on, I took the opportunity to enjoy a passing moment of aloneness. I slowed the horses to a walk, soaking in the way their hooves shifted quietly along a track of powdery white clay. I leaned back in the saddle, watching the outstretched branches of the walnut trees and their broad leaves glide over us. Like Tatar elders who had survived deportation and returned, these elegant trees had outlived the Soviet years and were obstinately rooted in Crimean soil.

Beyond the orchard we emerged from the shade and descended into the head of a gorge-like valley. Ears pricked and tongue out, Tigon craned his neck to look at the high slopes that now blocked much of the sky. Rising above were limestone bluffs running like ramparts along both our sides. The rock high up to our left was honeycombed with caves—the remnants of a seventh-century Byzantine stronghold that was taken over by the Tatars in the fourteenth century. The farther on we rode, the deeper we sank into this curious landform, and as the gorge narrowed we began to pass homes, stables, and even an Orthodox monastery carved out of the rock at the base of the bluffs.

Where the gorge seemed to have run its course, the cliffs converged and the track shrank to a narrow cobbled alleyway between old stone houses. Then, unexpectedly, it hooked sharply to the left, and a valley opened up, filled from wall to wall with a riot of minarets and red ceramic-tiled roofs. Right in front of us they mingled majestically with the bustle of cars and pedestrians in the dusty summer evening.

Bakchisaray was formerly the capital of the Crimean khanate and once an important crossroad of the Silk Road, where traders met from across the Black Sea, the steppes of Central Asia, Russia, and eastern Europe. In its heyday during the fifteenth and sixteenth centuries the town had boasted eighteen mosques and several important madrasas. Nowadays, it is the cultural center for returning Tatars and, as I would learn, a bottleneck of tourism, religion, and conflict. I would spend more than a week in Bakchisaray, but within the first twenty-four hours I had been introduced to the main settings and protagonists that came to dominate my stay.

Nestled among the cobbled streets of the old part of town lay the khan's palace. Known in Tatar as the *hanssaray*, it had been the seat of power for generations of Crimean khans dating back to the sixteenth century. On the one hand, the palace represented the sophistication of the Crimean Tatar khanate, which had once wielded much power, but on the other, now that it was a museum and part of a heritage park with a Russian director, it symbolized the passing of the Tatars' way of life into the archives of history and its once proud empire into subservience to Russia.

Out of sight of tourists at the other end of town—but still little more than a kilometre from the palace—lay the market. Here an ugly stand-off between Tatars and Russians was under way in which the same clashes of history documented at the palace were still being played out.

Lying between these two places, and caught in the crossfire, were my host, Volodya—impoverished, fiery, half Tatar, half Russian—and a Ukrainian girl named Anya, with whom I fell in love.

Ismet had arranged for Volodya to look after me in Bakchisaray, and so

I carried on down the steep cobbled street into the old town, where he led me through the grand wooden gates of the khan's palace. Inside, I rode Taskonir through an archway into the courtyard, where the last fragments of the evening sun cast golden light from over the cliffs above. As Tigon took the opportunity to bathe in a fountain, I lifted my gaze to the high wall of the palace and let my eyes wander down. Towering minarets inscribed in Arabic cast lean shadows across a courtyard of rose gardens, fountains, lawns, and shady trees. Adjoining the outer wall was the two-story palace itself, adorned with arches, long verandahs, and walls decorated with Islamic murals. In these luxurious headquarters the Crimean khans—blood descendants of Genghis Khan—had ruled one of the most powerful empires of eastern Europe. There was without question a sense of authenticity about the palace that transcended time and invited thoughts about what might have once been. At a closer look, though, tourist information signs nailed onto walls and museum-style displays were a reminder of the modern reality.

In 1736 Bakchisaray had been burned to the ground by the Russians, and when Catherine II's army completed the conquest of the peninsula in 1783, the last khan, Sahin Giray, took refuge in Turkey, where he was eventually executed. The palace had long become a defunct relic paraded by its captors as accommodation for important guests, including Catherine II herself. Two centuries on it was a major tourist attraction to which thousands of Russian tourists flocked each summer to marvel at the lair of their historic foe.

It was while the guards test-rode my horses that I noticed Anya. She stood by a rose garden in the back corner of the courtyard, busy brushing strokes onto canvas, her easel set up between us. Just from a glimpse of her bare, slender arms and golden hair I recognized her as a girl who had approached me as I had ridden down into the town. In fact, the image of her was still firmly entrenched in my mind: carrying an easel and a bag of paintbrushes, her blue eyes lit up by the low-angling sun, she had walked up to me and asked about my horses.

As I approached now she looked my way and put her brush down.

"About time you noticed me! You just walked into my painting!" she said, as we both struggled in vain to hold back smiles.

Anya was a twenty-four-year-old Ukrainian art student from Kiev. She had been given special permission to stay in the palace after hours to paint. I offered her a ride on Taskonir and for the next half hour nervously led her around the courtyard. Before I left, Anya and I agreed to meet in the city in the coming days.

At Volodya's house that night a rabbit was slaughtered in my honor, and we celebrated with cheap Russian vodka. My spirits were high: I had fallen for Anya, and in light of the last few hard days of riding, the rabbit was a veritable banquet.

Come morning, my feelings for Anya hadn't changed, but the reality around me was a lot more sobering. Volodya had been born in exile and now lived in a hovel he had built out of mud, reeds, scrap wood, glass bottles, and a few token bricks. Inside, there was just the one room with an old Russian divan that doubled as a bed for him, his wife, and their two children.

Volodya's mother, a Tatar, had been born in a house in the center of Bakchisaray, but on return from exile Volodya had been forced to settle in what had became known as the "seventh micro-region"—a self-proclaimed Tatar enclave (known in Russian as a *samozakhvat*) on the barren steppe above the gorge. To support his family, Volodya worked shifts at a tile factory in town, and his wife, who was Russian, made cushions stuffed with juniper shavings for tourists, receiving thirty kopeks for each. Their cross-cultural relationship did not make life any easier. "It's hard to hear when Tatar children tell my kids things like, 'We will butcher you. All Russians should be loaded up in cattle wagons and sent out, just as they did to us,' " Volodya's wife said. Compounding the difficult situation, as I would learn, was Volodya's addiction to cigarettes and alcohol.

Later that morning I visited the market for the first time. It was situated in the new center of Bakchisaray—a place with none of the allure I had seen the previous evening. Where the gorge spilled out into a wide dry valley, a hot summer wind blew dust through scattered Soviet apartment blocks and crooked wooden houses. Nineties-era shops were tacked on like afterthoughts, perused by token shoppers on foot. Beat-up Ladas drifted listlessly by.

At a central intersection, stretching across the road between an apartment block and a drugstore, was a picket line of demonstrators. Beyond them lay the entrance to the market and a makeshift barricade hung with the Tatar flag and an unmistakable banner: "Close the Market That Is Built on Our Bones!" To one side of the drugstore, a carpet had been laid down, and a group of men wearing traditional embroidered velvet skullcaps—known across Central Asia as the *tyubeteika*—were kneeling in prayer. A hundred or so elderly Tatars manned the picket line, and others gathered around a cauldron that filled the air with the aroma of boiled mutton.

Meanwhile, lurking in the shade of trees, in cars, and in buses on both sides of the picket line were dozens of heavily equipped *berkuts*, or riot police, their shields and truncheons at the ready. Another branch of police, special forces known as *bars*, were roaming about in flak jackets.

Ismet had informed the mejlis about my journey, and on approaching the protestors I found Akhmet, a high-ranking mejlis representative who had been expecting me. He was busy in negotiation with a local police constable but took the time to explain the crux of the issue. "There are eleven mausoleums here that house the graves of several generations of our khans and spiritual leaders who brought Islam to Crimea," he said. "They date back at least five hundred years. The market that was built on this holy site by Russians in the early nineties hasn't been around for more than fifteen years, and we want it removed."

Akhmet introduced me to a Tatar historian who took me beyond the picket line to the base of one of the mausoleums, a domed, octagonal monument built from stone. Nearby lay the vacant market, a ramshackle collection of insipid stands. Inside its buckled iron boundary fence stood another mausoleum—this one with a Russian-built pit toilet alongside.

The mausoleums were thought to be connected to the ancient city of Eski Yurt, which had been founded on the grave of the seventh-century Islamic saint Malik Ashtar—the first to have spread Islam in Crimea. It had subsequently become the cemetery for Tatar khans, and until Soviet times it attracted thousands of pilgrims annually.

In a provocative move, the market had been built during the death throes of the Soviet Union, and ever since then, Tatars had been lobbying the market's Russian director, Medvedev, to relocate it. They had put forth a plan for the mausoleums to be protected as part of the Bakchisaray Historical and Cultural Preserve. Medvedev had thus far refused, and only a few months before my arrival he had hired some men to start moving the boundary fence of the market out even further—with the rumored backing of the pro-Russian party Russki Blok and local Mafia.

It was this situation that had led to the violent confrontation I had seen on Islyam's footage back in Semfiropol. Medvedev had employed a band of thugs to smash through the protestors and reopen the market by force. Temporarily at least, Medvedev had won the day.

BY THE TIME I left the market the heat of the day had sapped the energy of the demonstrators and the tension had waned. Even the riot police had their helmets off and sat eating ice cream, their shields leaning up against trees.

I was determined to return to the market, but in the meantime I used the lull to meet with Anya. We spent the rest of the day together exploring the monasteries and ruins in the cliffs above the khan's palace. I talked a little about the problems at the market. As a Ukrainian accustomed to the imperialistic ways of Russia, she had some degree of sympathy for the Tatars, but on the other hand, like many Ukrainians, she had a poor understanding of the situation and was mostly impartial. I dropped the subject and savored the shady old quarters of the city, where there was little hint of conflict. Sunburned tourists flowed in on excursions from their resorts on the coast, and I was lost in the light, happy feeling of summer and romance. We spent the next two nights together in my tent, and hours in front of a campfire together with some of her student colleagues. In her arms I felt as though I were in a parallel world—a place where we could both have some time out from the palpable ethnic tension in Bak-chisaray, and I could rest from my journey.

On our second morning together I accompanied Anya to the station for the train to Kiev and kissed her goodbye. Our time together had been brief, but nonetheless, when the train pulled out of sight it left me feeling alone. We promised to remain in contact, and to meet up if possible. Anya had a dream of joining me somewhere, although realistically we weren't sure if that was possible: she was in the middle of working toward her master's degree.

In a somber mood I trundled away from the station. When I arrived at the market, however, I was promptly pulled out of my funk. The scene there was very different from how I had left it two days earlier. Now the picket line was choked with protestors, and the group of men camped outside the drugstore with their prayer mats had grown into such a crowd that there was only sitting room. The riot police, in turn, stretched across the road between the picket line and the market and were facing off against the swelling crowd, brandishing their shields.

I became acutely aware of glares from both the riot police and the Ta-tars. It was a delicate balance, being a foreigner seen to have an allegiance with one culture or the other—something that my time with Anya, a Slav, had only accentuated. Underneath I had felt a little traitorous abandoning the cause of the market to be with her, and Tatars, including Volodya, had been noticeably silent upon learning about our romance. On this day, however, I was relieved when a man from the crowd in front of the drug-store stood up and waved me over excitedly.

It was Islyam, the director of Tatar TV. He was looking sweaty and frazzled. Apparently the prime minister of Ukraine had flown to Crimea, and the mejlis was negotiating the final order for the market to be re-moved. Overnight, Tatars had rallied from across Crimea and were brac-ing for a showdown. "We are waiting for a decision," Islyam told me, "but, signature from the prime minister or no, we are going to smash the market down today, by ourselves if necessary!"

Just as he said it, there came a high-pitched whistling from the picket line, and around me the whole crowd of men, Islyam included, leaped to

their feet and rushed forward. Apparently someone had attacked the pick-
eters. I dashed after the rushing crowd but fell behind in the thrusting
mass of people. Suddenly I was yanked backward and fell flat on my
back—someone had nabbed me from behind and pulled me to the ground.

"Hey! Go back! Move out, Russian!" screamed the man who had grabbed
me, drawing back his fist above my face. A section of the crowd stopped
and circled, but just as they closed in there came a woman's voice. "No, no!
Leave him! He is one of ours. He is the Australian traveler!" The men
helped me up and invited me to join them, but I decided to hang back.

Watching from a distance, I saw that it wasn't a thug who had attacked
the picket line but a Russian pensioner. She was wielding her fists and
screaming, "Let me through! God! This is my home! Let me through to
my home!" According to Tatars, confrontations like these were part of a
campaign by Medvedev, who paid local Russians to act as provocateurs.

Over the next few hours I stuck close to Islyam as more provocations
unfolded and tensions rose. Tatar numbers were expanding. Rumor had it
Medvedev had hired a legion of thugs from Sevastopol, and that a group
of Cossacks—bent on fulfilling their historic role as protectors of Russia—
were coming from as far as Russia. Using wire, wood, and whatever they
could find, Tatars began to fortify their picket line in preparation for a
tense night.

I was invited to camp out with Islyam, but I had to decline, as I had
been invited to the khan's palace. The director of the Bakchisaray Historical and Cultural Preserve had arranged a special concert and dinner.

⸎

IN THE COOL of evening on a lawn at the back of the khan's palace courtyard, four musicians began to play. As I approached, wandering sounds from
a traditional flute, a long-necked lute, and a cimbalon mingled with the energetic notes of a conventional violin. The resulting harmony filtered up
through the shady trees above. I came to rest on the grass and felt my sweat
chill.

I gazed at the four men, each with their black olive-shaped eyes and wearing a golden embroidered tyubeteika. At the end of each song, they bowed their heads, bending elegantly at their waists, which were tightly wrapped in red cummerbunds.

The oldest of the men explained they had studied music in their youth at the conservatory in Tashkent and now played for the Crimean Philharmonic Orchestra. Since their return to Crimea, they had set about resurrecting traditional Tatar music and during a visit to archives in Istanbul discovered pieces dating back to the sixteenth century. It was these tunes they now brought to life.

The concert came to an end when Evegeniy Petrovich, the tall, charismatic Russian director of the Bakchisaray Historical and Cultural Preserve, arrived to take us to dinner. It was he who would be charged with the responsibility of looking after the site of the mausoleums—Eski Yurt—should the market be removed. In his presence, the musicians lost their happy glow.

"Evegeniy, why do the Russian tour guides purposely avoid us with their tourists? Today we earned almost nothing!" said the elder of the group.

Evegeniy smiled, rocking drunkenly on his feet, and ushered us out of the palace grounds. His distinguished silver hair and charming smile had no doubt reassured many disgruntled souls in his time.

In the nearby cheburekery (chebureks being the ubiquitous Uzbek meat pastry found right across the old Soviet Union), Evegeniy had assembled a large group of visiting historians, Tatar palace staffers, and other employees of the Bakchisaray Historical and Cultural Preserve. With everyone settled for dinner, he stood at the head of the table and shakily raised a glass of wine.

"It's my great, great honor to introduce you to a very unique person." The guests hushed. "A modern-day Marco Polo, speaker of fifteen languages, employee of the Royal Geographic Society, traveler on Mongolian horses, he carries half a sheep in his pocket. I welcome here tonight . . . Kimofi Pope!"

With that he threw open the toast, and I sat down trying to avoid the looks of adoration that now turned on me. Not knowing what to say, I took a large sip of wine.

The most senior historian at the table—who was already looking at the world through the prism of his wineglass—stood up to tell a tale of a different nature. "They found Hitler in the Amazon and brought him to court in Paris this year," he began. "The English decided that death by firing squad should be punishment. The French, the guillotine. The Americans, a hanging. Yet when they couldn't decide, they turned to the representative of Israel. He coolly told them: 'I don't know what the argument is about. The solution is simple—marry him off to a Crimean Tatar!'" With that he erupted in a deep, croaky laugh and downed a shot of vodka.

The far end of the table where the musicians sat was deathly silent.

A vodka glass slipped and fell, and alcohol was quickly poured anew for everyone.

When dinner was over we loaded into a bus and went to a disco to continue celebrating. Evegeniy drank endlessly, and in his euphoric stupor demanded the musicians bring out their instruments and play. As they played, their music drowned out by Russian pop, fluorescent disco lights lit up their surly looks in fragments of purple, green, and nauseating white.

It was some time before I realized the disco we were in was located at the intersection directly opposite the Tatars' picket line. Somewhere out there Islyam and his crew were battening down for another night in the open. Meanwhile, the man who would be responsible for the site of the mausoleums should the market be removed sat before me clapping his hands and rolling with laughter.

At midnight, when the musicians refused to play on, he wobbled over to me with a crazed look. "Tim, do you have your own separate room where you are staying? I mean, if you need a girl, twenty years old, it's no problem . . . Or how would you like having fifteen or twenty girls in one room? They just come to you to sniff you and touch you."

He had by this stage leaned right over close to my ear and was whispering, but then slumped back in a drunken silence.

NOT ONLY WERE the worlds that I passed between in Bakchisaray all surreally parallel, but they seemed to be simultaneously reaching climactic crescendos.

Back at the seventh micro-region that night, I passed a friend of Volodya's, Eldar, who was stumbling off with his bicycle and clutching his jaw. Inside his hut, Volodya lay as if in a coma on the divan, speckles of blood down his shirt, a cigarette butt floating in the vodka glass next to his head. His freckled ten-year-old son rushed to me in excitement. "Dad's head flew off! First Eldar went down, then Papa, but they didn't share with us the reason for the fight!"

When Volodya rose, battered and bruised, he was still desperately drunk. With his remaining weekly salary, which he had received the day before, he went to buy beer and credit for his prepaid mobile phone. He then began calling strangers and speaking nonsense until the credit dried up.

If the signs were ominous at Volodya's home, then it was nothing compared to the situation at the market.

I headed off hoping to meet Islyam, but a kilometre from the picket line, it was obvious I wouldn't be able to get through. The roads and shops had been shut down, and hundreds of police and soldiers were being bused in.

At an outer police line, muscle-bound Russians emerged cut and bloodied, boasting about the Tatars they had bashed. Beyond the police, Russian men of all ages paced about wielding sticks and planks of wood and a crowd of Russian women chanted abuse. The Russian version of Rambo, a bare-chested hulking brute of a man, flexed his sunburned pectorals and screamed, "I am ready! I am mad! And I am ready to face death to fight you Tatars in the Russian way!" There was even a band of Cossacks in army fatigues. The Tatars, meanwhile, vastly outnumbered, were surrounded by hundreds of riot police, upturned cars, and wire.

I rang Islyam, who explained that three hundred "fighters" had stormed the picket line. When pushed back by police, they had begun hurling concrete, steel, and rocks. One Tatar had been hit on the head and had nearly bled to death in the crowd before being retrieved. Many cars, including Islyam's, had been smashed, and their tires slit. For the time being there was a relative lull, but there were no signs of a resolution yet.

"It's too dangerous for you now. I can't get you in," Islyam told.

I decided that it was safer to walk home to the relative sanctuary of

Volodya's home. On the way, buses and cars full of Tatar men rocketed past into town. The word was out, and vehicles were roaming Tatar enclaves to recruit volunteer fighters.

By the time I arrived at Volodya's, smoke had begun to rise from the market, accompanied by occasional gunfire. Volodya's wife was in hysterics, tears streaming down her sunburned cheeks. The seventh micro-region was eerily quiet—children were locked indoors and houses deserted of men. Later, reports suggested that around fifteen hundred Tatars moved in to encircle the Russians.

I sat down and watched the Russian news. Crimea was in the headlines, as usual. The journalist commented, to pictures of a beautiful coastline, "These people are coming back here to Crimea because they like it here and because they lived here before 1944." Then they showed footage of a Tatar man hurling a rock at riot police.

As I withdrew to my bed it seemed inevitable that Bakchisaray was on the verge of war. The market had become an opportunity for Russians to settle old scores, and for the time being there was no end in sight.

IN THE MORNING I woke early and gathered my things. I craved being back on the steppe.

Before leaving, I rang Islyam. Overnight the army had moved in and cleared out both the Russians and the Tatars. Islyam was recovering at home. He was jubilant. "The prime minister signed! The market will be abolished!"

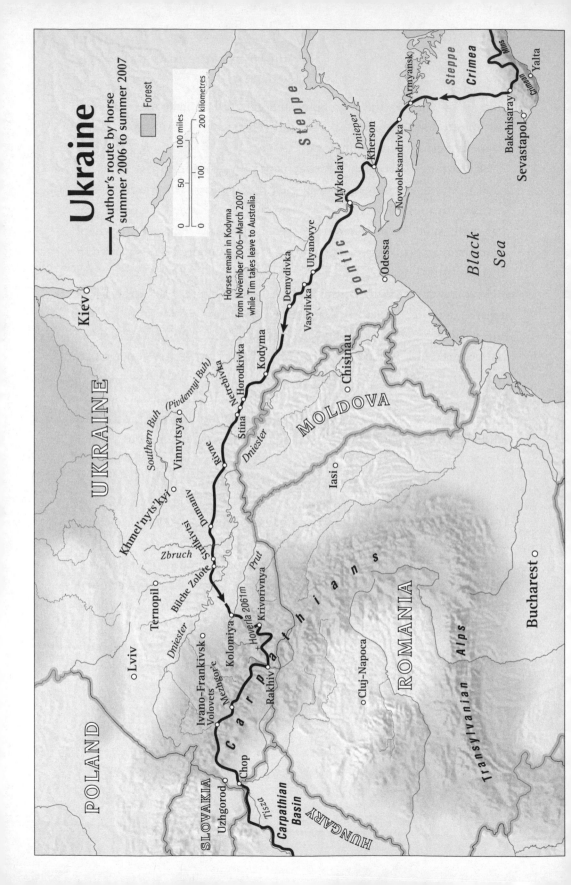

Ukraine

— Author's route by horse
   summer 2006 to summer 2007

▨ Forest

0   50   100 miles
0   100   200 kilometres

POLAND

SLOVAKIA

Uzhgorod
Chop
Tisza

Carpathian
Basin

HUNGARY

Volovets
Mezhgore
Ivano-Frankivsk
Rakhiv
Hovella 2061m
Krivorivnya
Kolomiya
Prut

Lviv

Ternopil
Bilche Zolote
Zbruch
Strilkivtsi
Dunaivtsi

Khmel'nyts'kyi

UKRAINE

Kiev

Vinnytsya

Rivne
Dunaiiivtsi

Southern Buh (Pivdennyi Buh)

Stina
Netrebivka
Horodkivka
Kodyma

Dniester

Dniester

Iasi

MOLDOVA

Chisinau

ROMANIA

Cluj-Napoca

Transylvanian Alps

Bucharest

Demydivka
Vasylivka
Ulyanovye

Horses remain in Kodyma
from November 2006–March 2007
while Tim takes leave to Australia.

Odessa

Mykolaiv

Pontic

Steppe

Kherson
Dniepet

Novooleksandrivka

Armyansk

Steppe
Crimea

Nins
Yalta

Bakchisaray
Chuman

Sevastapol

Black
Sea

21

CROSSROADS

FROM BAKCHISARAY I headed north through the arid steppe interior of Crimea and settled into a rhythm of riding by night, making camp by midday, and sleeping in the open under horse blankets. By following a canal that carried water from the Dnieper to the cities of Crimea, I was able to avoid towns and villages and make quick progress. As I rode, the tension and stress of the conflict began to dissipate.

Little more than a week took me to the far north of Crimea, where I woke late one night, half asleep, and gazed up at the dim profile of the horses. Taskonir stood over me, his ears bent forward, back leg cocked, and Kok's head resting on his wither. Tigon was curled up, breathing heavily, his bony spine hard up against my thigh. Time passed unmarked until a fart broke through camp. Ogonyok, who had evidently woken himself up with the noise, put his head down to munch on the sun-dried grass, followed by a quick shake of the mane and a stamp of the hoof. Tigon let out muffled barks in his sleep, and Taskonir's bottom lip quivered for some time until once again all was still.

It occurred to me that without the horses I would have lost my sanity on this journey long ago. Only from the solitude of the steppe, reconnected with them, did I feel ready to make sense of what had passed and make room for new horizons.

This night it was sinking in that after three intense months in Crimea, I would soon leave the peninsula for the mainland. Simultaneously, my third and final summer on the steppe was coming to a close. These milestones cemented the feeling that the vast bulk of the Eurasian steppe, which bulges out at its core in the oceanic spaces of Russia, Kazakhstan, and Mongolia, was now firmly behind, and all I had in front of me were the western fringes that taper off into a narrow prong in Hungary. With the softer climate of Ukraine nearly in my sights and the border of Hungary a mere 934 km away as the crow flies, it promised to be a piece of cake compared to what I'd been through. In fact, for the first time on my journey I was tempted by thoughts of the end. If all went smoothly, I could bank on crossing the Carpathians and reaching the Danube by early spring.

It was ironic, then, just how distant Hungary would prove to be in reality. What I could not have foreseen was that in Ukraine my journey would again be waylaid by events. In fact, another summer would come to pass before I could set my eyes on the finish, and this time the setback would be a personal loss far more profound than the journey itself.

For the time being, though, that was weeks away in the future, and as far as I knew, I was gathering momentum to make the final run. Gazing up at the stars, I felt a breath of cool air breeze through with its nightly relief, then rolled under the sweaty smell of the horse blankets and surrendered to sleep.

AT 3:30 A.M. the alarm clock sprang rudely to life, and as had become the routine, we were off within an hour, moving anonymously through the predawn darkness, the familiar dull ache throbbing up from my feet in the stirrups to my hips and butt.

When the black of the sky dissolved, it seemed the sun was rising just for us. Golden light spilled over the open steppe until I could check my bearing by the long shadows cast by our caravan. Tigon was off, a black speck bounding through the yellow grass, followed closely by dive-bombing birds. When I dismounted to pee, it triggered the three horses to do the same, and when Tigon homed back in he joined in, too.

The soft rays of friendly orange and yellow were deceptive. By 7:00 A.M. hot gusts thrashed at the grass and my eyes narrowed to slits. By lunchtime I had retired to the patchy shade of a lonely tree.

It took another day of riding through dry, hot conditions before we reached the narrow Isthmus of Perekop, which connects Crimea to the mainland. The modern territory of Ukraine that lay beyond was a land blessed with a relatively mild climate and an abundance of fertile soil, rivers, and forests—owing to which it was historically suited to an agrarian style of life.

Since the ninth century, the steppes of Ukraine had been a Slavic stronghold, and in the eleventh century they formed a key center of Kievan Rus, the most powerful state in Europe at the time. When the Mongols invaded in the thirteenth century, however, the state disintegrated, and for nearly three centuries Ukraine found itself under the rule of the Golden Horde. Ever since the dissolution of the Golden Horde, Ukraine had struggled to rekindle a sense of its greatness, forever in the shadow of Russia, Poland, and the Soviet Empire. Today it was a country ensconced in political chaos as the pro-national party that had been swept to power during the Orange Revolution of 2005 pitted its vision for integration with the European Union and NATO against those of the pro-Russian party that had recently gained control of parliament.

Kievan Rus and politics aside, what mattered to me at this point in time was that the perilous winters and scorching heat were safely behind us, and I was about to enter a world where I'd surely never have to worry about finding grass, grain, or water again. With Ukraine's many villages, I also hoped I could carry smaller loads of food and travel longer distances.

By contrast, I reflected, the prospects for Friar Carpini when he arrived in Ukraine in 1246 were altogether terrifying. Fresh from Europe and only just beginning his journey to Mongolia, it was in Ukraine that Carpini was warned about the treacherous lands ahead and forced to abandon his European horses because "Tartars have neither straw nor hay nor fodder, and they would all die." From Kiev, Carpini traveled southeast through the steppe of Ukraine and Russia on "the road to the barbarian nations." From there, he wrote, "we left with many tears, not knowing whether we traveled toward death or life." Ahead of Carpini stretched a land so vast and hostile that, on reading his account, one gets the impression that he went to painstaking lengths to convince readers he was telling the truth and not a fantasy.

The culture shock I anticipated, however, was essentially the reverse. Because I had traveled the long haul from Mongolia, Ukraine represented my first real glimpses of cultural Europe.

※

BEYOND THE INDUSTRIAL town of Armyansk I crossed onto the mainland and felt the first whisper of autumn. A cool breeze from the west rustled through the grass like some ghostly messenger and turned my sweat cold. The horses stopped to turn and gaze in its direction, and Tigon lifted his nose. The sun had done its summer's work and was moving on to new pastures. In its place thick, cottony clouds were filling the sky.

My own transition into autumn was not so subtle. On my first day on the mainland in Kherson Oblast a horse and cart spooked the horses into a wild bolt and I was forced to run 10 km to catch them. Ogonyok cut his leg badly on a broken glass bottle and was very nearly hit by traffic while crossing a bridge. Taskonir managed to run off with a full grain bag in his teeth and spread its entire contents on the ground.

Beyond the vast waters of the Dnieper River we were caught in an extraordinary deluge, and in the city of Mykolaiv my horses were confiscated by customs and veterinary officials, who said my permits were inadequate. After another round of vaccinations, being issued with Ukrainian animal passports, and a gift of a bottle of vodka to the head of veterinary control, the horses were released. It would be a month, however, before I got back in the saddle. Unexpectedly I had been selected as the *Australian Geographic* Adventurer of the Year, and as part of the award they were flying me to Sydney for the ceremony. The opportunity to see my family after two and a half years was too much to pass up despite the delays it would cause.

Leaving the horses at an equestrian center in Mykolaiv, I spent some days with Anya in Kiev, then, still dressed in my tattered riding boots and single change of shirt and trousers, found myself in front of a packed audience at the Maritime Museum in Sydney. A week passed in a whirlwind of media interviews, visits to sponsors, and two days at home, culminating with a luxurious dinner at the Australia Club in Sydney with Mum, Dad, and my great-uncle John Kearney. Although Dad in particular had felt uneasy about me throwing over my law studies at nineteen to pursue adventure, he had always supported me, and over oysters and champagne we celebrated the award as if it were ours together. He gave a short speech about what I had done, and in his swelling pride and approval I realized he had begun to see me as a man.

After staying together in a hotel on Sydney's Darling Harbor, I hugged Mum and Dad goodbye, then watched their taxi drive off until it was lost in the busy traffic of the city. It was the last time I would ever see my father.

※

BY THE TIME I had returned to Mykolaiv the air was crisp, the autumn leaves were alight with yellows and reds, and the horses had begun to grow their wooly winter coats. For the third year in a row I fitted my wide Mongolian stirrups, donned my winter boots, and prepared to set off with no one but winter expecting me beyond the horizon.

Anya had traveled down to Mykolaiv to see me off, and when the day came to leave, she walked alongside my caravan to a small forest on the outskirts, where we kissed goodbye. Both of us knew that we might never see each other again, and by the time we parted, both our faces were wet with salty tears.

From Mykolaiv I aimed to traverse southwest Ukraine before crossing the Carpathians and descending into Hungary. For the first few days

I charged across cultivated flats. The horses bristled with energy, and I sat high in the saddle watching Taskonir's wild mane thrash about and feeling his powerful chest absorb the shudders of pounding hooves.

We departed from all signs of main roads, and the flats grew into raised plains, dissected by deep, shadowy gullies and streams. Unlike on the Kuban in Russia, much of the land here that had been cultivated in Soviet times was overgrown and neglected, and those fields still in use had been deserted for winter. Sometimes I made my way cross-country using a compass, while other times I followed muddy lanes and tracks. Apart from the odd buckled Lada and horse and cart, only thin trails of smoke rising from villages in the valleys suggested signs of life.

The villages I did pass through presented a bleak picture of post-Soviet decline. Many of the houses had been hastily built in the 1930s and 1940s with tree branches, mud, and reeds and were now sinking unevenly into the ground. A great number of villages had only a handful of residents remaining, and some had been abandoned altogether. The majority of people who still lived in these hamlets were old babushkas and elderly men who looked as bent over and obsolete as the thatched-roof homes they stepped out of. Usually I would drift in during the morning or in the evening before camp in search of a well. As I rode through avenues of empty homes, it was clear the communities were receding as fast as the occupants were dying.

Beyond the village of Ulyanovye, where the only movement on the muddy street was a medieval-looking wooden cart, I rode through heavy mist and long grass until the land gave way to a valley. As the mist began to rise I looked down to a small huddle of homes chugging out smoke. The only person visible was a man walking behind a herd of cattle. He had not seen me.

From my vantage point in the saddle I was overcome by the vulnerability of the village. I felt I could have just pressed my heels into Taskonir's side and galloped down before anyone knew what or who was coming. The late autumn chill had lifted my energy significantly. The horses, too, had been raising their heads a little higher and were striding out with renewed alertness. Meanwhile, the settled world was withdrawing for a season of atrophy in the comfort of their homes. It occurred to me this natural trend had been exploited by nomads for thousands of years and perfected with cruel precision by the Mongols. It was, after all, in the winter of 1237, after the villagers had retreated from the fields and the Mongol horses were at their peak strength, that thousands of Mongol horseman emerged from the steppe to so infamously devastate the cities of Ryazan and later Vladimir. Entire towns were wiped off the map in those cold months when unsuspecting villagers retired for relative hibernation. In the city of Vladimir it is still remembered by Russians today that terrified townsfolk who had sheltered in the city's churches were burned alive.

For Ukrainians, the greatest moment of tragedy also fell in the wintry month of December. It was in 1240, as the frost settled, that the Mongols surrounded Kiev and within a matter of days laid waste to what had been the most powerful princedom of Russia and the capital of Kievan Rus. A measure of the devastation was recorded by Carpini some six years later, when he noted that the city was still littered with "countless human skulls and bones from the dead." "In fact," he wrote, "there are hardly two hundred houses there now."

It is true that this state of ruin was only part of the Mongol legacy. Conquest of Russia was backed up by 240 years of Genghisid rule, under which a sophisticated bureaucracy was introduced and commerce flourished. The Russian Orthodox Church, for instance, grew in material wealth during the Golden Horde period, and the fur trade was rerouted along north-south lines, allowing cities such as Moscow to enjoy unprecedented prosperity.[1] Nonetheless, the many benefits that Mongol rule would bring would have been cold comfort for those who endured the initial wrath.

After the crushing of Kiev, the Mongol army had continued across what is now Ukraine, setting up a summer camp just east of the Carpathian Mountains, lying in wait for the next winter of raiding and warfare to come.

The mist rolled back in, the village disappeared from view, and I rode on, unnoticed except by a couple of dogs that let out halfhearted barks.

Winter might once have been synonymous with the appearance of nomad hordes, but it seemed as though that chapter of history had long been forgotten here.

For another couple of days we continued on with energy and confidence, but unlike the Mongols and their army, I was alone and my feeling of empowerment waned. In the week since leaving Mykolaiv the horses hadn't had a rest and I had only been invited into a home once, and even then just for a cup of tea. When I asked the whereabouts of wells in villages, many would narrow their eyes and claim they didn't know. When I enquired whether anyone was willing to put me up for the night, the typical response was, "Sorry, I can't help you because I do not have space to shelter three horses."

One evening in a remote field I stopped by a broken-down truck. From under the hood, a hulking man emerged into the evening light. I noticed his powerful hands first, with their grease-stained, callused fingers—each as thick as a bratwurst. The way he fidgeted with a screwdriver as if it were as light and fragile as a toothpick suggested he had the potential for violence. Then came his face, bulging out of a long-necked woolen sweater, wide and round as a dinner plate. Set into the folds of his grimy skin were two small hazel eyes that now locked on to me.

He shook my hand absentmindedly as his cheeks, brows, and mouth began to bunch up in a way that didn't feel friendly. I started asking directions, but he cut me off.

"Give me at least one of your horses!"

"No," I replied. "These horses are going with me to Hungary!"

His eyes grew hard, and his face took on a righteous look. "Sure!" he grunted. "I know that you have stolen these horses, and so I will take them from you!"

There was a stand-off for a few moments, until he moved toward Ogonyok, behind me. Before he could reach the horse, I pulled on Ogonyok's lead rope, kicked my boots into Taskonir's side, and pulled away. I didn't turn around until the man and his broken-down truck had been swallowed up by the land.

That night I made camp in a hidden gully where I felt safe. In the coming days, however, I couldn't escape the feeling that while I might have shaken off this stranger, the land was imbued with the same sinister intentions as he was.

The following evening when I descended to the village of Vasylivka I was desperate. I had run out of grain and food, and the horses were exhausted. Some Uzbeks offered the horses a drink on the outskirts, but still no one was willing to put me up. Dark crowded in, sleet fell, my feet were numb in the stirrups, and I was told to go into the hills to the abandoned settlement of Mala Dvoryanka. "There is one man who still lives up there, and he can point you in the direction of water and grass," an old man told me.

The green beneath us turned to black, and after another hour's ride we were drawn to the lonely glow of a house. On our approach the sound of the door swinging open filled me with relief, but then two snarling dogs leaped out. Tigon launched into attack, a blinding flashlight flicked on, and above the raucous barking and snarling came swearing. I could just make out the silhouette of a man, then the pointy end of a rifle.

"Calm down, please! I came for advice on where to graze my horses and somewhere to camp!" I said angrily.

"Turn around, thief! Get out of here! I will shoot your dog just like that!" he screamed in a mix of Russian and Ukrainian.

I replied in Russian, "Okay! Okay! I'm leaving!"

I rode away and felt my way up a gully until safely hidden, and then I made camp.

My anger subsided only as the last of my pasta settled into my stomach. People here might have suspected me to be a thief or a Gypsy, but it gave me some sense of satisfaction that perhaps deep down in the Slavic psyche there was still recognition that horsemen from the east meant trouble.

IN THE MORNING the sun revealed thick, unruly pasture. Beneath the frozen yellow tops, the grass was still green near the roots. There was also a well in the old village of Mala Dvoryanka, and despite the risk of meeting the old man, I watered my horses there and decided to stay put for the day.

While the horses grazed I had just enough battery power to start my computer and connect the satellite phone to post an update to Australia. Before I could manage it, however, an email arrived in my inbox. It was from my father and addressed to me, my two brothers, Jonathan and Cameron, and my sister, Natalie. The subject line was "Sandy Point Van Sold," and it was written in a reflective tone I had rarely heard from him. In it he expressed his feelings about his early retirement. *As you know,* he said, *I took a step into the unknown last year . . . In retrospect the resignation probably wasn't a good idea financially . . . I struggle each day to try and determine what I should be attempting to reach forward for . . . and it is a major readjustment not having as a goal the care and maintenance of our children.*

For most of his career Dad had worked in outdoor education, first as a field leader, then as a lecturer, and eventually as founder of a degree program in sport and outdoor recreation at Monash University, Australia.[2] As children we were lucky to be taken out with university students on skiing, bushwalking, and sea-kayaking trips. But in the past ten or fifteen years the job had taken Dad into progressively more administrative roles, in which he had struggled with the internal politics of the workplace and a recent decision by management to relocate the program. These stresses were what had conspired to force him to consider early retirement.

The main subject of the email was the sale of his holiday cabin at Sandy Point—another point of sorrow for Dad. Sandy Point, a summer village on the Victorian coastline where his family was heavily involved in the local surf lifesaving club and owned a block of land, had been his stomping ground for most of his childhood and adult life. In 1999, however, his mother had pledged the block of land to one of Dad's brothers as a dying wish. This had caused a serious fracture between Dad's siblings and their father, who felt beholden to her promise. In the interceding years since then, Dad had, in part, resolved his feelings of dispossession by buying a simple cabin in Sandy Point caravan park—a permanently anchored caravan with built-on annex. But now he was writing to tell us he was forced to sell it for financial reasons.

Dad went on to press us to spend time with our grandfather while he was still clear of mind, and to learn from the schism between him, his siblings, and their parents. He wrote: *I can assure you that I do not want to be as isolated (distanced) from my children as mine have been as our family grew up . . . You are all in the prime of your life with many years of energetic activity to go, but once partnered and with children it would be fun to be near you.* The email finished, *I wish you well and look forward to sharing your ambitions, joys and sorrows and the sound of your voices in our house. Love, Andrew.*

The battery died and my screen went blank.

For most of the last two years, my home and childhood had seemed like another lifetime, a reality so detached it was in a parallel world that didn't belong. Now, however, I felt myself drawn into memories and feelings that cut to the present. My surroundings faded until I was back at Sandy Point, running along the beach and into the water with my brother Jon to catch a wave, Mum and Dad watching from the shore.

I recalled all the times that I had visited Dad at his university office and the long drives to get there and back home, when he would open up and vent all his frustrations, hopes, and ideas. It had been hard to weather his negative outbursts, but underneath there was a camaraderie during those trips that perhaps only a father and son can experience. He had resigned from his work toward the end of my stay in Kazakhstan, and I wondered with sadness and even guilt what it must have been like for him. We had all encouraged him to take the early retirement package he was being offered, yet now he was left at home alone, all four of his children pursuing their own lives.

What moved me most about the message, though, was the absence of anger. It disarmed all defenses and left me pining to tell him how grateful I was, how brave I thought he was for making the decision to resign, and how I sympathized.

My reflection was cut short by someone clearing his throat. Tigon woke with a growl, and I unzipped the tent door to meet the eyes of a startled cow herder.

"Do you have any cigarettes?" the man asked, trying to mask his curiosity.

I WAS THE first foreigner that Kolya had ever spoken to. He and his wife were from western Ukraine and had moved here to take up beekeeping. Later that evening when they had finished their village cow-herding duties, they returned to my camp to invite me to stay with them in Vasylivka.

My arrival at their home was a stark reminder of the settled world of Europe I had begun to enter. As I pulled in, Kolya invited my horses into a cramped barn, but even Taskonir pulled backward.

"Your poor horses!" Kolya exclaimed. "They have been out in the elements for so long they have forgotten what a stable is!"

I gave him a wry look. "The problem is that my horses have almost never been in a stable!"

Kolya shook his head and grinned, then took a longer look at my horses.

I'd become used to this misperception since arriving in mainland Ukraine. Some people had refused to take me overnight because they didn't have space in their barn and thought it cruel to make the horses stand out in the rain and cold.

Clearly Kolya had associated horses with stables all his life, and his innocent comment well illustrated that although Europeans had originally inherited horses from nomads of the steppe, they could not comprehend the extreme conditions that define the native environment of the horse, nor the horse's ability to survive in it. The horse, after all, evolved as a herd animal with a physiology honed for outrunning predators in the harsh climes of the Eurasian steppe. It was not naturally conditioned to either a stationary life isolated from other animals or a regimented diet of hay and grain.

It was difficult to explain to Kolya that to my horses his stables would have appeared more prison than refuge. Even more difficult to get across would have been that to me the stable symbolized the greatest difference between nomads and sedentary society: while nomads adapt their lives to the needs of their animals, migrating from pasture to pasture in symbiosis with nature, sedentary beings tend to control their animals and environment for their own convenience. In a similar vein, I felt it ironic that many times on my journey people had pitied me for living out in the elements. The truth was that after being so long on this journey, I found it hard to imagine living in a town or village, let alone a four-wall dwelling in a city.

That night I proudly tied the horses up outside and Kolya gave them generous piles of hay. In the morning, however, it was with a hint of hypocrisy that I found myself relishing the feel of my warm clean skin and the fresh sheets. The furnace was going and the smell of fried pork, buckwheat, and eggs wafted into my room. Outside, the first snow of the season had blanketed the earth. Life under the open sky wasn't as inviting as it had seemed the night before.

With some reluctance I saddled up and rode out over the frozen waves of mud in the streets of Vasylivka. Kolya walked with me to the outskirts, where my goodbye was marred when a man came hurrying up to us to ask if he could buy Taskonir. His dog attacked Tigon, and by the time we had separated them, blood was dripping from Tigon's mouth onto the snow.

Beyond Vasylivka I carried on through high open plains broken by the occasional gully. Bitten by frost, the land had lost its autumn gleam, and leaves on the odd trees that we passed were dull and brittle. By evening it was so cold I was forced to get off and walk to bring life back to my toes. It was only −2°C, but the moisture in the air and the ceaseless northwest wind were grinding me down.

The next day promised to be warmer, but by midmorning gray clouds swooped in and the headwind brought flurries of snow. My ropes turned stiff and frozen and the horses attempted to shy away.

Sometime in the afternoon we emerged from the plains like wild animals to cross the Odessa–Kiev freeway, then scurried our way back into

the hills to the village of Demydivka. Ostensibly I entered the village looking for water, but the cozy homes under their wreaths of smoke broke the
nomadic rebel in me.

At the first house a woman carrying the weight of middle age on her
hips came out wrapped in a scarf and coat. She hurried back inside and
emerged with a man bearing glazed, bloodshot eyes. He stopped a short
distance away, corrected the angle of his fur hat, then broke out in stac-
cato laughter.

"Tie up the horses! Fuck your mother and a donkey, too! This kind of
traveler comes once in a hundred years!" His hands were up in the air as
if praising the gods. "Nina!" he called to his wife. "We will feed the
horses beets, hay, straw! Prepare porridge for the dog! Get the borscht
ready! Tim, listen to me, I don't drink . . . Well, today I am because it is
thirty years since my father died. Tomorrow I will also drink, and then I
will stop. But come in, come in, you must be cold!"

Vasya, as he was known, had apparently only just raised a toast in memory of his late father when my caravan came clopping into town. It was an
event he wanted his children, grandchildren, and great-grandchildren to
know about. Who was I to argue?

With the horses tied and beets, hay, and grain raining down, we
rushed inside, where samohon (home-distilled vodka) was poured. There
was apparently no need for me to worry about my horses. "I am a gun
lover, you see!" he explained. "The special forces came to take away my
guns, but everyone in the village suspects, rightly, that they didn't find them
all! One *puck*," he said, pulling an imaginary trigger, "and the thieves will
all be gone in a second!"

The vigor of his words made him quite a coherent and pleasant
drunk—that is, until I stopped drinking and he carried on to finish the
2 litre soft drink bottle of home brew. By that time, I could not avoid con-
fronting the circumstances in which he, his two young children, and
their wife found themselves. The whitewashed walls and ceiling of their
tiny two-room house were coated in years of grime, smoke, and cooking
fat. It was better not to take shoes off, given all the muck on the floor. As
I lay down to rest and the world faded away, I was vaguely aware that the

boy had plucked out a gun from under Vasya's bed and was scampering about the house pretending to shoot.

After a shallow sleep I woke to suffocating wafts of stale samohon, body odor, and cigarettes. It was not the refuge, nor the sense of family, I'd been looking for.

For the next three days I rode into sleet and snow, became lost in a tangle of hills, and felt my spirits fall into a tailspin. In the town of Obzhyle I was greeted by drunken men driving a horse and cart. "Where the fuck! From where the fuck?" they hollered when they saw me. They were coarse and unhelpful, and I realized that while they marveled at my adventure, they did not identify with it—I had become a novelty.

I rode out fast, aiming to camp in the hills nearby, but as dark fell a Lada pulled up and a man in uniform stepped out demanding documents. I told him angrily that I did not have time, for it was getting late, but a second man emerged and took Taskonir by the reins. "Hand over your papers. *Now!*"

By the time they concluded I was legal, it was too dark to get safely out of town and find camp. Perhaps it was just the lack of sleep in the last few days, but I felt distraught and vulnerable. I told them that since they had held me up, they were responsible for finding me a place to stay. It was a mistake.

I was sent home with a drunk Gypsy bachelor, who after half a bottle of vodka outlined his plan to steal my horses. I broke out of his squalid hut in the middle of the night and slept on the frozen earth among the horses, which were tied up outside.

Another day took me to the town of Kodyma, where by chance Rodion, the brother of a Ukrainian friend of mine, had agreed to meet me. He had generously prearranged for my horses to be looked after at a collective farm with the help of the head of the local forestry department, Vladimir Sklyaruk.

For two days I enjoyed a respite, and when I left the weather had cleared somewhat. Still, when I rode out I felt directionless. The trees had finally been stripped of all life, and like my spirits, the autumn leaves skittered about in the breeze. I had a formidable distance to go to get to the Carpathians, and I wasn't sure how I could sustain my pace through the winter. I was also unsure how I fitted into this sedentary world. Irritated,

I tried calling Dad on his mobile via satellite, but time after time, the call went to voicemail. There was only one solution: it was time to grit it out and get this journey done.

⌗

TWO DAYS OUT from Kodyma I rode toward the sun as it was sinking from a clear peach sky. I passed a herd of cattle returning for the night, and noticed a horse and cart clopping along a track in the distance. A ways in front of us to the west the land planed off into a gully, and I reasoned that if I hurried, I could make it there for camp before dark.

Before speeding up, I reached into my backpack and pulled out the satellite phone. For some time now it had been beeping—a sign that I had accidentally left it on. As I went to switch it off, however, I noticed a new message.[3] It was from my brother Jon: *Tim! Call home please!*

I stopped, leaped from the saddle, and knelt in the grass. Clutching the handset, I dialed home and waited. When our family friend Peter Nicholson answered, it was obvious something was wrong. As the handset was carried to Mum, I could hear other familiar voices of friends.

Mum was in the bathroom when she picked up. "Tim?" Her voice crackled down the line, shaking. There was a long pause. I held my breath.

"It's Dad," she started, her voice strong, but in an instant it wavered and she began to cry. "He was in a car accident . . . I'm so sorry, Tim . . . he is dead . . . I can't bring him back."

⌗

IT'S NOT HARD to remember the first few moments after I hung up that evening, November 16, 2006, but they are hard to describe, and it's harder still to do them justice.

On the one hand, sitting there by the roadside at the feet of my horses, the journey that had consumed me for two and a half years evaporated as if it had never been. I couldn't breathe, and my back muscles heaved. I vomited two or three times, cried, and felt my body convulse. Inside, it was as if a bullet had ripped through me, cutting the tensioned cords that held me together, and they were recoiling, whipping at my interior.

But simultaneously there was a numbness and a surreal sense of calm and normality. I was still on a horse somewhere in Ukraine, and I needed to camp, find grass, and unsaddle. I fragmented into two distinct parts from that moment—the practical, steadying me, and the passenger.

Among the myriad thoughts competing for space in those first few moments, the predominant one was that I had to be alone, to be away from anyone who had not known my father. Somehow I knew that if I was quick about making camp, out on the steppe under the stars I had a fleeting chance of communion with Dad before he was gone.

In a gully somewhere I worked fast. Poles broke through sleeves in the tent, Tigon whined for his food, and the horses tried to bolt. For a fleeting moment it felt as though the two disjointed parts of me merged to focus and get the job done. But then the horses were tethered, the food was cooked and eaten, and I crumpled onto my canvas bag. I gazed up at the sky, and suddenly it was so big and so lonely. Where could he be? Did he know how to find me?

I wanted to know when Dad had died, how many hours I had been pretending that life was normal. I computed what Mum had told me, weighed up the time differences: he had been alive when I woke up but dead by lunch. My lungs seized again at the thought.

How many times had I called? How many times had he not answered? I could imagine his phone lighting up, my name coming through. Maybe when I made that last call he had still been alive, trapped in the wreckage, watching the phone. And all I could do was get angry and leave a message to say how pissed off I was that he wouldn't pick up!

Sleep didn't beckon. To sleep would have been to abandon him, and he had to be aware of me, he had to know that I was here. And yet the steadying hand of the other me guided and caressed until I couldn't keep my eyes open any longer.

When I awoke again, I felt frozen—the sleeping bag was half on. There was ice on the tent, and outside a sea of mist was gushing in and devouring us. It must have been about four in the morning. I picked up the phone again. This time I got Jon. We just cried. Then I talked to my sister, Natalie. The first thing she asked was, "Did you reply to his email?"

"No, I didn't," I replied.

"I didn't, either."

THERE WAS ONLY one thing to do: go back. Back to the spot where I had eaten lunch after he died, back to where I'd camped the previous day, when he was still alive. Back home, where I could return to the life I'd had as his son.

I packed faster than I had ever managed. To stop and think would be to let time carry on.

We trotted through the village under the cover of heavy mist, and before the sun could illuminate a world without Dad we were lost in the folds of the land. The sun gradually melted through, a silvery disc suspended in space. Delicate, frost-encrusted birch limbs fingered their way into reality. I pushed the horses harder, into a canter. Mist began to swirl, then above me a circle of clear sky turned peach. I craned my neck and twisted around but urged the horses on.

Dad, I'm coming!

I was catching up with him. But then Ogonyok pulled at the lead rope, I slowed, and the mist began to rise.

I lost Dad for some time. Then, as we entered a tract of forest, he seemed to return. I slowed to a walk, breathing in the tang of rotting leaves that littered the ground. Dad walked to my left in his shorts and hiking boots, carrying one of his weathered old daypacks. We stopped momentarily as he leaned over and lifted a plant from under a tree. Cradling it in his palm, he brought it over to me and held it up. I was back in the Australian bush, one of the many times when he'd turned to me and said, "Tim, isn't life amazing?" Back then I hadn't understood what he meant, though I could see from the look of fascination in his eyes that he was right. Now he looked up at me in the saddle, his eyes alight with the same sense of enchantment. We rode on together.

So many times by phone and email we had talked about him joining me on this adventure. Since resigning from work he had taken interest in the histories and cultures of the countries I traveled through and read many books on the subject. Nevertheless, neither of us had committed to the idea of him coming over. The naked forest glared angrily—I had missed the season of opportunity—and as the edge of the forest drew near I began to sob.

WHEN I WAS halfway back to Kodyma, Vladimir Sklyaruk met me and took my gear back by car. I'd phoned his family in the middle of the night, and he had promised at once to find a way to look after Tigon and the horses in my absence. I galloped past the lunch spot and camp and rode another 15 km into town.

The following dawn I fell into Anya's arms at the Kiev train station and about thirty hours later walked out through Australian customs—the same gates I had recently passed with so much celebration.

Then they were there: Mum with her pale face and wet blue eyes, Jon behind her, nervously grinding his teeth. I was the eldest child, and Jon was my junior by two years, although from an early age he had been much stronger and more athletic than me. As he leaned over and hugged my skinny frame there was a seniority in him I hadn't recognized before.

Natalie and Cameron were there, too, but it wasn't until we made the two-hour drive home that it felt like we were all finally reunited. And Natalie had some good news: although neither she, Jon, nor I had answered Dad's email, Cameron had. He had also made sure, by looking at Dad's email account, that his response had been read.

In the coming days it was obvious that Dad's death meant something unique and different to each of us, but in some ways the four of us were together in our grief. There was no one who could share what Mum must have been going through, however. Mum and Dad had been married for thirty years and had lived in the same country house in rural

Victoria since the year I was born. On the previous Thursday, the day of Dad's accident, Mum hadn't been expecting him home. He had spent the week helping out at a surf lifesaving camp at Sandy Point and had promised to be back on Friday morning, as the two of them would be attending a wedding in Canberra on Saturday.

Sometime in the early evening of Thursday there had been a knock at the front door. This was odd, since anyone who had been to our home knew that the back door was in fact the proper entrance.

It was the police. At about 4:30 P.M. that day there had been a crash on a stretch of the South Gippsland Highway—the road we traveled from home to Sandy Point. A man carrying Dad's identification was deceased.

"It can't be him! There must be some mix-up!" she'd told them.

Our neighbors, who had come over after seeing the police car, had helped Mum to an armchair and tried to calm her down.

In hindsight, Mum said, there were signs that something was going to happen. Every day of their married life she had been picking up after Dad—his clothes sprawled over the bedroom floor, the mess he'd left in the kitchen, his Ventolin inhaler not where it should have been. Yet when he'd left to go to Sandy Point, almost everything had been in its place. In the final weeks before his death he had also met with an unusually large number of old friends and acquaintances—mostly coincidental meetings, such as in the supermarket or at various functions. Then there was the email to us, and other subtle things—it was as if he had been unconsciously preparing to sign off.

Out in the garden I joined Dad's brother Kim, who had been liaising with the police, and learned something that Mum and the others had been keeping from me. "First, Tim, I want you to know that there was little chance for your Dad—it was a head-on collision," he told me. "People went to his aid within a few minutes, but he was trapped in the driver's seat and unconscious."

He took a deep breath.

"But not long after the crash, your dad's car started burning. They tried to get him out, but it was impossible. I am still trying to get details from the police. They think that someone checked for his pulse before the fire and he didn't have one, but we don't know. Only the autopsy will give us the answer."

The accident had been a tragedy for those in the other car as well. One woman had died and her husband had been airlifted to the hospital. Their granddaughter, who had Down syndrome, had been in the front seat and had survived, but with possible spinal injuries. No one yet knew how the accident had happened.

I passed out for some time in the afternoon and woke feeling groggy and disoriented. The house was strangely empty, and I stumbled down the hallway into the living room. Surely if I sat there long enough, something would break the silence—perhaps Dad would talk to me, or walk through the door.

As I closed my eyes I could hear the screen door open outside. In my mind I heard his work bags land on the floor and his shoes come off, but when I opened my eyes and looked up it was Mum. She had come running to hold me.

ELEVEN DAYS OF life without Dad.

The house was filled with guests, and we spent much of our time organizing the funeral. Unlike out on the steppe, in our Western world dying was complicated. Dad's body couldn't be released until the autopsy was finished, and until the death certificate arrived Mum's bank accounts were partially frozen. We were not allowed to see Dad.

Finally, though, we had chosen a coffin, Dad had been returned, and on the eve of the funeral I lay awake hearing nothing but the odd creak of a bed and the rustle of possums on the roof. We had several large specimens living up there; they were nocturnal animals, and slept in the attic during the day, but at this time of night you could hear them venturing out for food.

I was still suffering jet lag, but more than that I craved the calm of night, which held me close to Dad. I knew that when daybreak came it would bring with it terror, sobbing, guests, and frantic preparations. I'd come to think of my nightly vigil as a duty.

The darkness moved slowly until a *cack cack cack* from a magpie sounded, then the warbling of a hatchling. An ever so pale light cracked through the fronds of the giant cypress trees, and a thrush hopped by the window—so innocent and unaware that the world had stopped.

I couldn't lie there any longer.

From the back corner of the wooded yard I gazed out over the paddocks toward the emerald hills of the Strzelecki range. A fox and her cubs appeared, moving stealthily across the dew-laden grass. They were hurrying back to their den before the magic of dawn was eclipsed by the sun.

To the east I fixed my eyes on large eucalypts that stood with their limbs outstretched, silhouetted against the blanket fog. These ancient trees were what Dad loved, so much so that they were somehow inseparable from him. How could they still be here, continuing to exist as if everything remained as it had always been?

Finally I sat on an old cypress stump and watched the sun grow near. For a while it seemed like an even race between it and the mist to reach the horizon, but in the end the mist won, rising like a cloak from the land, embroiled in pinks and reds that glowed brighter and brighter. From the gap between the mist and the horizon, subtle rays of golden light began to feel their way over the land, rendering the dew a million glinting marbles. The deciduous trees around the house behind me lit up with their translucent, wafer-thin spring leaves. Then came the sun, this lifting yellow orb of life, so full of spirit yet indifferent and coldly calculating. It was rising for another day, one of millions and millions of cycles.

Then the sun was gone, hidden behind the fog. The sound of a crow. A breeze. The leaves in the trees beginning to move—they were no longer translucent, but opaque and dull. Everything was returning to the mundane, to the passing of time.

THE FUNERAL PASSED, then the wake, then the memorial service at his university, and gradually the visitors and letters of sympathy slowed to a trickle.

Sometime after Christmas Jon and I decided to board up the holes around the house where the pesky possums were getting inside to sleep in the attic. We did it late at night when they were out looking for food. As dawn broke I was woken by the sound of possums frantically scratching to get back in before the sun exposed them. Their days had begun just like any other, yet they had returned to find that their whole life had changed, and try as they might, there was no way back.

Since receiving the news about Dad, there had only been room to confront his death and what it meant, but as time wore on the journey reemerged. I received emails that Tigon was well but missing me. The horses, however, had been hastily left at the collective farm, where they were tied up in a barn with dairy cows. I wasn't sure if the men there had managed to remove their horseshoes, or how often they saw daylight. Fodder was scarce, and it was a big thing to ask strangers to feed three extra horses.

Come February I had to make a decision. If I left it much longer, I might not have horses to return to. But on the other hand, I was the eldest of four children and it didn't feel right to abandon everyone so soon. And in any case, my Ukrainian visa had expired, and I'd spent the last of my money on a plane ticket home. Underneath, though, I knew that Dad would have wanted me to continue, and I simply couldn't abandon my animals.

The answer came when I was offered work as the subject of a Discovery Channel promotion film. It was to be filmed over two days in March, and I was to be given a round-trip ticket to Dubai, valid for twelve months, as well as almost $2,000. From Dubai it was a relatively cheap and short plane trip to Kiev.

So on March 14, 2007, four months after arriving in Australia, I was back at Melbourne airport, feeling as if I had left my horses too long but was saying goodbye to Mum and the family too early.

Andrew John Cope, born on December 13, 1950, passed away on November 16, 2006. He was the oldest of five children. The autopsy report eventually determined that there was no sign of smoke inhalation in his throat or lungs; he had died on impact of a broken neck. At the coroner's hearing it was concluded that Andrew had veered into oncoming traffic. The coroner found that he had most likely fallen asleep at the wheel.

22

TAKING THE REINS

On A BRISK spring morning in central Ukraine a small crowd of workers was assembling by the buckled iron gates of Kodyma's collective farm. I stood with them, a compass strung from my neck and dressed in the patched trousers and faded Russian army hat that I had lived in for the better part of two and a half years but which, at this moment, felt like objects from a former life.

Among those gathered were the many generous people who had looked after my animals during my absence in Australia. Incredibly, for the four and a half months that I had been away the director of the collective had not charged me a cent. I shook his hand and presented him with an Australian oilskin coat. In a gesture recalling the Mongolian tradition of throwing milk to the sky, he then raised three toasts of vodka for a fortuitous journey to Hungary.

It was at that point I hauled myself up onto Taskonir, shouldered my backpack, and, with Tigon choking himself to get moving on the lead in front, felt my journey pulled back into motion.

At first I rode slowly and carefully through the outskirts of town, my body settling back into the saddle, hands and feet feeling their way instinctually around the reins and into the stirrups.

It was early April, the time of morning when the frosted-over furrowed earth in the fields was acquiescing to mud and the pall of smoke from wood fires and coal stoves was beginning to lift. We passed graying timber homes and snow-trampled stretches of pastureland that were yet to spring back after the post-winter thaw. To me, everything about this mash of brown and grays signaled a land at its lowest ebb, and it mirrored the way I felt internally. It wasn't a pleasant analogy, but one I had grown comfortable with—after all, it wouldn't have felt right to return to the bloom of spring or the gaiety of summer.

If my state mirrored that of the land, then the condition of the horses was a good metaphor for where my journey was at as a whole. Two weeks earlier I had arrived in Kodyma to find Kok, Taskonir, and Ogonyok in a cavernous cow barn where they had been tied up for the better part of four and a half months. Their muscles had atrophied, their hooves had grown out, and their winter coats were matted with muck. When I saw them, it had sunk in that to reach Hungary would not be a simple a matter of picking up from where I had left off. Though I had already traveled around 8,000 km from Mongolia, the momentum had dissipated, and ahead still loomed over 1,000 km to the Danube River, including a crossing of the high Carpathian Mountains. These initial few weeks would be as much a journey of spiritual and physical recovery as a passage through the landscapes and people of central and western Ukraine.

There remained one last but important moment for pause and reflection before I could truly get moving. Not far beyond Kodyma I turned onto a muddy trail and pulled the horses into a familiar meadow. Winter had preserved the ghostly footprint of my tent from the previous year. I dismounted and lay on the earth. It was the last place that I had slept and woken while Dad was alive.

It was just an insignificant patch of grass and weeds near a railway, but it was also the place where my life had been broken in two—life with a father, and life without. For the past five months I had been dealing only with the latter, and time, like my journey, had effectively stood still.

Beyond this point lay horizons where I had never been while Dad was alive. Without him the road ahead seemed more fraught with dangers than before. My guts twisted at one thought in particular—that somewhere in a village ahead, at some point in time, I would be asked the inevitable question: "Do you have parents?" On the steppe it had been a standard greeting that I found odd and even amusing. I'd answered without thinking.

Before remounting I noticed a solitary dandelion that had blossomed. With it firmly pressed into my breast pocket I moved on.

THAT NIGHT A snowstorm swooped in, and I spent the following day in camp listening to the snow rap against the tent, the rise and fall of Tigon's chest pressing into my side. When morning came the snow had stopped, and anticipation hung as heavy as the frost. Tigon lay next to me, feigning sleep, with one ear cocked and an eye half open. When I rose, he rose with me, and together we jammed our heads through the tent entrance. The sun was nudging its way into a deep blue sky. Golden fragments of light splintered through the snow-covered grass. There was a stillness that beckoned with the promise of the kind of crisp, calm weather that a horseman could only dream of.

After packing up I rode quietly through empty meadows and woodlands. A couple of hours later I crested a hill overlooking the village of Horodkivka. Cupolas of an Orthodox church reached gracefully above a huddle of timber homes—rather like a priest towering over his flock. As I rode down the hill I met a procession coming up. I pulled over to yield the way.

Leading the march was an elderly man bent forward carrying a heavy wooden cross. His face was a haggard topography of shadowy ruts draining tears from glassy blue eyes. Beyond him women carried the lid of a coffin, followed by a priest, who, with his flowing black robe and beard, seemed to glide rather than walk. Next rumbled an old truck with an open coffin in the back. The deceased was an elderly woman, the skin of her pale, uncovered face lightly warmed by the sun. Two children sat in the back holding her in place as the truck wobbled and rocked its way up the road to the grave.

As I turned to move on, the land ahead seemed touched by the beauty and sorrow of this traditional passage. It felt as if we, too, were passing through the gates into another world.

From Horodkivka I tracked west. I rose to high plains, then dipped into deep, meandering river valleys that flowed southward to the Dniester. Hamlets drew me away from heavier thoughts. Most were nestled on the steep valley sides and on riverbanks, tucked away from the cold wind. They were places far from main roads where the only movement to be seen were dogs running to the end of chains and babushkas bent over scattering seeds in furrowed plots, looking as twisted and knotted as old birch trees. I seldom stopped, registering only the occasional greeting.

In Dakhtaliya an old man yelled, "Hey, sell me your horses."

In the next village, Netrebivka: "Hey, Gypsy, where are you going?"

On the cobbled, windy streets of Hnatkiv: "What's this caravan?"

In Stina, a lady pointed in horror at my packhorses: "Hey, stop! You have lost your passengers! They must have fallen off!"

There were so many villages that sometimes these greetings were the only means of making sense of where I'd been and when. Perhaps my lacking clarity of mind was also because I felt withdrawn, unable to engage as normal. I tried to let my mind go blank and allow thoughts and feelings to come without force, relying on the land, the animals, and people to lift me.

The first inkling of a smile surfaced one morning as I lay in the tent. It had been another cold night, and I cautiously opened the tent flap so as not to give myself away. Outside, the horses were making the most of their newfound freedom.

Ogonyok was irrepressible, erupting in fly kicks, shaking his neck, and teasing the others into play fights. Taskonir had his regal reputation to uphold, but Kok was more than happy to join in, rearing on his hind legs and softly biting at Ogonyok's neck.

As the sun rose, the brittle frost softened and the needling air turned friendly and ambient. Taskonir dropped to the ground with a sigh, then stretched out on his side and closed his eyes. Kok joined him, lying opposite, followed by Ogonyok. Together they lay breathing in the promise of spring. The snow and rain had washed away all traces of their ordeal in the barn, and their bodies rippled and shone with vitality.

It was rare when the horses were so benign, and sensing this, Tigon took the opportunity to get up close and sniff around them. Then, as if it were one of his first days out of prison, he wriggled around on his back, paws punching at the air, chewing lazily on grass. When he was done with that he sprinted circles around camp and cocked his leg on everything in sight. Eventually he lay upside down playing dead—legs in a tangle, tongue hanging slack out of his jaws, and back legs wide apart, proudly displaying his jewels to the sky.

It was to be a charmed day. Not long after setting off, a wiry, little man pulled up in his ancient Lada and surveyed me with astonishment. "What's this? It's my dream! I've always wanted to travel like a free Cossack!" he exclaimed, grabbing my hand with both of his and shaking like a madman. "You are coming to my village! To Rivne! Follow me!"

Yanked rather than coaxed from my withdrawn state, I found myself that evening at a long wooden table jammed with burly farmers. "Pork fat is life! Sport is your grave!" they chuckled, slapping their bellies and pouring vodka. "Eat and drink! This isn't Russia, where they drink a lot and eat little. We *eat* a lot and *drink* a lot!" It was the beginning of two days of utter embrace by the villagers of Rivne.

My time in the village was marked by a particularly special visit to the local school. At the school's entrance the principal—a fiery lady with red permed hair—had ordered the children out into the front yard. There, as she shook my hand and kissed me on the cheek, Tigon proceeded to stick his snout under her dress. Teachers and students alike erupted in hysterics, then descended on Tigon. While tens of pairs of hands reached out to stroke him, he sat like a prince, then surrendered to a lying position, spreading his back legs in an effort to direct scratches to his belly.

When things had settled down I was ushered into a classroom where children with wide, uncorrupted eyes divided their attention between this funny Australian and the dog. I fielded questions for over an hour: "How many kilometres a day do you travel?" "What do you eat?" "Do you have a girlfriend?" "When do you wash?" "Is Tigon a father?" Their questions were simple and the right ones to ask. Unlike adults, who were full of astonishment that I hadn't been knocked over the head and killed along the way, they saw my adventure in all its simplicity. It reminded me that in truth, before setting off from Mongolia, I had never worried about death, bureaucracy, conflict, drunkards, or robbers. I had wanted to come here out of curiosity, to appeal to the better side of people whoever they were, and live the kind of dream that most forget when they grow up.

I left the school feeling light and unburdened in a way that, after the past few months, I could not remember.

꧁꧂

FROM RIVNE I carried on with such buoyancy that I was engrossed in thoughts other than about my father.

As I passed through back-to-back villages, it occurred to me the land was shrinking in scale, and with it the concept of the world held by local people. If in Kazakhstan the average distance between settlements had been 100 km, then here in Ukraine it was rarely more than a tenth of that. Yet it was often the case that people did not know the names of villages beyond the next one or two. A satellite image of the earth at night that I had with me well demonstrated the nature of the land I was entering. From Mongolia to Russia the Eurasian steppe was visible as one vast black empty space, ringed by a few dim lights on its fringes in Siberia and Central Asia. In Ukraine, the lights of towns, cities, and villages faded in, growing in intensity toward western Europe, which was ablaze. The higher the density of living, it seemed, the shorter were the boundaries of the known world for the people who lived there.

Another thing that began to strike me was that when I materialized in a village out of the forest, from across a field, or out of a gully, villagers were bewildered. Where had I come from? How? The penny dropped one day when I stopped to ask directions from a man on the edge of a village. I could see by the lay of the land, and from my map, that I could cut straight over a rise beyond the last houses, through a forest, and end up in the next little hamlet.

"No, you can't! I don't know about your map, but it's clearly wrong!" he said, a little angrily. "You need to go back the way you came and take the road over there."

I proceeded to follow my off-road route without issue. On the map I could see that the road he suggested would have taken me the long way round—almost twice as far.

Unlike a nomad, who from the back of a horse learned to read the lay of the land using its natural features, this villager had mapped out his world almost exclusively according to roads. This had blinded him to the natural paths in the environment. It would be easy to assume that this road culture was a modern product of the motorcar, yet that couldn't have been farther from the truth. After all, this man from whom I had asked directions had been at the helm of a horse and cart. When I asked him why he didn't ride, he replied, "Horses are for work! Not for fun!"

It was an apt illustration that Europeans from antiquity had been experts not at riding but in using carts, drays, sleds, and carriages. With a single animal, the settled farmer could transport hay, grain, and other produce, carry the whole family, and cultivate the land. For them this was a much more practical application of the horse than riding, although it did have one small drawback: they could travel only where their wheeled vehicle would go, and this limited their sensory experience of the landscape.

Riding on, I began to imagine the life of a villager as it might have been in medieval times. Most peasants would have been illiterate and would have rarely traveled beyond the boundaries of their parish—the root of the term *parochial*—and for those who did travel a considerable distance, they did so almost exclusively by road.

Meanwhile, for a nomad in the Mongol army in the thirteenth century, the world would have looked like a very different place. His concept of the world was an ever-expanding one as he traveled through diverse landscapes, experienced different cultures, heard a multitude of languages, and of course did so without being limited to roads. When the nomad horseman reached Europe, the knowledge and life experience he possessed would have been beyond comprehension of the insular European villagers. For them, just like for the man who rejected my map as being "incorrect," it would have seemed that the invading nomads were breaking the rules. In fact, the nomad ways, land, culture, and origin had been a mystery to Europeans for thousands of years before the arrival of Mongols and, despite the eternal waves of invasion, would remain so, it seemed, for centuries to come.

A WEEK OUT of Rivne I woke tired and hungry in a weed-infested gully. Tigon yawned, pricked his ears, realized there was no food on offer, and then tucked his nose back under his tail.

For five days straight we had been riding into bitterly cold wind and rain, and overnight fog had flooded the gully and snap-frozen my muddy boots and chaps. It might have been May, but winter was reluctant to let go.

After a breakfast of residual oatmeal scraped from the bottom of a pack box, I willed the horses down to a river valley in search of food and a rest. In the village of Dumaniv I had only just dismounted when a car pulled up at a cluster of adjacent homes. I approached nervously but had barely begun when the driver cut me off: "Don't even think about it! Sleep here! You will eat what we eat! Sleep where we sleep! We won't offer more, we won't offer less."

Valeri, as the man was known, led me home and doled out hay and grain. By nightfall I had scrubbed clean and sat reborn at the dinner table. Across from me sat Valeri, his father Volodomor, and his grandmother Ferona—three generations of a family, each of whom, I would learn over the course of the evening, was in some ways a unique product of their era.

Valeri, who was in his thirties, had recently come back from four years working as a laborer in Spain. Like thousands of others who had reached adulthood in the chaos of the 1990s, he had gone to the European Union in search of work but was now barred from returning because he had overstayed his visa. He was relying on the savings he had brought back to set himself up for the future.

In the formative years of Volodomor's life, such a scenario had been unimaginable. Born in 1950, he was schooled in the Soviet Union at the height of the Cold War and had served a long career in the army. In 1992 he had quit; in 1998 he "realized the big mistake" in his life and become Christian. Nowadays he was an evangelical preacher and had returned to the roots of his childhood in Dumaniv.

Both Valeri and Volodomor had fascinating stories to tell, but the person who interested me most was Volodomor's mother, Ferona. I'd been drawn to her ever since she greeted me at the doorway dressed in a black shawl that was as creased and wrinkled as the folds in her ancient face. She sat at the table practically jumping out of her skin. "I might be ninety-three, but I can still thread the eye of a needle, no sweat! And every day I go barefoot to the hills with my goats!"

Her body was miniature and shrunken, but in her eyes was the sparkle of youth. She opened a Bible. "I only learned to read at the age of eighty-three! My son taught me so that I could read the Bible before I die." With a giant magnifying glass trembling in her hand, she read aloud. I listened intently, astonished that before me sat a woman who had survived every violent convulsion of Ukraine's past century. By the time she turned thirty, she had witnessed the Bolshevik revolution, Ukraine's fleeting independence, Stalin's purges, and the horrors of World War II, navigating her way through these cataclysmic events in spite of, or perhaps partly because of, her illiteracy.

Like most survivors of her generation, she told me the event that had most affected her was the Holodomor, the famine of 1931 to 1933. Somehow most subjects of conversation with Ferona led back to her experience of this tragedy. Bearing parallels with the Great Zhut in Kazakhstan, the Holodomor had been triggered by the forced collectivization of Ukrainian farmers—a policy propagandized as a war on the kulaks, but which in reality was a means for the state to wrest control of agriculture, using the citizens as virtual slaves to produce grain that was then used to buy industrial equipment and patents from the West. Mass starvation began in the winter of 1931–32 after widespread crop failure. Stalin suspected sabotage and persecuted the farmers, who were now part of collectives.

"To keep us alive my father hid a bag of wheat in between the stones in the wall of our house. One day the Komsomols found it, and Papa was sent away to a labor camp in Russia. We never heard from him again. I survived on grass and the old leaves of sugar beets," Ferona told me.

As tragic as that winter had been, it paled in comparison to what followed. The summer harvest of 1932 was successful, but few collectives met the unrealistic grain quotas. Failure to meet targets was treated as treason and led to an all-out attack on the rural population. Grain was locked up in storehouses or sent to Russia while essential supplies to Ukrainian villagers were cut off. "Bread procurement officers" roamed villages searching for food. Mortars were ordered destroyed. By the middle of the winter of 1932–33, people in Dumaniv—like in thousands of villages and towns across the breadbasket of Russia and Ukraine—were dropping dead in the fields, on the roads, in their homes. Even then, Ferona explained, the authorities "came to ask for taxes on everything—the trees in our yard, our animals, all our possessions." When her family could pay no more they were evicted and locked in jail. The authorities stole everything remaining in their house, "even our sewing machine, bedding, and cooking items," she said.

Resembling the debate that goes on in Kazakhstan about the causes of the Great Zhut, there is broad disagreement—primarily between Russians and Ukrainians—about whether the Holodomor was a genocide or just a tragedy resulting from collectivization. For Ferona there was little doubt that the state did everything it could to thwart the survival of the rural Ukrainian population. At the height of the crisis, when the only way for many villagers to survive was to send their children to cities, a passport and registration system was introduced to keep collective farmers out of urban areas. The border with Russia was closed, and food imports were not allowed in.[1] Miron Dolot, in *Execution by Hunger: The Hidden Holocaust*, an eyewitness account from a survivor of the Holodomor, points out that when villagers resorted to eating cats and dogs, quotas for dog and cat skins were suddenly invented. Authorities went around shooting the animals, and the carcasses were guarded and left to rot. When people resorted to wild birds, rodents, and fish, Stalin proclaimed that all living things were owned by the state. In some cases, being alive was considered counterrevolutionary because it demonstrated that the collective farmers and their families were getting food from somewhere. By the summer of 1933, an estimated seven million Ukrainians had starved to death. Unbelievably, it was a tragedy unacknowledged by the Soviet Union until the late 1980s.[2]

In the morning Ferona took me down to the velvety grass by the riverbank with her four goats. She had promised to sing for me, and after tethering her little crew she put her hands together in prayer and wet her lips.

> I was born in Ukraine
> I lived here a long, long time
> Now they are sending me away
> What is happening to me?
> They will send me out of Ukraine
> They will send me away
> Oh, oi oi oi
> I am leaving small children behind
> And adults go away with me
> My small children are not ill
> Other people will feed them
> And I will be in Siberia
> Remembering my children.

From her crumpled, shrunken body came a deep, gravelly voice. It wavered a little at first but soon strengthened.

> And who's going to feed him
> When he'll be on his deathbed?
> And who's going to feed him?
> How is he going to live?

She brought her hands to her face, and, as though an unhealed wound were breaking open, her eyes cracked and tears came, running over her fragile eyelids and down the worn, eroded gullies of her cheeks. She edged close, clutched my hands, and searched my eyes for a fragment of consolation. But then her grip loosened and she surrendered to an empty gaze. Although millions had suffered with her, most had died long ago, lucky to survive just one of the tragic waves of madness that had swept Ukraine in the twentieth century.

THE SURROUNDINGS FELL away. Avoiding villages, I camped in hidden valleys and cut through fields and forests. At night I sat by the campfire feeling the cool air fall on my back and the glow of coals on my face. I listened to the horses grazing and watched the moon rise into clear, starry skies.

I tread a knife-edge of wonderment and gloom. While Ferona would probably pass away as peacefully as a fallen autumn leaf, Dad, who had lived in one of the safest countries on earth, had met a violent end. Was it destiny? Luck? Karma? Or was life's path random? How was it that Ferona embodied the optimism of the children from the school in Rivne even though she had seen the very worst of humankind?

It wasn't until one stormy afternoon several days west of Dumaniv that I was pulled out of my introspection again. I had reached the river Zbruch, a shallow flurry of water that had once been the border between the Russian and Polish empires. For many during the 1930s it had been a cruel demarcation line between life and death.

On the eastern bank, where I pulled up, Stalin's terror had reigned. On the far bank the churches had remained intact, the people had continued their farming traditions, and there had been little hint of a famine. Until World War II, in fact, the land west of the Zbruch had passed between the Austro-Hungarian and Polish empires but had never been part of Russia. It was only when the Red Army routed the Nazis that Ukrainian land as far as the plains of Hungary was absorbed by the Soviet Union. Nowadays the Zbruch is the border between Khmel'nyts'kyi Oblast and Ternopil Oblast and is one of the fault lines of the east-west cultural divide in modern Ukraine.

As I crossed the river and carried on through a village, rain bucketed down and dark brooding clouds swallowed the sun. Even in the dimness, through the frame of my tightly pulled hood, the atmosphere in the village at once felt different. There were tall two-story homes, a flaking old church that looked to be Catholic rather than Orthodox, and shopfronts built onto ornate buildings of an unfamiliar style. I rode through the main street, then up a muddy track between twisted wooden homes that took me out over a crop of winter-sown wheat. I hurried on another few hours toward the town of Bilche Zolote (the name means "white gold"). Ismet Zaatov from Crimea had contacted some friends along my route, and earlier I had received a message that the mayor of Bilche Zolote was awaiting my arrival.

The nature of my meeting with the mayor in Bilche Zolote proved characteristic of the man I came to know in coming days. Long after darkness had descended I was clopping along the main street wondering how I might find the mayor, when there came someone running into my path wearing a suit and tie. He had a chubby face, a stomach to match, and the stocky, square frame of a bulldog.

"Off you get! We're just about to start dinner!" he instructed in a raspy voice. Introductions had to wait as he seized me by the collar, asked someone to watch my horses, and ushered me inside a bar for a celebratory pint.

Come morning I was left with no doubt as to who was in charge. I had barely pried my eyes open when Yaroslav burst into the room in a frilly apron holding out a tray of steaming hot eggs, sausages, salad, bread, and tea. He dragged his nose over the feast in appreciation, then put it on my lap.

"Here you are, traveler! Courtesy of Bilche Zolote's first-class hotel!"

This was just the beginning of my time under the wing of the eccentric and at times overzealous mayor, who viewed my arrival as the chance to put his town on the map. Every moment was a photo opportunity, and in coming days he would treat me to aromatic baths, royal tours of the town's historical sights, feasts with local dignitaries, and even a school concert put on at his insistence. Although he possessed an overinflated sense of self-importance that tended to rub locals the wrong way, his enthusiasm and raw energy were infectious. I was more than happy for my journey to fall into his hands while I enjoyed the opportunity to recuperate physically and gather my first insights into western Ukraine.

My days in Bilche Zolote were centered on Yaroslav's office, where on my first visit he sat behind a large desk, directed me to a seat, and proclaimed that he was the "owner of this region" and that he didn't have to "answer to anyone." He was scheming to set up a national press conference based on my arrival and generally spent his time reaching for the phone and fax. His press release was titled "Great World-Famous Australian Traveler Arrives in Bilche Zolote." During the work session that first day, I trawled my eyes around his walls and shelves, which were plastered with flags, photos, books, and emblems, all in one way or another representative of the spectrum of Ukraine's divided politics and indicative of the crisis currently engulfing the country. Two small flags in a vase on his desk symbolized the main opposing forces at work: the flag of the pro-Western and NATO-aspiring Orange Revolution Party, and the flag of the Russian-leaning Party of the Regions.

Although the president of Ukraine at that time, Viktor Yushchenko, had been swept to power during the 2004–5 Orange Revolution, the Party of the Regions had since won a majority in parliamentary elections and installed Yushchenko's archenemy, Viktor Yanukovych, as prime minister. In the beginning of April 2007, only days before I flew back to Ukraine, Yushchenko had dismissed the government and called for fresh elections. Yanukovych was now contesting the decree in the constitutional court, and Kiev was once more flooded with thousands of demonstrators. In some Russian media there was talk of civil war and the potential for the country to split into separate states. The political deadlock reflected deep cultural divisions in Ukraine. In the west of the country, people were staunchly nationalist and identified themselves as European. In the Russian-colonized east and south, the population was predominantly Russian-speaking and -leaning.

As a western Ukrainian himself, Yaroslav's bipartisan display of flags was out of official decorum only—his true sentiment was embodied by a large black and red flag on the shelf. It was the historical banner of the Ukrainian Insurgent Army (UPA). Next to the UPA flag was a large portrait of the late Ukrainian nationalist Stepan Bandera. Lauded as a hero in the west but a villain in the east, Bandera was a divisive figure who had led a faction of the Ukrainian Nationalists Organization (OUN) whose ultimate aim in the 1930s and 1940s was to create an independent state in today's western Ukrainian provinces. The UPA was the military wing of the organization and had fought a guerrilla-style campaign first against the Poles and then against the Soviets until it disbanded in 1949. Bandera, who was eventually assassinated by KGB agents in Munich, had emerged in the wake of the collapse of the Soviet Union as a symbol of Ukrainian independence and anti-Russian sentiment.[3]

From here onward to Hungary I could expect more nationalist sentiment, and in the main I was sympathetic to western Ukrainians who were struggling to salvage their cultural identity. Most interesting for me, however, was that this cultural divide seemed broadly reminiscent of the fractious Slavic princedoms the Mongols had so famously exploited during their invasion all those centuries ago. Many Russians and Ukrainians had lamented to me that "if only" the Slavs could have unified, then the Mongols never would had advanced to Europe. Little, it seemed, had changed.

The first of many tours of Bilche Zolote got under way with typical gusto. In the "first-class" sanatorium I was ordered to strip off and enter a special pine-oil bath. Yaroslav stood over me cuddling one of the sanatorium's nurses, to whom Yaroslav had apparently lost his virginity in his youth. "That was thirty-seven years ago!" she yelped as Yaroslav moved to bury his face in her bosom. This was just one example of the mayor's rather lewd behavior, which went as far as climbing up a stone statue of an undressed woman and posing with his tongue caressing a giant nipple. On several occasions he told me that if I needed a girl, I only had to whisper the word.

Among the multiple other tours, one of the more memorable was riding through the countryside in a traditional horse wagon squeezed between two teenage girls dressed in traditional outfits. Yaroslav sat back, commanding the girls to sing. Between songs he told elaborate tales of his kingdom. The driver, who had been convinced to drag out his old horse and cart for the occasion, swore monotonously.

It was on the third evening that things began to spiral out of control. I was invited for dinner with the principal of the high school, and Yaroslav was adamant the horses remain grazing after dark on the soccer oval. "Don't worry! Nothing can happen in this town, it is mine! I will order the caretaker to guard the horses while we are gone!" But when we returned around midnight the caretaker was passed out, snoring. Ogonyok and Kok were gone.

In that moment Yaroslav's authority disintegrated. You could see a growing look of terror as it dawned on him that his grand PR plans were fast unraveling—half of the country's media were due to turn up for a press conference in the morning, and what they would get was a story about horse thievery!

As panic spread through us all, Yaroslav, the principal, and her husband took off in three different directions. The security guard was resigned. "What's the point? It's common knowledge that the horse will be at a meat factory by morning. You will never find them," he said.

I raced around blindly on Taskonir trying to pick up the scent, but after two hours all seemed lost . . . that was, until the sheriff phoned to report the sighting of a local leading two horses out of town. I later learned this person was an orphan with a history of crime who was currently on parole; being caught would have meant a long jail sentence. Word was that the sheriff managed to find him and convince him to return the horses, or at least that was what we came to believe, because at about 1:00 A.M. a mysterious figure came running through the street with my horses before letting them go and vanishing into the night.

Come the press conference I was itching to wrest control of my journey back from Yaroslav. After I finished giving interviews, there was one last event—the school concert. The poor principal, who had been told only the day before about the impending extravaganza, scrambled to get the kids in traditional dress. When the time came, Yaroslav changed into traditional clothes too and addressed the crowd with an exuberant speech. During the group photo, he leaped from the steps at the school entrance onto an unsuspecting Taskonir and paraded for the TV cameras with a fist punching into the sky.

In the afternoon I dug out my gear and attempted to ride off. It wasn't going to be that easy, though. On the way out I was serenaded by the local choir and offered vodka and food, and by the time I got going it was almost dark. I made it as far as a lake and thought I was in the clear—until 3:00 A.M., when there came shouting. I wearily zipped open the tent, and there in the pouring rain, with his leather jacket and "I Love Ukraine" T-shirt soaked through, was Yaroslav.

"It's such a beautiful place here, isn't it? I was so worried they would steal your horses! I came to protect you!" He had walked on foot for 10 km to reach me, and now looked in with crazed drunken eyes and dangled a pint-sized fish in my face. "Come and see the rest of my catch and I will make us fish soup! Only I'm wet—can I borrow a coat?"

I gave him my rain jacket and went back to sleep, but no sooner had I drifted off than I was woken by a bloodcurdling noise. Not far away under a little tarp shelter I discovered Yaroslav. He lay on the ground, covered in mud, curled up with his pet dog. The two of them had their noses pointed skyward and were howling a duet.

"Listen, Tim! This Bilche Zolote dog can sing! Where is your video camera?"

With what little strength I had left I rode out, and even when the howling faded I didn't look back.

⌗

A WEEK FROM Bilche Zolote I pulled into camp on the banks of the river Prut near the city of Kolomiya. The grass was long, the evening dry and dusty; the tender spring foliage on the trees fluttered in the breeze.

The last few days had felt like more of a recovery from Yaroslav than from Dad's passing, but either way the horses, Tigon, and I were rejuvenated. I felt ready to commit myself to the task at hand. As I gazed to the western horizon, there, embroiled in dark stormy clouds, was my first glimpse of the Carpathian Mountains.

23

AMONG THE
HUTSULS

"Where there is a Hutsul, there you will find a horse."

Vincenz Stanislaw, 1936
On the High Uplands: Sagas, Songs,
Tales and Legends of the Carpathians

BEYOND THE VILLAGE of Sheshory the mountains closed in and the sky shrank to a strip. I followed a river in a deep, narrow valley where steep slopes barbed with spiny spruce rose around my little caravan. In the late afternoon dark gray clouds avalanched from unseen peaks, flooding the valley and blotting out the sun. Thunder cracked, a gust of cold air hurtled past us, and a heavy rain tore down.

In the evening the sun made a fleeting reappearance, backlighting a bedraggled babushka who hobbled along the roadside carrying a sack of hand-cut grass on her back. She looked up at me with great concern.

"Are you off to the *polonina?*" She put her hand on her heart. "You are brave! May God be with you!"

The following morning I was no wiser as to what the word *polonina* meant—that would come later—but I was beginning to appreciate the well wishes. At the head of the valley in the village of Shepit, the road gave way to ridges and peaks with no obvious way through. I could either take a three-day detour back the way I had come and ride on via a main road, or I could try my luck at finding a path over the top.

Opting for the latter, I dismounted and set off up a slope that soon became so steep I could almost lean on it. With each step my panicked lungs sucked for air. Behind, the horses heaved and moaned, sweat dribbling down from the back of their ears, hooves slipping as rocks were dislodged and went clattering down.

Higher up I found a chute used by timber workers for sending logs down from the forest. The rains had turned it into a muddy trench, and after many falls I reached a grassy ledge and collapsed at the hooves of my horses. At first I lay clutching the lead ropes, feeling my eyeballs throb in time with my chest, but as my heart rate subsided I lifted my sights, and the difficulties faded. To the east, back the way we had come, the mountainside dropped away to the foothills of the Carpathians. Lined up like ocean swells were row upon row of forested ridges. The sky was clear, and my eyes floated effortlessly over the same crests and troughs through which we had struggled in recent days. Eventually my focus settled on the horizon where the land tapered off into steppe.

Two and a half years earlier I had perched on a similar slope in the Altai of eastern Kazakhstan and gazed over the steppe from the opposite direction. From such a height the modern age of machines, highways, and state borders had melted into insignificance. The Eurasian steppe had beckoned as a fenceless space that carried on unbroken for a vast distance to the Carpathians. I had visualized it as one giant kingdom, guarded in the east by the Altai and in the west by the Carpathians, beyond each of which lay the respective outposts of Mongolia and Hungary.

Around 7,250 km later, Ogonyok and Taskonir, who had shared that moment with me, were still here, and none of my enchantment from those early days had worn off. Only now, looking to the horizon, what had been an unknown I could recount in vivid detail. When I closed my eyes I could visualize every camp, every lunch stop, the contours of the land, and the faces I had met from the Altai to here.

I reached up to Tigon and scratched his chest. As I did he swung his eyes from the steppe to the steep slope ahead of us. Speckles of his saliva dropped onto my face, and I rolled over on my stomach to share the view of a new unknown.

Above us a rising blanket of mist was snagged on dense alpine forest. Every now and then pointy treetops tore a hole through it, offering fleeting glimpses of craggy peaks that form the periphery of the second-longest mountain range in Europe—a range that stretches in a horseshoe embrace around the frontiers of Poland, Slovakia, Ukraine, and Romania like Europe's insulation against the East.

Through this terrain the Mongols had once forged a path on their way to conquering Hungary. Setting off in the deep snows of winter in early 1241, they had somehow been able to navigate the labyrinth of forests and ridges and surge through the guarded high passes almost as if the mountains presented no barrier.

When King Bela IV of Hungary finally became convinced of the impending invasion, he naively hoped that cutting trees across the paths of the Carpathians and sending extra troops to man the forts would be enough to stop the Mongols, or at least give him time to prepare an army. But, as a measure of the sheer speed of the Mongol advance, only four days after Bela learned that the Mongols had attacked the Carpathian passes, news that they had fallen reached Buda. Once over the mountains, the Mongols flew across Hungary, covering 65 km a day, their advance ending in battles that would see half of Hungary's population wiped out and the defeat of some of the most professional and prestigious armies of Europe.

Nowadays the Carpathians stood in a different era, crisscrossed by asphalt highways that connect Ukraine with central Europe. Some of the famous passes through which the Mongols had forged, are now little more than scenic overlooks where roadside souvenir and fast-food sellers take advantage of through traffic.

Riding along such roads, I could not hope to appreciate what the Mongols achieved, nor rekindle a sense of what it might have been like for these hardy nomads crossing into Europe. My plan was to avoid roads where possible and travel through the highest and most rugged section of the Ukrainian Carpathians, where, I had learned recently, there existed something that was more likely to capture the spirit of the nomads than was a ride along a highway.

Back in Crimea, the eyes of Ismet Zaatov, the Tatar deputy minister for culture, had lit up when I mentioned the Carpathians. "Our brothers live there—the Hutsuls," he told me. "They are an example to us all, keeping their culture alive under the fists of the Russians. Most important for you are their horses, which they say are descendants of those left behind from the Mongols when they retreated from Europe in 1242."

Where the Mongols had succeeded in crossing the Carpathians, the invasion of tractors, combines, bulldozers, and the penetrating policies of the Soviet machine had apparently failed. According to Ismet, the Hutsuls were a unique ethnic group who lived in the most inaccessible valleys and alpine plains, relying on the forest and the herding of sheep and cattle for subsistence. Their land, Hoverla, orbiting around the tallest peak of the Ukrainian Carpathians, was broadly known as Hutsulshchyna, and while there is no consensus as to the origins of the Hutsuls, the various hypotheses gave me reason to be excited.

Some believe the name *Hutsul* is derived from the old Slavic term *kochul*, which means "nomad," and that they are possibly a Turkic people who fled to the mountains during the Mongol invasion of Russia. The more contemporary belief is that the name comes from the Romanian word *hotul*, meaning "outlaw," and that they were descendants of a Slavic people who had lived in the Carpathians since the fourth century.

"When you get there, Tim, please give me a call," Ismet had said. "I know the governor of the region, and I will make sure I arrange a special greeting for you."

* * *

THERE CAME A shout from somewhere above in the forest, then the thud of an axe on wood. My horses stood to attention, their ears pointed forward like pistols. I pulled myself up in a hurry. From the mist above, four stocky men and their similarly built horses materialized towing freshly cut logs. They struggled to arrest the slide of the timber before coming to an unsteady halt.

"Good morning, men! Can you show me the way over to Berezhnytsia?" I called, referring to a hamlet marked on the map on the far side of the ridge.

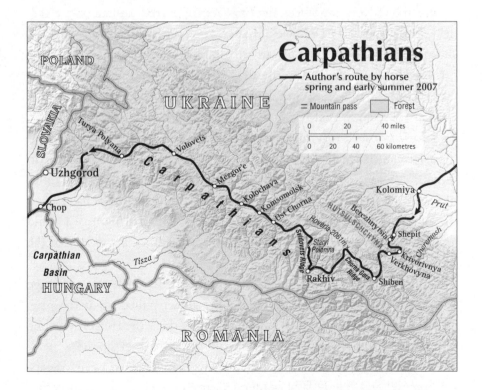

Like horsemen of the steppe, they took their time to respond, first running their eyes over my equipment and tilting their heads sideways to peer under the legs of my horses, checking their status. As always, attention narrowed down to Ogonyok, who they all agreed would make a fine timber-pulling horse.

It wasn't long before the youngest of the men unharnessed his horse, leaped on bareback, and led the way. We entered the forest via a track so narrow and crowded with crisscrossing branches that I was forced to dismount and follow the horses on foot. The fir trees and mist became ever denser, the sunlight withered, and Ogonyok struggled to squeeze between moss-laden trunks with his plastic pack boxes.

At the top of the ridge we came to a wind-raked saddle, then dropped beneath the cloud on the other side. When the mist had cleared, we brought the horses to a stop. From where we stood, the mountainside fell away into space. Across the valley on the opposite slopes, timber homes bordered by silver-gray fences and haystacks appeared painted onto a vertical canvas of green. The jingle of bells floated across to us from a flock of sheep making their way up toward an alpine meadow.

I had been accustomed to the drab, derelict collectives of Russia and Ukraine, and so Ismet's account of the Hutsuls had been hard to believe. But now, as I gazed down into this otherworldly valley, my doubts vanished.

Sometimes such rosy first impressions are fleeting. Not so here. Over the next month my developing picture of Hutsulshchyna would prove to remain true to this fairy-tale exterior—a place elevated from the realities of both my personal challenges and the issues of the societies I had passed through. I would find the land and its people so engrossing that I could temporarily forget about the past and live unconcerned about all that the future held.

My introduction to the Hutsul people began in earnest at a cottage practically at the tree line. The young horseman pulled up at the gate. "They will certainly take you in for the night—that's the Hutsul way!" he said, before using a twig for as a whip and galloping back up the slope.

True to the horseman's pledge, a portly woman followed by her sheepish husband and elderly father emerged and ushered me in. Even before they introduced themselves they had invited me to stay for a week. "First things first, though," the lady, named Maliya, said, hands on her generous hips. "You need a bath."

As it turned out, Berezhnytsia was not so much a village but a community of around eighty homes and corrals sparsely dotted about the high slopes at the head of this remote valley. To reach my host's cottage—like most others in Berezhnytsia—one needed to walk or ride along steep, ankle-breaking paths. The only evidence of the mechanical era was a deeply rutted track at the bottom of the valley, apparently bulldozed in the 1960s but rarely used.

To some it would have seemed a tough, isolated life, but not to Maliya. After I had washed, she fed me sour milk and blueberries and told me that they had "everything" in Hutsulshchyna. The cattle provided meat and milk, berries from the forest were plentiful, and every winter they harvested small fir trees, which they took to eastern Ukraine to sell as decorative New Year trees. Having traveled through regions where collectivization had wiped out untold thousands of hamlets and family farms, I found the independent life she described novel and difficult to comprehend.

I asked her how it could be, and Vasili, her father stepped in to explain. He told me that the Hutsuls had never surrendered their homes. After World War II the Soviet state had officially taken over the land, but when the Soviet Union fell, the property was returned to the original owners or their descendants. "We might be Ukrainian, but we are first and foremost Hutsuls," he said.

Judging by Maliya's two-story timber cottage built into a cutting on the slope, the Hutsuls had also dodged the attack on cultural identity and traditional craftsmanship that had devastated so many ethnic groups across Eurasia under Stalin. I let my eyes filter down from the steep angled roof of a structure that could only be described as a work of art. The ridging that ran along the hips of the roof was decorated with thousands of motifs cut from shiny zinc sheets. Most of these seemed to be in the form of eagles and men reaching to the sky. The zinc cladding on the gable was worked into an extravagant mural of circle, diamond, and star shapes and featured depictions of animals. There were lions—a tradition, according to Vasili, that dated to an era when these predators still roamed Europe—encircled by doves. Framing them were flowers, suns, and thousands of other patterns, the details of which were only obvious up close.

The interior of the house was something else. Doors featured multicolored glass panels, and the ceilings were awash with hand-painted peacocks, wrens, and a dizzying array of floral patterns. There were woven mats and rugs, hand-woven blankets, Orthodox Christian icons, wood carvings, and a range of hanging carpets. The centerpiece of the house was the furnace, painted a lurid purple with repeated themes of lions, birds, and deer.

With the two men shyly following in tow, Maliya took me to her room and pulled down a wooden picture frame with a black and white photo of a young couple in traditional dress. "These are my grandparents. Before deciding to build here, my grandfather watched carefully for the places where the cows liked to lie down. Once he found this place, he spent a night sleeping on the earth. According to Hutsul belief, if one dreams about cattle, then it is a sign the site is blessed."

Ivan, her husband, disappeared into the attic, then came back timidly holding an antique that wouldn't have been out of place in Mongolia. Carved with symmetrical lines, diamonds, and coils, it was a wooden saddle so small and delicate that Ivan could hold it up with two fingers. It was clearly designed for a short-backed horse. Vasili and Ivan were convinced of its origins: "Just like the horses and the saddles, there is Mongol influence among us Hutsuls! Some of us have high cheekbones and slanty eyes!" they chuckled.

There were untold centuries of history in this saddle, but Vasili sadly explained that the man who had crafted it had died thirty years before. "These days everyone in our valley rides bareback," he said. He now used the saddle for ferrying supplies to the house on a packhorse.

※

IN THE MORNING I stepped into the theater of high peaks and forest. I felt at ease. To see the horses grazing and Tigon off the leash brought a sense of calm and completeness I had not found in the villages and towns. I could sympathize with the words of Stanislaw Vincenz, an influential Polish writer who grew up among the Hutsuls at the turn of the twentieth century: "All they [the Hutsuls] know about towns is that they stink till you choke, that there is no water there, and nothing to be seen, and they are terribly short of room . . . A town is a calamity, a work of the devil." In the Hutsul uplands, according to him, "distances and journeys" were "not recounted in hours, nor—God forbid—in minutes, like trains, but in days and weeks." There was a sense of time here "not to be compared with foreign time."

For me there was nevertheless a pressing need to move on. For years I had been lobbying the Australian Broadcasting Corporation (ABC) to support a proposal for a documentary film about my journey. Just before my dad passed away, the ABC had promised a development grant sufficient to pay for veteran Australian adventure cinematographer Mike Dillon to join me and film the kind of shots impossible alone. He planned to spend two or three weeks with me on foot, and I had prearranged a rendezvous point not far from Berezhnytsia in a village called Krivorivnya. Although Mike wasn't due for a few days, word had it that the priest of Krivorivnya was awaiting my arrival.

It took a day to descend to the Cheremosh, a fast-moving river that carved a serpentine path through the bowels of the mountains. Compared to where I had just come from, the air was damp, the sky crowded in, and there was even an asphalt road. But as I rode into Krivorivnya, a string of homes built between the bottom of the slopes and the rapids of the Cheremosh, it was clear that the town was anything but the "work of the devil."

Striding up the street came a man so much larger than life that the mountains shrank around him. He stood 2 m tall and was built like an ox; his long, flowing dark hair and bushy beard were matched by a black robe dragging at his heels. He had eyebrows that spread over his face like the wings of an eagle, drawing attention to dark, deep-set eyes. In another life he had been a Hare Krishna devotee, but the large golden cross that bounced about his chest left no doubt as to his prevailing faith. In fact, if ever there was a reincarnation of Jesus Christ, then it was he who now had his eyes locked on me and was fast approaching.

"Ribaruk, Ivan, priest of Krivorivnya, welcome!" he bellowed. I surrendered my hand to his bear-like grip.

Ivan and I got along like old friends from the beginning. Nudging forty years of age, he was still bristling with a kind of rebellious youth, and out of his robes could well have been mistaken for a charismatic rock star. During his student days, mountaineering and travel had been his passion. In fact, it had been while climbing in the high Pamir Mountains of Tajikistan that he resolved to become a priest. "I reached a peak around six thousand metres high and realized that I didn't want to go down. Below it was full of problems that humans had created, and I just wanted to keep climbing up to the sky," he told me.

After completing theological studies, he had returned to the playground of his childhood in Krivorivnya, where at the young age of twenty-nine he was elected priest of the parish. He had since married a local poet, Oksana. These days Ivan did not have much time for mountaineering, but he still put his skills to good use. One of his chief responsibilities was to bless all the houses in the village and the outlying mountain communities—about six hundred—as well as the rivers, streams, and wells that were within the boundaries of his parish. To do this involved setting off on a two-week trekking expedition in winter every year.

I would spend a week in Krivorivnya, lodged at a guesthouse on the church grounds. During this time I came to appreciate that for Ivan, Ukrainian Orthodox Christianity—as opposed to the Russian denomination— was a profound symbol of Ukrainian independence. More specifically, his church in Krivorivnya had remained open since 1620, defying closures during Soviet times. With handwritten scriptures in the Hutsul dialect and traditions unique to the region, the church, as Ivan said, lay at the heart of Hutsul life and culture.

Only one day after arriving I returned with Ivan to Berezhnytsia, where a ceremony in honor of Saint Nikolai had been scheduled. To get there we joined a throng of babushkas, elderly men, and children hitching a ride on the back of a former army truck. On the last stretch of road before town the truck threatened to slide. Up on top we clung to swaying slabs of beer and soft drinks.

The wooden church where the celebration was to be held was situated at the base of the head of the valley. As we arrived, young and old were converging from the slopes. Elderly men steeled themselves down narrow paths on walking staffs, and babushkas straddled wooden fences. Some teenage boys rode horses down slopes so steep they nearly rested the back of their head on the horse's rump as they went.

It was the kind of clear day when the sky appears close, and in the unfiltered light, the traditional dress worn by the people glittered from afar. The men wore stiff bowler hats, known as krysani, and heavy, sheepskin vests, called kyptars, embellished with braided multicolored cords and all manner of shiny buttons, sequins, and metal studs. Some hats were more extravagant than others, covered by hundreds if not thousands of these bright spangles and topped off with feathers. The women wore long embroidered dresses and handcrafted jewelry ranging from gold and silver coin necklaces to glass beads fitted tightly around the throat. There was many a teary eye as this rush of color congregated. Ivan and Vasili—my hosts from earlier—were among them. "You see," Vasili said, "we Hutsuls don't just wear our clothes for show. They carry the soul of our ancestors and of our belief in God."

There was no clear cut beginning or end to the proceedings. The hundreds of people who had come to celebrate could not fit inside the church, and so there was a slow shuffling queue moving in through the door at the front and out another. Inside, Ivan and two other priests went through an exhaustive series of prayers and songs, acknowledging those who reached the front with a swinging thurible casting thick incense smoke. The interior of the church was filled with the same overwhelming color as Maliya's house, but with the addition of a sophisticated network of fluorescent green, purple, and white disco lights flashing robotically around the icons of Saint Nikolai.

It must have been two or three hours by the time Ivan, sweating like a shaman in a trance, led the congregation outside and stood before a wooden barrel of holy water. There, adorned with a silky orange and golden mantle, he held up a cross to the sky and went into deep whispers of prayer. When this was done he lowered the cross into the water before again raising it and patting it dry. As his prayers came to an end the crowd descended to drink from the barrel.

After the ceremony Ivan changed into simpler vestments, champagne was popped, violins were brought out, and we retired to a nearby cottage, where dance and song hummed through the wooden floors and walls. Our celebrations were rounded off by a visit to an eighty-four-year-old hatmaker called Vasil, who had been making traditional clothing from the age of sixteen. In his remote mountain abode, he invited me to a dark, hidden room in the attic. When he turned on a flashlight I realized that the hard wooden shape pushing against my thigh was a coffin.

"This is older than you are, boy!" he said, grinning. "Made of light wood, too, so that when they carry me out of here, they don't drop me! Every real Hutsul must make his own coffin by the time he is forty." He lifted the lid. There, laid out, was a traditional costume including boots, trousers, and a hat. Vasil shuffled around and brought out a metal head-stone plate engraved with his name and birth date. A blank space was set aside for the day of his passing. "Hutsuls don't fear death. But we must prepare to meet God, and for that it is expected you will be dressed in your best outfit."

On the way back down Ivan described a Hutsul legend: "When God was giving out land the Hutsuls turned up late and all that was left were these harsh, infertile mountains. However to compensate, he gave them generous helpings of creativity."

⸙

ON THE EVENING of May 25 a rather jet-lagged Mike piled out of a car with his backpack and camera gear. The lanky sixty-one-year-old Australian cut a humble figure. Soft-spoken, with wide blue eyes and wavy silver hair, he was dressed in worn cargo trousers, creased old boots, and a checkered shirt. I'd warned him about weight limits for baggage on the horses, and he had kept to his word, bringing only two sets of clothes.

Ahead of us lay a crossing of the Chorna Gora, a wall of peaks that rise in the heart of Hutsulshchyna, including Ukraine's highest mountain, Hoverla, at 2,061 km. In my short time in Krivorivnya, I had learned it was a place enshrined in local legend through songs and folklore about tales of high adventure—such as that of the eighteenth-century outlaw Oleksa Dobosz, known as the Robin Hood of the Hutsuls.[1]

Hutsul shepherds and their families had been making annual migrations to the high slopes on and around Chorna Gora for centuries. There in the summer months they grazed their animals in alpine meadows known as *polonina*. Most of the older folk in Krivorivnya had worked as shepherds on the Chorna Gora in their youth, and while they admired my plan to cross the peaks, they had stern warnings. "Every year shepherds are killed by lightning! You could be caught in a snowstorm! Eaten by wolves! Or, God forbid, lost in the forest—there are such big, dense forests that you can easily get lost for days."

Our send-off from Krivorivnya was marked by a traditional ceremony—an event Ivan said was reminiscent of the annual farewell for shepherds and their families traveling to the high slopes. With Ivan leading on foot, a drumroll, violins, and a long horn known as a *trembita* heralded our approach to the front gates of the village school.[2] As I urged the nervous horses closer, a group of pretty girls in traditional dress stepped forward with wreaths of crepe-paper flowers to tie to the horse's halters. When the horses shied away, the girls found a more appreciative recipient in Tigon. As all three wreaths were tied around his collar, he sat with his chin raised high.

Ivan had insisted we take someone to help us find our way across the highest peaks, and at his request a veteran mountaineer, Yuri Wadislow, and a man called Grigori from the mountain rescue squad had agreed to come. For the final part of the ceremony, Yuri, Grigori, Mike, and I lined up to be blessed. Ivan came to us one by one, said a prayer, and doused us with holy water. He blessed the horses, too, and said a prayer for Tigon.

It took a long day's ride to reach the outpost village of Shiben, which lay at the feet of the Chorna Gora. Along the way a thunderstorm smacked into the mountains, followed by a torrential downpour, turning the Cheremosh into a dirty brown torrent. The river had broken its banks and torn apart several timber bridges. If the conditions were so turbulent down here, it was daunting to imagine what it was like up high.

In the morning Mike, Yuri, and Grigori shouldered backpacks and we heaved our way up a forest path. We were not the only people making for the polonina, however. Not far into the trek a squall of curses and neighing rang out through the forest. Near the base of a particularly steep track I came across two Hutsul horses harnessed to a heavily laden cart. The cart had jackknifed and sat at right angles in the mud. The drunken cart drivers were beating the horses with straps and chains. They wanted to borrow my horses to help pull the cart up, and when I refused, the abuse turned on me. A man with a balding head and fiery eyes flew at Kok and Ogonyok with his fist: "Come here or I will cut you down the Bandera way!" When I backed away, the men calmed down a little and explained they were heading to a polonina known as Vesnyak, where they planned to live for three to four months. Cattle and sheep from Shiben had been driven up ahead.

Mike, Yuri, and the others caught up, and we carried on. That afternoon we reached the alpine meadows, and after overnighting in a cluster of knotted pines we began the climb in earnest.

Not far above camp we moved into a shroud of cloud and onto the top of the main ridge. The mist was so thick it felt like we were burrowing our way through the mountains, but at times when it thinned out I caught glimpses of the abyss that fell away on both sides. We paused by memorials to two young boys who had died the previous summer during a lightning storm. Those markers were the first of many we would see in the coming weeks.

When evening came we had been moving for almost ten hours, the mist had not lifted, and we were all feeling a little frayed. Grigori and Yuri had begun to bicker between themselves.

After pitching camp, Mike and I climbed up to a peak just in time to see the mist fall away and reveal our first full view of the Chorna Gora ridge. Like the twisted torso of a serpent, it stretched ahead, joining a series of peaks. Along the edges scabby snowdrifts formed cornices. Above it all hovered the distant dome of Hoverla.

The Carpathians weren't the tallest peaks in the world, but from here they had a grandeur befitting the history they had played theater to. Not only had the Mongols surged across these mountains, but the plethora of nomads before them—Huns, Scythians, and the Magyars, to name a few. In more recent times, as evidenced by stone markers we had seen along the ridge, it had also been the shifting boundary between the Austro-Hungarian and Polish empires, not to mention the scene of fierce fighting between Nazis and the Red Army.

In the morning we were back on the ridge. Clouds were colliding with the east face, then hurtling up like waves, breaking over the lip of the cliffs, and crashing down to the west. Unperturbed, Tigon spent most of the time scouring the slopes, appearing from time to time poised over great precipices of ice and rock. More than once he disappeared for an extended time, and I was sure, as I had been so many times before on my journey, that he was gone forever.

Just after lunch we reached the first of several impasses. The ridge had narrowed to a razorback where one slip on steep rock or snow meant that the entire caravan would tumble down. After scouting the route, we took a line along the eastern side of the ridge. The first section was around 50 m of rock, leading to a snowdrift. I began with Taskonir, watching as he nervously inched his way forward. His hooves scraped and slipped across the broad faces of the rocks but, fortunately, caught on to cracks and gaps. The last 10 m were the most delicate, requiring navigation down a ledge to a small flat rock. Taskonir studied the way ahead, then came down in a controlled slide, coming safely to rest at my feet.

Ogonyok was less elegant. He stood on the point of a rock with his front legs together, his half-tonne frame and 50 kg load teetering over the edge. With a tug on the lead rope he scraped and slipped his way down, miraculously landing on all fours at the bottom. Kok followed in similar fashion.

The snowdrift proved impossible to negotiate, and so there began an operation to get the horses up over the ridge to the far side, where it was rocky but free of snow. The whole procedure took a couple of hours, by which stage Yuri, who was inexperienced with horses and accustomed to mountaineering in far more dangerous terrain, became impatient, shouting, "Those Mongols certainly didn't come over this way, did they?"

Yuri and Grigori's bickering escalated as we continued. In the end, Yuri strode out ahead, refusing to listen to Grigori, and made his way straight up to the summit of a peak. An hour later we were staring down a face of steep, jagged rocks. Grigori had had enough. "I am going home! I warned you, Yuri! My body can't take any wasted effort!"

By the time we retreated, the sky had turned dark and the heavens opened. Although Mike, Grigori, and I shrank into our raincoats, Yuri came to life. "Tim, you waste time like you are a rich man! In the mountains every second counts!" He had thinly veiled his feelings about this several times. For him, packing carefully and allowing time for the horses to graze and rest were unnecessary. The concept of a multiyear journey and the sustainable cadence and patience it required was beyond him. "We will not get through now! We will have to cut our way through these bushes! People have become lost and died here!" His words were lost in the thunder and rain as I tied the horses up, my mind elsewhere.

If Yuri, who had traveled widely himself, was unable to appreciate the scale of my journey, then how could anyone in Europe have comprehended the Mongols or the threat they posed on the eve of their invasion of Hungary and Poland? By the time the Mongols had reached the Carpathians in 1241, they had already created the largest land empire in history and developed what was arguably the most sophisticated army of the era. Their exploits had included a defeat of much of China, Central Asia, Persia, and more recently Russia.[3] Among the sixty thousand hardened horsemen who had crossed through these mountains, it is not hard to imagine there were men who had been on continuous campaigns for twenty years or more. For them, the Carpathians must have been more like the backwater hills commonly found at home in Mongolia.

In Europe at the time, the truth is that although there was clear evidence of the formidable Mongol threat, few took it seriously. The countries firmly in the Mongols' sights—namely, Hungary and Poland—were more concerned with domestic squabbles, and farther afield Pope

A Kalmyk herder near Tavan Gashun, Kalmykia, Russia.

The Golden Temple in Elista, Kalmykia—the largest Buddhist temple in geographical Europe. Founded and completed in 2005. IGOR SHPILENOK

This Kalmyk man in the village of Ul'dyuchiny lived through the deportation of his people to Siberia during World War II, and their return to their homeland in 1957.

A male saiaga (*Saiga tatarica*) on the Kalmyk steppe. Its horns, much sought after as a Chinese flu remedy, have made it the target of rampant poaching. Saiga are now critically endangered. IGOR SHPILENOK

Luti (left) and his driver, Lokha—my unlikely saviors in Timashevsk, Krasnodar Krai, Russia.

A Cossack Ataman of the Kuban with his son, both in traditional dress.

Ogonyok, Taskonir, and Utebai happily grazing in one of the first fields I had seen on my journey . . . only moments before I am told that they have ruined a winter crop of barley. Stavropol Krai.

Cossacks of the Kuban, a once proud horseback society, have become cultivators of the hallowed *chernozem* (black soils).

Taskonir, Tigon, and I stand on the edge of the Karabi Jayla, Crimea, overlooking the Black Sea. The high plains of the Crimean Mountain range were once a summer haven for nomadic Tatars.

Me bathing in the Black Sea waters with the palomino gelding, Kok.

Seryoga, a Russian from Staryi Krym, spent two weeks leading me through the forest and mountains of Crimea.

Three elderly Crimean Tatar women who survived the deportation of their people to Central Asia and Siberia in 1944 and have returned. Here, they sit in near the picket line in Bakchisaray, where Tatars are lobbying for the removal of a market, built in the 1990s, from Eski Yurt—the site of an ancient city dating to the seventh century, where generations of spiritual leaders and Tatar khans are buried.

Riot police try to keep the peace in Bakchisaray.

The old quarters of Bakchisaray.

One of the Tatar musicians, who played a concert in the Khan's Palace, Bakchisaray.

One of the last photos of our family taken together with my father. I am standing with my brothers Cameron (left) and Jonathan (right). My sister, Natalie, my father, Andrew, and my mother, Anne, are seated, with our family dog, Pepper, who died during my early weeks in Kazakhstan. Photo taken November 2003, eight months before I began my journey.

Tigon looking for a pat from Ferona, the ninety-three-year-old babuskha in the village of Dumaniv, who learned to read at age eighty-three.

A Hutsul man in traditional dress at the church in Berezhnytsia on Saint Nikolai Day. The felt hats are known as *krysani*, and the heavy sheepskin vests are *kyptars*.

Ivan Ribaruk, the Hutsul priest of Krivorivnya who hosted me, finished the ceremony on Berezhnytsia. With him is eighty-four-year-old hat mater, Vasil.

Yuri Wadislow carefully guides my horses over a snowdrift high on the Chorna Gora ridge of the Carpathians, Western Ukraine.

Tigon poses on a peak in the Carpathians. By this stage of the journey, he has grown into adulthood, run probably more than 9,000 miles, and even become a father.

The tail end of the Svidovets ridge. I'm riding Taskonir and leading Ogonyok and Kok. Note the dog lead—sometimes necessary in Ukraine and Russia where there was a risk of him being shot by sheep herders or eating mouse poison in the fields.

Guadians of Hungarian nomadic heritage. Top left, Kassai Lajos, demonstrating his prowess as a horseback archer. Top right, Tamas Petrosko, who rode from Bashkiria in Russia to the Danube on horseback in honor of his ancestors. Below left, a Csikos horseman on the Hortobagy steppe. Below right, Istvan Vismeg, from Sarospatak.

Peter Kun's Kazakh yurt at his steppe ranch in the Hortobágy Puszta.

A Przewalskii stallion at a scientific reserve on the Hortobágy. The Przewalskii—a wild species of equine, known in Mongolian as *takhi*—is thought to be the closest living link to the original wild horse of the Eurasian steppe that was domesticated at least 5,500 years ago.

I dismount on the banks of the Danube—the end of the steppe, and the completion of my journey.

Gregory IX was at war with the Holy Roman Emperor, Frederick II. As a measure of the ignorance among European powers, Pope Gregory had suggested that the supposed Tatar advance was nothing more than a strategy on behalf of his enemies to "unite Christendom against the Lord Pope." When at the eleventh hour King Bela IV of Hungary finally realized the seriousness of the threat facing him, it was too late. Ironically, it seemed that the very Carpathians that ordinarily comforted Europeans with a sense of protection from the East had fatally insulated them from any real understanding of the foe that was approaching at a gallop.

The rain went on for two or three hours. I gave up waiting for it to stop and erected my tent. The horses stood stiffly. Mike retreated to his single-man, coffin-shaped tent, followed by Tigon. We went to bed too exhausted to cook a proper meal.

COME MORNING, THE tension between Yuri and Grigori had dissipated, and it became clear that the struggle of the journey across the Chorna Gora was also over. We found an easy path around the ridge and later passed below the mist-shrouded summit of Hoverla. Climbing the last short stretch to the top was out of the question with the horses.

At the first opportunity Grigori headed down a shortcut to the nearest village. Yuri, who had grown thin and tired, walked silently down the western flanks with us to a valley. The following day he hitched a ride into the town of Rakhiv with Mike and had gone by the time I arrived.

One last challenge lay ahead of me before the mountains promised to drop away to the more gentle mountains on the edge of the Hungarian plain: the crossing of a ridge known as Svidovets. I was confident of managing the Svidovets alone, and after the intensity of the experience with Yuri and Grigori I was relieved it would just be Mike and me for the next couple of weeks.

After restocking with supplies, Mike and I began the process of rising once more into the high mountains—I on horseback, he on foot. The summer heat was cranking up in Rakhiv, and it was a relief to return to the polonina, where the air was thinner and cooler and the sun's ferocity was vulnerable to as little as a single cloud.

On the second day we reached the exposed Svidovets ridge. The weather had stabilized, and we followed sheep tracks across soft green meadows. The terrain was less rocky than the Chorna Gora and better suited to grazing. The jingling of bells from sheep and cows was ever present, punctuated by the gruff commands of shepherds. Wiry men with the same jerky, bandy gait of their sheep sometimes stood in our way, resting on twisted old walking staffs. Their giant leathery hands looked too hardened to have any feeling.

On the evening of the second day we struck camp at a Hutsul summer station known as Staryi Polonina. We had planned to continue at first light, but by dinner Tigon was looking seriously ill. Curled up immobile on a horse blanket, he refused to stand or eat. His condition had been deteriorating for a couple of days. Mike joked that he was missing his girlfriend—a bitch from Krivorivnya with whom he had made friends— but it was more likely due to the raw pig lungs I had fed him in Rakhiv. For the next couple of days I rested Tigon and set the horses free to graze. The break proved an opportunity to learn about the life of the polonina we had heard so much about.

Staryi Polonina was separated into two quarters—one for a cow herding station, and another for sheep. We came to know the latter best. It was primarily run by two lanky seventeen-year-old boys, Bugdan and Vasil. Apart from guarding and grazing sheep, their job was to milk all four hundred animals three times a day—twice in daylight hours, and once at 4:00 A.M. After each session, they carried buckets of fresh milk to a cooking hut where milk was forever being boiled and churned, the curds and whey separated, and cheese hung up to drain. Once a week a horse and cart came to collect the cheese and take it down to the valley, where it was usually mixed with cow's milk and made into a feta-type cheese known as brinza.[4]

The boys had been coming to the polonina as long as they could remember, and the hardworking life in the mountain air had already sculpted

them into distinct adult characters. Vasil, the most striking, had long narrow limbs and wore black jeans that fell straight as timber planks down
his bony legs. His childlike body—so slight that when he crossed his arms
it was as if his shoulders were touching each other—seemed incongruent
with the aged look of his face. His front teeth were turning brown and his
cheeks were so gaunt that when he smiled, his face collapsed into a series
of deep, habitual wrinkles. He smoked regularly, and once I noticed him
fiddling with a cigarette in the corner of his mouth while he was milking
a sheep. He twitched it up and down until it fell out into the pail of milk.
He then simply dipped his hand in, put the cigarette back in his mouth,
winked at me, and continued.

After the evening milking session, Mike and I joined the boys for a
meal of maize porridge and sour cream, known as banosh, washed down
with homemade wine. Darkness was descending on the forests below, but
the afterglow of sunset still lit up the polonina. A feature of the station
was an old dead tree, the branches of which had been turned into a rack
for hanging utensils. Pots, pans, sifters, stirrers, ladles, and many other
items shone a ghostly silver against the sky. When the stars came out, Vasil
pointed across the valley to a distant polonina where a fire lit up the night.
"Over there they have bears. That's why they need to keep the fire burning," he said in a deep husky voice.

"And what about here?" I asked.

"Here? Wolves are a regular audience!" he chuckled. "But we aren't
afraid of wolves and bears. And this work is a holiday compared to winter, when we work with horses hauling logs through the forest."

During daytime the polonina was a friendly place that would have
beckoned with adventure and fun for any young boy. But as the blanket of
cool air dropped and the slopes turned black, the sky loomed vast and the
mountains became a place for grown men. Vasil and Bugdan fired up stoves
in cubicle-like huts where they barely had enough room to lie down in. The
sheep settled, and as all fell quiet the huts seemed to shrink until they were
nothing more than specks, as lonely as the stars.

At 1:00 A.M. that night I listened from the comfort of my sleeping bag as dogs barked, my horses whinnied, and the sheep rose to flee. Come morning we learned that wolves had emerged from the forest edge. The boys had been up all night.

The responsibility carried by Bugdan and Vasil left a deep impression on Mike and me, and for days afterward neither of us could help reflecting that on their narrow shoulders also weighed the traditions of an entire people. In Ukraine, the people of the Carpathians were renowned as poor, and for every Hutsul boy like Bugdan and Vasil, there were probably ten who had left to try their luck in the cities.

⊞⊞

WITH TIGON BACK to health we set off again, and a day and a half beyond Staryi Polonina we climbed beyond a snowfield to reach the highest point of the Svidovets. On the way a hailstorm converged and the mist closed in, stealing away the view in a single swoop. When the worst had passed I dismounted and led the horses along a narrow ridge, watching as the rain came in waves and mist ebbed and flowed.

Late in the afternoon the wind dropped and the mist began to sink. A freshened blue sky was unveiled and the grassy but sheer ridge glistened emerald, appearing to float above the clouds. Just as the sun angled down into our eyes there came an apparition—the shape of fifty horses rising through the mist, their silhouettes coming to a standstill right before us. After some time a horse stepped nervously forward with its head up and nostrils flaring. It seemed to be readying to strike, but then nibbled gently on Ogonyok's mane instead. Pressing on, the herd followed in a symphony of whinnies, snorts, and the rhythmic beat of hooves. Their coarse, split manes, large heads, and thick short necks were all outward signs of their Mongolian origins. Tigon strode out as if he were the proud leader, and when the herd lost interest and stole away at a gallop, he pretended he had gallantly chased them away, shooting an aggressive bark in their direction.

We walked on until the sky turned the same rosy pink as Mike's cheeks—we had both taken a shot of sugar beet vodka to warm up earlier in the day. Then in a small meadow atop of the ridge we called it a day. I sat admiring the horses as they rolled about the luscious green. Tigon came sprinting when he heard the ritual bang of my cooking pot, and we shared, as always, a slice of pig fat before putting on dinner to cook. All day I had been overwhelmed by the sense of freedom. Up here, away from roads and fences, it occurred to me that because my horses were free, they had nowhere to run. We had everything necessary—fresh air, water, open space, and an abundance of grass. In these circumstances it didn't make sense to tie a dog up or fence a horse in.

Mike set up the tripod to film the sun as it slid below the horizon. The mist had pooled deep below, and for the first time it was clear we had nearly reached the end of the ridge. Ahead of us it twisted and fell as a spur to the same kind of low, forested foothills through which I had entered the Carpathians from the east. Far beneath us was a river valley collecting tributes from the many converging slopes on its snaking path to the plains of Hungary.

"Tim, this might be your last real mountain campsite," Mike said, pulling himself away from the viewfinder.

I took out my diary and felt the cold fall. I thought about Dad; I thought about where I had come from in the last three years, and indeed what I had experienced in the last few weeks. Then I thought about going down from here. Mike was right—this tail end of the Svidovets was the end of the polonina, the end of Hutsulshchyna, and the last real mountain between us and the Danube. I was about to enter another world, and it was hard to think that I might not ever share this kind of wild landscape with my little family of horses again.

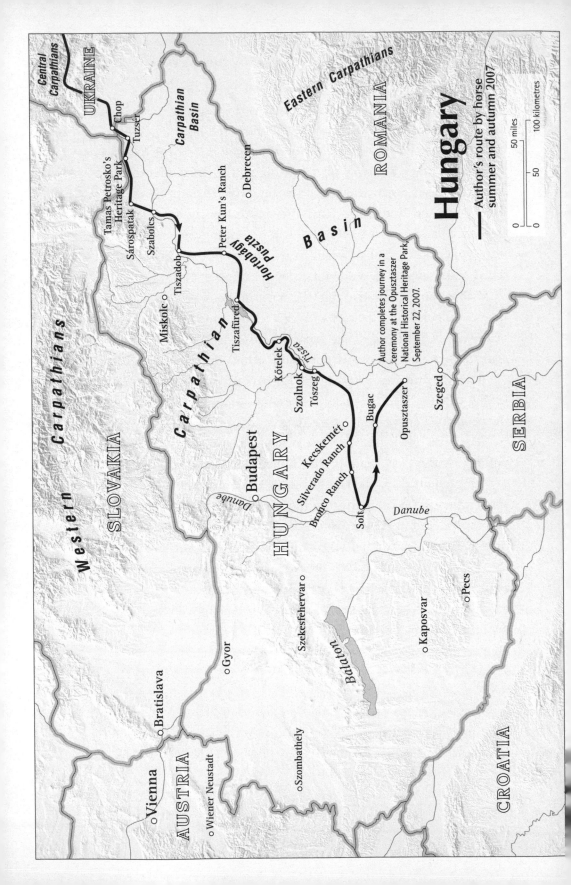

Hungary

— Author's route by horse
  summer and autumn 2007

Central Carpathians

UKRAINE

Chop
Tuzsér

Carpathian Basin

Tamas Petrosko's
Heritage Park
Sárospatak
Szabolcs

Tiszadob
Peter Kun's Ranch

Horotbágy Puszta

Debrecen

Eastern Carpathians

ROMANIA

Basin

Miskolc

Carpathian

Tiszafüred

Kötelek

Tisza

Szolnok
Tószeg

Author completes journey in a
ceremony at the Opusztaszer
National Historical Heritage Park,
September 22, 2007.

Kecskemét
Silverado Ranch

Bugac

Opusztaszer

Szeged

SERBIA

Bronco Ranch

Budapest

Danube

HUNGARY

Solt

Danube

Western Carpathians

SLOVAKIA

Györ

Szekesfehervar

Balaton

Kaposvar

Pecs

Bratislava

Szombathely

Vienna

Wiener Neustadt

AUSTRIA

CROATIA

50 miles

100 kilometres

50

24

THE END
OF THE WORLD

"The keeping of herds on free range is not more 'primitive' than the other method, nor is it more sophisticated. It is simply a quite different approach to the problem . . ."

—Miklos Jankovich, *They Rode into Europe:*
  The Fruitful Exchange in the Arts of
  Horsemanship Between East and West

IN THE SUMMER of 1240, the Mongol army was resting in the shadows of the Carpathians, poised to invade central Europe. Ever since the grand kurultai of 1235 in Mongolia, they had been steadily conquering territory to the west under the leadership of the veteran general Subodei and Genghis Khan's grandson Batu.[1] In 1238 they had defeated the powerful nomadic Kipchaks—known in Europe as the Cumans, and henceforth in this book by this name—and after fattening their horses on the rich steppe grasslands between the Sea of Azov and the Caspian Sea, they went on to subjugate Russia, culminating with the siege of Kiev.[2]

Despite overwhelming evidence of the Mongols' superior military and the threat they posed, the reality was that Europe was still a deeply fractured political landscape. The Mongolians—experts in gathering detailed intelligence—were fully aware of the infighting and ready to exploit it.

Hungary was first and foremost in the Mongols' sights. A country in the heart of the so-called Carpathian Basin, it offered the strategic gates to Central Europe and the most suitable country in Europe for grazing their army of horses. There was also a convenient pretext for invading: during the Mongols' conquest of the Cumans, forty thousand nomad families had fled to Hungary, where King Bela IV had offered them refuge in return for conversion to Catholicism. Aware of this, Batu had issued the king a grave warning: "I command you to send them [Cumans] away, for by taking them away from me you have become my enemy. It is easier for them to flee than it is for your people. They live in tents, while you live in houses and cities. So how do you escape my hands?"[3]

Although it is unlikely that Hungary's neighbors—Poland, Bohemia, and Germany—were capable of uniting to block the Mongol invasion of Hungary, Batu and Subodei were taking no chances. In early February 1241, soldiers under the command of the Mongol leaders Baidar and Orda were sent on a campaign into Poland. On March 18 they defeated the thirty-thousand-strong army of King Boleslaw IV, which had among its ranks some of Europe's most professional soldiers.[4] On Palm Sunday a few days later, the Mongols burned Krakow, then carried on into Silesia to face Duke Henry II, who was supported by German knights. Drawing the knights into an ambush near the town of Liegentz, the Mongols attacked with a technique of horseback archery not practiced in Europe, where close range fighting was the norm. The Mongols shot from afar, sometimes using smoke to disorient their enemy. Although the knights' heavy armor offered some protection, it proved cumbersome in the face of the speed, endurance, and agility of the Mongols, who were lightly protected and rode small but strong horses; the Mongolian conquest of Europe is thought to have heralded the end of heavy battle horses and knights and the beginning of light horse cavalry. By the end of the battle Duke Henry's head had been cut off and paraded on a pike. As evidence of the defeat, nine large sacks of ears were collected and sent to Batu and Subodei.

While the Poles were occupied with Baidar and Orda's forces, Batu and Subodei attacked Hungary. Batu's central column of soldiers descended from the Carpathians onto the plains and swiftly defeated a Hungarian army on March 11. Two smaller columns moved along Batu's flanks; the northern column was credited with traveling an astonishing 70 km a day through the snow.

As the Mongols advanced, Hungary fell into internal strife. The Cumans were already unpopular due to their nomadic ways, which clashed with the sedentary, agriculture-based way of life, and now King Bela's detractors spread a rumor that the nomadic Cumans were allied with the Mongols. Cuman royalty, including the leader, Kotian, were murdered, and an uprising against the unwelcome nomadic guests spread across the country. The Cumans, who were steppe nomads familiar with Mongol warfare and who under other circumstances might have bolstered the Hungarian defenses, fled south to Bulgaria, murdering Hungarians en route.

By March 15, Batu's forces had arrived near Buda on the Danube and were soon joined by the two other columns from the north and south. On the far bank of the Danube, Bela gathered his army, which some estimate was as large as eighty thousand. On April 9, the same day as the Battle of Liegentz in Silesia, Bela's army began moving north from Pest for an attack on the Mongols. In a tactic typical of steppe warfare, Batu and Subodei feigned retreat, leading the Hungarian army to the plain of Mohi—a place previously chosen by the Mongols—near the confluence of the Tisza and Sajo rivers. While the Mongol army melted away into the forests, Bela set up camp on the plain, fortifying the camp with a ring of wagons linked by chains. Bela reasoned the only access the Mongols had was via a single bridge across the river, which he arranged to be guarded by a thousand men.

Bela's actions played into the hands of the Mongols. The following day, when Batu began attacking via the bridge, Subodei took a troop of men upstream, where they crossed the river and set about surprising Bela from the rear. When Batu's army breached the bridge, the Hungarians inflicted

serious losses on the Mongol army, but when Subodei appeared from behind, Bela's army was trapped. With the Hungarians encircled, the Mongols withdrew and employed catapults, sending burning tar and naphtha
raining down inside the fortress of wagons. The Mongols then intentionally created a gap in their defenses to the west, encouraging Hungarian
soldiers to escape. As planned, what began as a few soldiers riding for
their lives became a mass retreat. The Mongols closed in on this spread-
out line of soldiers and cut them down. The killing is believed to have
gone on for two days, during which about sixty-five thousand Hungarian
soldiers were put to death. King Bela managed to escape to Zagreb, from
where he was pursued to an island off the Adriatic coast. The detachment
of the Mongols charged with the task of hunting him conquered their
way through Slovenia, Croatia, and Bosnia in the process.

The following winter, 1241–42, the Mongols were using Hungary as a
base for furthering their campaign into Europe. In what was an unusually
cold year, the army was able to cross the frozen Danube and carry on into
Austria, where they invaded the town of Wiener Neustadt, just south of Vienna. Eccentric accounts from a heretic priest who resided there provide
some insight into the terror and confusion Mongols wrought. Yvo de Nar-
bonne, as he was known, recorded the following about the fate of the locals:

> Without any difference or respect of condition, fortune, sexe, or
> age, were by manifold cruelties, all of them destroyed; with
> whose carcasses, the Tartarian chieftains, and their brutish and
> savage followers, glutting themselves as with delicious cakes, left
> nothing for vultures but the bare bones . . . the beautiful they
> devoured not, but smothered them, lamenting and scritching,
> with forced and unnatural ravishments. Like barbarous miscre-
> ants, they deflowered virgins until they died of exhaustion and
> cutting off their tender Paps to present for dainties unto their
> chiefs, they engorged themselves with their bodies.[5]

Regardless of the embellished and imagined details—some of which
were born of religious ideology, but also no doubt a result of Mongolian

propaganda designed to spread fear—such accounts provide some insight into what appeared to lie in store for the rest of Europe. It seemed nothing could stop the Mongols from carrying on deep into the heart of Catholicism and beyond. In the end, though, there will only ever be speculation, for in March 1242 news reached the Mongols that the grand khan, Ogodei, had died in Mongolia. Batu, Subodei, and their army began to withdraw east for the election of a new leader, reaching their homeland in 1243.[6] Although the Mongol Empire would hold together for another century, and the Golden Horde for 240 years more, the Mongols would never return to Hungary, nor realize their aspirations for domination of central and western Europe.

AS DEFTLY DESCRIBED by Jack Weatherford in his book *Genghis Khan and the Making of the Modern World*, the initial destruction caused by Mongols during their conquests usually "yielded to an unprecedented rise in cultural communication, expanded trade, and improved civilization." Although it is broadly true that the territories the Mongols conquered were incorporated into their empire and enjoyed the stability and relative prosperity that followed, Hungary could be considered an exception. Followed by the rapid withdrawal, the conquest must have appeared to be the kind of senseless murder and destruction for which Mongols (and nomads in general) have been largely remembered in Europe.

Given the devastation wreaked on Hungary, it might be expected that someone like me, arriving in the spirit of the Mongols, could not expect a particularly warm reception. Yet in the dying light of the warm summer evening on the Hungarian-Ukrainian border, the atmosphere was anything but unwelcoming.

Inside the veterinary control building that lay beyond immigration, János Lóska was excited. Within the tight coils of the Hungarian's short blond hair, there seemed to exist the same spring-loaded energy of his bulging forearms and legs. János was a horse breeder, a former member of the Hungarian national eventing team, and currently the president of the Hungarian Equestrian Tourism Association. For months I had been corresponding with him by email, and he had pledged to do all he could to help get my horses across the border into his country. In the few weeks since I had said farewell to Mike in the Carpathians and dropped down to the Hungarian plains, János's help had been instrumental in navigating the European Union's tough quarantine regulations.

Standing over the veterinarians as they inspected my animals and documents, János urged them on with a look of unwavering determination. When the last of the documents was stamped, he grabbed my sweaty arm with an iron grip and spoke to me in hushed English: "Nothing can stop us now! Nothing!"

We celebrated with beer that János's son brought to us, and I rode the horses to the nearby town of Tuzsér, where they were taken in by a family. Tigon and I climbed into János's BMW and were rocketed away to his home. I clung to Tigon in the backseat, drawn toward sleep yet determined not to miss a single waking moment. At one stage the journey was broken by a fuel stop, during which I stumbled into the gas station convenience store and picked up a hot dog. The bright lights, sanitized walls and floor, and plastic-sealed "food on the go" were a startling novelty and a measure of how far I had come.

In the morning the scale of János's support became clear. He had already promised a public finale for my journey, and now spread out a map of Hungary to plot the route he had prearranged. I was to travel southwest across the great plain of Hungary, known as Hortobágy, then roughly along the meandering banks of the Tisza River to the center of the country before turning west to the Danube. "I have ridden every corner of this country by horse, and I can ensure that you will never have to ride on a road if you follow my directions," he said proudly.

The vision that János had for this last chapter of my journey was one of my caravan being escorted and hosted by Hungarian horsemen and -women along a network of tracks and trails, and where possible cross-country. He had friends and acquaintances ready to take me in and guide me through, and planned to ride with me whenever he could. He estimated it would take between four and six weeks to make it to the Danube.

Although Hungary had been an eastern frontier for Catholicism since the eleventh century, and was indeed a sedentary society at the time of the Mongol invasion, it had for a much longer period of time been the western bulwark of steppe nomad culture. Forming the westernmost tip of the Eurasian steppe, its plains had, since antiquity, been roamed by nomads with their yurts, horses, sheep, and cattle in a fashion not dissimilar to those of the Mongolian plateau today. The Indo-Aryan Scythians were one of the first known nomads to reside in Hungary, and it is well known that in the fifth century the Huns, united under Attila, had used Hungary as their platform to invade the Roman Empire. Following them came the Avars, another steppe people who are believed to have introduced the stirrup (which had been developed in Asia) to Europe. Modern-day Hungarians are thought to be descended from the last known nomadic people from the east to migrate to the Hungarian plains, the Magyars.[7] There is an ongoing dispute about the origins of the Magyars, whose language is more closely related to the Finno-Ugric group than the Turkic languages that predominate on the steppe. It is safe to say, however, that they came riding out of their homeland somewhere in the vicinity of modern Bashkiria—also known as Bashkortostan—near the southern Urals of Russia. Under their leader, Arpád, the Magyars officially founded the nation of Hungary in 896 and spent the best part of the next century raiding deep into Europe, defeating armies of Italy, France, and Germany.

I had long read about the nomadic history of Hungary but hadn't held out high hopes of finding Hungarians with whom my journey resonated. By the time the Mongols invaded, Magyars had not been nomadic for almost three hundred years. This reflected a unique feature of Hungary—on the fine line between temperate Europe and the Eurasian steppe, it had always been a kind of bridge between two worlds, characterized by a fusion of both sedentary and nomadic customs. In the long run, a settled way of life had come to dominate, and in the twenty-first century Hungary was firmly part of the European Union, gravitating—politically at least—to the

West, and more renowned for its grand cultural capital, Budapest, than for its steppe heartland.

Yet there was little doubt that János's support for me came because I was honoring the heritage of his own ancestors by riding horses from Asia into Europe. With time I would learn that among many Hungarians, wounds from the Mongol invasion had long healed, and for them the Mongols, Huns, Scythians, and Magyars had all coalesced into a broad brotherhood of horseback, nomadic peoples.

Emblematic of the significance that my journey held for János was that he didn't hesitate to tell me where I should hold the ceremony for the end of my journey. "There is only one choice, if you really want to make it the Hungarian way. And that is Opusztaszer. There I will really be able to make you a hero!"

THE FIRST OF my hosts in Hungary was a man very familiar with Opusztaszer. I met Tamas Petrosko half a day's ride from Tuzsér. Wearing traditional regalia, he rode toward me in a saddle draped with a full sheepskin, tail and all. In his sixties, he had slightly sunken shoulders and a hard, toughened frame rounded out by a belly.

"You come the Magyar way! I also ride this route!" he said in a patchwork of English and Russian, leaning over from his horse and giving me a hug.

In 1996 Tamas had been part of a small group of Hungarians who carried out a 4,200 km journey in honor of the great migration of his people. With a backup truck carrying supplies, they had ridden horses from Bashkiria in the southern Urals through Russia and Ukraine before crossing through the Carpathians onto the Hungarian plain. The end of their journey had been celebrated with a ceremony in Opusztaszer, which, according to Tamas, was the "spiritual center" of the country. It was in this nondescript town on the sandy steppe, just 90 km east of the Danube, that the Magyars' leader, Arpád, had officially founded the modern nation.

Tamas's quest had by no means ended there. On return from his journey, he had been inspired to set up a tourist park in honor of his Hungarian ancestors. I would spend several days with him on a sweeping property that featured yurts, a Mongolian ovoo, and a shaman's hut marked at the entrance by the skulls of a horse and a cow. Out in the field flocks of long-haired Hungarian sheep and a herd of horned Hungarian cattle grazed. It was Tamas's dream to inspire young Hungarians to incorporate the spirit of their nomad ancestors into their identity—an aim that he fulfilled with summer camps where children came to ride and live as nomads might once have done.

In the context of greater Hungarian society, Tamas may well have been considered an eccentric, but as I rode onward over the coming days and weeks, I came to think it would not be an inflation of the truth to suggest that he was part of a groundswell of Hungarians—albeit a minority—who were not merely conscious of their nomadic heritage but hungering for a connection to the life of their horse-borne ancestors.

In Hungary, where there were no mountains or deserts and there was plentiful grass and water, my meetings with these people took over from the geographical challenges as the driving narrative of my journey. Joining me from Tamas's farm, for instance, was István Vismeg, a burly high school physical education teacher with unkempt, shoulder-length black hair and a hint of the East in his eyes. In a wild ride through backstreets, along forest trails, and across fields, he took me to a monument near the town of Sárospatak that had recently been built on an ancient Magyar gravesite. It was a pyramid onto which was embellished a mosaic of the path of Hungarians from horseback warriors who migrated from the East to settled Christians.

"Archaeologists discovered this important graveyard fifty years ago—they believe there was some kind of battle here when Arpád conquered the Carpathian Basin, but it was only two years ago that this site was rescued from farmers. Our governments have hidden and disrespected our history . . . they've protected the buildings of the Austro-Hungarian Empire, yet left the graves of our founding fathers to be plowed over," he told me.

The collapse of the Iron Curtain had provided freedom for Hungarians to reevaluate the Communist version of history, which had emphasized Hungary's rise as a sophisticated European society and treated nomads with some hostility. Now, as the country shifted its allegiance to the West, there was a determination to rediscover and preserve the unique nomadic identity of Hungarians before the tide of European cultural and economic norms swallowed the country.

From Sárospatak in Hungary's northeast, István guided me through rolling countryside to the historic town of Szabolcs and handed me over to my next host, a short, rotund man named Geyser. A self-proclaimed shaman, Geyser greeted me with a ceremony complete with drums and chanting in the center of a thousand-year-old earthen fortress. I camped there and celebrated into the night with Geyser, István, and a saddle maker who specialized in Arpád-era saddles. After many glasses of the national drink, pálinka—a kind of schnapps—Geyser became even more animated. He argued a point with the saddle maker that the true Hungarian origins were to be found in the Huns, rather than the Magyars, and began beating his drum and chanting. "The Hun way! You have come the Hun way. We are Huns! One sky, one big blue sky, the Huns, the stars, the sky. Earth, water, sky."

Among Hungarian horsemen and -women there was a raft of conflicting opinions about which era of history embodied the most authentic Hungarian culture—not unlike the competing philosophies I'd witnessed in Kalmykia among those striving to revive a sense of culture and identity. Another character I met who was convinced of his Hunnic origins was Kassai Lajos. Kassai had resurrected the art of horseback archery and turned it into an international martial arts discipline. Through years of research he had developed bows and archery techniques reflecting various nomad eras. He had become somewhat of a cult figure, with thousands of followers and his own institutionalized training center, called The Valley. Watching him galloping and shooting off six arrows in just ten seconds, hitting the target every time, one could only imagine the intimidating sight of a group of Mongols or Magyars charging into Europe. Ironically, this horseback archery skill was one that Mongols had since lost. Among Kassai's many ambitions was to travel there and reintroduce the art.

When I rode out from Szabolcs and waved goodbye to Geyser, I was still only four days' ride into my Hungarian journey. Ahead lay a further

five weeks of encounters that are too numerous to recount here. Suffice it
to say that the entourage—arranged by János—proved to include individuals ranging from wealthy businessmen to academics, stud farm owners, and simple farmers; though they often held opposing views, all had
their own unique way of incorporating something of the steppe culture
into their modern lives. Among these many people, one man in particular, Peter Kun, had a profound impact on me. My encounter with him was
the kind of watershed moment I had not expected but nevertheless always
hoped for.

At the time I met with Peter, I had ridden seven long days from the
Ukrainian border, at first as far west as Tizsadob in Hungary's northeast,
then rapidly south with János. On my second afternoon with János we
rode out under the glare of the sun onto a vast golden plain. Squinting
hard, I could make out the appearance of cattle and sheep inching across
the horizon, cutting in and out of focus in the wobble of heat mirage.

We had reached the Hortobágy—a vast plain of eastern Hungary considered the last great remnant of arid grasslands in the Carpathian Basin
and home to the only remaining mounted herdsmen of Hungary. The
Csikós, as they are known, are to this day predominantly graziers of cattle
and sheep, renowned as skilled horsemen who, among many tricks, can
make their horses lie down on command—a tactic the Mongol army was
famed to have done in order to remain unseen.

It was just as we idled up to a well and Tigon returned to his old trick
of bathing in the drinking trough that Peter Kun came cantering in. Sitting straight-backed astride an Arab horse, his long hair neatly tied in a
ponytail, the thirty-five-year-old cast his almond eyes at once to my horses,
then to Tigon.

"Your dog is tazi! And your horses are dzhabe!"

I nodded in disbelief. Not a soul had recognized the very specific Kazakh breeds of my animals since I left their homeland more then eighteen
months earlier.

It was not a lucky guess. Claiming to be descended from the nomadic
Cumans, who had fought the Mongols before fleeing to Hungary for refuge, Peter had had a fascination for everything nomadic since he was a

child. As a university student he had excelled in ancient Turkic history, learned to speak Mongolian and Kazakh, and at the age of seventeen spent a year living in Mongolia. He had gone on to complete a doctorate comparing Hungarian and Mongolian horsemanship and had produced a popular documentary about the Kazakhs of remote western Mongolia.

Peter had been offered a job in the Hungarian embassy in Ulaanbaatar but instead decided to follow what he called a "true Hungarian life." He had bought up cattle, sheep, and horses and moved to a traditional Hungarian homestead on the Hortobágy. Peter now split his time between lecturing at a university and tending his herds. "In Mongolia and Kazakhstan I can go to feel something of how my ancestors once lived. At the university in the city I can teach about our Hungarian heritage, and here on the *puszta*"—the Hungarian term for the steppe—"I can really live in line with my origin," he told. Leaning down out of the saddle, he plucked a piece of wormwood plant and brought it to his nose. "When I smell this wormwood, I feel like I am back out on the wild steppes of Kazakhstan and Mongolia . . . and that's because this is still the big Eurasian steppe, the same one where you began."

Riding onward, Peter and I passed shepherds tending to sheep and cattle, and lonely old barns and ranches with reed-thatched roofs. There were also traditional wells that operated using a weighted lever to extract water, nodding against the sky like majestic old oil well pump jacks. In such open and flat terrain the sky was dominating, and beneath us the earth a mere crust. From time to time, fine clouds of choking dust and pulverized dung wafted through.

With no paths, roads, or fences, we rode five abreast—János, his son Marti, Peter, myself, and Ogonyok, who had decided of his own volition to join us in the front. János, being his exuberant self, led us into a full gallop, and for a few fleeting moments it felt as if we were flying effortlessly over the land. Embodying the sentiment of all Hungarian horsemen I met, János veered over next to me and shouted: "The day there are fences in Hungary is the day that this is not my country. I will leave."

An hour or two brought us to Peter's ranch. It was a huddle of horse and sheep yards, with a barn and house cast like an island in a pale brown sea of steppe. A Kazakh yurt stood out front. At first I spotted what appeared to be a pile of old matted sheepskins lying in the shade of its northern wall, but these presently rose and transformed into the figures of two indignant-looking dogs the size of small bears. They were a breed known as komondor, which is a corruption of the Hungarian term for "Cuman's dog." Their long white dreadlocked coat, the likes of which I had never seen, was so thick, it was rumored even wolves were unable to penetrate to the flesh.

After János and his son had loaded their horses into a waiting trailer and departed, Peter brought me a piece of rope, slung it over my forearm, and began to tie a knot. I knew in advance what his special demonstration was going to be. On the very first night of my journey, now more than three years ago, a Mongolian herder, Damba, had spent an hour teaching a knot that he assured me I had to know. A kind of reverse bowline, it could be tied with lightning speed, always held fast, and no matter what force was applied, could be quickly and easily untied. It was an indispensable knot I had used for everything from tethering horses to tying improvised reins and fastening pack loads.

During my first winter on the steppe I had begun to realize the cultural significance of the special knot. In Kazakhstan, herders had looked on with astonishment and asked where I had learned it; it was, after all, a Kazakh knot. In Kalmykia, more than a year later, I encountered the same reaction from a Kalmyk craftsman, who termed it a Kalmyk knot. Now, just as I predicted, Peter tied the very same knot and claimed it for his own people: "You know, we say that if you don't know this knot, then you are not a horseman . . . In western Hungary, beyond the Danube and the great Eurasian steppe, no one knows this knot. We call it the Cumanian knot."

After a meal of mutton and a good serving of pálinka, I lay down to rest on a sheepskin in Peter's yurt. Outside, the wind gently pushed against the felt walls. A horse somewhere cleared its nose, and a bleating sheep stirred. Through a narrow gap in the felt of the ceiling, glimmers of moonlight filtered down, illuminating a wolf skin, horsewhip, and bow that hung from the wall. Next to me, his head resting on an old stirrup, Tigon was fast asleep and in a dream, paws twitching.

There were many connections that I had learned of between the modern-day cultures of the steppe, yet I had never dreamed that among them was something I had carried with me from day one. To me, this simple knot not only tied together immense stretches of steppe but symbolized the relationship between human and the horse that underpinned nomadic life.

AT SUNRISE I joined Peter as he saw off his herd of long-haired Hungarian sheep and gray cattle. A bandy-legged shepherd who wore a wide black hat slowly moved them out with the crack of a whip and a chorus of whistles and shouts. Then we opened the gates of the horse yard and watched as Peter's herd thundered off, leaving a cloud of dust suspended in the morning light.

By 9:00 A.M. everything had settled, and the sun brought such stifling heat it had quashed the spirits of the most exuberant young horses.

"It's too hot to step outside," said Peter mischievously. "In fact, it is so hot the only reason to step outside today is to see the *takhi*."

Unbeknown to me, Peter had arranged a visit to a rare reserve where herds of Przewalskii horses (known in Mongolian as takhi) live with minimal human interference. As the only surviving wild horse of Eurasia, the takhi may closely resemble the equines that were first domesticated by hunter-gatherers. Access to the takhi reserve was ordinarily restricted to scientists, but Peter had been able to get permission for me through his connections.

After we had followed hoofprints for half an hour or so, the crest of a slight rise fell away to a series of reedy waterholes and marshes. There, mingling by the water, were around sixty or seventy takhi, all of which displayed distinctive zebra-striped legs, short manes, and dun-colored coats.

Peter pointed to a commotion on the far side of the water hole. A stallion had set upon a younger competitor, which now galloped off. At first the younger horse darted right and left before plunging headlong into the water. The pursuing stallion crashed in behind, nipping at the fleeing competitor. On our side of the water hole the pursuit continued. The stallions shot past a mare that was leading her foals along the water's edge, and careened out into the steppe. My attention returned to the water hole, where there had been a collective decision to move on. The water's surface was shattered by a frenzy of hooves as the herd pulsated through the water, then out onto hard ground.

It was the first time I'd laid eyes on takhi, and it struck me that before us was a scene that could at once have been something taken from prehistory, but also still be seen in any given valley in Mongolia on a hot summer's day.

The takhi's barrel-like chests and trunk-thick necks were a feature of the constitution of my own horses, Taskonir and Ogonyok, reflective of the endurance and hardiness that had carried me safely to Hungary. The speed of the stallions was a reminder of the equine's unparalleled ability to take flight and reach as much as 70 kph in seconds—a trait that had developed as the horse evolved over millions of years and which eventually opened up a new era of communication, travel, trade, and warfare for humans.[8] Even the way the takhi opportunistically took bites at reeds on the move was reminiscent of the greedy Ogonyok. At heart, horses were nomadic, and their ability to travel long distances enabled them to roam far and wide for feed and water, eating on the move.

I could not help but reflect that the very qualities of the takhi I was bearing witness to had facilitated the creation of some of the world's greatest empires, from those of the distant past, such the Scythian, Roman, and Mongol, through to the making of the New World. Although nomadic life could not be sustained far beyond the Danube, the horse and a nomadic style of light horsemanship had been adopted by Europeans and taken to the Americas, Australia, and Africa, where men had conquered from the saddle with same advantage that earlier nomads had once used to great effect in Eurasia.[9] For better or worse, the horse, together with humans, had been on a journey through time that had not just contributed to the world but helped define society in every inhabited continent.

After the excursion to see the takhi I returned to Peter's place for several more days. When finally I saddled up to leave, he plucked hair from each of my horses, gifted me with a Mongolian sweat stick, and told me: "I am so happy to have met you, and I hope we have strong connections in future. In your mind, your head, you think and act like a nomad even though you are from Australia."

I rode on with my sails filled. With my mind lingering on thoughts of the takhi and the experience of sleeping out in the Hortobágy in Peter's yurt, the complexities I'd encountered in recent months and years seemed to melt away, and I found myself reunited with the basic ingredients of the land from which I had begun.

For seven days straight my caravan traveled south along the Tisza River, covering as much as 50 km from one host to the next. Tigon was a rod of muscle and could sustain long sprints at over 40 kph. A quick dip in any number of oases along the way—river, trough, drain, or puddle—and it was as if he had been recharged. At night the horses were spoiled with hay and grain, and in the mornings they routinely broke into frolic. Taskonir, who had once been so desperately thin that some people had said he would not make it to the Russian border alive, now pig rooted, thrashed his head about, and nipped at his juniors with mighty aggression. In the evenings, I took Taskonir out without so much as a saddle or even a halter. It had taken me a year on the road to feel confident enough to gallop, and another year before we reached the kind of fattening grass where I was tempted to try. Here, though, the issues of water, grass, and distance had fallen behind us. Holding on to Taskonir's mane, with my bare toes tucked into the fur on his belly, I took him for long, exhilarating gallops. As he leaned forward and the earth began to rush beneath, I was overcome by an uncanny sensation that time was slowing down. Details of the environment passed through my field of vision with lucidity. I sat straight and still, legs wrapped around Taskonir's chest, my rear not lifting a centimetre from his spine. These same animals that I had been terrified of in the beginning had transformed me. I could not imagine life without them.

The momentum of the ride from Peter's farm carried me to the village of Tószeg, from where I was escorted straight west for two days by a party of horsemen whom János had described as "cowboys." He was not exaggerating. Riding American quarter horses, they turned up with their lassos, long leather chaps, spurs, bulging belt buckles, and broad cowboy hats. Leading them was a man they called "Sheriff'—a wealthy software programmer who admitted to having watched too many John Wayne movies as a child. En route with them, I stayed in the unique Hungarian institution of a horse-friendly hotel. While the horses overnighted in stables, I slept with Tigon in the luxury of my own chandelier-hung room.

It was only as I rode on unescorted from Sheriff's ranch that my buoyancy began to wane. Immersed in the rush of movement and with my time filled daily with new characters, I had barely taken note of how rapidly I was crossing the country. It was hard to believe, but it was already September, and I was now just two days' ride from the Danube.

So often during the earlier part of the journey, when Hungary had seemed impossibly beyond reach, I had dreamed about a time like this, when I was nearing the end. Mostly I imagined the day my horses would no longer have the burden of carrying me. After all they had done, I wanted desperately to offer them a land where there would be certainty of pasture. There had been many times when it seemed that my ambition to give my horses a deserving retirement would remain just that—and some horses hadn't made it. I was still haunted by the gray horse, Kok, whom I had left behind with an infected hoof more than a year ago in Kalmykia. I hadn't had the nerve to call to find out what his fate had been. Somehow, though, I'd brought the rest of my team through. Ogonyok and Taskonir had been with me for almost three years—a prospect that had seemed improbable when the old man in Pugachevo from whom I had bought Taskonir asked me to send him a photo from the Danube. Yet now that I was in this place of relative richness, it felt all too soon, too quick.

After a gentle ride west from Sheriff's farm through undulating sand hills and forest, I craved setting up camp in the open steppe to take stock, but it was not to be. My last night before the Danube was to be spent at another Western-style stud farm, the Bronco Ranch. My arrival happened to coincide with a Saturday and a gathering of Western horseman. Instead of pulling into camp, I rode in among a throng of suburbanites and loudspeakers that alternately played country-western music and rang out with commentary. There was barrel racing, sliding, and a beer-swilling crowd adorned in the same outfits as Sheriff's cowboys.

After being met by a man called Tibor, who was one of Sheriff's train-
ers and caretakers, I unloaded and took Taskonir and Tigon on a ride. I
trotted out of the ranch and into the forest, where I found a small, sandy
meadow and lay with Taskonir's rope lax in my hand. I tried to focus my
concentration on the sunset and let the steppe soothe me as it had done so
many hundreds of times before, but from one direction the constant hum
of distant motorcycles and cars was unending, and from the other, music
from the Bronco Ranch crept its way through the forest.

A legend I'd been told about the makings of Hungary gripped me. At
the end of the Magyars' epic voyage from the East in search of a new
homeland, it is said, they offered a white horse to the existing rulers of
the land in return for a bundle of grass and a jug of Danubian water. It
was a deeply meaningful exchange: water and grass were the essential
ingredients of life, and the Carpathian Basin offered the kind of quantity
that any nomad would yearn for. In the end, that eternal search for pasture and water, which tied people to the rhythms of the land, was what
defined nomads for me—not their dual capacity for devastating feats of
war and empire building, which can be found among the history of many
nations and cultures.

Explicit in the Hungarian legend, though, was a conundrum that I was
only now beginning to grasp: the quest for better pasture had ultimately
lured nomads—just as it had me—to this land on the border of Europe
and the steppe that was not suited to a pure nomadic existence. By buying
into a world of abundance, the Magyars were trading away their white
horse, a symbol of their nomad way of life and the animals that they had
sought to nourish in the first place. Like nomads who had come before
them, their saddles would be replaced over time with wagons, plows, and
scythes, their vast herds with cultivated fields, and the yurt with permanent homes. In a land of such riches, there was, after all, no driving im-
petus to keep moving.

I thought about it for some time—about what it meant for Hungary's
unique past, then what it spelled for my future. Hungary was the high-
water mark of the steppe—a place of historical stalemate between those
of the saddle and those of the plow. Even the Mongols, who had struck

deep into settled lands and administered their rule, had not been able to sustain nomadic life beyond the great grasslands and deserts whence they had come.

And therein lay my dilemma. The journey had changed me, and I'd fulfilled my dream of riding from Mongolia to Europe, learning to see the world through nomad's eyes. Yet if nomadism didn't belong in temperate Europe, or indeed my home in Australia, then could I really carry what I had learned beyond the Danube?

I wasn't at all sure, and it worried me that people back home might not be able to relate to who I had become. I found some cause for optimism in the example of Peter Kun, who seemed to have been able to embrace the advantages of the modern, settled world while also living according to his nomad heritage. But then again, I was Australian, with Anglo-European origins—wouldn't it feel contrived to live as he did? Then it occurred to me that perhaps part of the answer lay in the raucous music drifting through the trees from the Bronco Ranch. The truth was that a part of the nomad legacy had never stopped radiating beyond the steppe. In the deserts of Mexico and the mountains and prairies of the United States, a sophisticated horse culture had developed, resting on the accumulated wisdom of untold people over untold centuries. It was strange, in a way, that Tibor, Sheriff, and others were reimporting a style of horsemanship in which the shadow of their own ancestors was inextricably woven. And yet it seemed to me proof that the virtues of freedom and independence for which the cowboy of the American West had become glorified—and which were at the core of steppe life—were universal. It was a thought that would at least provide some comfort as I moved on from here.

FROM BRONCO TO the village of Solt on the Danube was a mere 25 km. It was to be my last day of westward travel, and my last alone.

As I traveled roughly parallel with the M52 freeway, the steppe came in dribs and drabs. When there appeared open spaces I went into a trot, but then a ditch, a road, or a cornfield would stop us. In the evening I passed through Solt, disturbing a few dogs, a cyclist, and a pedestrian. From there it was a hop, skip, and jump to the flood embankment, from which we soon dropped down to lush green flats and arrived at the river. In front of me lay a wide swath of silty brown water stretching to the far bank. Not much beyond that lay the beginning of fences, walls, roads, and cities. From the south, a tourist ferry was chugging up against the current. I resisted the pull of Taskonir's head at first, but then let the reins go and watched as all the horses drank. Even Tigon carefully walked his way in and lapped it up.

That night I camped for just the second time in Hungary. Deep into the early hours of morning I retraced in my mind every day of travel since I had set off three and a half years earlier. Give or take one or two campsites, I could remember every step of the way. It was not a journey as such, but had become my life. And yet there was no escaping the reality that it was already fading. The hoofmarks of my horses in Kazakhstan would have already long gone by now, the bushes I crushed rejuvenated, the grass my horses eaten regrown. Some of the people I had met had even passed away. Never again would the horses feel the packsaddle on their backs. Tigon would never again know the freedom of running day in and day out.

As I had felt when I was leaving my life in Australia behind and heading to Mongolia, I knew that a part of me was dying.

JUST AS IT was hard to say precisely when the summer came to an end and when autumn fully took hold, my journey did not come to a close in one time in one place. There were, rather, many endings, and later many new beginnings.

Originally I had flirted with the idea of coming to a close in Budapest, but decided that finishing in a metropolis where the Mongols were still remembered almost singularly for their destruction was not fitting. The rather anonymous stretch of Danube near Solt offered a personal finish and symbolized the edge of the steppe. It was, however, a very solitary and rather anticlimactic ending.

The other significant ending was to be in Opusztaszer—just as János had planned. As the site where Arpád had founded the nation of nomadic Magyars in 896, it was symbolic of Hungary's enduring role in the history of the Eurasian steppe. Perhaps just as important, it was a place where I could celebrate with others.

The day after reaching Solt and the Danube, I packed my things and made my way to Budapest's international airport. There, stumbling a little disoriented out through immigration, was my brother Jon. During my journey there were times when he had wanted to join me but didn't. In the wake of Dad's death, he had been determined to come for at least the finish.

For the four days it took to ride from the Danube southeast to Opusztaszer, he traveled with me. On the first day, he went by foot, running this way and that, snapping photos, and taking in all the details—it was only his second time outside Australia, and his first in Europe. At dusk he approached me with a smile. "Look, there are so many frogs! I have one!" He opened his hands to reveal a squirming, mud-coated little specimen. Standing there at my side, with his daypack on and face full of wonderment, he was the spitting image of Dad—or at least the vision I had had of my father walking by my side, the day after he had died.

For the second day of riding János came to lead us on a trail more than 5 km long. We carried on well after darkness, and just as we approached an equine-friendly hotel for the night, there came a familiar voice.

"Tigon! It's really you!"

Ahead of us, Tigon was the first of our troupe to greet my mother. Also waiting there was Graeme Cook, a longtime family friend and neighbor who had been the first person to put me on a horse four years earlier. My childhood mate Mark Wallace was there, too, with his partner, Nadia.

The next two days were something of a dream. To ride with family and friends by my side, with my caravan of horses still intact, gave me a feeling of togetherness that I knew would never be repeated in exactly the same way.

My last camp was a mere 10 km from the finish line. A night of what I had hoped to be reflection became one of minor drama: Tigon had rolled in something dead earlier in the day, and I spent hours trying to wash him with shampoo and water.

For the finale at the national heritage park in Opusztaszer, the Kazakh and Mongolian embassies had sent representations, along with the deputy ambassador from the Australian mission in Budapest. Gordon Naysmith, a roguish old Scot who in his youth had ridden from south to north through Africa and into Europe, arrived as the representative of the Long Riders Guild. Then there were tens and tens of others—some were friends from Europe, including old friends Sandy and Rita Cooper from Scotland, but mostly they were Hungarians who had hosted me along the way.

As the remaining distance of my journey dwindled, I felt carried forward on a wave of emotion. The last few steps were made through a guard of honor formed by Hungarian horsemen in traditional regalia.

When the formal side of the ceremony was over, the celebration moved to a yurt camp nearby, where that night the smell of goulash, the splash of pálinka, and the neighing of horses mingled till morning.

At one stage, Attila Cseppento, the owner of the yurt camp, pulled me aside with a gleam in his eye that was definitely part pálinka. "Tim Cook— first night of travel you sleep in yurt tent. Last night of travel you sleep in Hungary, yurt tent." He looked at me now, almost ready to cry, but shook his head slowly. "Beautiful, it's beautiful."

EPILOGUE

SEPTEMBER 22, 2007, the day I rode into the national heritage park at Opusztaszer in Hungary, was one of the most fulfilling of my life. More than three years after setting off from Mongolia, I had achieved my dream to ride by horse across the Eurasian steppe to the Danube. There to share the moment with me were my mother, my brother, friends old and new, representatives of cultures across the steppe, and of course my family of animals.

That same day, however, also marked the beginning of a process of what I could best describe as the surrender and shedding—not always voluntarily—of much of what had come to define my life on the steppe.

During my time in Hungary I had thought long and hard about what I would do with the horses after I had finished. I'd considered giving them to Peter Kun or Tamas Petrasko, but in the end I was persuaded by a suggestion from János Loska that I give them to an orphanage in the small village of Tiszadob. I had stayed at the orphanage en route, and the director, Aranka Illes, explained that they had been trying to set up a riding program for the orphans for many years. At the end ceremony I handed over the horses to Aranka and several children who had traveled to greet me. The next morning the horses were loaded into horse trailers and driven off, and I was left with a now useless array of horse tack.

It had never been within the realm of possibility to bring the horses back home to Australia, and so I had long expected this day. I had, however, harbored hopes of bringing Tigon home with me, so it was somewhat devastating to discover that getting him into Australia from Hungary would cost around $10,000—a nearly impossible sum of money at the best of times, but particularly at that point because I was broke. Additionally, Tigon would need to become a resident of the European Union before being eligible to apply for a permit to enter Australia's strict quarantine, and that would require him to stay in Hungary for a minimum of another six months. János took Tigon home, generously offering to keep him at his horse farm.

Six weeks later I put my bags down at my mother's country house in Gippsland, Australia, and entered a world where I savored being in familiar surrounds and close to my family. Still, a part of me felt in exile, and I found it difficult to understand the relevance of all I had learned and witnessed. I realized almost at once that readapting to life in Australia, particularly without my animals, would be much more difficult than the challenges of being a novice horseman on the steppe. The hardest stage was yet to come. Little more than a month after arrival, several of my journals—which I had cradled across the length of the steppe—were stolen from my car in St. Kilda, Melbourne, outside my sister's apartment. A campaign of appeals through media and with leaflets and reward posters proved to be of no avail. The grief I felt from this is difficult to describe, but suffice it to say that I felt as if someone had robbed me of a part of my life.

The months following the loss of these journals were a low I would never wish to return to, but they also became the turnaround point for me on the long path to reconciling a sense of the significance of the journey for myself, and, most important, beginning the catharsis of turning my experiences into something of relevance to other people.

With editor Michael Balson, my brother Cameron, and producer Richard Dennison, I began working through 140 hours of video that I had taken over the course of the journey, with the aim of making a film series for television broadcast. Simultaneously, I began putting my journey in writing—a process that was tinged with grief in the beginning because of the loss of some of my journals. As I began to write, however, I found myself so immersed in my experiences that I only had to feel the contours of my saddle—which is still infused with the smell of my horses and the steppe—get a whiff of wood smoke, feel the breeze wash over the hills near my mother's home, catch a glimpse of a horse in a paddock, or hear the sound of a distant dog barking to feel transported back to the steppe. Where diaries were lacking, I realized I was also fortunate to be able to draw on maps, photos, and other writings I had done at the time. Most important, I began reestablishing contact with many of the friends I had made across the steppe—both through correspondence and, in some cases, by visiting them. In the middle of 2008, I took up an impromptu request by World Expeditions to guide a trekking journey in Mongolia, at which time I met with many of the people who had seen me off in the saddle all those years before, including Gansukh Baatarsuren and Tseren Enebish and her family and relatives. It was to be the first of a series of trips to Mongolia I have undertaken annually since.

Toward the end of 2008, things began progressing quickly. In the fall I found myself in North America after accepting an invitation as a presenter to attend a travel and adventure festival in Montreal. On the way back to Australia, I stopped over in Washington, D.C., from where I traveled to New York with literary agent Gail Ross and met with several publishers in Manhattan, among which were editor Anton Mueller and publisher George Gibson of Bloomsbury. Within a couple of months I had a contract.

During 2008 I missed Tigon greatly and kept in close contact with János Loska about his well-being. There were many stories of mischief to be recounted, such as when Tigon followed a passing horseman for a day and took all the farm dogs with him. János lamented that he had had to send a taxi to pick them all up. True to form, Tigon became a father at János's farm, and one of the offspring was given to the Tiszadob orphanage, where he was named Tigi.

In November 2008, more than twelve months after I had last seen Tigon, I received a letter in the mail. It was from Australian Quarantine—a permit for Tigon to enter Australia had been granted! I was still without money, however, and the catch was that it would expire within a month. I happened to be in Perth at the time, staying with my friends Rob and Rachel Devling, and with the help of Mike Wood of Mountain Designs, I was able to arrange a special fund-raising presentation. The response was overwhelming, and with a sold-out theater of people who had come to listen to my story, $8,000 was raised in just one night.

In early December 2008, Tigon was taken from Budapest to the Vienna airport by Hungarian veterinarian Edit Budik. From there he was flown to the United Arab Emirates and loaded onto an Australia-bound flight to Melbourne. On December 12, 2008, Tigon showed no hesitation as he came bounding out of his quarantine enclosure to meet me (although he then ignored me for half an hour while he chewed on a marrow bone that I had brought as a welcome gift). In January 2009, when I sat down in earnest to begin the long journey of writing the book, Tigon was by my side, and I was well on the way to bridging the great divide between life in Australia and life on the steppe.

Since that time, much has happened, both for me and for the many people on the steppe with whom I still share a close connection.

In August 2009, I made the first of several trekking journeys back to the Kharkhiraa-Turgen mountain region of western Mongolia, in cooperation with Tseren Enebish and World Expeditions. There, we hired Dashnyam as our head camelier and guide to make the same trek I had done with him over the high pass. It was a wonderful experience to reunite with Dashnyam and his family and tell him news of my journey to the Danube. Dashnyam's circumstances had changed little since I had said farewell to him on a cold autumn morning in 2004. He was still living a marginal existence with very few animals to support his many children. I had hoped to see the horse I had gifted him, Saartai Zeerd, but he explained that the horse had become old and his family had eaten him the previous winter. More recently, his one and only other horse had been stolen, and so he was all but horseless. With the help of the trekkers on the initial 2009 journey, we raised enough tips additional to his salary for him to buy a new horse—and in later years a second horse and a camel. Since then, Dashnyam has become a grandfather—his daughter, whom I had photographed in 2004 (seen on page 5 of the first photo insert), gave birth to a boy in the spring of 2012.

Two other important things happened for me in the summer of 2009. After many trials and tribulations, I received news that ZDF, the national broadcaster of Germany, acting on behalf of the ARTE channel, had granted funding for a three-hour documentary series about my journey. ABC in Australia soon followed with their support of a version of the series, and I spent much of the next year working on the film, which was titled On the Trail of Genghis Khan (Auf den Spuren der Nomaden in German). The series has since been broadcast in several countries and languages.

The other important event was that I met a young Mongolian woman, Khorloo Batpurev, with whom I fell in love. I would spend the summers of 2010 and 2011 in Mongolia, guiding my annual trip and writing my book in Ulaanbaatar, where I shared an apartment with Khorloo. Since then, we have remained mostly in Australia—Khorloo concentrating on her studies, and me on my book.

During the writing, I have followed with great interest the unfolding circumstances of the lives of many whom I met on the steppe. None are more important to me than Aset from Zhana Zhol, who accompanied me in the winter of 2004–5, and Baitak and his friends in Akbakai.

It wasn't until a year after Aset traveled with me in Kazakhstan that he told me he had spent fourteen years of his life in jail. At the age of just twenty, while working as a taxi driver, he had been involved in a brawl and accidentally broken the jaw of a policeman. He hadn't mentioned it at the time because he feared it would scare me off. Since my journey with him, Aset has moved from the village of Zhana Zhol into the city of Oskemen, where he lives with his wife and disabled son, Guanz. Back in 2005 I was able to return the saddle that he sold to me, but it has to date gone unused in his new city life. Guanz is doing well, now studying at university. I have promised to send more updates about his former pup, Tigon, and hope to visit them again one day.

Baitak and his wife, Rosa, left Akbakai in 2006. After selling his horses and home, Baitak bought a herd of sheep and goats and at the time of this writing runs a cafe on the main highway between Almaty and Astana. When Baitak left Akbakai, he took the alcoholics Grisha and Vitka with him. Vitka continued his ways with vodka and returned to Akbakai, where he died in the autumn of 2006 of a combination of malnutrition and alcohol poisoning; Baitak arranged a funeral for him. Grisha worked as a welder for some time but then went missing, and Baitak has not heard from him since.

Madagol, the herder who looked after my horses that winter in Akbakai, never recovered from the broken leg he incurred in his fall, and he now lives in Moiynkum with his son and daughter-in-law. His wife died of cancer at age fifty-three in the winter of 2007–8.

In terms of gold mining in Akbakai, Baitak tells me that things have since been cleaned up. In 2004 about half of the city's three thousand residents apparently had been involved in gold theft. The mine is now in private hands and security guards are harder to buy out. He tells me that only 10 percent of people are now stealing, and that as a consequence, the black market price for gold has increased by more than 300 percent.

In the years between the finishing of the trip and the publishing of this book, it is worth noting some of the political and economic changes across some countries of the Eurasian steppe through which I traveled. In the political sphere, Vladimir Putin stepped down as president of Russia in 2008 to become prime minister but has since returned to his role as president. Of the many "color revolutions" among former Soviet states, all have been reversed. In Kyrgyzstan, the Tulip Revolution, which ousted President Akayev in 2005, brought some semblance of stability for just five years until the 2010 so-called Second Kyrgyz Revolution, which was followed by violent interethnic conflict in which as many as two thousand people, mostly ethnic Uzbeks, were killed. In Ukraine, Viktor Yanukovych, from the Russian-leaning Party of Regions, came to power in 2010 and has reversed many of the reforms of his Orange Revolution predecessor, Viktor Yushchenko. Yulia Tymashenko, who at the time of my travels in Ukraine was in a bitter power struggle with both Yushchenko and Yanukovych, is currently languishing in prison after being found guilty of abuse of office when brokering the 2009 gas deal with Russia—a case that is widely regarded as politically motivated. In Kazakhstan, on the other hand, Nursultan Nazarbayev remains in power and has essentially become president for life after the parliament passed a constitutional amendment allowing him to run for president as many times as he chooses.

These political changes I've outlined, as turbulent as some may have been, probably have not brought much influence to bear on the trajectory of life and culture of the steppe peoples as I encountered them during my journey (although in Ukraine it is true that the Ukrainian language and culture have undoubtedly been dealt a blow by Yanukovych's pro-Russian policies). In Mongolia, however, it may be a different story, for it is a country that has recently seen, and will no doubt undergo, a dramatic economic shift.

In 2001 copper and gold deposits worth an estimated $350 billion were discovered in the southern Gobi Desert. After many years of political wrangling and negotiation, an investment agreement on the development of the deposit—which is known as Oyu Tolgoi—was reached in 2009 between the government of Mongolia and the mining corporations Rio Tinto and Ivanhoe Mines (now Turquoise Hill). Commercial mining at Oyu Tolgoi, which is expected to be one of the five largest mines on the planet, is scheduled to begin operation in 2013, and at full production will provide an estimated 30 percent of GDP for Mongolia.

Oyu Tolgoi is not the only big mine under development in Mongolia. Tavan Tolgoi, also in the Gobi, is thought to be one of the largest unexploited reserves of coking coal in the world. This is not to mention the untold smaller mining projects currently under way across the country.

Given the scale of Mongolia's resources, and the investment that has been poured into the mining sector in recent times, it is not hard to imagine that a transformation must now course through Mongolian society. Nonetheless, the economic statistics are mind-boggling. In 2011 Mongolia was the fastest-growing economy in the world—the GDP had increased from $1 billion in 2001 to $11 billion just a decade later. Even compared to 2004 when I set off on my journey, the Ulaanbaatar of 2013 is unrecognizable. At rush hour, the city's roads are jammed with a chaotic sprawl of traffic, among which one cannot avoid the spectacle of fleets of luxury vehicles. The Soviet-era apartments that once loomed large over the city's suburbs are fast being outnumbered by new developments, which include gated communities and multistory office blocks in the city center—many of which have been built in anticipation of the mining production to come.

With a boom of this kind, it comes as no surprise that there are many allegations of corruption against Mongolia's politicians, complaints about the lack of transparency of deals with multinational mining companies, and rumors of foreign companies taking advantage of Mongolia's inexperience in dealing with such large-scale projects. Then there is the problem of high inflation and the growing wealth gap between rich and poor, and questions over the environmental impact of mining. For one, the scale of mining being developed requires vast quantities of water—a fragile resource in the Gobi and one that is key to the survival of nomads.

Much of what is happening in Mongolia resembles the early stages of Kazakhstan's oil boom, only in a country with a population of just 3.2 million—many of whom are still nomadic—the effect is bound to be more profound. And this inevitably raises the question of what this will bring to bear on the nomad's economy and culture. No matter how ethically mining is managed, there is, of course, a very real risk in the long term of the marginalization of nomadic life and, ultimately, its slow demise.

Whatever may await in the future, though, for many, such as Dashnyam in western Mongolia, the fast pace of change in Ulaanbaatar is worlds away. And at the present time the constitution of Mongolia still prohibits the privatization of grazing lands—that is, with the exception of mining leases and areas suitable for crop farming. For the time being, the ancient rhythms of steppe life that revolve around the horse reign supreme in the Mongolian countryside.

Returning to notes of a more personal nature, in 2006, the year before I reached the Danube, Kathrin Nienhaus, with whom I had begun the journey, married Frank Bender. We remained in contact, and Kathrin has been a great support, ranging from her counseling at the time of my father's death to helping me trawl through details of our time together in Mongolia for the purposes of this book.

It is also of note that Gansukh Baatarsuren, the young Mongolian man who helped me buy my first horses, splits his time between Mongolia and Australia with his Australian partner, Sonya. We remain good friends.

And a word about my animals in Hungary. In the years since I left the horses at the orphanage, Aranka has kept in touch, sending photos and updates of the horses, and the orphans who have learned to ride on them. Not long after I left Hungary, the soccer oval was permanently transformed into the horses' paddock. A measure of how long my book has been in the works, however, is that at the time of writing, Taskonir, who is now probably into his twenties, has been retired from work. Kok unfortunately suffered some kind of injury to one of his legs and is lame. Ogonyok continues to be ridden by the children. Tigi, Tigon's progeny, unfortunately went walkabout one day and never returned.

Lastly, plans for the future. I have many dreams of traveling in northwest China, Central Asia, and even Australia, mostly on foot, with animals. I'm also interested in the origins and migrations through time of the Roma people (Gypsies), and on a different note, I dream of writing a children's book about Tigon and visiting my horses. I have begun a program of taking Australian students to Mongolia and raising money for the school in the village of Khovd, and I hope to continue this.

In the meantime, however, I am going to take a breath and enjoy the experience of new and opening horizons with the completion of this book. After that, I will probably take a long walk with my four-legged companion to think about it.

—Tim Cope
April 9, 2013

ACKNOWLEDGMENTS

WHAT BEGAN AS a plan to ride horses for eighteen months from Mongolia to Hungary has shaped and consumed my life for a decade.

Broadly speaking, there have been three stages—the preparation, the journey, and the digesting of the experience, including the making of a film series, but mostly the writing of this book. At every stage, help, support, and encouragement from others have allowed me to go forward.

Some of these people to whom I owe my gratitude I have lost contact with, partly because while I have been consumed with the journey, they have long moved on in their lives; others are still close friends; and some, I am sad to say, did not live to see the end of this project.

In the early stages I owe many thanks to my parents—Anne Cope, and the late Andrew Cope—and my then-girlfriend, Kathrin Nienhaus (now Kathrin Bender-Nienhaus). My great-uncle and great-aunt, John and Alison Kearney, have supported me throughout my travels over the years and offered crucial moral and financial assistance.

The horse world is a varied, and confounding one for the uninitiated, and there were individuals who helped guide me into it. CuChullaine O'Reilly, a founding member of the Long Riders Guild, responded at once to my request for advice, offering generous wisdom, a sympathetic ear, and encouragement that not only equipped me with the knowledge to travel by horse but inspired me to carry on with what I learned far beyond the Danube and write this book. His colleague, Long Rider and author Jeremy James, also offered some guidance.

In Australia, Cath and Steve Baird of Bogong Horseback Adventures generously gave me my first taste of horse riding—a packhorse trip in the Victorian Alps. In Western Australia, Brent, Sam, and Sascha Watson of Horses and Horsemen provided training, then advice throughout my journey. They introduced me to equine vet extraordinaire Sheila Greenwell, who donated a veterinary kit and throughout the journey offered life-saving vet services by correspondence.

Then there are those who helped me in the countries I traveled. Old friends Tseren Enebish of Mongolia and her husband, Rik Idema, Tseren's elderly mother, and her cousin Bayara Mishig hosted and guided me through the difficult early stages in Ulaanbaatar. Gansukh Baatarsuren, a young enthusiast of Mongolian history and horsemanship, helped me buy my horses and was an endless source of nomadic cultural insight.

In Kazakhstan I stayed with some seventy families, but in particular I'd like to thank Evegeniy and Misha Yurckenkov in Oskemen, Aset and his son Guanz (who generously offered me Tigon), Baitak in Akbakai, and Dauren Izmagulov and Azamat Sagenov in Atyrau. I'm also particularly grateful to Kosibek Erzgalev, the minister for agriculture in Western Kazakhstan, and his team, who helped me get my horses into Russia. In Almaty, thanks go to Rosa and Vadim Khaibullina of Tour Asia for visa- and logistics-related assistance, and to Gaukhar Konuspayeva for putting me in touch with many helpful contacts.

In Russia I was supported by Dr. Anna Lushchekina of the Russian Academy of Science, journalist Inna Manturova, and Dr. Liudmilla Kiseleva. Liudmilla, a professor of biology and an environmental activist, unfortunately was killed in a car accident in suspicious circumstances only a couple of weeks before the end of my journey. I'd also like to thank Yuri at the Kalmykian Wild Animal Center, the Kalmykian Institute for Humanitarian Sciences, and Nikolai Vladimorivich Luti and all his crew in Timashevsk. In the winter of 2005–6, I traveled to Crimea to renew my Russian visa. I was hosted for a month in Sevastopol by my surrogate Russian grandmother, Baba Galya, whom I had befriended in 2000 while cycling in northern Russia. Her daughter Shura, grandchildren Olya and Dima, and son-in-law Sasha Shishkin, kindly looked after me for a month. Sasha died suddenly of cancer in 2007. Baba Galya passed away on November 24, 2008, just shy of her eightieth birthday.

In Crimea, thanks go to Ismet Zaatov, deputy minister for culture of Crimea, and to Ira of Argamak Horse Center, near Feodosiya, and her helping hand Sascha, who has unfortunately since been killed in a horse accident.

In Ukraine itself, thanks to Anya Summets for her love and support, particularly during the period after my father's death, and to Vladimir Sklyaruk and his family in Kodyma, who arranged for Tigon and the horses to be looked after while I returned to Australia after my father's passing. In the Carpathians, Ivan Ribaruk remains a good friend. I was fortunate in Hungary to have broad support from many. I am indebted to János Loska, who single-handedly arranged my journey across the border into Hungary and then to the Danube, as well as the special ceremony for the finish in Opusztaszer. Peter Kun, István Vismeg, and Tamas Petrosko also deserve special mention.

The last stage of my journey, from the Danube until now, has been the longest, and in many ways the most trying. I owe great thanks to my mother, Anne, for sheltering me for the best part of two years after I returned home. Mum has supported me through the highs and lows I have experienced while coming to terms with the end of one journey and the beginning of new challenges. Likewise, thanks go to my brothers, Cameron and Jonathan, and my sister, Natalie. Family friends the Cooks, Wallaces, and Nicholsons have been great supporters of our family, particularly since the passing of my father.

It goes without saying that I owe much to my father for introducing me to the outdoors and doing everything he could to support me on my path to adventure and writing, even when it involved abandoning my law degree at university—something that did not sit comfortably with him at the time.

The book has been a major thread of my life for nearly four years. I have written it in many places. I began writing at the Drouin South home of our longtime family friends, the Wallaces, who kindly offered use of their study. Then I went off on solo writing "expeditions," such as when I was invited by Andrew Faulknor (aka Viktor) to his property in the Strzeleckis, where I wrote by day in a shed and slept in a tent at night with Tigon. Some of this book was written in Mongolia, and in November 2011 I was given a Fleck Fellowship to write in the artists' colony at the Banff Centre for Creativity, Canada. The last part was written mostly in Tawonga in the Victorian Alps, Australia, where I have had very understanding landlords in Helen and Glen McIlroy, forever patient and supportive friends in the Van der Ploeg family, and a trusty canine sitting on the couch by my side and demanding a run at the end of every writing day.

Through all of this time, I am thankful for the patience and belief of my literary agents, Benython Oldfield in Australia and Gail and Howard in Washington, D.C., and my publisher, George Gibson, in New York, who was willing to go out on a limb and commission this book from an unknown, rather disheveled Australian.

Anton Mueller, my editor, has lived through the journey, and although it has been via correspondence between New York and Australia, I feel like he has accompanied me for every hoofstep. Anton has both encouraged and challenged me during the writing process, and I feel indebted to him for the personal growth I have experienced as a result; the book simply would not be as it is without his input. During the writing of this book—and the cutting, which has involved reducing the original manuscript by almost half—I have also enjoyed the generous feedback of longtime friend and travel companion Dr. Chris Hatherly. Then there is the person closest to me, who has had to live through all the ups and downs. My girlfriend, Khorloo Batpurev, did not know me when I carried out the journey, but she has had to weather every challenge as I have relived them. It's also true that while I have long since returned from the steppes, I have not been 100 percent present at home, either. Thank you, Khorloo, for all your love and care, and for sticking this long journey out.

There are many other friends and supporters who have helped me greatly, including my former English and history teacher Rob Devling, longtime friends Cordell Scaife, Ben Kozel, and Todd Tai, and more recent friend Joss Stewart. Thanks to the many others not mentioned here.

Lastly, it would never have been possible to carry out this journey without the support of sponsors. I would like to thank the following:

MAIN SPONSORS
Iridium, satellite phone communications
Internetrix.net, particularly support from Daniel Rowan
Saxtons Speaking Bureau, especially Nannette and Winston Moulton
The Australian Geographic Society

MEDIUM-LEVEL SPONSORS

Bogong Horseback Adventures (Victoria, Australia)

Horses and Horsemen (Margaret River, Western Australia)

Odyssey Travel

Mountain Designs

Spelean Australia, distributors of such brands as MSR, Therma-Rest, and Platypus

Reflex Sports

Fujifilm, with special thanks to Graham Carter and Darren at CPL Digital Services, Melbourne. Fujifilm and CPL were responsible for supplying the transparency film for my photography (a range of Astia, Provia, and Velvia slide film) and the reproduction for this book.

Inspired Orthotic Solutions, with a thank-you to Jason Nichols

Equip Health Solutions

Dick Smith Foods, with special thanks to Dick Smith

Mobile Power

MINOR SPONSORS

Baffin Polar Proven, Nungar Knots, Ortlieb, Leatherman, Magellan, Mountain Horse, Bates Saddles, Energizer, Custom Pack Rigging, Lonely Planet.

NOTES

CHAPTER 1: MONGOLIAN DREAMING

1 This is only an approximate distance that I traveled, which is not to say that it is 10,000 km as the crow flies from Mongolia to the Danube River in Hungary.

2 In time sedentary society would also adopt the horse and use it to great advantage, but for those early earth-tillers who suffered the wrath of raiding nomad hordes, there is no doubt that the horse was an inseparable symbol of the devastation of war. It is surely no coincidence that in the New Testament it is horses that carry the four beasts of the apocalypse: conquest, war, famine, and death. The legend of the centaur—the mythical creature that is half man, half horse—is probably further indication of just how alien horses and nomads initially were to sedentary society. *Centaur* literally means "those who herd cattle," and while there are many theories as to its origin, one suggestion is that it originates from Scythian incursions into Thrace in ancient Greece.

3 Originally from the *Chronica Majora*, written by Matthew Paris in the thirteenth century. I read it in the Introductory Notice of *The Journey of William of Rubruck to the Eastern Parts of the World 1253–55, with Two Accounts of the Earlier Journey of John of Plan De Carpine*, trans. and ed. W.W. Rockhill (London, 1900; repr. Asian Educational Services, 1998), xiv, xv.

4 *Ammianus Marcellinus*, Book 31, trans. Walter Hamilton (Hammondsworth, UK: Penguin, 1986), quoted in Erik Hildinger, *Warriors of the Steppe: A Military History of Central Asia 500 BC to 1700 AD* (New York: Da Capo Press, 2001), 57, 58.

5 During the Mongol reign, travel from east to west was not limited to nomads and armies. A Nestorian Christian from China, Rabban Saums, who set out on a pilgrimage to Jerusalem, became the effective Mongol ambassador in Europe and had audiences with King Philip the Fair of France in Paris, King Edward I of England in Bordeaux, and the Pope.

6 This drew author Gabriel Ronay to speculate in his book *The Tartar Khan's Englishman* that the Englishman had probably been Master Robert Eracles—an

English knight and former adviser of King John who had been exiled and eventually picked up by Mongol talent scouts and taken to Mongolia.

7 It is worth clarifying that although Hungary was indeed emerging from Soviet rule, it had long been a settled nation. In fact the Magyars—who had arrived on horseback from the east in the ninth century—were already a sedentary Christian society at the time of the Mongolian invasion in the thirteenth century.

CHAPTER 2: THE LAST NOMAD NATION

1 Although the upper Orkhon was effectively Genghis Khan's administrative capital, particularly from 1220 onward, it was his son Ogodei who is considered the founder of Kharkhorin in the years following Genghis's death. Genghis's grandson Khubilai later built a capital for the Yuan dynasty (greater China and Mongolia), Khanbalikh (also known as Ta-tu or Dadu). Khanbalikh stood on the approximate site of modern Beijing.

2 There is some dispute about Genghis Khan's birth year. I am assuming his birth date is the same as that referenced by Mongolians today, 1162.

3 The Borjigins were part of the Mongol tribe, which also included the Taijut clan.

4 The Tatars were a tribe that had emerged in the eighth century as one of the most powerful on the eastern steppe, but their power had begun to wane by the twelfth century. They were one of the Borjigins' enemies.

5 The vast majority of my journey would be through the former territory of the Khanate of the Golden Horde.

CHAPTER 3: WOLF TOTEM

1 *The Secret History of the Mongols*—a mix of factual history and folklore documenting the rise of the Mongol Empire—was written for the Mongol royal family some time after Genghis Khan's death in 1227. It is the oldest surviving Mongolian literary work.

CHAPTER 4: A FINE LINE TO THE WEST

1 The severe nature of these fleshy wounds was later diagnosed as a symptom of Cushing's syndrome.

2 As recounted in Jack Weatherford's *Genghis Khan and the Making of the Modern World*, the wartime spirit banner, and therefore soul, of Genghis Khan was protected by his descendants until the Stalin purges of Mongolia in the 1930s, when it disappeared.

3 In retrospect, this concept of mine might have been a little unfair. In a tradition known as *tuvar*, nomad families in Mongolia are still known to leave their grazing lands and move out on extended horseback journeys with their herds in search of better pasture. This is particularly true of nomads from Uvs Aimag during times of drought. Tuvar dates back to the very earliest of nomads, whose eternal journeys in quest of better pastures took them across the breadth of the Eurasian steppe. Whether coincidence or not, the word *tuvar* is still used by Crimean Tatars; it means "cattle" or "livestock."

4 Hints of this can be found in the term *Oirat* itself, which some historians believe originates from an earlier name, Dorben Oord, meaning "the allied four." The Mongol tribes farther east, meanwhile, sometimes referred to themselves as the Dochin Mongols, meaning "forty Mongols."

5 In a possible throwback to this historical division, it is nowadays common to hear Mongolians from the central regions insult the Durvuds, who form the majority in Uvs Aimag, by calling them *Khun Bish*, meaning "inhuman."

CHAPTER 5: KHARKHIRAA: THE ROARING RIVER MOUNTAIN

1 *Hun*, pronounced "khun," is modern Mongolian for "person," and this has been used as evidence by some historians to prove the Mongolian origins of the Huns. In 2011, Mongolia officially celebrated the 2,200th anniversary of the Hunnic (Xiognu) empire.

2 This border between Uvs Aimag and Kosh Agach in Siberia was, ironically, opened for the first time to foreigners later the same year I was traveling. In 2011, the border with China in the southwest was opened for foreigners. China would have been my preferred route to Kazakhstan.

CHAPTER 6: STALIN'S SHAMBALA

1 The Golden Horde is also known as the Kipchak khanate or the Ulus of Jochi.

2. From Tom Stacey's introduction to Mukhamet Shayakhmetov, *The Silent Steppe: The Memoir of a Kazakh Nomad Under Stalin* (New York: Overlook/Rookery, 2007), ix.

3 This was not a policy unique to the Soviet era. Dostoyevsky was also sent to prison in Semipalatinsk in 1862, where he wrote *Memoirs from the House of the Dead*. The Ukrainian artist Shevchenko also served a term in Orsk in 1847.

4 A kurultai historically was a political and military council of ancient Mongol and Turkic chiefs and khans. The root of the word means "meeting" in Mongolian.

5 Claire Burgess Watson has since written a book about her journey from Mongolia to Turkmenistan, *Silk Route Adventure: On Horseback in the Heart of Asia.*

6 By contrast, at that time a horse in Mongolia started at $80, and a *good* horse there was no more than $150.

7 According to the formula I have used elsewhere in the book for transliterating Kazakh terms to English, Taskonir would more correctly be *Taskonyr* (*Tas* meaning rock, and *konyr* meaning brown). But in the interests of pronunciation, given how centrally this horse featured on my journey, I have stuck with Taskonir.

CHAPTER 7: ZUD

1 It is with an irony not lost on many Kazakhs, then, that it was Lenin's recognition of ethnicities—attachments that he thought would dissolve over time with the brotherhood of Soviets—that eventually heralded the independent state of Kazakhstan.

2 Many historians believe that if the initial policy had confiscated animals from just the bai, and not the middle class and poor, the famine would not have occurred.

3 The Kazakh professor Talas Omarbekov, who worked on the 1997 senate commission into the famine, came across a telegram sent in 1933 from the administration of Kostanai Oblast to the central government: "We cannot fulfill our quota of meat supply of pigs. In the entire oblast there is left just one pig."

4 Collectives run by ethnic Russians and Cossacks tended to have a much lower attrition rate, because their heritage as agrarian farmers allowed them to adapt to the conditions much better than Kazakhs, who knew only nomadic life.

5 Official figures from the time suggest that cattle numbers declined from 6.5 million to fewer than one million. Sheep declined from 18.5 million to just 1.5 million.

6 *Aul* was originally used for Kazakh settlements, as opposed to those founded by Russian settlers, which are known as *derevnye* (village), and separate from

collective farms. Up until the 1950s there was a substantial difference in living conditions between a village and an aul. Russians, with their history as cultivators, were much more easily able to adapt to running state-owned farms, while Kazakhs had neither the same equipment nor the experience and were given less-arable land, so their auls were much poorer. Therefore there was a stigma attached to the word *aul*, which still persists in some ways to the present.

From here on, for the purposes of the book, I will refer to any small Kazakh settlement based on agriculture as an *aul*, no matter whether it was initially a former state farm or collective, Russian-founded or not.

It is also worth noting that at the time of Soviet collectivization, anyone whose family was branded kulak or bai were forbidden to reside in collectives. *Aul* therefore also came to mean the forced settlements of Kazakh nomads outside the collectives.

7 Frederick Burnaby—a British soldier, writer, and undercover spy agent in the era of the Great Game—was told of a similar phenomena in 1875 during his horseback journey from Russia, south through the Kazakh steppes to Khiva. He wrote: "A tartar who is a rich man can find himself a beggar the next. This comes from the frequent snowstorms, when the thermometer sometimes descends to around −40 to −45°C; but more often from some slight thaw taking place for perhaps a few hours. This is sufficient to ruin whole districts. The ground becomes covered with an impenetrable coating of ice, and the horses simply die of starvation, not being able to kick away the frozen substance, as they do the snow from the grass beneath their hoofs." From Burnaby's *A Ride to Khiva: Travels and Adventures in Central Asia*, 148.

8 Since I finished my journey, Mongolia has been hit by another severe zud. In the winter of 2009–10, about 80 percent of the country's territory was covered with a snow blanket of 20–60 cm, and in Uvs Aimag a period of extreme cold, with nighttime temperatures as low as −48°C, endured for almost fifty days. Nine thousand families lost their entire herds, while an additional thirty-three thousand suffered a 50 percent loss. The Ministry of Food, Agriculture, and Light Industry reported 2,127,393 head of livestock lost as of February 9, 2010 (188,270 horses, cattle, and camels and 1,939,123 goats and sheep). The ministry predicted that livestock losses might reach 4 million before the end of winter. But by May 2010, the United Nations reported that 8 million, or about 17 percent of the country's entire livestock, had died.

9 Note that the famine in Kazakhstan under Stalin is known in Russian language as *Veliki Dzhut* (Great Zhut), but in Kazakh the famine is officially known as *asharshylyk*.

10 Later I heard that the Hazara of Afghanistan—descendants of Mongols who conquered the region in the thirteenth century—have the same horse care method, although the same can't be said for Pashtuns and other non-Mongol peoples in that country.

11 The most infamous flight for survival occurred in the spring of 1723 when the Zhungars—Oirat Mongols—nearly wiped out the entire Kazakh population of the Talas region in the middle of a seasonal migration. Those who survived fled to refuge in the overcrowded oases of Bukhara and Samarkand in present-day Uzbekistan. To this day the events are remembered as Aktaban Shubyryndy— "running" (fleeing) to "the bone" (of the foot)—a saying sometimes used in reference to the exodus of Kazakhs to China in the twentieth century during Stalin's collectivization policies and the subsequent famine.

12 There is a legend about the dombra that is linked to the Mongol Empire. The story goes that Jochi, the eldest son of Genghis Khan, promised to pour melted lead down the throat of whoever brought bad news about his son. His son was killed on a hunt by a stampeding wounded ass (known in Kazakh as a *kulan* and in Mongolian as *khulan*). Although everybody was afraid to tell the news to Jochi, there was one musician who agreed to advise of the accident by composing and playing a piece on a dombra. Jochi understood every detail and instead of pouring the lead down the musician's throat ordered it to be poured over the body of the dombra. The hot lead made the soundhole on the instrument that it has today.

13 In Mongolian, the name *Tarbagatai* translates to something like "marmot mountains."

CHAPTER 8: TOKYM KAGU BASTAN

1 Reflecting the blend of old beliefs with the more recently adopted Muslim customs, these days "mounting *ashami*" is often practiced in auls at the time of circumcision. The boys are paraded around the village on horseback to symbolize their coming of age.

2 Above the ranks of akyn were the *jyrau*, who represented an entire people and were advisers to the great khans. They performed *kui* or *terme* (musical recitatives) in everyday life, some of which were many thousands of lines long. Many of these *kuis* recall such events as Alexander the Great's arrival on the Syr Darya (classically known as the Jaxartes River), the Mongols, the Zhungars, and the arrival of Russians on their land.

3 Their observation was not without reason. They told me about a fisherman who had recently died of thirst after his motorcycle broke down during a poaching trip to the lake somewhere nearby. And in the afternoon that day two Russian men turned up briefly looking for water. They had been stuck out on the lake edge for more than a week after their motorcycle broke down. Emaciated and exhausted, they told stories of drinking the saline water, which had made them more and more thirsty, until they had miraculously gotten the bike going again.

4 For some time now I had been sensing that *Oralman* was a derogatory term, as if they considered these people an impure underclass who weren't genuine Kazakhs.

5 In a strange twist, three years later I met an Australian who cast some light on these rumors about police that I would hear time and time again during my travels in Kazakhstan. This Australian had set up a company in Azerbaijan and had once sent a Scottish employee to Kazakhstan on business. According the Scotsman, he had been arrested while near Aktau in western Kazakhstan, driven into the desert, and strangled before the police took off with his wallet. It was apparently only by feigning death that he had survived at all. He managed to wander back into an aul for help.

6 Most of the emissaries of the Tsar were Cossacks.

CHAPTER 9: BALKHASH

1 Over vodka I learned these policemen worked as security guards at a nearby abandoned military base. A year earlier the weapons storage facility at the base had exploded, very nearly killing the workers inside. I later spoke to a man who managed to rescue several military employees by car in the nick of time. For kilometres around there was still debris to be found, and many of the local people had discovered that shards of an orange substance could be used effectively as fire lighters. This was a reminder of hundreds of Soviet military relics

that remain in the steppes of Kazakhstan, where military zones occupy vast stretches of country.

CHAPTER 10: WIFE STEALING AND OTHER LEGENDS OF TASARAL

1 It is also true that existing Slavic settlers from colonial times already made up an estimated 40 percent of the population in 1917.

2 The loss of the Kazakh language was consequently rapid—by 1989, it was estimated that 40 percent of Kazakhs no longer had a proficient grasp of their own language, and three-quarters of Kazakh urban dwellers did not use their native tongue in daily life. Russian, as Dave Bhavna explains, was "more than just a survival tool; it also became a source of personal and collective empowerment and an emblem of becoming 'cultured' and 'civilized.'"

3 In Mongolia it is nine generations.

CHAPTER 11: THE STARVING STEPPE

1 The maps I primarily relied on were tactical pilotage charts that I had managed to buy from a map shop in Adelaide, Australia.

2 This is recounted by Peter Hopkirk in *Foreign Devils on the Silk Road: The Search for the Lost Treasures of Central Asia.*

CHAPTER 12: THE PLACE THAT GOD FORGOT

1 Saksaul was scarce and the wood so dense and twisted that the only way to split it was by smashing it on rocks in winter, when the frozen wood would shatter on impact.

2 According to Ron Stodghill's article for the *New York Times*, "Oil, Cash and Corruption," Nov. 5, 2006, the money was also allegedly channeled to the head of the oil ministry.

3 The autumn slaughter, known as *kuzdyk*, is also celebrated. In summer the slaughter is known as *szhazdyk*, although it is not usually celebrated with ceremony, as in summer dairy products become the staple.

4 CuChullaine O'Reilly regards this as the first international meeting of long riders in history, with riders traveling from all five continents. I was the first to be made a fellow while still on an expedition and "in the saddle."

CHAPTER 13: OTAMAL

1 There was a subtle warning about this in the saying "By spring, fat stock grows thin, and by spring thin stock's nothing" (from Mukhamet Shayakhmetov's book *The Silent Steppe*).

2 I later understood that long farewells, gazing after the departing guest, or the traveler looking back was considered bad luck. In western and central Kazakhstan in particular, I was regularly abandoned and left alone on the day of departure, and until I understood this lore, I felt that I had offended my hosts in some way.

3 Upon reading *The Silent Steppe* I was deeply moved by Mukhamet Shayakhmetov's description of riding alone through a deserted valley the year after nomads had been forced into collectivization: "Until the previous autumn, the valley had been crammed almost full of the nomadic aul who regularly spent each autumn and spring there, to the extent that there could be arguments over whose livestock had the right to graze where. But now it was completely deserted and eerily silent. The people who used to live here had all joined collective farms, and were mostly living together in centralised winter stopping places or in make-shift camps on the ploughed fields; and as there was now enough pasture near these farm centers for the depleted herds of livestock, it no longer made sense to drive them to deserted pastures such a distance away." Mukhamet Shayakhmetov, *The Silent Steppe: The Memoir of a Kazakh Nomad Under Stalin* (New York: Overlook/Rookery, 2007), 65.

4 In times past, anyone who could recount forty generations was held in particularly high status in society.

5 The Kazakh nation had emerged in the sixteenth century as a unity of three confederations of tribes or juzes: the Ula Juz (Elder Horde) in the Jeti-Su (Seven Rivers region) in southern Kazakhstan, the Kishi Juz (Junior Horde) of the arid deserts of the west, and the Orta Juz (Middle Horde) of the north, center, and east.

6 Statistics paint the scale of change in Kazakhstan through the twentieth century. In 1897—thirty years before Kazakhs were forced into collectives—only 7 percent of the Kazakh population had lived settled lives. Nowadays only 9.6 percent of Kazakhs worked on the land, roughly 5 percent of whom, like this family, were thought to carry on a nomadic or semi-nomadic way of life.

7 Beshbarmak is customarily followed by meat broth mixed with dried curd.

8 A fatty sheep tail is the equivalent of a modern-day pacifier and is still used that way among Mongolians as well. Kazakhs also believed that touching a baby's body with a fatty rump will bring wealth.

9 In Mongolia today, it is still in fact the custom never to compliment a baby but to call it "ugly" so as not to cast a spell of bad luck.

CHAPTER 14: SHIPS OF THE DESERT

1 The Khwarezm Empire, which bordered the Mongol Empire, stretched across what is historically known as Transoxiana, which roughly includes the modern states of Iran, Turkmenistan, Uzbekistan, and parts of Kazakhstan, Tajikistan, Afghanistan, and Pakistan.

2 Alexander the Great had in fact fought a famous battle on its banks in 329 BCE with Scythian nomads. Tamerlane (also known as Timur and "Timur the Lame"), of Turkic descent, attempted to evoke the legacy of Genghis Khan in the second half of the fourteenth century, restoring rule over much of the territory that the Mongols had earlier conquered, including the Chaghatai khanate in Central Asia, remnants of the Ilkhanate in Persia, and the Golden Horde on the Pontic-Caspian steppe as far as Russia. He also attempted to reestablish rule over China.

3 In the summer heat it was also the case that injuries to the horses were more prone to infection, and this kept me additionally occupied. At this point of the journey Ogonyok had an infected cut above his left eye, and a pressure sore on his back—probably the result of heat, combined with tying down the pack load too tightly. I gave him an anti-inflammatory and antibiotics, made some adjustments to the saddle, and could only hope his condition did not deteriorate.

4 Although by 2005 most of these ships had reportedly been salvaged for scrap metal, some still stood as sad memorials in what had once been Aralsk's busy port.

5 As some measure of the fallout caused by the shrinking of the Aral Sea, Anton Schneider, an ethnic German who grew up in Kazakhstan, has recently written to me, describing how, in the 1990s, desperate refugees from Aralsk—fleeing disease, and unemployment—turned up in his aul of lugovoy, about 1,200 km from the Aral Sea. From what Anton recalls, the Aral Sea refugees lived in tents

on the outskirts of their village. Anton's father and many others in the aul had great sympathy for these poor people. Eventually the local government gave them land to build new homes on.

6 To help address the situation from the Kazakh side of the border, in 2005 a scheme was under way to build a dam along the southern tip of the northern Aral Lake and hence capture all the outflow of the Syr Darya. This guaranteed some rebound in the northern lake and the potential for the limited reintroduction of the fishing industry.

7 The expedition was officially said to be a scientific expedition to the Aral Sea. The mission of rescuing slaves, however, was also a cover for the real intention, which was to conquer Khiva.

8 I will always remember one morning after a long night ride when we had been forced to divert from the river course. Upon discovering a shallow, spring-fed puddle barely a centimetre deep, Harvette had moved in slowly, dipped her long arched neck, and brought her lips ever so carefully to the surface, whereupon she began to suck in the water without stirring up any visible sediment. When the horses came galloping impatiently over, Taskonir stomped about, turning the puddle into a mud bath before the others were able to drink.

CHAPTER 15: THE OIL ROAD

1 Some commentators, such as Lutz Kleveman in his book *The New Great Game: Blood and Oil in Central Asia*, suggest that by 2020 Kazakhstan could rival Saudi Arabia, exporting as much as 10 million barrels of oil a day.

2 Lutz Kleveman in *The New Great Game: Blood and Oil in Central Asia* alleges that $120 million of this was discovered in accounts under the names of Nazarbayev's children and relatives. Soon after these revelations Nazarbayev had the parliament pass a law making him immune from prosecution for anything he may have done in office.

3 At the time of my journey there were several known incidents of rioting and violence. Weeks prior to my arrival in Kulsary there was a riot between Turkish and Kazakh employees at Tengiz. In December 2011, at least fourteen people were known to be killed when oil workers of the Ozenmunaigas company—based farther south in the town of Zhanaozen—went on strike due to unpaid hazard pay, rioted, and were fired upon by police.

4 In Kazakh, *kok* means "green," but it is also a word used to describe the color of a gray horse.

5 My visa eventually came through successfully, but not before I was taken in by police in the town of Ganushkino, who threatened to hold me until I could produce my passport. In the end I was rescued by a local former politician who agreed to be my guarantor.

6 They were Karakalpaks—a Turkic people closely related to Kazakhs who were nowadays a minority in their own semi-autonomous republic of Karakalpakstan.

7 *Kyl* means "horse" and *terlek* means "summer deel" or, in old-fashioned language, can apparently also mean "underwear."

8 After her operation, Kathrin had also proposed visiting me in Almaty, but I had jettisoned the idea because I knew I would be occupied with the visa and other tasks.

9 Tengiz-Chevroil is the name of the company run by Chevron together with the Kazakh government to exploit the Tengiz oil deposits.

CHAPTER 16: LOST HORDES IN EUROPE

1 It is also acknowledged by historians that the majority of the Kalmyks who remained behind were of the Durvud tribe, and they had elected to stay there.

2 In the fifteenth century, the Oirats had usurped the Genghisid Mongols (also known as the Eastern Mongols) and gone on to found the empire of Zhungaria, which at its peak stretched from Lake Baikal in the northeast to Lake Balkhash in the west and the Great Wall of China in the south.

3 The Kalmyk khanate held sway from the Zhem, across the northern shores of the Caspian Sea, to the Terek River in what is present-day southern Russia.

4 In one campaign in 1711 the Kalmyks attacked the Nogais, who, since being pushed out of the Lower Volga, had moved west to the Kuban steppe and become vassals of the Ottomans. In four days of fighting it is believed the Kalmyks caused the deaths of almost 40,000 and wiped out the entire male population of the Kuban Nogais. They also took 22,000 people captive—the majority of whom were women and children—and stole 190,000 horses and 220,000 sheep.

5 It is so called because of the lack of snow cover on this steppe in the winter.

6 This particular Chechen farmer, whom I did not meet, was said to have lost two houses, a truck, and a semi trailer in the recent riots.

7 This works out to about 150,000–200,000 individuals.

8 I later met a Kalmyk man who told stories about his time as a teenager helping to herd Kalmyk livestock to the eastern banks of the Volga in an attempt to stop them from falling into the hands of the Nazis. "They were never returned to us after the war," he said sadly. "Probably those Kazakhs still have them."

CHAPTER 17: COSSACK BORDERLANDS

1 Kurgans are found across Central Asia, Siberia, and eastern Europe. They were common among many nomad societies on the steppe, including that of the Scythians. According to the Oxford English Dictionary, the word is derived from a Tatar term meaning "fortress."

2 The capital of the Golden Horde, Sarai, was established on the Volga River. The Pontic-Caspian steppe, where vast numbers of horses could be kept in close proximity to Russia, enabled the Mongols and their successors to preserve their military superiority over their vassals.

3 Nothing further is known of Jebe, and it is assumed he died soon after arrival back in Central Asia, but the young Subodei would go on for another twenty-five years, long after Genghis had died, expanding the Mongol Empire to its zenith and again wreaking devastation on the princedoms of Russia.

4 A decade after Russia defeated the largest Cossack army, the Zaporizhian Sich, the Cossack army was reinstated to help efforts in the Russo-Ottoman War of 1787–92. Russia later granted Cossacks the lands of the Kuban for their contribution. Twenty-five thousand Cossack soldiers moved to the Kuban, founding the Kuban Cossack society that still lives there today.

5 In one case the entire populations of three Kuban towns, totaling 45,600 people, were deported. Later, as more than 3 million tonnes of wheat were kept in government storehouses, up to 4.5 million peasants across Ukraine and Kuban starved to death.

6 Home-distilled vodka in Russian is known as *samogon*, but Cossacks use the Ukrainian variation of the word, *samohon* (Kuban Cossacks generally speak a dialect closer to Ukrainian than Russian). The large bottles they serve with corncob corks are known additionally as *suliya*. Ordinary vodka in Cossack dialect is also known by the Ukrainian term, *horilka*.

CHAPTER 19: WHERE TWO WORLDS MEET

1 For me, the most intriguing symbol of the unique cultural dualism of Pantica- paeum was an excavated tomb that lay in the hills overlooking Kerch. The so- called Tsar's Kurgan or Royal Kurgan, a 22 m earth-covered dome, appeared from the exterior like a typical Scythian burial mound—the kind I'd seen regularly elsewhere. Yet the excavated opening revealed an arrowhead-shaped tunnel and a chamber constructed with impressively hand-hewn sandstone blocks that bore the hallmarks of the ancient Greek. The tomb was not of a nomad but of a Bosphorian king.

2 The Crimean khanate was founded in 1430 by Batu Khan's brother's descen- dant, Hajji Giray.

3 After conquering Baghdad in 1258, Hulegu Khan (Genghis Khan's grandson), of the Ilkhanate declared war on Egypt. Mongol advances were halted by the Mamluks, however, who defeated them in the Battle of Ain Jalut. It was the first of several major battles with the Mamluks, including the First and Second Battles of Homs.

4 It is also true that Mongol aristocracies assimilated with the culture of their subjects—at the turn of the fourteenth century, for example, the Golden Horde officially converted to Islam, breaking the tradition of Mongol rulers adhering to shamanism.

5 After weeks of protests and blockades it was reported that the NATO ship sailed home without unloading. The day after my trip to the city, the front page of the newspaper had two headline stories: "Australian Reaches Crimea from Mongolia by Horse" and "Crimeans Say No to NATO."

6 Sourced from Erik Hildinger, *Warriors of the Steppe: A Military History of Central Asia 500 BC to 1700 AD* (New York: Da Capo Press, 2001), 205.

CHAPTER 20: THE RETURN OF THE CRIMEAN TATARS

1 Translated from an original Crimean verse by Rustem Ali. Sourced from Edward A. Allworth, *The Tatars of Crimea: Return to the Homeland* (Durham, NC: Duke University Press, 1998), 5.

2 From here on I will use *Tatars* and *Crimean Tatars* interchangeably, although Crimean Tatars are a distinct people from other Tatars, such as the Kazan or Volga Tatars.

3 There was wide agreement among historians that the real reason for Stalin's decision to exile the Tatars had been his fear of their historical alliance with the Turks.

CHAPTER 21: CROSSROADS

1 Contemporary historians, such as Charles J. Halperin, argue that even after throwing off the so-called Tatar yoke, Russia inherited Mongol military and economic models that helped enable the Muscovite state to unite the northeastern Slavs.

2 His most spoken-about experiences were during a year at Mankato University in Minnesota, where he studied for his master's degree.

3 Text messages could be sent to my phone via an email address.

CHAPTER 22: TAKING THE REINS

1 When reports of famine reached the West and relief supplies were sent to the border, they were turned back, and Moscow announced that there was no famine.

2 In November 2006, the same month that my father died, the Ukrainian president brought to power through the Orange Revolution, Viktor Yushchenko, had finally pushed through a decree that the famine had been genocide. At the time of this writing, however, Yushchenko's archenemy, pro-Russian politician Viktor Yanukovych, is in power and has reversed this decree, recognizing the Holodomor only as a human tragedy.

3 Such were the high emotions surrounding Bandera that one of Yushchenko's last acts as president in January 2010 was to posthumously award Bandera status as a "Hero of Ukraine." Months later Yanukovych had the award overturned. At the time of writing, the award has been officially annulled, although Stepan's grandson, who received it on his behalf, has not been asked to return it.

CHAPTER 23: AMONG THE HUTSULS

1 In times gone by, Hoverla had even been a site of religious sacrifice—the higher the Hutsul climbed to carry out the sacrifice, the more respect they would have from the community. There was one legend I heard about a man who had carried a white bull on his back all the way to the top to be slaughtered.

2 According to tradition, this unique horn was always made from a pine or spruce tree that had been struck by lightning, and it was bound by birch bark collected from trees growing beneath waterfalls. The trembita—which is quite unlike the better-known alpenhorn of the European Alps—was then used to send signals across the high slopes for everything from weddings to communication between herders.

3 Although Genghis Khan had died fourteen years earlier, his son Ogodei, together with Genghis's loyal general Subodei, had resolved to carry out Genghis's wish for world domination.

4 Later on I was approached frequently by villagers who asked how much I was selling brinza for—they assumed that I was a shepherd bringing it down from the polonina.

CHAPTER 24: THE END OF THE WORLD

1 Batu was the second son of Jochi, who was himself Genghis Khan's eldest son. Batu became khan of the Golden Horde.

2 The Kipchaks were known as Cumans in Latin and Polovtsy in Russian. For the remainder of this chapter, I will use the term Cumans, since this is historically how the Europeans referred to them. Those Cumans who survived the onslaught and accepted Mongolian suzerainty became central to Batu Khan's Golden Horde (also known as the Kipchak Khanate).

3 This is an excerpt from the letter delivered from Batu Khan to King Bela IV. The original is believed to have been in Mongolian, but this is part of one of many different versions—all subtly different—translated from Latin. Gabriel Ronay, in The Tartar Khan's Englishman, even suggests that it was possibly the Mongol's mysterious English diplomat who penned the letter. The translation version I have used here is sourced from Leo De Hartog, Genghis Khan, Conqueror of the World. Folio Edition. (Berkeley: University of California Press, 2005), 176. (Note however, Hartog did not include the last line that I have here: "So how do you escape my hands.")

4 Many of these elite soldiers had fought against the Seljuks during the Crusades and were part of military orders including the Knights Templar, the Knights of the Hospital of Saint John of Jerusalem, the Teutonic Knights, and the Brothers of the Sword.

5 Sourced from Gabriel Ronay, *The Tartar Khan's Englishman* (London: Cassell, 1978), 11.

6 It is also said that divisions between Batu and other family members influenced the decision to abandon plans for Europe. Additionally, the retreat may be partially explained by the fact that although the Hungarian plain was well suited for horses, it wasn't large enough to support the sheer number of Mongol mounts. This, some historians suggest, would have forced the army to eventually return to the more familiar steppe of the former Cumanian territories anyway.

7 In the centuries following the arrival of the Magyars in Hungary there was a belief that somewhere between the Volga and the Urals existed an ancient "greater Hungary. " In 1236, a Dominican friar, Julian, claimed to have reached it and met people who spoke fluent Hungarian. The following year he once more set out east but on arrival in Suzdal in Russia was told that the eastern Hungarian nation had been wiped out by the Mongols. The existence of this nation remains a mystery.

8 In his remarkable book *The Centaur Legacy*, Bjarke Rinke writes that the "neurophysiological merging of horse and man" resulted in a "super predator equipped with the ambition of man and the speed of the horse." Bjarke Rink, *The Centaur Legacy: How Equine Speed and Human Intelligence Shaped the Course of History* (Zurich: Long Riders Guild Press, 2004), 29.

9 In his book *Guns, Germs, and Steel: The Fates of Human Societies* (New York: W.W. Norton & Company, 1999), Jarred Diamond points out that "the most direct contribution of plant and animal domestication to wars of conquest was from Eurasia's horses, whose military role made them the jeeps and Sherman tanks of ancient warfare" (91).

   In relation to the Spanish conquest of South America, he also writes of the "tremendous advantage that Spaniards gained from their horses." Reminiscent of the advantage that the nomads of the steppe had over the armies from sedentary Europe the "shock of a horse's charge, its maneuverability, the speed of attack that it permitted and the raised and protected platform that it provided left foot soldiers nearly helpless in the open" (76).

GLOSSARY

FOR THE BENEFIT of readers I have created a glossary of common and important foreign terms used in the text. I have categorized them according to the country of origin of the term. Separately I have provided a list of the Mongol khans and military leaders referred to in the book. There are also lists of other important historical figures, and steppe peoples and empires.

A note about transliteration: there are various formulas for transliterating Mongolian, Kazakh (which is a Turkic language), Russian, and Ukrainian to English. In some cases I have decided to stick with the most commonly found spelling in English, particularly for historical figures. Genghis Khan is a good example—that spelling is widely known in the English-speaking world, even though his name is more accurately transliterated from Mongolian as Chinggis Khaan or Jenghiz Khan.

For Kazakh terms, there is a convention of writing the Kazakh letter к as q, in English, but for ease of reading I have retained this as K. So for example, Qyzylorda becomes Kyzylorda.

In the majority of cases, whether they relate to people, places, or other terminology, I have tried to stick with the spelling that most closely resembles pronunciation in the indigenous tongue.

Note that the letter ы which is similarly pronounced in Kazakh, Russian, and Ukrainian as a hard, unrounded i (such as in the word silly) is transliterated in my book as y.

MONGOLIAN TERMS

Aaruul A traditional dairy product made from dried curd, commonly found among steppe cultures. Known in Kazakh as kurt.

Aimag Traditionally meaning "tribe" in Turkic and Mongolian; now describes administrative subdivisions of Mongolia.

Airag Fermented mare's milk. Also known across the steppe by the Turkic term kumys (sometimes spelled "koumiss").

Boortsog A deep fried dough common among steppe cultures. Known in Kazakh as *baursak*.

Borts Meat cut into strips and hung to dry from the ceiling of a ger or yurt, then crushed.

Deel Long-sleeved long robe traditionally worn by Mongolians and many other peoples of the steppe; held in place by a belt or sash.

Ger Portable tent of steppe nomads, constructed with collapsible lattice walls and roof poles that support an insulating layer of wool felt. More broadly known as a yurt (note that apart from my Mongolian chapters, I have used the term *yurt* in my book to refer to these tents).

Khan Title of a sovereign or military ruler among the Turkic-Mongol societies of the steppe and Central Asia. Also known in Mongolian as khaan or kahn, or by the Turkic term *kagan*.

Nermel arkhi Clear alcoholic beverage, usually distilled from yak or cow's milk; commonly known by outsiders as "Mongol vodka."

Nomkhon Calm, still; often used in relation to a good-natured, quiet horse.

Nuur Lake.

Ovoo Mongolian cairn of rocks and sometimes timber, often found on passes and mountaintops; sites of worship for travelers to pause and venerate the mountains, and offer acknowledgment and prayer to tengri.

Tavan tolgoi mal Five-animal herd (sheep, goat, camel, horse, and yak/cattle); symbol of wealth and prestige among nomads.

Tengri Supreme deity many ancient steppe cultures once worshipped, including Mongolians, many Turkic nomad peoples of Central Asia, and even Hungarians. "Tengrism," which has features of shamanism, animism, totemism, and ancestor worship, is recognized as once having been an organized religion. In what is now modern-day Kazakhstan, Tengrism survived an invasion of Christianity in the sixth century, then Judaism in the seventh. Between the twelfth and fifteenth centuries, Tengrism competed with Islam and was ultimately superseded. In Mongolia today, many Mongolians practice a blend of Buddhism and worship of tengri. Tengri—known as Tenger in modern Mongolian—is also the the term for "sky."

Uul Mountain.

Zud Particularly harsh winter of the steppe that usually leads to heavy losses of livestock. There are a variety of types of zud, ranging from very cold winters, winters with lots of snow or ice, or even *harin zud*—black Zud—when there is no snow at all. Zuds are known in Kazakh language as *zhut*, and in Russian as *dzhut*.

KAZAKH TERMS

Airan Fermented cow's milk.

Akim Mayor; head of local government.

Ak-shi A variety of grass (*Achnatherum splendens* or *Stipa splendens*) that grows on the steppe in tall, tight tussocks and which is used for many Kazakh handicrafts and practical applications in nomad life.

Akyn A talented musical performer traditionally chosen to represent a certain kinship group or family among Kazakhs.

Aul Historically, a community of nomads who camped together in vicinity of a single region, and sometime migrated together. Nowadays used to describe a Kazakh village.

Barimta Traditional form of justice in nomad society that ordinarily involved avenging a crime by stealing the offender's livestock and keeping it for ransom until the dispute was resolved.

Batyr Honorific title given to a Kazakh warrior hero. A baytr was part of the *aksuyet*, aristocracy of Kazakh nomadic society.

Baursak Deep-fried dough meal of Kazakh nomads. Same as boortsog in Mongolian.

Beshbarmak Meaning "five fingers" (because of the way the meal is eaten with one's hands), the Kazakh national dish of meat and boiled squares of pastry, often cooked with wild onion.

Biys Traditional title of elected leader or judge in Kazakh society; part of the *aksuyet*, aristocracy of Kazakh nomadic society.

Buran Fierce windstorms of the steppe, accompanied by a whiteout that can last for days. Known in Mongolian as *shuurgan zud*.

Chaban Kazakh nomad herder.

Dastarkhan Traditional low table of Kazakh nomads; also, table mat spread out on the ground or floor; or, more generally, Kazakh tradition of hospitality.

Dombra Traditional long-necked, two-stringed lute of the Kazakhs.

Dzhabe Kazakh breed of horse renowned for its endurance, strength, and ability to hold its weight even when fodder is scarce. My horses Taskonir and Ogonyok were both of the dzhabe breed. Kazakhs say that their nation was "built on the back of the dzhabe."

Jalau Summer pasture. Same as *jayla* in Crimean Tatar language.

Jeti-su Fertile region of southeast Kazakhstan between Lake Balkhash and the Tien Shan Mountains, known as *semirechye* in Russian. It owes its name to the "seven waters" (or rivers) that flow through the region from the Tien Shan to Lake Balkhash. The Jeti-su has historically been a strategically valued region for empires of Central Asia.

Juz A confederation of nomad tribes, of which there are three that make up the nation of Kazakhstan. The *Ula Juz* (Elder Horde), *Kishi Juz* (Junior Horde), and the *Orta Juz* (Middle Horde).

Kalym Bride-price.

Kstau Winter quarters of Kazakh nomads, usually a semipermanent mud-brick house with corrals for the animals.

Kumys Fermented mare's milk; also written in English as "koumiss." Same as *airag* in Mongolian.

Kurt A traditional dairy product made from dried curd, commonly found among steppe cultures. Same as *aaruul* in Mongolian.

Kurultai Political and military council of ancient Mongol and Turkic chiefs and khans. The root of the word *kural* or *khural* means "meeting" in the Mongolian language, as in "Great State Khural."

Kyl terlek Saddle blanket woven from horsetail hair. Although it is a Kazakh term, it roughly means "summer deel (or underwear) for horse" in Mongolian—evidence perhaps of a wide tradition of its use in the past.

Oralman Expatriate Kazakh whose ancestors fled Kazakhstan during times of war or to escape the privations of the Stalin era; expatriates who have returned to Kazakhstan since the collapse of the Soviet Union.

Otamal Sudden cold snap that usually occurs in mid-March, just when it appears the winter has passed.

Saksaul Small, bush-like tree (*Haloxylon* spp.) of the arid steppes and deserts of Eurasia; traditionally played an important role in nomad life as a source of firewood, shelter, and, in emergencies, even water.

Shubat Camel milk.

Tazi A sight hound of Central Asia renowned for its ability to run over long distances; traditionally used for hunting fox and hare. Due to its nature as a quiet, short-haired dog, it is the only breed Kazakhs—as nominal Muslims—allowed into their dwellings. Tigon's father was a purebred Tazi.

Zhut Particularly harsh winter of the steppe that usually leads to heavy livestock losses. Same as *zud* in Mongolian and *dzhut* in Russian.

RUSSIAN TERMS

Babushka Grandmother, old woman.

Banya A kind of traditional sauna used for bathing and washing.

Chernozem Rich "black soils" found in southern Russia, Ukraine, and some northern parts of Kazakhstan.

Dacha The summer villages of city people across the Soviet Union, used primarily for growing vegetables to supply families through winter.

Krai Administrative division of Russia, historically describes territories that were on the frontier of the Russian empire. Equivalent to a province or state, and holds the same status as an *oblast*.

Kulaks Originally used to describe independent and relatively prosperous peasant farmers of the early twentieth century in Russia, but after the Bolshevik revolution described any farmer not handing over his property to the state.

Lada Soviet (and now Russian) make of car.

Moskvich Small sedan car of the Soviet era.

Oblast Administrative division in Slavic countries (and Kazakhstan), equivalent to a province or state.

Solonchak Salt marshes, salt pans, salt flats.

Ural motorbike Sidecar motorcycle that was a workhorse in Soviet times and is still widely used across the former Soviet Union.

Valenki Traditional knee-high felt boots.

COSSACK TERMS

Ataman Leader; may range from administrator of a regional community to the commander of a Cossack army (as was the case during the Russian Empire).

Horilka Vodka; technically a Ukrainian term.

Khutor Traditionally meaning a single farming homestead but came to describe small Cossack settlements that were not big enough to warrant a church.

Samohon Home-brewed vodka; technically a Ukrainian term.

Stanitsa Traditionally, a unit of economic and political organization among Cossacks; has come to describe Cossack towns and regional centers large enough to support a church.

CRIMEAN TATAR TERMS

Jayla Summer pasture of nomads, generally used to describe the various alpine uplands of the Crimean Mountains. Same meaning as *jalau* in Kazakh.

Mejlis Central executive body of the kurultai of Crimean Tatars, founded in 1991; acts as a representative body for the Crimean Tatars to the Ukrainian central government, the Crimean government, and international bodies.

UKRAINIAN TERMS

Horilka Vodka.

Krysani traditional stiff bowler hats of the Hutsuls.

Kyptars traditional heavy sheepskin vests of the Hutsuls, usually embellished with colorful braided cords, buttons, sequins, and studs.

Polonina High alpine pastures of the Carpathians, used by the Hutsul people for summer grazing of their livestock.

Samohon Home-brewed vodka.

HUNGARIAN TERMS

Komondor Traditional Hungarian breed of dog renowned for its long, matted white coat.

Pálinka traditional Hungarian fruit brandy.

Puszta Steppe.

MONGOLIAN KHANS AND MILITARY LEADERS OF THE MONGOL EMPIRE MENTIONED IN THIS BOOK

Arikboke Grandson of Genghis Khan, the youngest son of Tolui. In 1260–64 Arikboke fought against his brother Khubilai for ascendancy to the throne of the grand khan of the Mongol Empire. He was defeated, and died in 1266.

Batu Khan Grandson of Genghis Khan, and son of Jochi. Ruler of the Golden Horde (including the territories of Russia) from 1227 until his death in 1255.

Genghis Khan United the Mongolian and Turkic tribes of the Mongolian plateau and in 1206 founded the Mongol Empire; considered to have conquered more territory in his lifetime than any other single conqueror in history. Born in 1162, died in 1227.

Hulegu Khan Grandson of Genghis Khan, son of Tolui, who founded the Ilkhanate of Persia. Hulegu died in 1265.

Jebe One of Genghis Khan's most important commanders, who, together with Subodei, led the first Mongol conquest of Russia in 1223. Jebe is thought to have died some time after this campaign en route back to Central Asia. In Mongolian, Jebe is *zev*, meaning "arrow."

Jochi Oldest son of Genghis Khan. After his father's death he was given the westernmost lands conquered in Genghis Khan's lifetime, from the Irtysh to the Ural River; his descendants went on to rule the Golden Horde (also known as the Ulus of Jochi, or the Kipchak Khanate.) Jochi died in 1227, the same year as his father.

Khubilai Khan Grandson of Genghis Khan, son of Tolui; became the leader of the Yuan Dynasty, the territories of which included China and Mongolia. Established the khanate's summer capital, Xanadu, and the Yuan Dynasty capital, Khanbalikh. Khubilai fought a brief war against his brother, Arikboke, in the 1260s for the ascendancy to the throne of the grand khan of the Mongol empire. Khubilai was victorious and is considered to have ruled the Yuan dynasty from the 1260s until his death in 1294.

Ogodei Khan Third son of Genghis Khan; ascended to the throne of the grand khan of the Mongol Empire in 1229, oversaw Mongol expansion into Europe. When news of Ogodei's death in 1241 reached the Mongol armies, the Mongols withdrew and retreated east to elect a new leader.

Subodei Genghis Khan's chief military strategist and commander. After the death of Genghis, Subodei oversaw Mongol expansion into Russia and eastern Europe and was later assigned to lead campaigns against the Song Dynasty in China. Regarded as one of the greatest military minds in history, he died in 1248 in Mongolia at the age of seventy-two. His name is transliterated more correctly from Mongolian as *Subatai*.

OTHER IMPORTANT FIGURES OF STEPPE HISTORY MENTIONED IN THIS BOOK

Alim Khan Emir of Bukhara from 1911 until 1920, when he was deposed by the Soviet army and forced to flee to exile in Afghanistan, where he died in 1944. Thought to be the last direct descendant of Genghis Khan to hold sway as a national ruler.

Arpád Nomad leader of the Magyars (Hungarians) from 895 to 907. Under his rule, the Magyars settled the Carpathian Basin and laid the foundations of the nation of Hungary.

Bela IV Ruler of Hungary at the time of the 1241 Mongol invasion of eastern Europe; escaped and returned to successfully govern Hungary after the retreat of the Mongols to Asia.

Hajji Giray Descendant of Batu Khan's brother; founded the Crimean khanate sometime around 1430. The Giray dynasty survived until annexation of Crimea to Russia in the late eighteenth century.

Inalchuk Governor of the town of Otrar on the Syr Darya River during the reign of Muhammad II and the Khwarezm Empire. He enraged Genghis Khan by executing a 450-man merchant caravan sent from Mongolia to Otrar in 1218. Otrar was the first city to be crushed by the Mongol campaign against Khwarezm in 1219–1220. Inalchuk was put to death by molten silver poured in the eyes and ears.

Kotian Khan of the nomadic Kipchaks (also known as Cumans) at the time of the Mongol invasion of Russia and Europe. During the initial Mongol raid in 1223, Kotian sought military alliances with several princedoms of Kievan Rus but was nevertheless heavily defeated during a battle on the Little Kalka River. In 1238 when the Mongols returned, the Kipchaks were again defeated, and Kotian, together with 40,000 nomad families sought refuge in Hungary. It was on the pretext of King Bela IV of Hungary harboring these Kipchaks that the Mongols invaded Hungary in 1241.

Muhammad II Sultan of the Khwarezm Empire, the territory of which stretched across Transoxiana, roughly including the modern states of Iran, Turkmenistan, Uzbekistan, and parts of Kazakhstan, Tadjikistan, Afghanistan, and Pakistan. Khwarezm was crushed by Genghis Khan's army in 1219–1220. Muhummad fled to an islet on the Caspian coast but died of pneumonia in the winter of 1220–1221.

Sahin Giray Last khan of the Crimean khanate.

Tamerlane Turkic ruler from Central Asia who attempted to evoke the legacy of Genghis Khan in the second half of the fourteenth century; restored rule over much of the territory Mongols had conquered earlier. Also known as Timur and "Timur the Lame," Tamerlane died in 1405.

Tayang Khan Leader of the Naimans, who were defeated by Genghis Khan's army in 1204. Also known as "Taibuqa," he was mortally wounded in this battle.

Ubashi Khan Eighteenth-century khan of the Kalmyks; led the disastrous exodus of Kalmyks from the Caspian Steppe back to China and Mongolia in 1771.

Yanibeg Khan Distant descendant of Jochi; ruled the Golden Horde from 1341 to 1357.

IMPORTANT STEPPE PEOPLES

Borjigin Clan that was part of the Mongol tribe that inhabited the steppe and forests of northern Mongolia between the Onon and Kherlen Rivers; the clan of Genghis Khan.

Botai An ancient steppe people of what is northern Kazakhstan today (Akmola Oblast); credited with being the first culture to domesticate the wild horse, c. 3700–3100 BCE.

Huns Renowned horseback warriors who appeared on the Russian steppe and the Hungarian plain in the fourth century CE and in the fifth century, under the rule of Attila the Hun, threatened the Roman Empire, Persia, and much of Europe with their invasions.

Kalmyks Descendants of Oirat Mongols who migrated to the Caspian steppe in the early part of the seventeenth century and formed the Kalmyk Khanate.

Khoton A small Mongolian minority, most of whom live a traditional nomad life in the Kharkhiraa-Turgen mountain region of Western Mongolia.

Kipchaks Powerful Turkic people of the steppe who at times held sway from Siberia and Central Asia to the Balkans. The Mongols defeated the Kipchaks during their westward expansion into Europe, and 40,000 Kipchak families fled to Hungary for refuge. The Golden Horde is also referred to as the Kipchak Khanate. Kipchaks are known as "Cumans" in Latin, and "Polovtsy" in Russian. Note I have used the term *Cumans* in the Hungarian chapter, for this is how they were known to Europeans.

Magyars Nomadic people believed to originate from somewhere in the vicinity of Bashkiria (also known as Bashkortostan) near the southern Urals of Russia; conquered the Carpathian Basin in the end of the ninth century and, under the leadership of Arpád, founded the nation of Hungary in 896.

Mamluks Powerful military caste of medieval Egypt who seized the sultanate of Egypt and Syria and dealt the Mongol some of its first major defeats. The Mamluks were primarily of Kipchak origin—nomads of the steppe with a wealth of experience in the tactics of Mongol warfare who had been traded to Egypt as slaves.

Naimans Turkic tribe of western Mongolia; one of the most powerful tribes on the Mongolian steppe at the end of the twelfth century at the time of Genghis Khan's rise. The Naimans and the Keraits alike were Nestorian Christians. After their 1204 defeat by Genghis Khan's army, the Naimans fled west into what are now the steppes of Kazakhstan, where, under their leader Kuchlug (the son of Tayang Khan), they struck alliance with the Kara-Khitans. The Naimans were again defeated by the Mongols during the conquest of Khwarezm. Today there are around 400,000 Naimans in Kazakhstan, mostly in the east. They are part of the Orta Juz (Middle Horde) confederation of tribes. I met with Naiman nomads migrating to the Betpak Dala from the river Chu.

Nogais Descendants of Mongol and Turkic tribes who rose to power on the Caspian Steppe in the wake of the collapse of the Golden Horde. Nogais were allied with the Crimean Khanate, and many migrated to Crimea, where they served as cavalry for the Crimean Khan (in fact Crimean Tatars who resided on the steppe of Crimea are known as Nogais). The Kalmyks displaced the Nogais from the Caspian steppe in the first half of the seventeenth century. Nogais today reside mostly in the northern Caucausus, Crimea, and Turkey. There is also a tribe of Nogais who are part of the Kishi Juz (Junior Horde) of Kazakhs.

Oirat Mongols A confederation of the Choros, Durvud, Torghut, and Khoshut tribes of western Mongolia, believed to have originated from the forests of southern Siberia; fought fiercely against Genghis Khan and later formed their own empire, Zhungaria. As the power of Zhungaria waned in the early part of the seventeenth century, some tribes migrated west to the Caspian Steppe, where they founded the Khanate of Kalmykia and became known as Kalmyks. In 1771, the Kalmyks made a tragic exodus back to Asia during which many died en route through the Kazakh steppes. The Zhungarian Empire was vanquished by the Qing Dynasty between 1755 and 1757. Today, Oirats primarily reside in western Mongolia and China, and in the republic of Kalmykia (Russia).

Scythians Diverse group of sophisticated nomadic and seminomadic cultures stretching from Hungary to the Altai Mountains from around the seventh to the fourth century BCE. Their war tactics of feigned retreat and skill as mounted archers—described by Herodotus—bear a striking similarity with the Mongols. The Scythians were renowned for their gold art and the elaborate burial mounds known as kurgans, still found widely on the steppe.

Xiongnu Nomadic people of Inner Asia who ruled an empire in greater Mongolia during the Iron Age from the third to the first century BCE. Although the origin of the Xiongnu is subject to ongoing controversy and debate, many historians believe they were the original Hunnic people, whose descendants charged into Europe centuries later under the helm of Attilla.

CRIMEAN TATAR TRIBES

Nogais Tatars who were primarily pastoral nomads on the steppe of Crimea.

Tatas Tatars who inhabited the forested mountains of Crimea, renowned for their European features.

Yaliboyu Crimean Tatars who lived as traders and fishermen on the coast of Crimea.

KAZAKH JUZES (HORDES)

Kishi Juz (Junior Horde) Confederation of tribes in the arid deserts of western Kazakhstan between the Aral Sea and Caspian Sea.

Orta Juz (Middle Horde) Confederation of tribes in the north, center, and east of Kazakhstan, and many of the Kazakhs of Xinjiang province in China.

Ula Juz (Elder Horde) Confederation of tribes in the Jeti-Su region in southeast Kazakhstan.

THE MONGOL KHANATES

Chaghatai Khanate Founded by Chaghatai, Genghis Khan's second son, and ruled by his descendants; extended from the Amu Darya to the Altai Mountains.

Golden Horde Khanate composed of territories of what is nowadays Kazakhstan, Russia, Ukraine, and the Caucasus, ruled initially by Jochi Khan but expanded to its zenith under his son, Batu Khan.

Ilkhanate Khanate primarily comprising territories of Persia, founded by Hulegu Khan (Genghis Khan's grandson) and ruled by his descendants until the mid-fourteenth century.

Yuan Dynasty Khanate that included approximate territories of modern China, Mongolia, and Korea; ruled by Khubilai Khan from 1260 to 1294.

SELECT BIBLIOGRAPHY

NONFICTION

Allworth, Edward A. *The Tatars of Crimea: Return to the Homeland*. Durham, NC: Duke University Press Books, 1998.

Burnaby, Frederick. *A Ride to Khiva: Travels and Adventures in Central Asia*. Oxford: Oxford University Press, 2002.

Carpini, Giovanni di Plan. *The Story of the Mongols Whom We Call the Tartars*. Wellesley, MA: Branden Books, 1996.

Conquest, Robert. *The Harvest of Sorrow: Soviet Collectivization and the Terror-Famine*. New York: Oxford University Press, 1987.

Dave, Bhavna. *Kazakhstan: Ethnicity, Language and Power*. London: Routledge, 2007.

Dolot, Miron. *Execution by Hunger: The Hidden Holocaust*. New York: W. W. Norton, 1987.

Gray, John. *Kazakhstan: A Review of Farm Restructuring*. Herndon, VA: World Bank Publications, 2000.

Halperin, Charles J. *Russia and the Golden Horde: The Mongol Impact on Medieval Russian History*. Bloomington: Indiana University Press, 1985.

Hartog, Leo De. *Genghis Khan, Conqueror of the World*. Folio Edition. Berkeley: University of California Press, 2005.

Haslund, Henning. *Mongolian Adventure: 1920s Danger and Escape Among the Mounted Nomads of Central Asia*. Zurich: Long Riders Guild Press, 2001.

Hildinger, Erik. *Warriors of the Steppe: A Military History of Central Asia 500 BC to 1700 AD*. New York: Da Capo Press, 2001.

Hopkirk, Peter. *Foreign Devils on the Silk Road*. Amherst: University of Massachusetts Press, 1980.

————. *The Great Game: The Struggle for Empire in Central Asia*. New York: Kodansha International, 1992.

Jankovich, Miklos. *They Rode into Europe: The Fruitful Exchange in the Arts of Horsemanship Between East and West*. Zurich: Long Riders Guild Press, 2007.

Khodarkovsky, Michael. *Where Two Worlds Met: The Russian State and the Kalmyk Nomads 1600–1771*. Ithaca, NY: Cornell University Press, 2006.

Kleveman, Lutz. *The New Great Game: Blood and Oil in Central Asia*. London: Atlantic Books, 2004.

Maclean, Fitzroy. *Eastern Approaches*. London: Penguin Books, 1991.

Manz, Beatrice Forbes. *Tamerlane: His Rise and Rule*. Folio ed. Berkeley: University of California Press, 2005.

Martin, Virginia. *Law and Custom in the Steppe: The Kazakhs of the Middle Horde and Russian Colonialism in the Nineteenth Century*. Richmond, Surrey, UK: Routledge, 2001.

Rink, Bjarke. *The Centaur Legacy: How Equine Speed and Human Intelligence Shaped the Course of History*. Zurich: Long Riders Guild Press, 2004.

Rockhill, W. W. *The Journey of William of Rubruck to the Eastern Parts of the World, 1253–55*. Asian Educational Services, 1998.

Ronay, Gabriel. *The Tartar Khan's Englishman*. London: Cassell, 1978.

Rossabi, Morris. *Khubilai Khan: His Life and Times*. Folio ed. Berkeley: University of California Press, 2005.

Shayakhmetov, Mukhamet. *The Silent Steppe: The Memoir of a Kazakh Nomad Under Stalin*. New York: Overlook/Rookery, 2007.

Uehling, Greta Lynn. *Beyond Memory: The Crimean Tatars' Deportation and Return*. New York: Palgrave Macmillan, 2004.

Weatherford, Jack. *Genghis Khan and the Making of the Modern World*. New York: Three Rivers Press, 2004.

FICTION
Rong, Jiang. *Wolf Totem*. London: Penguin Books, 2009.

Stanislaw, Vincenz, *On the High Uplands: Sagas, Songs, Tales and Legends of the Carpathians*. Roy Publishers, 1955.

Tolstoy, Leo. *The Cossacks and Other Stories*. London: Penguin Classics, 2007.

EQUESTRIAN TRAVEL RESOURCES

For anyone interested in the practical side of equestrian travel, I recommend consulting the Long Riders Guild at www.thelongridersguild .com.

A comprehensive list of historical equestrian adventure and practical guides to horse packing can also be found at www.horsetravel books.com.

A full list of my personal equipment can be found on my website, www.timcopejourneys.com

INDEX

TIM COPE, F.R.G.S., is an adventurer, author, film-maker and motivational speaker with a special interest in Central Asia and the states of the former Soviet Union. He has studied as a wilderness guide in the Finnish and Russian subarctic, ridden a bicycle across Russia to China and rowed a boat along the Yenisey River through Siberia to the Arctic Ocean. He is the author of *Off the Rails: Moscow to Beijing on Recumbent Bikes* and is the creator of several documentary films, including the award-winning series 'The Trail of Genghis Khan', which covers the journey of this book. He lives in Victoria, Australia.

www.timcopejourneys.com